WORLDCOMP'13

July 22-25, 2013

Las Vegas Nevada, USA

www.world-academy-of-science.org

PROCEEDINGS OF THE 2013 INTERNATIONAL CONFERENCE ON GENETIC AND EVOLUTIONARY METHODS

GEM 2013

Editors

Hamid R. Arabnia
Ray R. Hashemi
George Jandieri
Ashu M. G. Solo
Fernando G. Tinetti

AF519499

FIREWALL MEDIA
(An Imprint of Laxmi Publications Pvt. Ltd.)
An ISO 9001:2008 Company

BENGALURU • CHENNAI • COCHIN • GUWAHATI • HYDERABAD
JALANDHAR • KOLKATA • LUCKNOW • MUMBAI • RANCHI • NEW DELHI
BOSTON (USA) • ACCRA (GHANA) • NAIROBI (KENYA)

This volume contains papers presented at The 2013 International Conference on Genetic and Evolutionary Methods (GEM'13). Their inclusion in this publication does not necessarily constitute endorsements by editors or by the publisher.

Branches

	Branch	Telephone	
✆	Bengaluru	080-26 75 69 30	
✆	Chennai	044-24 34 47 26,	24 35 95 07
✆	Cochin	0484-237 70 04,	405 13 03
✆	Guwahati	0361-254 36 69,	251 38 81
✆	Hyderabad	040-27 55 53 83,	27 55 53 93
✆	Jalandhar	0181-222 12 72	
✆	Kolkata	033-22 27 43 84	
✆	Lucknow	0522-220 99 16	
✆	Mumbai	022-24 91 54 15,	24 92 78 69
✆	Ranchi	0651-220 44 64	

PUBLISHED IN INDIA BY

FIREWALL MEDIA
(An Imprint of Laxmi Publications Pvt. Ltd.)

An ISO 9001:2008 Company
113, GOLDEN HOUSE, DARYAGANJ,
NEW DELHI - 110002, INDIA
Telephone : 91-11-4353 2500, 4353 2501
Fax : 91-11-2325 2572, 4353 2528
www.laxmipublications.com info@laxmipublications.com

C—
Printed at:

Foreword

It gives us great pleasure to introduce this collection of papers to be presented at the 2013 International Conference on Genetic and Evolutionary Methods (GEM'13), July 22 through 25, 2013, at The New Tropicana Hotel, Las Vegas, USA.

An important mission of the World Congress in Computer Science, Computer Engineering, and Applied Computing (a federated congress to which this conference is affiliated with) includes *"Providing a unique platform for a diverse community of constituents composed of scholars, researchers, developers, educators, and practitioners. The Congress makes concerted effort to reach out to participants affiliated with diverse entities (such as: universities, institutions, corporations, government agencies, and research centers/labs) from all over the world. The congress also attempts to connect participants from institutions that have **teaching** as their main mission with those who are affiliated with institutions that have **research** as their main mission. The congress uses a quota system to achieve its institution and geography diversity objectives."* By any definition of diversity, this congress is among the most diverse scientific meeting in USA. We are proud to report that this federated congress has authors and participants from 82 different nations representing variety of personal and scientific experiences that arise from differences in culture and values. As can be seen (see below), the program committee of this conference as well as the program committee of all other tracks of the federated congress are as diverse as its authors and participants.

The program committee would like to thank all those who submitted papers for consideration. Each submitted paper was peer-reviewed by two experts in the field for originality, significance, clarity, impact, and soundness. In cases of contradictory recommendations, a member of the conference program committee was charged to make the final decision; often, this involved seeking help from additional referees. In addition, papers whose authors included a member of the conference program committee were evaluated using the double-blinded review process. One exception to the above evaluation process was for papers that were submitted directly to chairs/organizers of pre-approved sessions/workshops; in these cases, the chairs/organizers were responsible for the evaluation of such submissions. The overall paper acceptance rate for regular papers was 31%; 7% of the remaining papers were accepted as poster papers (at the time of this writing, we had not yet received the acceptance rate for a few individual tracks.)

We are very grateful to the many colleagues who offered their services in organizing the conference. In particular, we would like to thank the members of the Program Committee of GEM'13, members of the congress Steering Committee, and members of the committees of federated congress tracks that have topics within the scope of GEM. Many individuals listed below, will be requested after the conference to provide their expertise and services for selecting papers for publication (extended versions) in journal special issues as well as for publication in a set of research books (to be prepared for publishers including: Springer, Elsevier, BMC, and others).

- *Dr. Alireza Abbasi; University of New South Wales (UNSW), Canberra, Australia*
- *Dr. Selim Aissi (World Congress Steering Committee); formerly, Chief Strategist - Security, Intel Corp., USA; Senior Business Leader & Head of Global Enterprise Security Architecture, Visa Corporation, USA*
- *Prof. Babak Akhgar (World Congress Steering Committee); Fellow of the British Computer Society, CITP; Professor of Informatics; Co-Director of CENTRIC (Centre of Excellence in Terrorism, Resilience, Intelligence & organised Crime research), Sheffield Hallam University, Sheffield, UK*
- *Prof. Nizar Al-Holou (World Congress Steering Committee); Professor and Chair, ECE Department; Vice Chair, IEEE/SEM-Computer Chapter; University of Detroit Mercy, Detroit, Michigan, USA*
- *Prof. Hamid R. Arabnia (World Congress Steering Committee); Professor, Computer Science; Editor-in-Chief, The Journal of Supercomputing (Springer); Elected Fellow, Int'l Society of Intelligent Biological Medicine (ISIBM); The University of Georgia, Department of Computer Science, USA*
- *Peyman Arebi; Department of Computer Engineering, Technical and Vocational University, Bushehr, Iran*
- *Prof. Ezendu Ariwa (Publicity Vice-Chair); Chair, IEEE Consumer Electronics Chapter, UK&RI; Visiting Professor, Gulf University, Bahrain*
- *Prof. Juan Jose Martinez Castillo; Director of The Acantelys Research Group and Coordinator of the Computer Engineering Department, Universidad Gran Mariscal de Ayacucho, Venezuela*

- *Prof. Juan Cuadrado-Gallego; Universidad de Alcala, Edificio Politecnico, Madrid, Spain; Ecole de technologie superieure, University of Quebec, Canada*
- *Prof. Kevin Daimi (World Congress Steering Committee); Director, Computer Science and Software Engineering Programs; Department of Mathematics, Computer Science and Software Engineering; University of Detroit Mercy, Detroit, Michigan, USA*
- *Prof. Debasis Giri (IPCV); Haldia Institute of Technology, ICARE Complex, HIT Campus, Haldia, India*
- *Prof. Ray Hashemi (Session Chair, GEM); Professor of Computer Science and Information Technology, Armstrong Atlantic State University, Savannah, Georgia, USA*
- *Prof. George Jandieri (World Congress Steering Committee); Georgian Technical University, Tbilisi, Georgia; Chief Scientist, The Institute of Cybernetics, Georgian Academy of Science, Georgia; Editorial Board Member: International Journal of Microwaves and Optical Technology, The Open Atmospheric Science Journal, American Journal of Remote Sensing, Georgia*
- *Prof. Dong Hwa Kim; Department of Electronic and Control Engineering, Hanbat National University, Korea; Visiting Professor, Budapest University of Technology and Economic, Hungary; International Einstein awardee for Scientific achievement (2010)*
- *Prof. Dattatraya V. Kodavade (World Congress Steering Committee); Head of Computer Science and Engineering, D.K.T.E Society's Textile & Engineering Institute, Ichalkaranji, Maharashtra State, India*
- *Prof. B. Raja Sarath Kumar; Principal, Lenora College of Engineering, Andhra Pradesh, India*
- *Prof. Kun Chang Lee (World Congress Steering Committee); Professor of MIS & WCU Professor of Creativity Science, Business School & Dept of Interaction Science, Sungkyunkwan University, South Korea*
- *Dr. Bala Krishna Maddali; University School of IT, GGS Indraprastha University, India*
- *Dr. Veenu Mangat; Information Technology, University Institute of Engineering and Technology, Panjab University, Chandigarh, India*
- *Muhammad Naufal Bin Mansor; Intelligent Signal Processing Group (ISP), University Malaysia Perlis, Kangar, Perlis, Malaysia*
- *Dr. Tao Mao; Oracle America, Inc., Santa Clara, California, USA*
- *Prof. George Markowsky (World Congress Steering Committee); Professor and Associate Director, School of Computing and Information Science; Chair International Advisory Board of IEEE IDAACS; Director 2013 Northeast Collegiate Cyber Defense Competition; Cooperating Professor Mathematics and Statistics Department UMaine; Cooperating Professor School of Policy & International Affairs UMaine; University of Maine, Orono, Maine, USA*
- *Dr. Sara Moein; Editorial Board, International Journal of Science and Technology; Faculty of Engineering, MultiMedia University, Malaysia*
- *Dr. Ali Mostafaeipour; Industrial Engineering Department, Yazd University, Iran*
- *Dr. Saurabh Mukherjee; Department of Computer Science, Banasthali University, Banasthali, India*
- *Prof. G. N. Pandey (World Congress Steering Committee); Vice-Chancellor, Arunachal University of Studies, Arunachal Pradesh, India; Adjunct Professor, Indian Institute of Information Technology, Allahabad, India*
- *Prof. James J. (Jong Hyuk) Park (World Congress Steering Committee); Professor of Computer Science and Engineering, Seoul National University of Science and Technology (SeoulTech), Korea; President, KITCS; President, FTRA; Editor-in-Chiefs: HCIS, JoC and IJITCC Journals*
- *Dr. Satish Penmatsa; Computer Science, University of Maryland - Eastern Shore, Maryland, USA*
- *Prof. Junfeng Qu; Clayton State University, Morrow, Georgia, USA*
- *Prof. B. V. A. N. S. S. Prabhakar Rao (ICAI); School of Computing Science and Engineering, VIT University, Chennai Campus, India*
- *Dr. Liang Shi; Senior Researcher, McAfee, USA*
- *Dr. Kok Swee Sim; Faculty of Engineering and Technology, Jalan Ayer Keroh Lama, Melaka, Malaysia*
- *Ashu M. G. Solo, (Publicity Chair); Fellow of British Computer Society, Principal/R&D Engineer, Maverick Technologies America Inc., USA*
- *Prof. Fernando G. Tinetti (World Congress Steering Committee); School of Computer Science, Universidad Nacional de La Plata, La Plata, Argentina; Co-editor, Journal of Computer Science and Technology (JCS&T)*
- *Dr. Predrag Tosic (World Congress Steering Committee); Microsoft, Washington, USA*
- *Prof. Vladimir Volkov (World Congress Steering Committee); The Bonch-Bruevich State University of Telecommunications, Saint-Petersburg, Russia*
- *Prof. Jongwook Woo; Director, High-Performance Information Computing Center (HiPiC), Computer Information Systems Department, California State University, Los Angeles, California, USA*
- *Prof. Jane You (Vice-Chair of IPCV); The Hong Kong Polytechnic University, Hong Kong*

As Sponsors-at-large, partners, and/or organizers each of the followings (separated by semicolons) provided help for at least one track of the World Congress: Aldebaran Robotics Inc., USA (http://www.aldebaran-robotics.com); Altera Corporation, USA (http://www.altera.com/); Computer Science Research, Education, and Applications Press (CSREA); Impulse Accelerated Technologies, Inc., USA (http://www.impulseaccelerated.com/); NVIDIA Corporation, USA (http://www.nvidia.com/object/about-nvidia.html); Parallella Community, Supercomputing for Everyone, USA (http://forums.parallella.org/); Pico Computing, Inc., USA (http://picocomputing.com/); SemiWiki.com, The Semiconductor Wiki Project, USA (http://www.semiwiki.com/); Solarflare Communications, Inc., USA (http://www.solarflare.com/); Stream Computing, Performance Engineers, The Netherlands (http://streamcomputing.eu/); Taylor & Francis, UK (http://www.taylorandfrancis.com/); US Chapter of World Academy of Science (http://www.world-academy-of-science.org/) ; and WEBestSOL & Webest Solutions Ltd, UK (http://webestsol.com/). In addition, a number of university faculty members and their staff (names appear on the cover of the set of proceedings), several publishers of computer science and computer engineering books and journals, chapters and/or task forces of computer science associations/organizations from 5 countries, and developers of high-performance machines and systems provided significant help in organizing the conference as well as providing some resources. We are grateful to them all.

We express our gratitude to keynote, invited, and individual conference/tracks and tutorial speakers - the list of speakers appears on the conference web site. We would also like to thank the followings: UCMSS (Universal Conference Management Systems & Support, California, USA) for managing all aspects of the conference; Dr. Tim Field of APC for managing the printing of the proceedings; and the staff of the New Tropicana Hotel in Las Vegas for the professional service they provided. Last but not least, we would like to thank the Co-Editors of GEM'13: Prof. Hamid R. Arabnia, Prof. Ray R. Hashemi, Prof. George Jandieri, Ashu M. G. Solo, and Prof. Fernando G. Tinetti.

We present the proceedings of GEM'13

Steering Committee, 2013
http://www.world-academy-of-science.org/

Contents

SESSION: MULTI-OBJECTIVE OPTIMIZATION + COMBINATORIAL OPTIMIZATION + AGENT-BASED ALGORITHMS + COMPUTATIONAL BIOLOGY

SESSION: SWARM OPTIMIZATION ALGORITHMS AND APPLICATIONS

SESSION: EVOLUTIONAY ALGORITHMS AND STRATEGIES

SESSION: GENETIC ALGORITHMS AND APPLICATIONS + GENETIC PROGRAMMING

SESSION: EVOLUTIONARY OPTIMIZATION AND GENETIC ALGORITHMS

SESSION

MULTI-OBJECTIVE OPTIMIZATION + COMBINATORIAL OPTIMIZATION + AGENT-BASED ALGORITHMS + COMPUTATIONAL BIOLOGY

Chair(s)

TBA

Emergent System Effects from Microscopic Evasion Choices in a Predator-Prey Simulation

Chris J. Scogings
Computer Science
Massey University - Albany Campus
North Shore 102-904, Auckland
New Zealand
email: c.scogings@massey.ac.nz

Ken A. Hawick
Computer Science
Massey University - Albany Campus
North Shore 102-904, Auckland
New Zealand
email: k.a.hawick@massey.ac.nz

April 2013

ABSTRACT

A wide range of predator evasion strategies have been reported for several real predator-prey systems in the wild. We investigate predator evasion in a system of many simulated animal agents. Our model is capable of simulating the emergent effects arising from around a million individual microscopic agents which make individual intelligent choices based on their local information. We find oscillatory and other system wide effects arising from enhanced abilities of prey to evade their predators. We compare some of these effects to real predator-prey observed patterns of behaviour. We find additional oscillatory effects arising when prey can evolve towards different levels of evasive behaviour.

KEY WORDS

agent-based model; animat; overcrowding; prey evasion; evolved behaviour; intelligent agents.

1 Introduction

Predator-prey systems are often identified in nature and some of the effects understood from direct observation. Many of the system wide emergent effects are however still poorly understood, but can be probed using computer simulations. In this paper we investigate emergent oscillatory phenomena arising from population fluctuations when prey are able to evade predators.

Agent-based "Artificial life" models that simulate predator-prey systems are well known [1–5]. Such models consisted of agents that were entirely virtual and did not attempt to model real animals. Further work moved towards a modicum of real animal behaviour leading to the term "animats" [6, 7] being used for agents that attempt to model some aspect of real animal behaviour including flocking [8], sentinels [9] and termites [10].

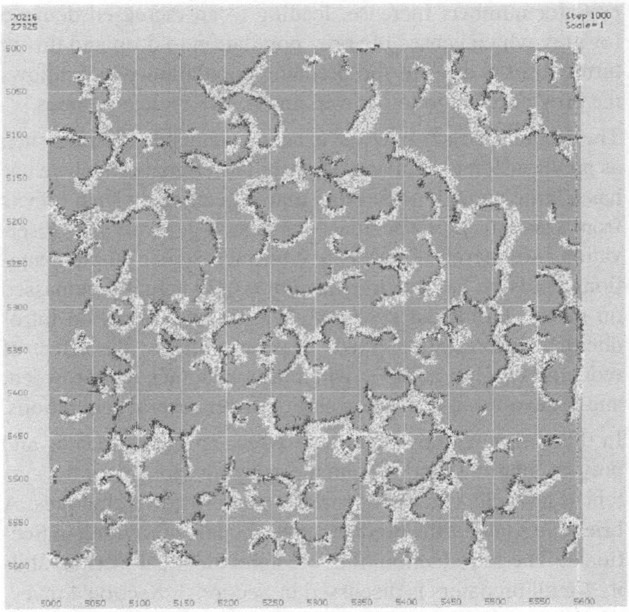

Figure 1: The situation at step 900 of a typical run showing animats on a square grassed area. Predators are black and prey are white. Various macro-clusters, including spiral formations, have emerged.

Many agent-based models focus on "emergence" – the complex and often unexplained patterns and clusters that emerge from the interactions of many agents at the local level. In predator-prey models, emergence can take the form of the defensive spirals and other features discussed in [11] and shown in Figure 1.

One aspect of real predator-prey behaviour is the use of evasion techniques by prey [12–14] and how such evasion capabilities affect both predators and prey. Of particular interest to this investigation is that large numbers of prey can lead to overcrowding which reduces the ability of individual prey to evade predators. Examples include: predators that employ a "sit-and-wait" technique will usually benefit from overcrowded prey [15]; prey that rely on hiding in burrows can have hiding places reduced by overcrowding [16]; and antelope in large herds are less vigilant than those in smaller groups [17].

As the foundation for an investigation into prey evasion, this paper makes use of a well-established spatial predator-prey model [18]. The model consists of a flat plain on which large numbers of animats reproduce, feed, flee predators or hunt prey and eventually die. The model reproduces the repetitive cycle of behaviour that is well known from predator-prey equation-based models such as the Lotka-Volterra equations [19]. Predators kill prey and, if prey is plentiful, the predator numbers increase, leading to an increased demand for prey which causes the prey population to drop and this in turn causes a drop in the predator population which allows the prey population to recover, and so the cycle continues.

The model abstracts over the exact mechanisms for traits such as prey evasion to evolve or appear. The animat model we use has a large enough population that we can study such effects from a statistical perspective over several generations. Observations are therefore insensitive to microscopic implementation details on how such behaviour would actually be passed on in real biological systems. We present results on introducing: different (but fixed) evasion abilities; the effect of reducing evasion abilities when prey becomes overcrowded; and the evolution of evasion abilities over several generations.

In this paper we investigate the effect on both predator and prey populations, and thus on the carrying capacity of the system as a whole, when prey make use of evasion techniques. A brief overview of the predator-prey model is provided in Section 2. The introduction of a fixed and identical evasion ability for all predators is discussed in Section 3. Section 4 investigates the effects of a reduction in prey evasion ability due to prey overcrowding. Section 5 allows prey to evolve the evasion ability through mutation across generations and investigates how the evolutionary process affects both the predator and prey populations. We discuss the implications of traits such as evasion on the overall system in Section 6 and offer some conclusions and ideas for future work in Section 7.

2 The Predator-Prey Animat Model

The model contains two groups of interacting agents (or "animats") – the predators and the prey. Every animat maintains its current state including: current health; current age; and an x-y location on the flat, 2-dimensional map. Every animat also carries a set of rules (depending on species). The rule sets are listed in Table 1.

Table 1: Animat Rule Sets in Priority Order

Rules for predator animats:	Rules for prey animats:
1. breed if health $> 50\%$ and mate adjacent	1. flee from predator if predator is adjacent
2. eat prey if health $< 50\%$ and prey adjacent	2. graze (eat grass) if health $< 50\%$
3. seek mate if health $> 50\%$	3. breed if health $> 50\%$ and mate adjacent
4. seek prey if health $< 50\%$	4. seek mate if health $> 50\%$
5. randomly move to any adjacent position	5. randomly move to any adjacent position

Each animat is initialised with the current age set to zero. The age is incremented at every time step of the simulation and when it reaches a pre-set maximum the animat "dies of old age" and is removed. When a new animat is produced, its current health value is set to the health of its parent. From then on, the current health is reduced at each time step and if it reaches zero the animat "starves to death". If an animat eats then the current health value is increased by a certain amount. The concepts of health values and animats eating behaviours are discussed in [20].

Prey eat "grass" which is placed at specific locations on the map – usually in a contiguous area. Grass has a fixed "nutritional value" and this is the number of health points that prey receive when executing the graze rule. In these experiments grass has a value of 45. Thus if a prey animat has 5% health and executes the graze rule, the animat's health would increase to 50%. However, if a prey animat with 75% health executed the graze rule the animat's health would rise to 100% as current health may not exceed 100%. The experiments discussed in this paper are situated on a large square "grassed area" which explains why the diagrams showing animat locations have a distinct edge. Containing the animats is useful as it prevents populations becoming unmanageable and also limits the area of the (otherwise unbounded) grid in which the animats exist. Previous work [21] has shown that these limitations do not affect the emergent patterns and clusters of the model.

Predators eat prey but only do so if the predator is "hungry" (i.e. the current health is less than 50%) and the prey is adjacent to the predator. Early on in the development of the model, a problem was identified whereby several predators simultaneously consumed the same prey animat. This led to the situation where a large number of predators could be sustained by an unrealistically small number of prey. This problem was solved by immediately removing "consumed" prey from the list of available animats in the given time step. Animats are updated in a random order which removes any spatial artifacts from the sweep order. The process is thus a two-phase system in which the variables for all animats are updated after all rules have been executed. A full discussion of this (and other) methods of updating agent-based models can be found in [22].

Rules are considered in a strict priority order. Each time-step, every animat attempts to execute the first rule in its rule set. However, most rules have conditions and often cannot be executed. For example, predators can only eat prey if prey are adjacent. If the conditions for the first rule can not be satisfied, the animat attempts to execute the next rule in the set and so on. Breeding only has a certain chance of success. This is a simple alternative to factoring in a host of complicated parameters including birth defects, nutrition, adequate shelter and so on. Changing the chances of a successful birth can dramatically alter the number of animats and can sometimes cause the extinction of all animats. For these experiments the chance of a successful birth was set to 15% for predators and 80% for prey.

3 Experiment 1 – Evasion Values

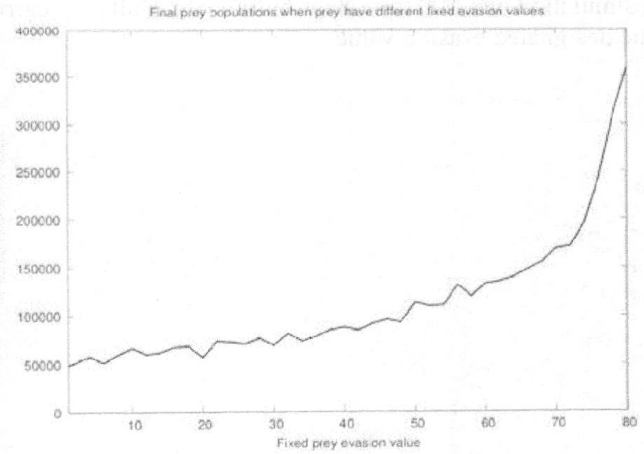

Figure 2: Plot showing the effects of fixed prey evasion values on prey populations. As evasion becomes more effective, predators catch less prey allowing the prey population to increase.

In this experiment, prey evasion of predators was introduced into the model in the following way: each prey agent was assigned an "evasion value" which is an integer value in the range 0 to 99. The evasion value is the percentage chance that the prey will evade a predator. Hence, for example, there is a 10% chance that prey will evade a predator when the prey animat has an evasion level of 10 and there is an 80% chance that prey will evade a predator when the prey animat has an evasion level of 80, and so on.

Prey evasion is checked during the execution of a predator's "eat" rule. When a predator is adjacent to prey and executes the "eat" rule, the chance of prey evasion is calculated. If the prey successfully evades the predator, the predator does not eat and thus does not receive the increased health from eating.

At the start of any simulation, all prey receive the same initial evasion value. The model can then be run in one of two ways: either every prey animat always carries the initial evasion value, i.e. all prey are clones of the initial prey; or the evasion level is allowed to mutate and evolve from one generation to the next.

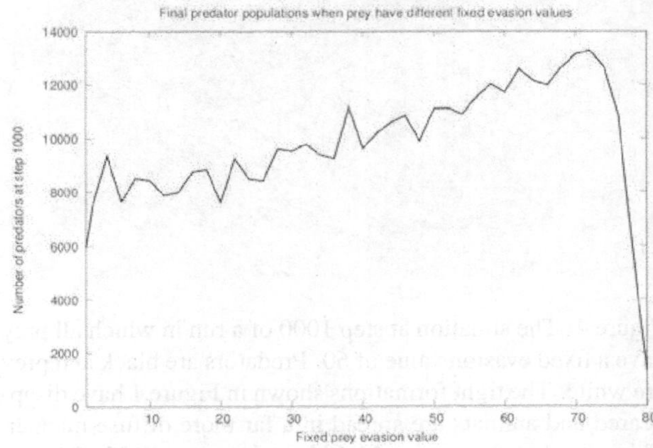

Figure 3: Plot showing the effects of fixed prey evasion values on predator populations. As evasion becomes more effective, predators catch less prey causing the prey population to increase and in turn making it easier for predators to find more prey. The predator population thus also increases – at least initially.

In this experiment, only the initial evasion values were used (all prey were identical clones). This enabled an analysis of the effect on both prey and predator populations of an evasion value that was fixed across the prey population. Several fixed evasion values were tested and the results are shown in Figure 2 (prey population) and Figure 3 (predator population). Each data point in the graphs is the final population figure at the end of a simulation of 1,000 time steps during which all prey carried the designated evasion value.

There is a distinct change in the emerging formations of animats during these experiments. Figure 4 shows the situation during a run where all prey have a fixed evasion value of 60. Because prey now have considerable success in evading predators, the animat clusters have taken on a more diffuse nature with prey in larger clusters. There are also small regions where predators have died out and only prey remain. This situation should be compared with Figure 1 in which prey have an evasion value of zero.

An unexpected outcome of this experiment is that the predator population initially benefits from increasing the prey evasion value, even though increased evasion values mean that

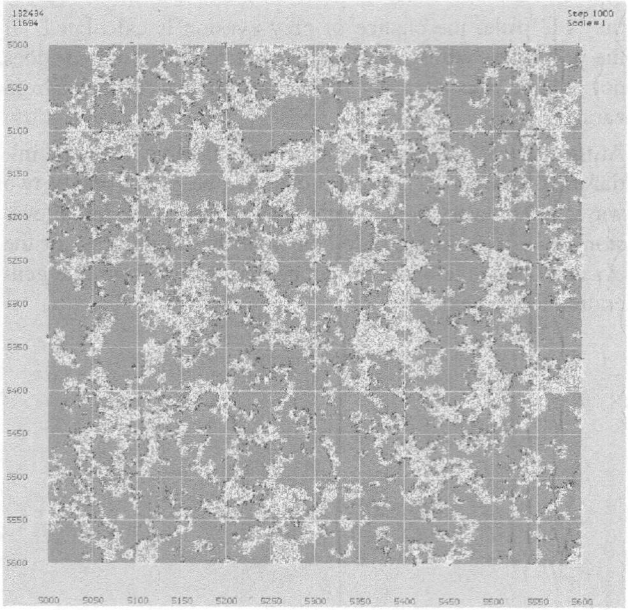

Figure 4: The situation at step 1000 of a run in which all prey have a fixed evasion value of 60. Predators are black and prey are white. The tight formations shown in Figure 1 have disappeared and animats are spread in a far more diffuse manner. This screen shot contains 11,694 predators and 132,434 prey animats.

individual predators catch less prey. The reason for this is that the increased evasion chance allows individual prey to escape and breed, thus increasing the prey population. This increased prey population, in turn, provides predators with more available prey and thus the predator population also increases, following the well known boom-bust population phenomena [23].

However, when the prey evasion value reaches values above 70, individual prey becomes too difficult to catch and predators can not catch enough to sustain themselves. Thus, from this point on, there is a rapid downward trend in predator numbers and a corresponding increase in prey population.

4 Experiment 2 – Overcrowding

Experiment 1 in section 3 established that both predators and prey benefit from prey evasion up to the point when the prey evasion value moves above 70. Once the value is greater than 70, prey can successfully evade predators most of the time leading to predators starving and the predator population becoming unsustainable.

In real animal populations, prey evasion does not reach such levels as some other factor usually intervenes to prevent this. These may include: predators evolving speed or other attributes that reduce prey evasion effectiveness, predators switching to other prey, or overcrowding of prey leading to a reduction in the ability to evade predators [15, 17, 24].

In this experiment, we assume that when the prey population exceeds 50,000 the prey will become overcrowded and that this overcrowding leads to a reduction in the prey evasion value. At this stage, the reduction is uniform across the prey population but future work may include making the reduction dependent on local factors. The formula used to calculate the reduction is (where N is the total prey population):

```
if (N > 50,000) then:
  reduction = (N - 50,000) / 1,800
else:
  reduction = 0
```

The reduction is then applied to the evasion value for each prey animat.

Once again, all prey were assigned a fixed prey evasion value and offspring were clones, i.e. every prey animat only ever carries the initial fixed evasion value. Several fixed evasion values were tested and the results are shown in Figure 5 (prey population) and Figure 6 (predator population). Each data point in the graphs is the final population figure at the end of a simulation of 1,000 time steps during which all prey carried the designated evasion value.

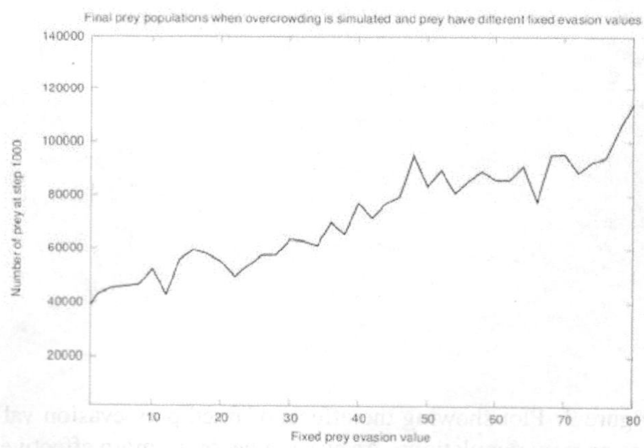

Figure 5: Plot showing the effects of fixed prey evasion values on prey populations. Predators are assumed to benefit from prey overcrowding and prey evasion values are reduced if the population is over 50,000. As evasion becomes more effective, predators catch less prey causing the prey population to increase.

The effects of prey overcrowding are clearly shown in Figure 5 where the prey populations never climb above 120,000. This should be compared with the situation in which prey overcrowding was ignored and prey populations reached figures in excess of 350,000 – see Figure 2. Figure 6 shows the benefits to the predator population of prey overcrowding in

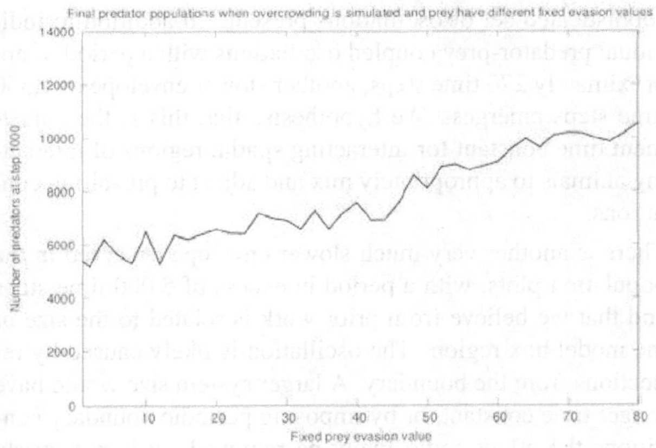

Figure 6: Plot showing the effects of fixed prey evasion values on predator populations. Predators are assumed to benefit from prey overcrowding and prey evasion values are reduced if the population is over 50,000. As evasion becomes more effective, predators catch less prey causing the prey population to increase and in turn making it easier for predators to find more prey. The predator population thus also increases.

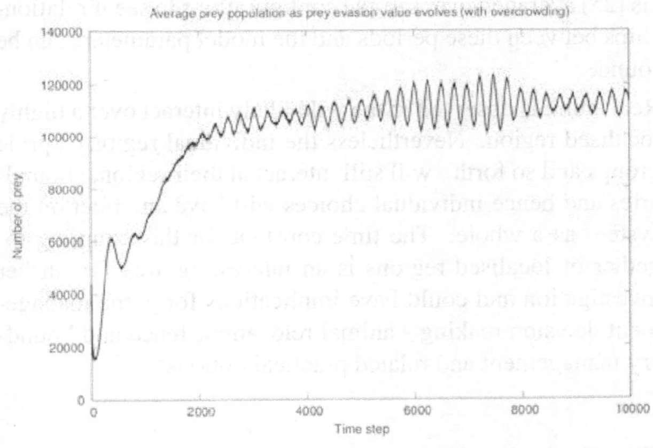

Figure 7: Plot showing the effect on the prey population as prey evasion values are allowed to evolve naturally over time. All prey were initially assigned an evasion value of 0. The overcrowding reduction is applied to evasion values, as described in Experiment 2 in section 4. The plot shows the average population over ten runs with different random number seeds.

that predators are always able to catch enough to eat and to increase their population, even when prey evasion values are above 70.

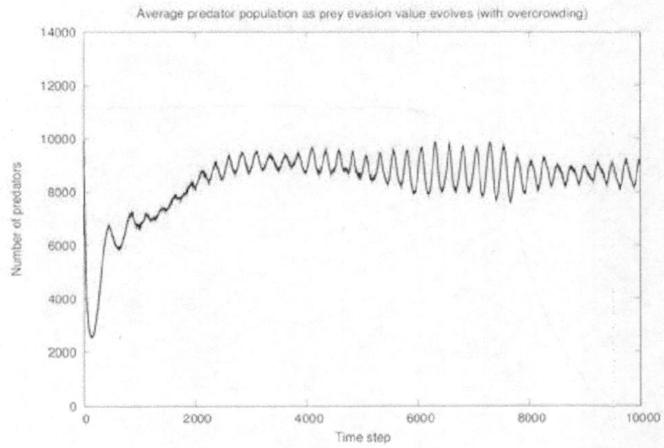

Figure 8: Plot showing the effect on the predator population as prey evasion values are allowed to evolve naturally over time. All prey were initially assigned an evasion value of 0. The overcrowding reduction is applied to evasion values, as described in Experiment 2 in section 4. The plot shows the average population over ten runs with different random number seeds.

5 Experiment 3 – Evolution of Evasion

Experiment 1 in section 3 established that different (fixed) prey evasion values affected both the predator and prey populations. In particular if the evasion value was too high (above 70) it became impossible for predators to sustain themselves and the prey population consequently increased dramatically. Experiment 2 in section 4 showed that both predator and prey populations could be stabilized by introducing a reduction in prey evasion values based on the size of the prey population.

This experiment investigates what happens when prey are allowed to evolve an evasion value. In this experiment, all prey were initially assigned an evasion value of 0 but evasion values were allowed to evolve due to mutation. When a new prey animat is produced, it inherits the evasion value of its parent but makes a random change to the evasion value (mutation). This change can be as much as 5 more or less than the inherited evasion value. For example, if an existing prey animat has an evasion value of 25 its offspring can have evasion values anywhere in the range from 20 up to 30. However, prey evasion values are restricted to a minimum of 0 and a maximum of 99.

Figure 7 and Figure 8 show the average populations of prey and predators respectively over time as the evasion values mutate and evolve within the prey population. Evasion values initially climb rapidly as individual prey mutate to a higher evasion value, enabling them to more easily evade predators and thereby survive to produce more offspring. However, the prey population increases to the point where prey become overcrowded and a reduction is applied to the evasion values.

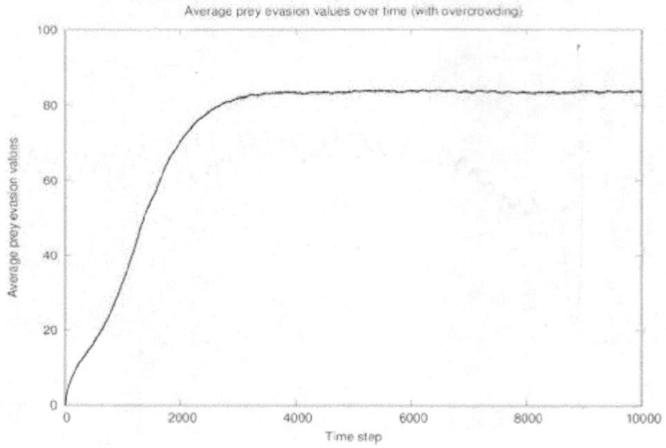

Figure 9: Plot showing how the prey evasion values evolved over the simulations shown in Figure 7 and Figure 8.

This enables predators to more easily catch prey and thus stabilizes the populations in the typical "boom-bust" oscillations characteristic of predator-prey models [23].

Figure 9 shows the change in the average prey evasion value over time. There is an initial increase followed by a steady state as the populations stabilize. The curve is quite smooth, albeit with continued fluctuations superposed as animats adjust their evasiveness locally.

6 Discussion

An interesting and important general observation concerns the interplay between what strategies work well for individual agents and what works best for the system as a whole. As figures 2 and 3 show, a prey species that is good at predator evasion may well survive initially but this can lead to massive over population levels of prey which in turn lead to a massive increase in predators before the whole system crashes. Predators then wipe out all prey before dying themselves of subsequent starvation. In many other variations of the core model we have found that such crashes are often avoided and the spatial model "equilibrates" and settles to finite dynamic mean population values around which stable and regular oscillations occur.

As the experiments in section 4 showed, a more realistic prey evasion probability does allow the system to reach a dynamic equilibrium mean values without complete extinction crashes occurring. In general if the spatial model system is large enough, even modestly large patches of local extinction can be tolerated and the system as a whole will recover. There are no obvious systematics to the fluctuations in the plots of section 4.

The most interesting case is when individual animats are able to adjust their microscopic behaviours and we observe a more sophisticated set of oscillations present. In addition to individual predator-prey coupled oscillations with a period of approximately 270 time steps, another slower envelope of 1,350 time steps emerges. We hypothesise that this is the adjustment time constant for interacting spatial regions of interacting animats to appropriately mix and adjust to prevailing conditions.

There is another very much slower envelope observed in the population plots, with a period in excess of 5,000 time steps and that we believe from prior work is related to the size of the model box region. The oscillation is likely caused by reflections from the boundary. A larger system size would have longer time constant, or by imposing periodic boundary conditions the effect could likely be removed. It is not overly influential for this study of evasion effects however. Figure 4 suggests that at any given time there are a number of relatively localised subsystems of interacting predators and prey in the model system. If a local extinction does occur, then stragglers colonize and take over that empty region and so the overall system - providing it is large enough - will not suffer total extinction, due to local fluctuations. A systemic effect such as massive over success of, for example, prey (as found in Experiment 1 in section 3) is necessary for a complete crash.

There is scope for a more detailed Fourier time-series analysis [25] averaged over sample configurations to see if relationships between these periods and the model parameters can be found.

Real animals observed in the wild likely interact over a highly localised region. Nevertheless the individual regions - pride groups and so forth - will still interact at their regional boundaries and hence individual choices will have an effect on the system as a whole. The time constant for this coupling together of localised regions is an interesting area for further investigation and could have implications for game management decision making - animal relocation; fence and boundary management and related practical options.

7 Conclusion

We have shown how predator evasion can be incorporated into an individual agent-based "animat" model to produce a number of emergent effects on the system as a whole. These include: over population of prey followed by over predation and subsequent system wide population crashes; and longer-term approach to a dynamic mean equilibrium around which stable spatial fluctuations are possible.

We have also observed the superposition of oscillations which we hypothesize is due to a new regional effect caused by local adjustments by individual animats within a region. We have shown how our rule-based model supports individual animats evolving traits and effectively adjusting a model parameter to reach a dynamic equilibrium that is stable against whole system crashes.

We believe there is ample scope for a more extensive quantitative analysis to further investigate interactions between localised regions. It may also be possible to investigate an imposition of deliberate boundary walls or isolation artifacts such as fences and animal group relocations, both in the model as well as in real predator-prey systems.

References

[1] Adami, C.: On modeling life. In Brooks, R., Maes, P., eds.: Proc. Artificial Life IV, MIT Press (1994) 269–274

[2] Ray, T.: An approach to the synthesis of life. Artificial Life II, Santa Fe Institute Studies in the Sciences of Complexity **xi** (1991) 371–408

[3] Holland, J.H.: Echoing emergence: Objectives, rough definitions, and speculations for echo-class models. In Cowan, G.A., Pines, D., Meltzer, D., eds.: Complexity: Metaphors, Models and Reality. Addison-Wesley, Reading, MA (1994) 309–342

[4] Tyrrell, T., Mayhew, J.E.W.: Computer simulation of an animal environment. In Meyer, J.A., Wilson, S.W., eds.: From Animals to Animats, Proceedings of the First International Conference on Simulation of Adaptive Behavior. (1991) 263–272

[5] Yaeger, L.: Computational genetice, physiology. metabolism, neural systems, learning, vision and behavior or polyworld: Life in a new context. In Langton, C., ed.: Proc Artificial Life III Conference. (1994)

[6] Wilson, S.W.: The animat path to AI. In Meyer, J.A., Wilson, S., eds.: From Animals to Animats 1: Proceedings of The First International Conference on Simulation of Adaptive Behavior, Cambridge, MA: The MIT Press/Bradford Books (1991) 15–21

[7] Ziemke, T., Balkenius, C., Hallam, J., eds.: From Animals to Animats 12 - 12th Int. Conf. on Simulation of Adaptive Behaviour (SAB 2012). Number 7426 in LNAI, Odense, Denkmark, Springer (2012)

[8] Fine, B.T., Shell, D.A.: Examining the information requirements for flocking motion. In: From Animals to Animats 12 - Proc. 12th Int. Conf. on Simulation of Adaptive Behaviours (SAB2012). Number 7426 in LNAI, Odense, Denmark, Springer (2012) 442–452

[9] Scogings, C.J., Hawick, K.A.: An investigation into the effects of sentinels on animat collectives. In: Proc. Nineteenth IASTED Int. Conf on Applied Simulation and Modelling (ASM 2011). Number 715-095, Crete, Greece, IASTED (2011) 221–226 CSTN-121.

[10] Scogings, C.J., Hawick, K.A.: Simulating intelligent emergent behaviour amongst termites to repair breaches in nest walls. In: Proc. Int. Conf on Computational Intelligence (CI2010), Maui, Hawaii, IASTED (2010) 125–132

[11] Hawick, K.A., Scogings, C.J., James, H.A.: Defensive spiral emergence in a predator-prey model. Complexity International **12** (2008) 1–10 ISSN 1320-0682.

[12] Woodbury, P.: The geometry of predator avoidance by the blue crab, callinectes sapidus rathbun. Animal Behaviour **34** (1986) 28–37

[13] Harper, D., Blake, R.: Energetics of piscivorous predator-prey interactions. Theoretical Biology **134** (1988) 59–76

[14] Weihs, D., Webb, P.: Optimal avoidance and evasion tactics in predator-prey interactions. Theoretical Biology **106** (1984) 189–206

[15] Beauchamp, G., Ruxton, G.: Changes in antipredator vigilance over time caused by a war of attrition between predator and prey. Behavioral Ecology **23** (2012) 265–270

[16] Hugie, D.M.: A waiting game between the black-bellied plover and its fiddler crab prey. Animal Behaviour **67** (2004) 823–831

[17] Scheel, D.: Watching for lions in the grass: the usefulness of scanning and its effects during hunts. Animal Behaviour **46** (1993) 695–704

[18] Scogings, C.J., Hawick, K.A., James, H.A.: Tools and techniques for optimisation of microscopic artificial life simulation models. In Nyongesa, H., ed.: Proceedings of the Sixth IASTED International Conference on Modelling, Simulation, and Optimization, Gabarone, Botswana, IASTED (2006) 90–95

[19] Lotka, A.J.: Elements of Physical Biology. Williams & Williams, Baltimore (1925)

[20] Scogings, C.J., Hawick, K.A., James, H.A.: Tuning growth stability in an animat agent model. In: Proceedings of the 16th IASTED International Conference in Applied Simulation and Modelling (ASM 2007). Number 581-094, Palma de Mallorca, Spain, IASTED (2007) 312–317

[21] Scogings, C.J., Hawick, K.A.: Global constraints and diffusion in a localised animat agent model. In: Proc. IASTED Int. Conf. on Applied Simulation and Modelling, Corfu, Greece, IASTED (2008) 14–19

[22] James, H.A., Scogings, C.J., Hawick, K.A.: Parallel synchronization issues in simulating artifical life. In Gonzalez, T., ed.: Proc. 16th IASTED Int. Conf. on Parallel and Distributed Computing and Systems (PDCS), Cambridge, MA, USA, IASTED (2004) 815–820 ISSN 1925-7937; ISBN 0-88986-421-7.

[23] Volterra, V.: Variazioni e fluttuazioni del numero d'individui in specie animali conviventi. Mem. R. Accad. Naz. dei Lincei, Ser VI **2** (1926)

[24] Jackson, A., Beauchamp, G., Broom, M., Ruxton, G.: Evolution of anti-predator traits in response to a flexible targeting strategy by predators. Proc. R. Soc. B. **273** (2006) 1055–1062

[25] Grafakos, L.: Nodern Fourier Analysis. Springer (2009)

Increasing the Density of Multi-Objective Multi-Modal Solutions using Clustering and Pareto Estimation Techniques

R. Kudikala, I. Giagkiozis, and P.J. Fleming
Department of Automatic Control and Systems Engineering,
The University of Sheffield, Sheffield - S1 3JD, UK

Abstract—*For continuous multi-objective optimization problems there exists an infinite number of solutions on the Pareto-optimal front. A multi-objective evolutionary algorithm attempts to find a representative set of the Pareto-optimal solutions. In the case of multi-objective multi-modal problems, there exist multiple decision vectors which map to identical objective vectors on Pareto front. Many multi-objective evolutionary algorithms fail to find and preserve all of the multi-modal solutions in the non-dominated solutions set. Finding more of the available multi-modal solutions would give the decision maker a greater selection when choosing between solutions. In this paper, we present an extended version of the Pareto estimation method, to increase the density of the multi-objective multi-modal solutions. The method uses clustering analysis to identify and separate different clusters in the decision variables space which correspond to the multi-modal Pareto optimal solutions. Then Pareto estimation procedure is employed for these individual clusters, there by increasing the density of available multi-modal solutions. The proposed method has been tested on experimental test functions and is shown to be successful.*

Keywords: Multi-objective optimization, multi-objective multi-modal problems, cluster analysis, genetic algorithms.

1. Introduction

Many multi-objective evolutionary algorithms (MOEAs) fail to find and preserve all of the multi-modal solutions in the non-dominated solutions set [1]. Due to the incorporation of diversity operators in MOEA, they will assign low fitness values to solutions that are densely clustered in objective space, which will eventually lead to their elimination from the population. Hence they can identify only one set of decision vectors out of the multi-modal solutions and converge to any one of the global optima out of multiple global optima present in the multi-objective multi-modal problems. Finding the multi-modal solutions would allow the decision maker a greater choice when choosing between solutions. For example, in chemical process optimization the decision maker would want to know about different temperature settings for which the process can deliver the same results [2].

In this work, we present an extended version of the Pareto estimation method [3], which can be used to increase the number of multi-modal solutions. The method uses clustering analysis to identify and separate different clusters in the decision variables space which correspond to the multi-modal Pareto optimal solutions. Then Pareto estimation procedure is employed for these individual clusters, therefore increasing the density of available multi-modal solutions in multi-objective problems.

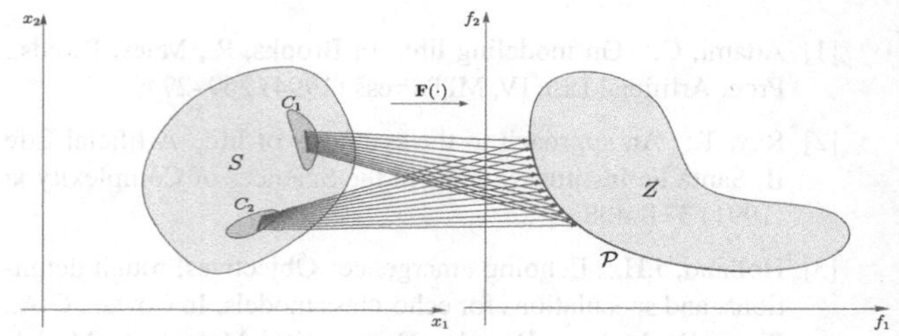

Fig. 1: A many to one objective function. The two sets C_1 and C_2 map to the same Pareto optimal solutions in the Pareto optimal set $\mathcal{P}$.

The remainder of this paper is organized as follows. In Section 2 a general definition of a multi-objective optimization problem and key concepts and definitions are provided. Section 3 presents Pareto estimation method and in Section 4 the extended Pareto estimation method with clustering is described for multi-objective multi-modal problems. In Section 5 the method is tested against a multi-objective multi-modal test problem with three cases and these tests are reported in Section 6. This paper is summarized and concluded in Section 7.

2. Problems with Multiple Global Optima

A multi-objective problem (MOP) is defined as:

$$\min_{\mathbf{x}} \mathbf{F}(\mathbf{x}) = (f_1(\mathbf{x}), f_2(\mathbf{x}), \ldots, f_k(\mathbf{x})), \quad \text{subject to } \mathbf{x} \in S, \tag{1}$$

where k describes the multiplicity of scalar objective functions $f(\cdot)$ and S is the *feasible region*. The vector of variables, $\mathbf{x}$, in this context is often referred to as decision vector while $\mathbf{z} = \mathbf{F}(\mathbf{x})$ is referred to as objective vector. An implicit assumption is that the individual scalar objective functions in (1) are mutually *competing*. The objective function described in (1) can in some cases be a many-to-one mapping. Namely, there exist $\mathbf{x}, \mathbf{y} \in S$ and $\mathbf{x} \neq \mathbf{y}$ that map to the same objective vector, $\mathbf{F}(\mathbf{x}) = \mathbf{F}(\mathbf{y})$. This can especially impact the optimization algorithm when the objective function is many-to-one in the domain of Pareto optimal solutions, see *Fig. 1*. In this case, the same Pareto optimal objective vector can be obtained for more than one decision vector.

If the above assumptions hold then only a partial ordering can be defined unambiguously. Namely, when comparing two decision vectors $\mathbf{x}, \tilde{\mathbf{x}} \in S$, it can so happen that their corresponding objective vectors are incomparable. In practice, this situation is resolved by a decision maker who will select one solution over all others, thus inducing a form of complete ordering. However this ordering is mostly subjective, even in the case that utility functions [4] are used to ease the work of the DM. In the absence of a DM a usual assumption is that the relative importance of the objectives, f_i, is unknown hence it is reasonable to obtain several non-comparable solutions. The problem of inducing partial ordering in Euclidean spaces was initially studied by Edgeworth [5], and later further expanded by Pareto [6]. The relations introduced by Pareto are defined as follows for a minimization problem:

Definition 1: A decision vector $\mathbf{x}^\star \in S$ is said to **weakly dominate** a decision vector $\mathbf{x}$ iff $f_i(\mathbf{x}^\star) \leq f_i(\mathbf{x}), \forall i \in \{1, 2, \ldots, k\}$ and $f_i(\mathbf{x}^\star) < f_i(\mathbf{x})$, for at least one $i \in \{1, 2, \ldots, k\}$ then $\mathbf{x}^\star \preceq \mathbf{x}$.

Definition 2: A decision vector $\mathbf{x}^\star \in S$ is said to **dominate** a decision vector $\mathbf{x}$ iff $f_i(\mathbf{x}^\star) < f_i(\mathbf{x}), \ \forall i \in \{1, 2, \ldots, k\}$ then $\mathbf{x}^\star \prec \mathbf{x}$.

Definition 3: A decision vector $\mathbf{x}^\star \in S$ is said to be **Pareto optimal** if there is no other decision vector $\mathbf{x} \in S$ such that $f_i(\mathbf{x}) \leq f_i(\mathbf{x}^\star), \ \forall i \in \{1, 2, \ldots, k\}$ and $f_i(\mathbf{x}) < f_i(\mathbf{x}^\star)$, for at least one $i \in \{1, 2, \ldots, k\}$.

Definition 4: Let $\mathbf{F} : S \rightarrow Z$, with $S \in \mathbb{R}^n$ and $Z \in \mathbb{R}^k$. If S is the feasible region then the set Z is the feasible region in objective space. Given a set $\mathbf{A} \subset Z$, the **non-dominated set** is defined as $\mathcal{P} = \{\mathbf{z} : \nexists \tilde{\mathbf{z}} \preceq \mathbf{z}, \forall \tilde{\mathbf{z}} \in \mathbf{A}\}$. If $\mathbf{A}$ is the entire feasible region in the objective space, Z, then the set $\mathcal{P}$ is called the **Pareto optimal set** (PS) or **Pareto Front** (PF). Any element $\mathbf{z} \in Z$ is referred to as **objective vector**.

Definition 5: The **ideal objective vector**, $\mathbf{z}^\star$, is the vector with elements $(\inf(f_1), \ldots, \inf(f_k))$ [7, pp. 16].

Definition 6: The **nadir objective vector**, $\mathbf{z}^{nd}$, is the vector with elements $(\sup(f_1), \ldots, \sup(f_k))$, subject to f_i be elements of objective vectors in the Pareto optimal set [7, pp. 16].

Definition 7: The **convex hull** [8, pp. 24] of the set $C = \{\mathbf{e}_1, \ldots, \mathbf{e}_k\}$, denoted as $\mathbf{conv}\, C$, where $\mathbf{e}_i$ is a $k \times 1$ vector of zeros with 1 on the ith position, is referred to as $\mathbf{CH_I}$.

Definition 8: The **extended convex hull** ($\mathbf{EH_I}$) of the set C, is the union of CH_I and the points in the affine space of the set C produced by the projection of a Pareto optimal front, with ideal vector $\mathbf{0}$ and nadir vector $\mathbf{1}$, onto the hyper-surface of C.

Definition 9: Two decision vectors $\mathbf{x}, \mathbf{y} \in S$ are said to be **multi-modal solutions** if they satisfy $\mathbf{x} \neq \mathbf{y}$, and $\mathbf{F}(\mathbf{x}) = \mathbf{F}(\mathbf{y})$ for all $i = 1, \ldots, k$.

3. Pareto Estimation Method

3.1 Motivation

Consider the following problem. At the end of an optimization run on a multi-objective optimization problem we have a set of solutions that approximate the Pareto optimal front. Subsequently, these solutions are presented to a decision maker (DM) who can identify a few candidate solutions that are of interest, however, he would prefer a solution in the vicinity of the aforementioned solutions. In this case the analyst does not have many options and would either restart the optimization in hope that the preferred solution of the decision maker is obtained. An alternative is to use an interactive method such as, progressive preference articulation [9]. These alternatives present a number of difficulties of which the most obvious one is that the computational load is increasing disproportionately to the expected gain as there is absolutely no guarantee that the preferred solutions will be obtained. This consideration may lead the decision maker to abandon all the above scenarios and simply select one solution from the already existing Pareto set approximation.

The Pareto estimation method (PE) initially introduced in [3] resolves, to some extent, this issue by allowing the decision maker to explore more solutions in the vicinity of already obtained ones without resorting to further optimization. Specifically, Pareto estimation gives positive answer to the question: "Given a set of Pareto optimal solutions, obtained by any optimization algorithm, can specific solutions on the Pareto front be obtained that are not part of the initially obtained Pareto set?".

3.2 Overview

In [3] it was shown that using the Pareto estimation method the number of Pareto optimal solutions can be increased in specific regions of interest. Pareto estimation was applied to a 3-objective portfolio optimization problem successfully targeting two regions where the optimization algorithm used could not obtain solutions across 20 optimization runs. However, one of the assumptions in [3] was that the objective function is one-to-one, or at least that this condition obtains for the mapping between the Pareto set in decision and objective space. If this condition doesn't hold the artificial neural network used would face difficulties as for the same objective vector it would have to produce two or more output vectors simultaneously, see *Fig. 3*. In the rest of this section we briefly describe the Pareto estimation method and then explain the motivation for the extension introduced in this work. For a more complete description of the original version of the Pareto estimation method the reader is referred to [3].

A major motivation for the introduction of PE has been that Pareto optimal solutions can be obtained in specific regions of the Pareto front without the need to resort to additional optimization runs. Although there is no guarantee that such solutions will be produced the success rate of PE on a set of difficult test problems illustrated that the relative cost of

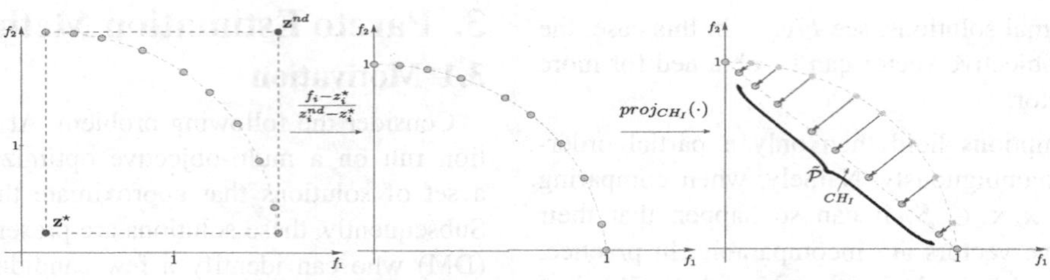

Fig. 2: Illustration of the Π^{-1} mapping for a hypothetical Pareto set $\mathcal{P}$.

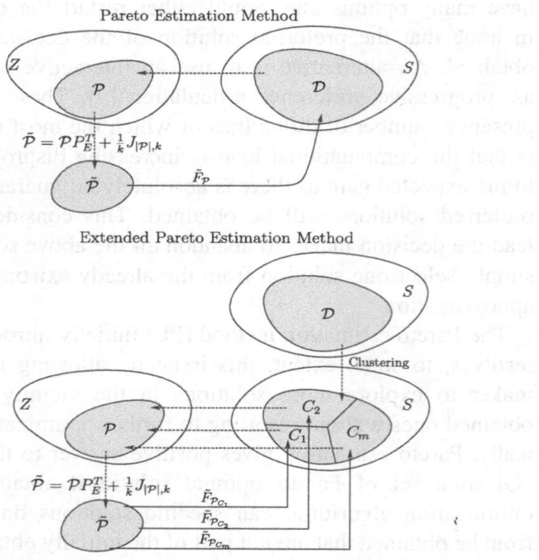

Fig. 3: The original version of the Pareto estimation method (top). The extended Pareto estimation method first clusters the Pareto optimal decision variable vectors and identifies a NN for every one (bottom).

applying PE before another method is justified [3]. PE depends on the ability to identify a relationship (mapping) from Pareto optimal solutions in objective space to decision space. This relationship can then be manipulated to produce solutions in specific parts of the Pareto front. We refer to this mapping as, $F_{\mathcal{P}}$, whose domain of definition is the set of Pareto optimal objective vectors, $\mathcal{P}$, and its range their corresponding decision variable vectors $\mathcal{D}$,

$$F_{\mathcal{P}} : \mathcal{P} \to \mathcal{D}. \tag{2}$$

We elected originally to use a radial basis neural network as it has been shown that it has competitive performance compared to the alternatives, see [10]. The theoretical argument that supports PE is was presented initially in [11], [12] and was later used by Zhang et al. [13] to create RM-MEDA, a regularity-based estimation of distribution algorithm. The argument is that for continuous multi-objective problems the Pareto optimal set is a piecewise continuous manifold in decision space. This effectively enables the identification of the mapping in (2).

3.3 Pareto Estimation - General Procedure

Pareto estimation is comprised of three main parts:

- A transformation of the Pareto optimal solutions in objective space, $\Pi^{-1} : \mathcal{P} \to \tilde{\mathcal{P}}$.
- The identification of the relationship, $F_{\tilde{\mathcal{P}}} : \tilde{\mathcal{P}} \to \mathcal{D}$, where $\mathcal{D}$ are decision vectors corresponding to Pareto optimal objective vectors, $\mathcal{P}$.
- The generation of a set, $\mathcal{E}$, and its use with the $F_{\tilde{\mathcal{P}}}$ mapping to generate a set of estimated decision vectors, $\mathcal{D}_{\mathcal{E}}$.

The first part is essentially a projection of the set $\mathcal{P}$ onto the CH_I. This is essential as it simplifies the task of generating the set $\mathcal{E}$ to a large degree, see *Fig. 2*. Prior to application of the projection the set $\mathcal{P}$ is normalized using,

$$\tilde{f}_i = \frac{f_i - \mathbf{z}_i^\star}{\mathbf{z}_i^{nd} - \mathbf{z}_i^\star}, \tag{3}$$

where $\mathbf{z}^\star$ and $\mathbf{z}^{nd}$ can be estimated from the Pareto optimal set $\mathcal{P}$. Using the normalization in (3) the objectives in $\mathcal{P}$ are restricted in the range $[0, 1]$ as shown in *Fig. 2*. Consequently the normalized objective vectors are projected onto CH_I as follows,

$$\tilde{\mathcal{P}} = \mathcal{P} P_E^T + \frac{1}{k} J_{|\mathcal{P}|,k}. \tag{4}$$

The matrix $J_{|\mathcal{P}|,k}$ is a $|\mathcal{P}| \times k$ unit matrix and P_E is a projection matrix obtained as:

$$P_E = H(H^T H)^{-1} H^T,$$
$$H = \left(\mathbf{e}_1 - \frac{1}{k}\mathbf{1} \cdots \mathbf{e}_{k-1} - \frac{1}{k}\mathbf{1} \right), \tag{5}$$

where $\mathbf{e}_i$ is a vector of zeros with its ith element set to 1. Next the artificial neural network (ANN) which is employed to identify the mapping $F_{\mathcal{P}}$, is created (see [3]), using $\tilde{\mathcal{P}}$ and $\mathcal{D}$ as the training inputs and outputs respectively.

When the ANN has been trained, it then can be used for creating more Pareto optimal solutions in specific regions on the PF given a set, $\mathcal{E}$, is supplied as input. $\mathcal{E}$ can be generated in one of two ways:

- In a specific region, presumably that is of interest to the decision maker.
- On the entire CH_I, which if PE is successful will cover the entire Pareto front.

In this paper, we employ the second method as it illustrates the ability of PE and its extended version presented here, to successfully identify Pareto optimal solutions across the entire front. It should be noted however that we envisage that the usage of PE would be to target specific parts of the PF as seen in [3].

4. Clustering and Pareto Estimation for Multi-Objective Multi-Modal Solutions

In the case of multi-objective multi-modal problems, there exists multiple decision vectors which result in identical objective vectors on Pareto front as shown in *Fig. 1*. This corresponds to the many-to-one mapping of the multiple decision vectors in $\mathcal{D}$ to the objective vectors in $\mathcal{P}$. The decision vectors corresponding to each multi-modal optimal fronts (Pareto front) originate from different clusters $\mathcal{C}_m$ in decision variable space $\mathcal{D}$. The ANN relationship will fail to produce the one-to-many mapping of $\tilde{F}_{\tilde{\mathcal{P}}} : \tilde{\mathcal{P}} \rightarrow \mathcal{D}$. It will generate any one but not all of the multi-modal solutions. In order to overcome this problem, the different clusters $\mathcal{C}_m$ of multi-modal solutions present in the non-dominated set can be identified and separated using a clustering algorithm. The obtained clusters of decision vectors $\mathcal{C}_m$ and corresponding objective vectors in $\mathcal{P}$ will have one-to-one mapping between decision variable space and objective space for the Pareto front. Once the different clusters of decision vectors $\mathcal{C}_m$ are separated, the ANN can be trained for the individual cluster of solutions $\mathcal{C}_m$ and $\tilde{\mathcal{P}}$ to identify number of one-to-one mappings $\tilde{F}_{\tilde{\mathcal{P}}_{\mathcal{C}_m}} : \tilde{\mathcal{P}} \rightarrow \mathcal{C}_m$.

Most clustering algorithms need the number of output clusters to be pre-specified as an input to the algorithm. In general we do not know a priori the number of clusters available in the data set. Bezdek and Hathaway developed a visual assessment of cluster tendency (VAT) method [14], to identify potential clusters in a data set. Here the pair-wise dissimilarities between the n individuals of the data set are estimated and reordered,so that all the neighbouring individuals are consecutively ordered. The reordered $n \times n$ matrix of pair-wise dissimilarities is displayed as an intensity image with $n \times n$ pixels. Clusters are indicated by dark blocks of pixels along the diagonal of the image. However, the VAT method is too computationally costly for larger data sets. Wang et al., [15], proposed an improved VAT (iVAT) and an automated VAT (aVAT) methods to automatically determine the number of clusters and cluster separation based on the difference between diagonal blocks and off-diagonal blocks in the image of the reordered dissimilarity matrix. In this paper, the iVAT and aVAT [15] methods are used for identifying different clusters of decision vectors $\mathcal{C}_m$ in $\mathcal{D}$, which correspond to multi-modal solutions in the objective space $\mathcal{P}$. The steps involved in clustering and Pareto estimation of multi-objective multi-modal solutions are summarised as follows:

Step 1 Extract, $\mathcal{P}$, the non-dominated individuals obtained at the end run of an optimization algorithm, and, $\mathcal{D}$ the associated decision vectors.

Step 2 Perform clustering analysis on the obtained decision variable vectors $\mathcal{D}$ using a clustering algorithm.

Step 3 The obtained clusters of decision vectors $\mathcal{C}_m$ and corresponding objective vectors $\mathcal{P}_{\mathcal{C}_m}$ will have one-to-one mapping between decision variable space and objective space.

Step 4 For each individual cluster normalize $\mathcal{P}$ using (3).

Step 5 Project the normalized $\mathcal{P}$ onto the the $k-1$ hyperplane defined by the set of vectors $\{\mathbf{e}_1, \ldots, \mathbf{e}_{k-1}\}$ using (5) and (4), to produce $\tilde{\mathcal{P}}$.

Step 6 Identify the mapping $\tilde{F}_{\tilde{\mathcal{P}}_{\mathcal{C}_m}} : \tilde{\mathcal{P}} \rightarrow \mathcal{C}_m$ using $\tilde{\mathcal{P}}$ and $\mathcal{C}_m$ as inputs and outputs, respectively, and use these to train the ANN.

Step 7 Create the set $\mathcal{E}$. In this work this is a set of evenly spaced convex vectors.

Step 8 Use the set $\mathcal{E}$ as inputs to the ANN created in Step 5, to obtain estimates of decision vectors $\mathcal{C}_{\mathcal{E}}$.

Step 9 All the sets $\mathcal{C}_{\mathcal{E}}$ can be used with the objective function $\mathbf{F}(\cdot)$ to verify that the produced solutions are non-dominated and acceptable.

5. Experimental Setting

We employed the following multi-objective multi-modal test functions as seen in [1].

$$\begin{aligned} \mathbf{F}(\mathbf{x}) &= (f_1(\mathbf{x}), f_2(\mathbf{x})) \\ &= \left(\sum_{i=1}^{n} \sin(\pi x_i), \sum_{i=1}^{n} \cos(\pi x_i) \right) \qquad (6) \\ & x_i \in [0, 6], i = 1, 2, ..., n. \end{aligned}$$

The above objective functions are chosen since both objectives are in conflict with each other and will have a trade-off in the objective space. For the minimization case, the above problem will have a known Pareto front which varies between $-\sum_{i=1}^{n} i$ to 0, where i is the number of decision variables chosen. The above problem is also a multi-objective multi-modal problem. The two objective functions are periodic functions with a period of 2. They will have efficient frontiers which correspond to the Pareto-optimal solutions for all the decision variable values varying in the ranges $x_i \in [2r + 1, 2r + 3/2]$, where r is an integer.

Deb and Tiwari [1] developed a generic evolutionary algorithm: Omni-optimizer, which incorporates restricted selection and crowding measure utilizing both objective and variable space information to find and preserve a well distributed multi-modal solutions. Here we use Omni-optimizer for solving the multi-objective multi-modal test problem in all three cases. Also we employ the ratio of the inverted generational distance, $D_R(\cdot, \cdot)$ and the ratio of the mean nearest neighbour distance $S_R(\cdot, \cdot)$ as well as the C-Metric. Due to space limitations we cannot include a description of these metrics, the reader is referred to [3].

6. Results and Discussion

In this paper, we are considering three test cases of the multi-objective multi-modal optimization problem (6) with different numbers of variables and population sizes in the optimization.

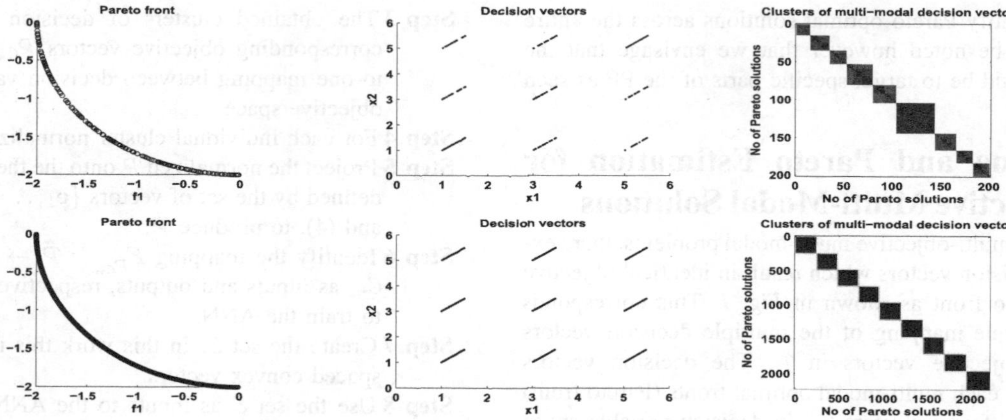

Fig. 4: Case I: Non-dominated solutions obtained with Omni-optimizer (top) and extended Pareto estimation methods (bottom) in objective space, decision variable space and image of clusters.

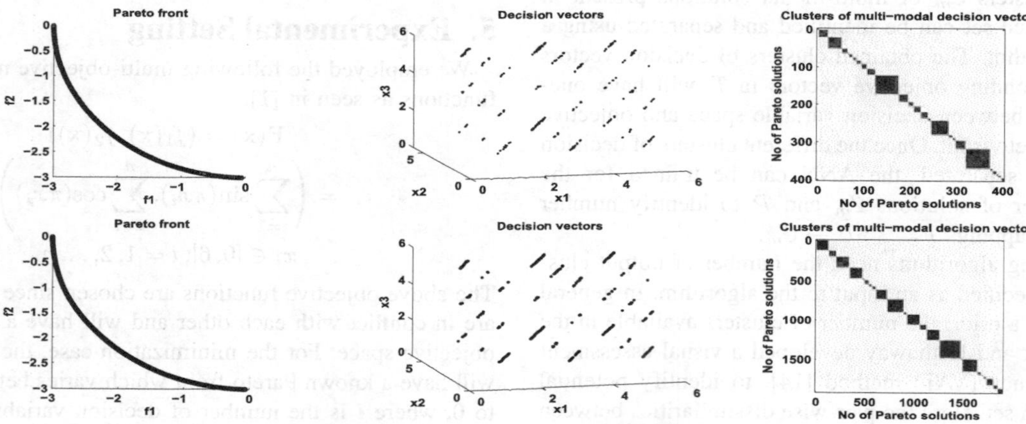

Fig. 5: Case II: Non-dominated solutions obtained with Omni-optimizer (top) and extended Pareto estimation methods (bottom) in objective space, decision variable space and image of clusters.

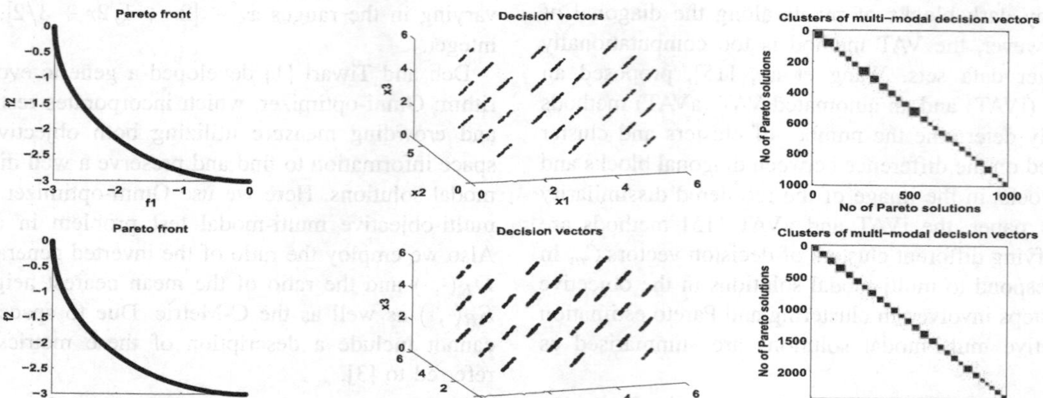

Fig. 6: Case III: Non-dominated solutions obtained with Omni-optimizer (top) and extended Pareto estimation methods (bottom) in objective space, decision variable space and image of clusters.

6.1 CASE I

In the Case I, we have chosen two decision variables $x_i \in [0,6], i = 1,2.$ for the optimization problem (6). Within the range of these two variables the problem will have nine multi-modal optimal fronts. We have set the population size to be 200 and run the optimizer for 500 generations. For the optimizer, finding the global Pareto front is not so difficult in this problem. However, finding all the multi-modal global Pareto fronts with good distribution of solutions in corresponding decision vector ranges is very difficult. In this particular instance, the Omni-optimizer [1] is able to find all nine multi-modal optimal fronts with 200 Pareto solutions with a good distribution of decision vectors in all ranges of $x_i \in [2r+1, 2r+3/2]$, where $i = 1,2$ and $r = 0,1,2$. *Fig. 4* shows the obtained Pareto optimal solutions in top three sub-plots.

Cluster analysis using iVAT and aVAT [15] methods is performed for the obtained Pareto optimal decision vectors. The reordered dissimilarity matrix of 200 decision vectors is displayed as 200 x 200 image with gray scaling in right hand side sub-plot. The dark blocks appearing on the diagonal of the image represent individual clusters; the size of each dark block, represent number of individuals present in each cluster. It can be seen from this plot, that each cluster (dark block) has atleast 18 individual solutions. After separating these clusters of decision vectors, the procedure for Pareto estimation is executed. For each cluster, the ANN is trained to find the one-to-one mapping between objective space and decision vector space. Then this ANN is used to estimate 300 solutions in each cluster.

The quality of mapping estimated by ANN is highly dependent on the supplied training decision vectors. If the training data has a sufficient number of vectors, well distributed, then the ANN will estimate a better mapping, otherwise, the mapping estimated by ANN will be deceptive and may not generate good solutions in the Pareto estimation process. After combining all the solutions obtained from individual Pareto estimations, we perform non-dominated sorting to remove any dominated solutions from the set. At the end we have obtained around 2 300 non-dominated solutions out of 2 700 solutions estimated. In *Fig. 4* the bottom sub-plots show plots for objective vectors, decision vectors and gray scale image of the dissimilarity matrix of estimated solutions. It can be seen from these sub-plots, that Pareto estimation along with clustering is successfully able to find many solutions for the multi-objective multi-modal problem.

6.2 CASE II

In Case II, we have chosen the same objective functions with three decision variables $x_i \in [0,6], i = 1,2,3..$ Within the range of these three variables the problem will have 27 multi-modal optimal fronts each one corresponding to $x_i \in [2r+1, 2r+3/2]$, where $i = 1,2,3$ and $r = 0,1,2$.

We have set 400 as the population size and run the optimizer for 500 generations. The obtained 400 non-dominated solutions are shown in the top three sub-plots *Fig. 5*. The optimizer has found all 27 multi-modal Pareto fronts, however, it is not able to obtain good distribution of solutions in all the corresponding decision vectors ranges. This can be easily observed from the image of clusters, in which some clusters have more than 70 solutions, where as some clusters got very less number of decision vectors around 2 or 3.

We applied Pareto estimation to each cluster of solutions, tried to estimate 200 solutions for each cluster. After combining the solutions estimated from all the clusters, non-dominated sorting is performed to get the non-dominated solutions. Around 1 950 solutions found to be non-dominated out of 5 400 estimated solutions. The method is able to estimate around 150 to 200 non-dominated solutions in some clusters, but failed to estimate more solutions in clusters where there are insufficient number of solution used for training the ANN. In *Fig. 5* the bottom three sub plots show the estimated non-dominated solutions, in objective space, decision variable space and image of clusters. (Note: Here the order of clusters in top and bottom images is not same.)

6.3 CASE III

In Case III, we have chosen the same objective functions with three decision variables $x_i \in [0,6], i = 1,2,3.$, but now increase the population size to 1 000 in optimization and run the optimizer for 500 generations. The obtained 1 000 non-dominated solutions are shown in *Fig. 6* top three subplots. The optimizer has found all 27 multi-modal Pareto fronts and is now able to obtain a good distribution of solutions in all the corresponding decision vectors ranges. This can be easily observed from the image of clusters, in which clusters have solutions in the range of 20 to 60 solutions per cluster.

We applied Pareto estimation to each cluster of solutions and tried to estimate 150 solutions for each cluster. After combining the solutions estimated from all the clusters, non-dominated sorting is performed to get the non-dominated solutions. Around 3 000 solutions were found to be non-dominated out of 4 050 estimated solutions. The method is able to estimate around 100 to 150 non-dominated solutions in each cluster. In *Fig. 6* the lower three sub-plots show the estimated non-dominated solutions, in objective space, decision variable space and image of clusters. It can be seen that, a very good distribution of non-dominated solutions is obtained from the Pareto estimation. (Note: Here the order of clusters in top and bottom images is not same.)

Tables 1 and 2 summarize the various test metric computed for the non-dominated solutions before and after the Pareto estimation in all the three cases I, II, and III. These metrics indicated that the proposed method is able to estimate well distributed non-dominated solutions close to the true Pareto front, when compare to non-dominated solutions obtained from the Omni-optimizer.

Table 1: $D_R(\mathcal{P}, \mathcal{P}_\mathcal{E})$ and $S_R(\mathcal{P}, \mathcal{P}_\mathcal{E})$ values of the obtained solutions by OMNI-optimizer, $\mathcal{P}$, and the estimated set, $\mathcal{P}_\mathcal{E}$, by the extended Pareto estimation method.

	IGD Ratio			ESSm Ratio		
Problem	min	mean	std	min	mean	std
Case I	5.2689	6.3300	0.5565	9.1278	11.3150	1.3969
Case II	1.8721	2.3615	0.2722	5.0175	5.6117	0.3843
Case III	1.8316	2.2347	0.1524	2.4162	2.9601	0.2344

Table 2: C-Metric values of the solutions obtained by OMNI-optimizer, $\mathcal{P}$, and the estimated set, $\mathcal{P}_\mathcal{E}$, using the extended Pareto estimation method.

	$C(\mathcal{P}_\mathcal{E}, \mathcal{P})$			$C(\mathcal{P}, \mathcal{P}_\mathcal{E})$		
Problem	min	mean	std	min	mean	std
Case I	0.4900	0.5848	0.0433	0.0000	0.0100	0.0042
Case II	0.4525	0.5200	0.0273	0.0000	0.0000	0.0000
Case III	0.5900	0.6154	0.0216	0.0000	0.0000	0.0000

7. Conclusions

For continuous multi-objective optimization problems, there exist an infinite number of solutions on the Pareto-optimal front. A multi-objective evolutionary algorithm (MOEA) attempts to find a representative set of the Pareto-optimal solutions. If the decision maker is not satisfied with the representative set found by the MOEA, and wants to explore different solutions available on the Pareto front, the MOEA needs to be re-run, which will increase the number of function evaluations without providing any guarantees that a suitable solution will be identified. In this case, the Pareto estimation method can prove useful in order to increase the density of available non-dominated solutions in particular regions or the entire Pareto front. However, in the case of multi-objective multi-modal problems, the Pareto estimation method is not able to identify the one-to-many mapping of the objective vectors to decision variables vectors.

In this paper, we have introduced an extended version of the Pareto estimation method, to increase the density of multi-objective multi-modal solutions. The method uses clustering analysis to identify and separate different clusters in the decision variable space which correspond to the multi-modal Pareto optimal solutions. These individual clusters are then used to estimate the relation between objective space to decision space using an ANN. Instead of a single network, as is the case in the Pareto estimation method, we employ a network for each individual cluster. These are then employed to estimate more solutions for the selected cluster, presumably by the decision maker, or all cluster. For testing purposes we have employed the latter method in this work.

The proposed method has been tested on experimental test functions, with three different case studies. We have used Omni-optimizer [1] to solve the test problem in three cases, and iVAT and aVAT [15] methods to identify different clusters of solutions in the cluster analysis. In all cases, the extended Pareto estimation method has successfully found many non-dominated solutions corresponding to different multi-modal solutions. The success of the proposed method highly depends on the number of solutions available in an individual cluster for training and estimating the one-to-one mapping between objective space and decision vector space. In case II, the method failed to improve density of the solutions in the clusters with a small number of individuals. However, it has improved the density of solutions in the remaining clusters representing multi-modal solutions to the test problem. We leave for future work the evaluation of the proposed method on a real-world system architecture design problems, which have a tendency to have multi-model solutions.

8. Acknowledgements

The first author wishes to acknowledge the financial support of Rolls-Royce plc and EPSRC through a Dorothy Hodgkin Postgraduate Award (DHPA).

References

[1] K. Deb and S. Tiwari, "Omni-optimizer: A generic evolutionary algorithm for single and multi-objective optimization," *European Journal of Operational Research*, vol. 185, no. 3, pp. 1062–1087, 2008.

[2] A. Tarafder, G. Rangaiah, and A. K. Ray, "A study of finding many desirable solutions in multiobjective optimization of chemical processes," *Computers & chemical engineering*, vol. 31, no. 10, pp. 1257–1271, 2007.

[3] I. Giagkiozis and P. Fleming, "Increasing the Density of Available Pareto Optimal Solutions," Department of Automatic Control and Systems Engineering, The University of Sheffield, Research Report No. 1028, November 2012.

[4] C. Vira and Y. Haimes, *Multiobjective Decision Making: Theory and Methodology*. North-Holland, 1983, no. 8.

[5] F. Edgeworth, *Mathematical Psychics: An Essay on the Application of Mathematics to the Moral Sciences*. CK Paul, 1881, no. 10.

[6] V. Pareto, "Cours D'Économie Politique," 1896.

[7] K. Miettinen, *Nonlinear Multiobjective Optimization*. Springer, 1999, vol. 12.

[8] S. Boyd and L. Vandenberghe, *Convex Optimization*. Cambridge University Press, 2004.

[9] C. Fonseca and P. Fleming, "Multiobjective Optimization and Multiple Constraint Handling with Evolutionary Algorithms. I. A Unified Formulation," *IEEE Transactions on Systems, Man and Cybernetics, Part A: Systems and Humans*, vol. 28, no. 1, pp. 26–37, 1998.

[10] Y. Jin, "A Comprehensive Survey of Fitness Approximation in Evolutionary Computation," *Soft Computing - A Fusion of Foundations, Methodologies and Applications*, vol. 9, pp. 3–12, 2005.

[11] Y. Jin and B. Sendhoff, "Connectedness, Regularity and the Success of Local Search in Evolutionary Multi-Objective Optimization," in *Congress on Evolutionary Computation*, vol. 3, dec. 2003, pp. 910 – 1917.

[12] O. Schütze, S. Mostaghim, M. Dellnitz, and J. Teich, "Covering Pareto Sets by Multilevel Evolutionary Subdivision Techniques," in *Evolutionary Multi-Criterion Optimization*, ser. Lecture Notes in Computer Science. Springer Berlin / Heidelberg, 2003, vol. 2632, pp. 10–10.

[13] Q. Zhang, A. Zhou, and Y. Jin, "RM-MEDA: A Regularity Model-Based Multiobjective Estimation of Distribution Algorithm," *IEEE Transactions on Evolutionary Computation*, vol. 12, no. 1, pp. 41–63, 2008.

[14] J. C. Bezdek and R. J. Hathaway, "Vat: A tool for visual assessment of (cluster) tendency," in *Proceedings of the 2002 International Joint Conference on Neural Networks, 2002. IJCNN'02.*, vol. 3. IEEE, 2002, pp. 2225–2230.

[15] L. Wang, U. Nguyen, J. Bezdek, C. Leckie, and K. Ramamohanarao, "iVat and aVat: Enhanced visual analysis for cluster tendency assessment," *Advances in Knowledge Discovery and Data Mining*, pp. 16–27, 2010.

Cancer Genome Assembly and Alignment

Michael Shan-Hui Ho[1], Kun-Yu Hung[2], Yu-Shiang Gen[1], Chaochang Chiu[3] and Tsung-Hua Lu [1]
[1]Department of Electric Engineering, NTPU, New Taipei City, Taiwan, ROC
[2]Department of Information Management, MCU, Taoyuan Country, Taiwan, ROC
[3]Department of Information Management, YZU, Taoyuan Country, Taiwan, ROC

Abstract— *Cancer is defined as a disease that involves changes or mutations in the cell genome. The underlying cause of mutations leading to cancer is DNA damage. Cancer genome sequencing includes cancer genome assembly and cancer genome alignment is through early detection improving survival opportunity of cancer patients. In this research, a bioinformatics approach is proposed to solve cancer genome sequencing by constructing De Bruijn Graphs along with using the Euler Path for finding an optimal cancer genome reassembly and the Smith – Waterman scoring matrix for cancer genome alignment optimization.*

Keywords: Cancer Genome Assembly, Cancer Genome Alignment, Bioinformatics Computing, De Bruijn Graphs, Smith – Waterman Matrix

1 Introduction

Cancer is an important public health concern around the world. Cancer is defined as a disease that involves changes or mutations in the cell genome. These changes (mutations) produce proteins that disrupt the delicate cellular balance between cell division and quiescence, resulting in cells that keep dividing to form cancers. The underlying cause of mutations leading to cancer is DNA damage.

DNA damage In human cells, the estimated average number of DNA damages occurring per hour is about 800, and the number per day is about 19,200 [1]. Under normal circumstances, a healthy cells repair virtually all of these damages. Damages that are not repaired are termed mutations. When a single cell acquires enough mutations in the DNA sequence of relevant 'cancer gene(s)' it begins to behave in an abnormal way characteristic of cancer. Cancer genome sequencing includes cancer genome assembly and cancer genome alignment is through early detection improving survival opportunity of cancer patients.

2 Cancer genome assembly

For the last 30 years, fragment assembly followed the ''overlap–layout–consensus'' paradigm [2]. Although this approach proved to be useful in assembling clones, it faces difficulties in genomic shotgun assembly: the algorithms often unable to resolve repeats even in prokaryotic genomes. So, in the past decade, there has been a newly approach: instead of ''overlap–layout–consensus'' paradigm, the new algorithm is based on the notion of the De Bruijn graph and transform the cancer genome assembly problem into an Euler super path problem [3].

2.1 The De Bruijn graphs

Dutch mathematician Nicolaas De Bruijn finds a cyclic sequence of letters taken from a given alphabet for which every possible word of a certain length (k) appears as a string of consecutive characters in the cyclic sequence exactly once. [4][5]

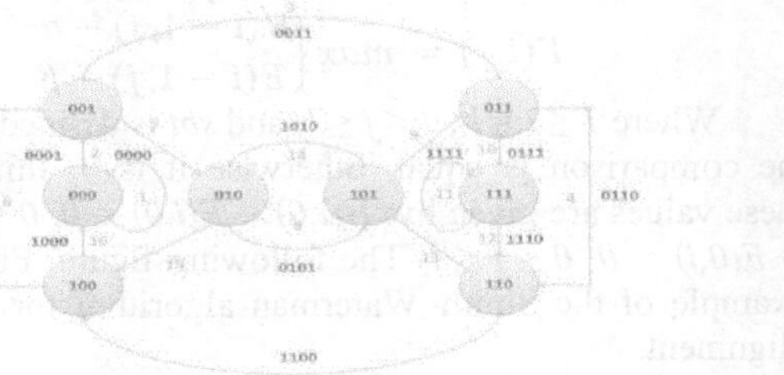

Figure 1: De Bruijn graph.

There exist n^k *k*-mers in an alphabet containing n symbols. If our alphabet is instead 0 and 1, then all possible 3-mers are simply given by all eight 3-digit binary numbers: 000, 001, 010, 011, 100, 101, 110 and 111. The circular superstring 0001110100 not only contains all 3-mers but also is as short as possible, as it contains each 3-mer exactly once shown in Figure 1.

2.2 The Euler path problem

The Euler path problem, having been considered as *one-stroke* drawing problem, is a path in a graph which visits every edge exactly once. Euler proved that a necessary condition for the existence of Eulerian circuits is that all vertices in the graph have an even degree. If there are no vertices of odd degree, all Eulerian paths are circuits. If there are exactly two vertices of odd degree, all Eulerian path start at one of them and end at the other.

3 Cancer genome alignment

Cancer genome alignment is a way of arranging the genome sequences of DNA to identify regions of similarity that may be a consequence of functional, structural, or evolutionary relationships between the sequences [6]. If two sequences in an alignment share a common ancestor, mismatches can be interpreted as point mutations and gaps as insertion or deletion mutations introduced in one or both lineages in the time since they diverged from one another.

3.1 Smith–Waterman algorithm

The Smith–Waterman algorithm [7] finds the most similar subsequences of two sequences by dynamic programming. The algorithm compares two sequences by computing a distance that represents the minimal cost of transforming one segment into another. The function of smith-waterman algorithm is as following: Consider two strings S_1 and S_2 of length l_1 and l_2. To identify common subsequences, the Smith – Waterman algorithm computes the similarity $H(i,j)$ of two sequences ending at position i and j of the two sequences S_1 and S_2. The computation of $H(i,j)$ is given by the following recurrences:

$$H(i,j) = max \begin{cases} 0 \\ E(i,j) \\ F(i,j) \\ H(i-1,j-1) + sbt\left(S_{1_i}, S_{2_j}\right) \end{cases}$$

$$E(i,j) = max \begin{cases} H(i,j-1) - \alpha \\ E(i,j-1) - \beta \end{cases}$$

$$F(i,j) = max \begin{cases} H(i-1,j) - \alpha \\ E(i-1,j) - \beta \end{cases}$$

Where $1 \leq i \leq l_1$, $1 \leq j \leq l_2$ and sbt is defined as value 2 if the comparison is equal, otherwise it is 0. Initialization of these values are given by: $H(i,0) = E(i,0) = 0$, $0 \leq i \leq l_1$, $H(0,j) = F(0,j) = 0$, $0 \leq j \leq l_2$ The following figure, Figure 2, is an example of the Smith–Waterman algorithm for two genome alignment.

		A	T	C	T	C	G	T	A	T	G	A	T	G
	0	0	0	0	0	0	0	0	0	0	0	0	0	0
G	0	0	0	0	0	0	2	2	1	0	0	2	1	0
T	0	0	2	1	2	1	1	4	3	2	1	1	3	2
C	0	0	1	4	3	4	3	3	3	2	1	0	2	2
T	0	0	2	3	6	5	4	5	4	5	4	3	2	1
A	0	2	2	2	5	5	4	4	7	6	5	6	5	4
T	0	1	4	3	4	4	4	6	5	9	8	7	8	7
C	0	0	3	6	5	6	5	5	5	8	8	7	7	7
A	0	2	2	5	5	5	5	4	7	7	7	10	9	8
C	0	1	1	4	4	7	6	5	6	6	6	9	9	8

Figure 2: Example of the Smith–Waterman

4 DNA computation with sticker-based

The sticker-based model employs two basic groups of single-stranded DNA molecules in its representation of a bit string. Consider a memory strand N bases in length subdivided into K non-overlapping regions each M bases long (thus, $N \geq M * K$). Each region is identified with exactly one bit position (or equivalently one Boolean variable) during the course of the computation. Each memory strand along with its annealed stickers (if any) represents one bit string shown in Figure 3.

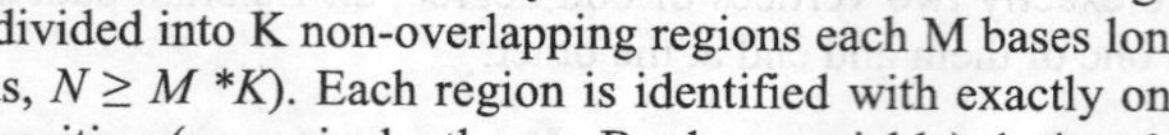

Figure 3: Memory strands of the sticker model

In Table 1, a two-bit sticker ($s_{m,1}$ and $s_{m,2}$) model is used to represent letters A, G, C, T.

Table 1: Two-bit sticker-based model

$s_{m,1}$	$s_{m,2}$	Letter of mth site
0	0	A
0	1	G
1	0	C
1	1	T

5 DNA manipulations

DNA Manipulations is also called Adleman-Liption model. A test tube is a set of molecules of DNA (a multi-set of finite strings over the alphabet {A, C, G, T}. In this subsection, DNA Model of computation has eight biological operations, shown as following:

1. ***Extract.*** Given a tube P and a short single strand of DNA, S, the operation produces two tubes $+(P,S)$ and $-(P,S)$, where $+(P,S)$is all of the molecules of DNA in P which contain S as a sub-strand and$-(P,S)$ is all of the molecules of DNA in P which do not contain S.
2. ***Merge.*** Given tubes P_1 and P_2, yield (P_1, P_2), where (P_1, P_2) = P_1 P_2. This operation is used to pour two tubes into one, without any change in the individual strands.
3. ***Detect.*** Given a tube P, if P includes at least one DNA molecule we have 'yes', and if P contains no DNA molecule we have 'no'.
4. ***Discard.*** Given a tube P, the operation discards P.
5. ***Amplify.*** Given a tube P, the operation, *Amplify* (P, P_1, P_2), will produce two new tubes $P_1$and P_2 so that P_1, and P_2 are totally a copy of P (P_1, and P_2 are now identical) and P becomes an empty tube.
6. ***Append.*** Given a tube P containing a short strand of DNA, Z, and the operation will append A onto the end of every strand in P.
7. ***Append-head.*** Given a tube P containing a short strand of DNA, Z, and the operation will append A onto the head of every strand in P.
8. ***Read.*** Given a tube P, the operation is used to describe a single molecule, which is contained in tube P. Even if P contains many different molecules each encoding a different set of bases, the operation can give an explicit description of exactly one of them.

6 Construction of bio-logic and bio-arithmetic bioinformatics circuitry

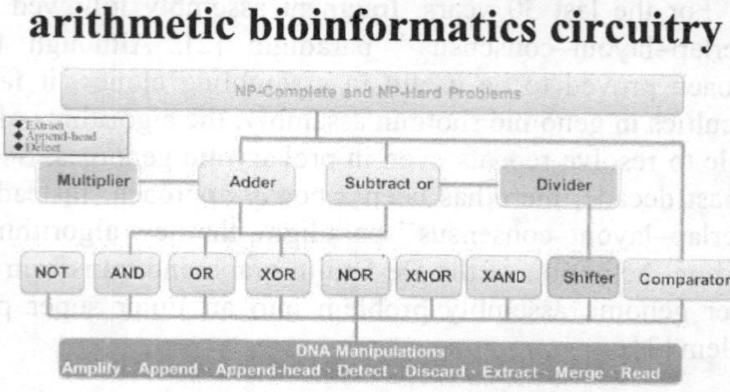

Figure 4: Bio-logic molecular computing model

We use logic truth tables to optimize and complete logic bio-circuit operations that can construct most basic DNA logic circuits. These DNA logic circuits (gates) work in test tubes to implement basic logic operations. These gates are AND, OR, XOR, etc. All operations of Optimal Bioinformatics Logic Computing are shown in Figure 4.

6.1 And operation on bioinformatics computing

The AND operation of a bit with two input Boolean variables U and V generates a result of 1 if both U and V are 1. However, if either U or V, or both, are zero, then the result is 0. The $\wedge$ symbol represents the AND operation. Assume that two one-bit binary numbers, U_k and V_k, for $1 \le k \le n$ are applied to represent first and second inputs for the AND operation of a bit respectively. The AND_k for $1 \le k \le n$ represents the output for the AND operation of a bit. The logic circuitry of parallel AND on one bit is shown in Figure 5. The corresponding truth table of the one-bit AND is shown in Table 2.

Table 2: The truth table of the one-bit AND

Input		Output
U_k	V_k	$AND_k = U_k \wedge V_k$
0	0	0
0	1	0
1	0	0
1	1	1

Figure 5: Logic circuitry of parallel AND on one bit

ParallelOneBitAND(T_0, U_k, V_k, AND_k)
$T_1^{U=1} = +(T_0, U_k^1)$ and $T_1^{U=0} = -(T_0, U_k^1)$.
$T_2^{U=1,V=1} = +(T_1^{U=1}, V_k^1)$ and $T_2^{U=1,V=0} = -(T_1^{U=1}, V_k^1)$
$T_2^{U=0,V=1} = +(T_1^{U=0}, V_k^1)$ and $T_2^{U=0,V=0} = -(T_1^{U=0}, V_k^1)$
If (*Detect*($T_2^{U=1,V=1}$) = = "yes") **then**
Append-head($T_2^{U=1,V=1}$, AND_k^1) **EndIf**
If (*Detect*($T_2^{U=1,V=0}$) = = "yes") **then**
Append-head($T_2^{U=1,V=0}$, AND_k^0) **EndIf**
If (*Detect*($T_2^{U=0,V=1}$) = = "yes") **then**
Append-head($T_2^{U=0,V=1}$, AND_k^0) **EndIf**
If (*Detect*($T_2^{U=0,V=0}$) = = "yes") **then**
Append-head($T_2^{U=0,V=0}$, AND_k^0) **EndIf**
$T_0 = \cup(T_2^{U=1,V=1}, T_2^{U=1,V=0}, T_2^{U=0,V=1}, T_2^{U=0,V=0})$
EndAlgorithm

Figure 6: Parallel AND operation of a bit algorithm

6.2 OR operation on bioinformatics computing

The OR operation of a bit with two input Boolean variables U and V produces a result of 1 if U or V, or both, are 1. However, if both U and V are zero, then the result is 0. A plus sign + (logical sum) or $\vee$ symbol is normally applied to represent OR. Assume that two one-bit binary numbers, U_k and V_k, for $1 \le k \le n$ are applied to represent first and second inputs for the OR operation of a bit respectively. The OR_k for $1 \le k \le n$ represents the output for the OR operation of a bit. The logic circuitry of parallel OR on one bit is shown in Figure 7. The corresponding truth table of the one-bit OR is shown in Table 3.

Table 3: The truth table of the one-bit OR

Input		Output
U_k	V_k	$OR_k = U_k \vee V_k$
0	0	0
0	1	1
1	0	1
1	1	1

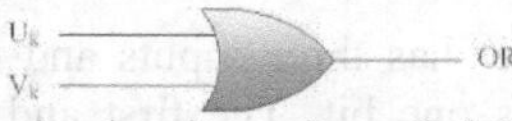

Figure 7: Logic circuitry of parallel OR on one bit

ParallelOneBitOR(T_0, U_k, V_k, OR_k)
$T_1^{U=1} = +(T_0, U_k^1)$ and $T_1^{U=0} = -(T_0, U_k^1)$.
$T_2^{U=1,V=1} = +(T_1^{U=1}, V_k^1)$ and $T_2^{U=1,V=0} = -(T_1^{U=1}, V_k^1)$
$T_2^{U=0,V=1} = +(T_1^{U=0}, V_k^1)$ and $T_2^{U=0,V=0} = -(T_1^{U=0}, V_k^1)$
If (*Detect*($T_2^{U=1,V=1}$) = = "yes") **then**
Append-head($T_2^{U=1,V=1}$, OR_k^1) **EndIf**
If (*Detect*($T_2^{U=1,V=0}$) = = "yes") **then**
Append-head($T_2^{U=1,V=0}$, OR_k^1) **EndIf**
If (*Detect*($T_2^{U=0,V=1}$) = = "yes") **then**
Append-head($T_2^{U=0,V=1}$, OR_k^1) **EndIf**
If (*Detect*($T_2^{U=0,V=0}$) = = "yes") **then**
Append-head($T_2^{U=0,V=0}$, OR_k^0) **EndIf**
$T_0 = \cup(T_2^{U=1,V=1}, T_2^{U=1,V=0}, T_2^{U=0,V=1}, T_2^{U=0,V=0})$
EndAlgorithm

Figure 8: Parallel OR operation of a bit algorithm

6.3 XOR operation on bioinformatics computing

The Exclusive-OR (XOR) operation of a bit with two input Boolean variables U and V generates an output of 1 if both U and V are different values and 0 if they are the same values. The $\oplus$ symbol represents the XOR. Assume that two one-bit binary numbers, U_k and V_k, for $1 \le k \le n$ are applied to represent first and second inputs for the XOR operation of a bit respectively. The representation of the superscript denotes the value of variable (e.g. U_k^1 denotes U_k=1, U_k^0 denotes U_k=0). The S_k for $1 \le k \le n$ represents the output for the XOR operation of a bit. The logic circuitry of parallel XOR on one bit is shown in Figure 9. The corresponding truth table of the one-bit XOR is shown in Table 4:

Table 4: The truth table of the one-bit XOR

Input		Output
U_k	V_k	$XOR_k = U_k \oplus V_k$
0	0	0
0	1	1
1	0	1
1	1	0

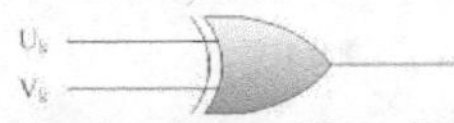

Figure 9: Logic circuitry of Parallel XOR on one bit

ParallelOneBitXOR(T_0, U_k, V_k, XOR_k)
$T_1^{U=1} = +(T_0, U_k^1)$ and $T_1^{U=0} = -(T_0, U_k^1)$.
$T_2^{U=1,V=1} = +(T_1^{U=1}, V_k^1)$ and $T_2^{U=1,V=0} = -(T_1^{U=1}, V_k^1)$
$T_2^{U=0,V=1} = +(T_1^{U=0}, V_k^1)$ and $T_2^{U=0,V=0} = -(T_1^{U=0}, V_k^1)$
If (*Detect*($T_2^{U=1,V=1}$) = = "yes") **then**
Append-head($T_2^{U=1,V=1}$, XOR_k^0) **EndIf**
If (*Detect*($T_2^{U=1,V=0}$) = = "yes") **then**
Append-head($T_2^{U=1,V=0}$, XOR_k^1) **EndIf**
If (*Detect*($T_2^{U=0,V=1}$) = = "yes") **then**
Append-head($T_2^{U=0,V=1}$, XOR_k^1) **EndIf**

If (*Detect*($T_2^{U=0,V=0}$) = = "yes") **then**
Append-head($T_2^{U=0,V=0}$, XOR_k^0) **EndIf**
$T_0 = \cup(T_2^{U=1,V=1}, T_2^{U=1,V=0}, T_2^{U=0,V=1}, T_2^{U=0,V=0})$.
EndAlgorithm

Figure 10: Parallel XOR operation of a bit algorithm

6.4 Bio-arithmetic parallel adder on one bit

A one-bit adder has three inputs and two outputs. Each input and output is one bit. The first and second input bits represent augend and addend, denoted by U_k and V_k, for $1 \le k \le n$. The last input represents the carry, denoted by C_k, for $1 \le k \le n$. The first output represents the sum of the augend, addend and carry, denoted by S_k, for $1 \le k \le n$. Then, the second output represents the carry which is generated by the sum of the augend, addend and carry, denoted by C_{k+1}. This carry becomes the input of next one-bit adder. The logic circuitry of parallel adder on one bit is shown in Figure 11, and the truth table of the one-bit adder is shown in Table 5.

Table 5: The truth table of the one-bit adder

Input			output	
C_k	U_k	V_k	$S_k = U_k \oplus V_k \oplus C_k$	$C_{k-1} = (U_k \wedge V_k) \vee (U_k \wedge C_k) \vee (V_k \wedge C_k)$
0	0	0	0	0
0	0	1	1	0
0	1	0	1	0
0	1	1	0	1
1	0	0	1	0
1	0	1	0	1
1	1	0	0	1
1	1	1	1	1

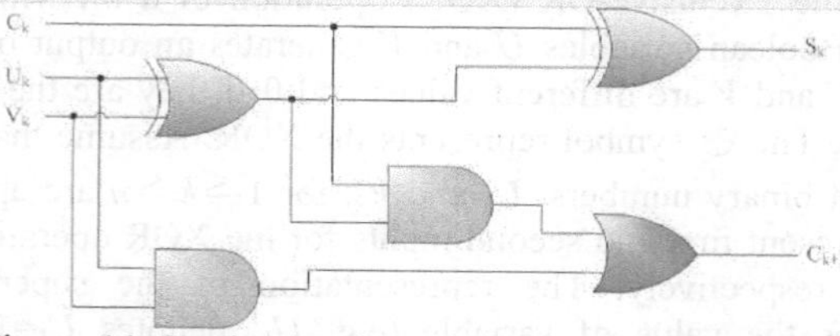

Figure 11: Logic circuitry of parallel adder on one bit

Based upon the logic circuitry in Figure 11, we can derive the bio-algorithm of parallel adder on one bit in Figure 12.

ParallelOneBitAdder(T_0, U_k, V_k, C_k)
ParallelOneBitXOR(T_0, U_k, V_k, XOR_k)
ParallelOneBitXOR(T_0, XOR_k, C_k, S_k)
ParallelOneBitAND(T_0, U_k, V_k, AND_k^1)
ParallelOneBitAND(T_0, C_k, V_k, AND_k^2)
ParallelOneBitAND(T_0, U_k, C_k, AND_k^3)
ParallelOneBitOR(T_0, AND_k^1, AND_k^2, OR_k^1)
ParallelOneBitOR(T_0, OR_k^1, AND_k^3, OR_k^2)
$T_1 = +(T_0, OR_k{}^{2^1})$ and $T_2 = -(T_0, OR_k{}^{2^0})$
If(*Detect*(T_1)=="yes") **then**
Append-head (T_1, C_{k+1}^1) **EndIf**
If(*Detect*(T_2)=="yes") **then**
Append-head (T_2, C_{k+1}^0) **EndIf**
$T_0 = \cup(T_1, T_2)$
EndAlgorithm

Figure 12: Parallel adder algorithm on one bit

6.5 Bio-arithmetic parallel adder on n bits

In this section, we use the bio-arithmetic adder on one bit to construct the Parallel Adder.

ParallelAdder(T_0, U, V, n)
Append(T_0, C_1^0)
For k=1 to *n*
ParallelOneBitAdder(T_0, U_k, V_k, C_k)
EndFor
EndAlgorithm

Figure 13: Parallel adder algorithm

6.6 Bio-arithmetic parallel comparator on one bit

The following algorithm is applied to compare stickers from T_a and T_b. Tube $T_0^=$ is the first parameter and includes comparison outcome to pass to algorithm ParallelComparator ($T_0^{EDGE\_temp}$, $T_0^{overlay}$, T_a, T_b, m, n, g, b). Tube T_a and T_b contain two compared fragments individually. Number p represents the site on T_a ($s_{1,1}s_{1,2}\cdot\ .\ .\ s_{p,1}\ s_{p,2}\cdot\ .\ .\ s_{m,1}s_{m,2}$) for $1 \le p \le q$ and number d represents the site on T_b ($s_{1,1}s_{1,2}\cdot\ .\ .\ s_{d,1}\ s_{d,2}\cdot\ .\ .\ s_{m,1}s_{m,2}$) for $1 \le d \le q$. Algorithm for parallel execution is shown in Figure 14.

OneBitComparator($T_0^=$, T_a, T_b, p, d)
$T_1^{1st\_on} = +(T_a, s_{p,1}{}^1)$ and $T_1^{1st\_off} = -(T_a, s_{p,1}{}^1)$
$T_2^{2nd\_on} = +(T_a, s_{p,2}{}^1)$ and $T_2^{2nd\_off} = -(T_a, s_{p,2}{}^1)$
$T_3^{1st\_on} = +(T_b, s_{d,1}{}^1)$ and $T_3^{1st\_off} = -(T_b, s_{d,1}{}^1)$
$T_4^{2nd\_on} = +(T_b, s_{d,2}{}^1)$ and $T_4^{2nd\_off} = -(T_b, s_{d,2}{}^1)$
If (*Detect*($T_1^{1st\_on}$)='*yes*' and *Detect*($T_3^{1st\_on}$)='*yes*') **then**
If(*Detect*($T_2^{2nd\_on}$)='*yes*' and *Detect*($T_4^{2nd\_on}$)='*yes*') **then**
$T_0^= = \cup(T_0^=, T_1^{1st\_on}, T_3^{1st\_on}, T_2^{2nd\_on}, T_4^{2nd\_on})$ **EndIf EndIf**
If (*Detect*($T_1^{1st\_on}$) = '*yes*' and *Detect*($T_3^{1st\_on}$) = '*yes*') **then**
If(*Detect*($T_2^{2nd\_off}$)='*yes*' and *Detect*($T_4^{2nd\_off}$)='*yes*') **then**
$T_0^= = \cup(T_0^=, T_1^{1st\_on}, T_3^{1st\_on}, T_2^{2nd\_off}, T_4^{2nd\_off})$ **EndIf EndIf**
If(*Detect*($T_1^{1st\_off}$) = '*yes*' and *Detect*($T_3^{1st\_off}$) = '*yes*') **then**
If(*Detect*($T_2^{2nd\_on}$)='*yes*' and *Detect*($T_4^{2nd\_on}$)='*yes*') **then**
$T_0^= = \cup(T_0^=, T_1^{1st\_off}, T_3^{1st\_off}, T_2^{2nd\_on}, T_4^{2nd\_on})$ **EndIf EndIf**
If(*Detect*($T_1^{1st\_off}$) = '*yes*' and *Detect*($T_3^{1st\_off}$) = '*yes*') **then**
If(*Detect*($T_2^{2nd\_off}$)='*yes*' and *Detect*($T_4^{2nd\_off}$)='*yes*') **then**
$T_0^= = \cup(T_0^=, T_1^{1st\_off}, T_3^{1st\_off}, T_2^{2nd\_off}, T_4^{2nd\_off})$ **EndIf EndIf**
EndAlgorithm

Figure 14: Parallel comparator for one bit

6.7 Bio-arithmetic parallel comparator on n bits

The following algorithm, ParallelComparator (T_0, T_0 *overlay*, T_a, T_b, m, n, g, b), is an n-bit comparator. The algorithm use "O" in a sticker-based model to represent four condition by calling function OneBitComparator (T_0=, T_a, T_b, p, $g+d$) and get equal statement. For every bit $O_{p,g}$ represents one success match between $s_{p,1}$, $s_{p,2}$ from T_a and $s_{g,1}$, $s_{g,2}$ from T_b. $O_{p,g}$ would store this comparing result in tube T_0overlay. The number m and n are regarded as the start and last site of fragment which contained in T_a. Number g and number b are regarded as the start and last site of fragment which contained in T_b. That is to say, the bit x_g to x_b in tube T_b are all 1. Algorithm for parallel execution is shown in Figure 15.

ParallelComparator(T_0, $T_0^{overlay}$, T_a, T_b, m, n, g, b)
For d =0 to Min(n-m,b-g)
For p=n **downto** m
OneBitComparator($T_0^=$, T_a, T_b, p, $g+d$)
If (*Detect*($T_0^=$)="yes") **then**
Append($T_0^{overlay}$, $O_{p,g+d}{}^1$)
Discard($T_0^=$) **EndIf**
EndFor
EndFor
If (*Detect*($T_0^{overlay}$)="yes") **then**

```
T0=∪(T0, T0^overlay) EndIf
Discard(T0^overlay)
EndAlgorithm
```

Figure 15: parallel comparator for n bit

7 Proposed bioinformatics approach for solving cancer genome squencing problem

7.1 Proposed optimal bioinformatics algorithms for solving cancer genome assembly

In the beginning, De Bruijn cancer genome assembly bioinformatics graphs are constructed and then a modified bioinformatics approach is using the Euler path to find an optimal solution for solving the cancer genome assembly.

Assume that x_m is a q-bit binary number, which is applied to represent q elements. Every bit x_m represent the *m*th element in S for $1 \le m \le q$. We define xm1 denotes the value of x_m is 1 and x_m^0 represent the value of x_m to be 0. The following algorithm is used to construct sticker-based cancer genome assembly bioinformatics solution space for 2^q possible fragments of a q-element set S shown in figure 16.

```
Init(T0, q)
(1) For m = 1 to q
    (1a) Amplify(T0, T1, T2)
    (1b) Append(T1, xm^1)
    (1c) Append(T2, xm^0)
    (1d) T0 = ∪(T1, T2)
    EndFor
EndAlgorithm
```

Figure 16: Bio-logical parallel n-bit init algorithm

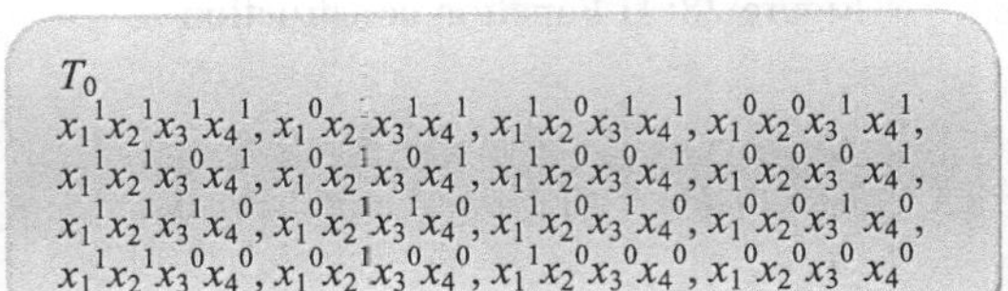

Figure 17: Example of figure 16

The De Bruijn solution space of k-tuple - 1 fragments in tube T_0 is constructed in Figure 18. Each fragment denotes one vertex in the De Bruijn graph.

```
ParallelDeBruijnSolutionSpace(T0, k, q)
For m = 1 to q – k+2
    (1)T3= +(T0, xm^1) and T4= –(T0, xm^1)
    For n = m to m + k – 2
        (2a)T5= +(T3, xn^1) and T6= –(T3, xn^1)
        (2b)Amplify(T5, T3, T3^backup)
    End For
    (3)If (m +k -1< =q) Then
        For n = q downto m +k -1
            (3a)T7= +(T5, xn^1) and T8= –(T5, xn^1)
            (3b) Amplify(T8, T5, T5^backup)
        End For
      Else If
        T8 = ∪(T8, T5)
    End If
    (4)Append-head(T8, Bm)
    (5)Tsolution_space = ∪(Tsolution_space, T8)
    (6)T0 = ∪(T0, T4)
End For
EndAlgorithm
```

Figure 18: Parallel De Bruijn solution space

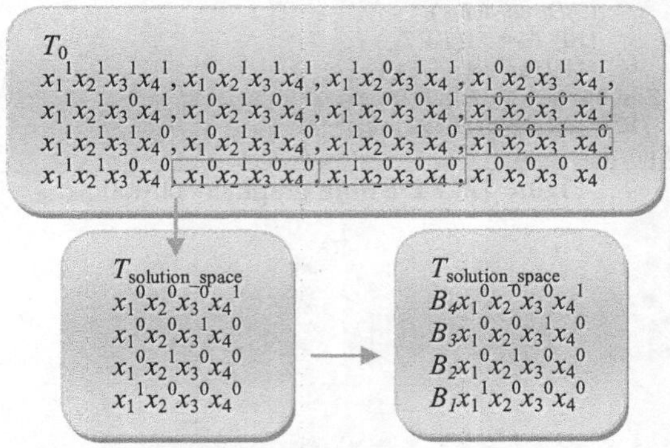

Figure 19: Effctive solution space from figure 18

Figure 20 appends stickers in the head of each fragment in the effective solution space.

```
ParallelStickerAppended(TSticker, Tsolution_space , q)
(1)For n = q downto 1
    (1a)T3= +(TSticker, xn^1)and T4= –(TSticker, xn^1)
    If (Xn = A) Then
        (1b)Append-head(T3, sn,2^0) and Append-head(T3, sn,1^0)
        (1c)TSticker= ∪(T3, T4)
    Else If (Xn = G) Then
        (1d)Append-head(T3, sn,2^1) and Append-head(T3, sn,1^0)
        (1e)TSticker= ∪(T3, T4)
    Else If (Xn = C) Then
        (1f)Append-head(T3, sn,2^0) and Append-head(T3, sn,1^1)
        (1g)TSticker= ∪(T3, T4)
    Else If (Xn = T) Then
        (1h)Append-head(T3, sn,2^1) and Append-head(T3, sn,1^1)
        (1i)TSticker= ∪(T3, T4) End If
EndFor
EndAlgorithm
```

Figure 20: Two-bit sticker model construction

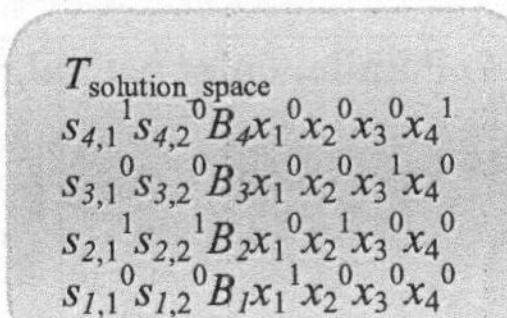

Figure 21: Example of two-bit sticker model

The algorithm in Figure 22 creates the De Bruijn bioinformatics graph. This algorithm merges the repeated vertex into one in the De Bruijn bioinformatics graph. Symbol "In_i" is used to indicate the *i*th repeated vertex.

```
ParallelConstructDBGraph(TDB_graph, TSticker, q)
(1)T9 = +( TSticker, B1) and T10 = –(TSticker, B1)
(2)Append-head(T9, In1)
(3)For i = 2 to size of T10
    (3a)T11 = +(T10, Bi) and T12 = –(T10, Bi)
(4)For j = 1 to size of T9
    (4a)T13 = +(T9, Bj) and T14 = –(T9, Bj)
    (4b)ParallelComparator(T0^table,T13,T11,i, j, k)
    (5)If (Detect(T0^table ) = "yes") then
        (5a)Append-head(T13, Ini)
        (5b)T9 = ∪(T13, T14)
        (5c)Discard(T13, T14)
        Terminate the execution of the loop   End If
```

(6)$T_9 = \cup(T_{13}, T_{14})$
(7)*Discard*(T_{13}, T_{14}) **End For**
(8)**If** (*Detect*(T_0^{table}) = "no") **then**
(8a)*Append-head*(T_{11}, In_i)
(8b)$T_9 = \cup(T_9, T_{11})$ **End If**
(9)*Discard*(T_{10})
(10) $T_{10} = \cup(T_{10}, T_{12})$
(11)*Discard*(T_{11}, T_{12})
End For
(12)$T_{DBGraph} = \cup(T_{DBGraph}, T_9)$
EndAlgorithm

Figure 22: De Bruijn graph construction

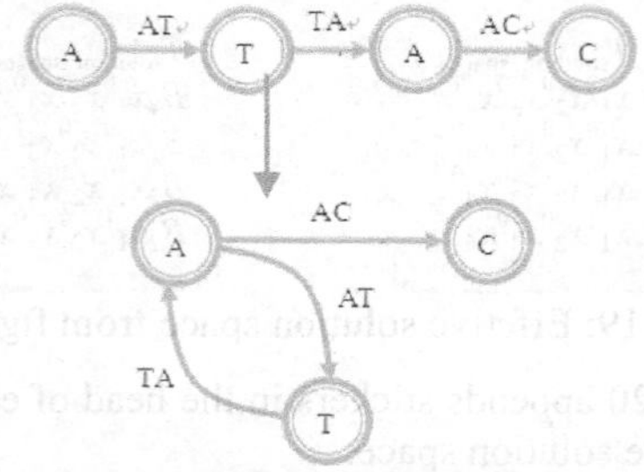

Figure 23: Example of De Bruijn graph construction

The algorithm in Figure 24 constructs an optimal path using the modified Euler bioinformatics path approach.

ParallelEulerPath$(T_{DB\_graph}, T_{Routing}, q, k)$
For m = 1 to q-k+1
$T_{13} = +(T_{DBGraph}, In_m)$ and $T_{14} = -(T_{DBGraph}, In_m)$
For $n = q$-k+1
$T_{15} = +(T_{13}, B_n)$ and $T_{16} = -(T_{13}, B_n)$
If (*Detect*(T_{15}) = "YES") **then**
Append$(T_{Routing}, B_n)$
Discard(T_{15}, T_{16})
Terminate the execution of the loop
End If
Discard(T_{15}, T_{16})
End For
$T_{DBGraph} = \cup(T_{13}, T_{14})$
End For
EndAlgorithm

Figure 24: Parallel euler path algorithm

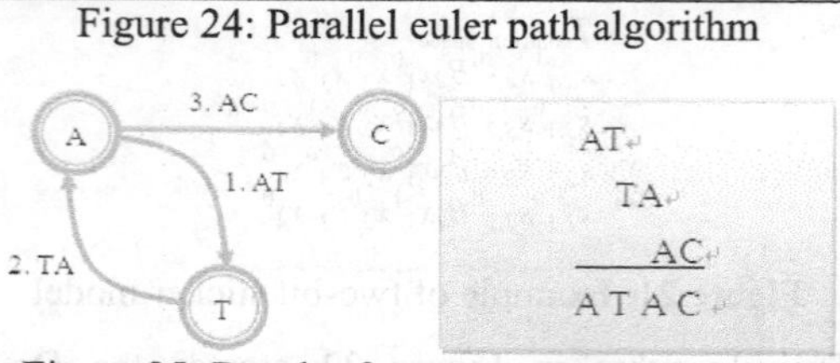

Figure 25: Result of cancer genome assembly

7.2 Proposed optimal bioinformatics algorithms for solving cancer genome alignment

The resolution for the proposed cancer genome bioinformatics alignment is using the modified Smith – Waterman algorithms to construct a Smith – Waterman matrix for solving cancer genome alignment. Here two strings "ATAC" and "AAAC" are used as an example. The algorithm in Figure 26 constructs the Smith – Waterman matrix.

ParallelSmithWatermanMatrix$(T_{matrix}, T_{test}, T_{target}, q, k)$
For $m = 1$ *to* q
For $n = 1$ *to* k
(1) **ParallelConstructHFunction**$(T^H, T_{matrix}, T_{test}, T_{target}, q, k)$
(2) **ParallelStickerComparator**$(T_0^{table}, T_{test}, T_{target}, m, n)$
(3) **If** (*Detect*(T_0^{table}) = "yes") **then**
(3a)**ParallelAdder**$(T^>, T^>, 2, n)$
(3b)*Append*$(T_{matrix}, X_mY_nZ_{T^>})$ **Else**
(3c)**ParallelSubtractor**$(T^>, T^>, 1, n)$
(3d)*Append*$(T_{matrix}, X_mY_nZ_{T^>})$
End If
End For
End For
End Algorithm

Figure 26: Smith – Waterman matrix construction

		A	A	A	C
	0	0	0	0	0
A	0	2	2	2	1
T	0	1	1	1	1
A	0	2	3	3	2
C	0	1	2	2	5

Figure 27: Example of Smith – Waterman matrix.

The algorithm in Figure 28 produces the score function of Smith–Waterman algorithm in tube T^H using the H function to score every comparison bit in the Smith – Waterman matrix.

ParallelConstructHFunction$(T^H, T_{matrix}, T_{test}, T_{target}, q, k)$
(1)**ParallelConstructHFunction**$(T^H, T_{matrix}, T_{test}, T_{target}, q, k, i\text{-}1, j\text{-}1)$
(2)**ParallelConstructEFunction**$(T^E, T_{test}, T_{target}, q, k\ i, j\text{-}1)$
(3)**ParallelConstructFFunction**$(T^F, T_{test}, T_{target}, q, k\ i\text{-}1, j)$
(4)**ParallelComparator**$(T^=, T^<, T^>, T^H, T^E, n)$
If (*Detect*$(T_0^<)$ = "yes") **then**
(4a)**ParallelComparator**$(T^=, T^<, T^>, T^E, T^F, n)$
Else If (*Detect*$(T_0^>)$ = "yes") **then**
(4b)**ParallelComparator**$(T^=, T^<, T^>, T^H, T^F, n)$
End If
End Algorithm

Figure 28: H Function construction

		A	A	A	C
	H(i-1,j-1)	E(i,j-1)	0	0	0
A	F(i-1,j)	(i,j)			
T	0				
A	0				
C	0				

Figure 29: H scoring of Smith – Waterman matrix

The algorithm in Figure 30 produces the score function of Smith–Waterman algorithm in tube T^E using the E function to score every comparison bit in the Smith – Waterman matrix.

ParallelConstructEFunction$(T^E, T_{matrix}, T_{test}, T_{target}, q, k)$
ParallelConstructHFunction$(T^H, T_{matrix}, T_{test}, T_{target}, q, k, i, j\text{-}1)$
ParallelConstructEFunction$(T^E, T_{test}, T_{target}, q, k\ i, j\text{-}1)$
ParallelSubtractor(T^H, T^H, α, n)
ParallelSubtractor(T^E, T^E, β, n)
ParallelComparator$(T^=, T^<, T^>, T^H, T^E, n)$
End Algorithm

Figure 30: E Function construction

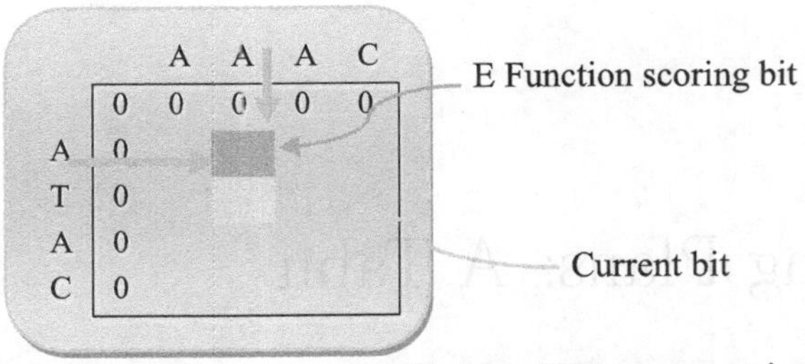

Figure 31: E scoring of Smith – Waterman matrix

The algorithm in Figure 32 produces the score function of Smith–Waterman algorithm in tube T^F using the F function to score every comparison bit in the Smith – Waterman matrix.

ParallelConstructFFunction(T^F, T_{matrix}, T_{test}, T_{target}, q, k)
(1)**ParallelConstructHFunction**(T^H, T_{matrix}, T_{test}, T_{target}, q, k, i-1, j)
(2)**ParallelConstructFFunction**(T^F, T_{test}, T_{target}, q, k i-1, j)
(3)**ParallelSubtractor**(T^H, T^H, α, n)
(4)**ParallelSubtractor**(T^F, T^F, β, n)
(5)**ParallelComparator**($T^=$, $T^<$, $T^>$, T^H, T^F, n)
End Algorithm

Figure 32: F Function construction

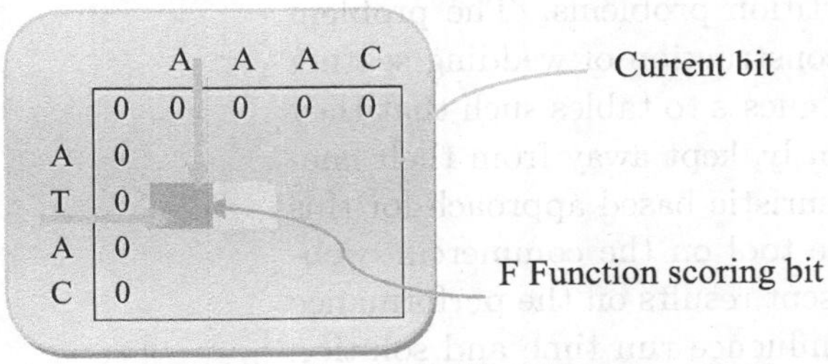

Figure 33: F scoring of Smith – Waterman matrix

The algorithm in Figure 34 finds an optimal path by computing a Smith – Waterman scoring matrix.

ParallelTraceBackPath (T_{matrix}, i, j, q, k)
$T_1 = +(T_{matrix}, X_l^1)$ and $T_2 = -(T_{matrix}, X_l^1)$
$T_3 = +(T_1, Y_l^1)$ and $T_4 = -(T_1, Y_n^1)$
For m = *1* **to** q
For n = *1* **to** k
$T_5 = +(T_{matrix}, X_m^1)$ and $T_6 = -(T_{matrix}, X_m^1)$
$T_7 = +(T_1, Y_n^1)$ and $T_8 = -(T_1, Y_n^1)$
ParallelComparator($T_R^=$, $T_R^<$, $T_R^>$, T_3, T_7, n)
If (*Detect*($T_R^>$) = "yes") **then**
Discard($T_R^>$)
$T_{trace} = \cup(T_{trace}, T_R^>)$ **End If**
End For
End For
For n = *1* **to** k
$T_9 = +(T_{trace}, X_{m-1}^1)$ and $T_{10} = -(T_{trace}, X_{m-1}^1)$
$T_{11} = +(T_{trace}, Y_{n-1}^1)$ and $T_{12} = -(T_{trace}, Y_{n-1}^1)$
$T_{13} = +(T_{11}, X_{m-1}^1)$ and $T_{14} = -(T_{11}, X_{m-1}^1)$
ParallelComparator($T_R^=$, $T_R^<$, $T_R^>$, T_9, T_{11}, n)
If (*Detect*($T_0^<$) = "yes") **then**
ParallelComparator($T^=$, $T^<$, $T^>$, T_{11}, T_{13}, n)
Else If (*Detect*($T_0^>$) = "yes") **then**
ParallelComparator($T^=$, $T^<$, $T^>$, T_9, T_{13}, n)
End If
$T_{trace} = \cup(T_{trace}, T_R^>)$
End For
EndAlgorithm

Figure 34: An optimal alignment path using Smith – Waterman scoring matrix

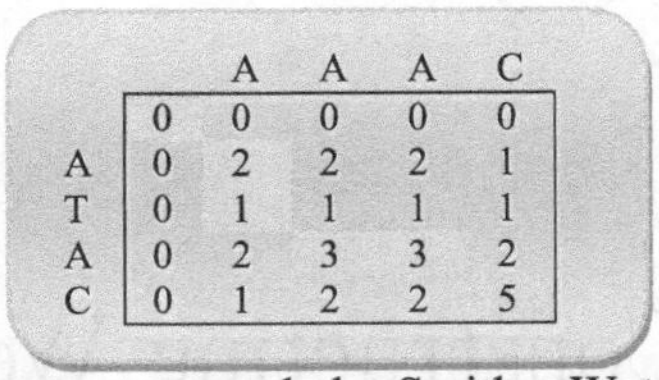

Figure 35: Alignment example by Smith – Waterman matrix

8 Conclusions

Cancer is one of the most common causes of death worldwide. The underlying cause of mutations leading to cancer is DNA damage. The best opportunity for improving survival of cancer patients is through early detection, when curative surgical resection is possible. By using cancer genome assembly and alignment can solve the cancer genome sequencing problem and can early detect the DNA of cancer damage. Both cancer genome assembly and alignment problems are NP-complete. To resolve these issues, we first break cancer DNA sequences into DNA fragments. A modified and enhanced De Bruijn cancer genome assembly graphs is constructed. Finally, an optimal Euler path is found for solving the cancer genome assembly. Secondly, an enhanced Smith - Waterman scoring matrix is used to compare the reassembled path of the two new reassembled DNA (test cancer DNA and target DNA) and determine whether the test DNA is damaged or not. This research work fully utilizing parallelism presents a clear evidence of the ability of bioinformatics computing for solving cancer DNA sequence assembly and alignment more efficient. The experimental results of cancer genome assembly can be found in O(n^3) polynomial bound. And the experimental results of cancer genome alignment is also in O($n*m$) polynomial bound.

9 References

[1] Venturi, M; Hambly, RJ; Glinghammar, B; Rafter, JJ; Rowland, IR. *Genotoxic activity in human faecal water and the role of bile acids: a study using the alkaline comet assay*. Carcinogenesis, 1997, 18, 2353-2359.

[2] Pevzner P. A., Tang Haixu. *Fragment Assembly with Double-Barreled Data*. Bioinformatics，2001，17 (1): 225—233.

[3] Pevzner P., *1-Tuple DNA Sequencing：Computer Analysis*. Journal of Bimolecular Structure and Dynamics, 1989, 7(1):63-73.

[4] Algorithms for de novo short read assembly using De Bruijn graphs Daniel R. Zerbino and Ewan Birney

[5] W. Bains and G.C. Smith [1988]. A novel method for nucleic acid sequence determination. *Journal of Theoretical Biology 135*, 303–307

[6] Mount DM. (2004). *Bioinformatics: Sequence and Genome Analysis* (2nd ed.). Cold Spring Harbor Laboratory Press: Cold Spring Harbor, NY. ISBN 0-87969-608-7

[7] T.F. Smith and M.S. Waterman, "Identification of common molecular subsequences," J. Mol. Biol. pp. 195–197, 1981

Constructing Wedding Seating Plans: A Tabu Subject

Rhyd Lewis*
Cardiff School of Mathematics,
Cardiff Univerity, CF10 4AG, WALES.
Email: lewisR9@cf.ac.uk; Tel: +44 (0)2920 874856.

Abstract

This paper examines an interesting combinatorial optimisation problem that generalises both the graph colouring and k-partition problems. The problem has an interesting practical application in the construction of wedding seating plans, where we seek to assign equal numbers of guests to tables such that they are sat near friends and, perhaps more importantly, kept away from their enemies. We describe an effective two-stage metaheuristic-based approach for this problem which is currently used with the online tool on the commercial website www.weddingseatplanner.com. We also present results on the performance of this algorithm, indicating what factors can influence run time and solution quality.

Keywords: Combinatorial Optimisation; Metaheuristics; Graph Colouring; Partitioning.

1 Introduction

The Wedding Seating Problem (WSP) involves taking a set of wedding guests and assigning them to tables so that the following constraints are met:

- Guests belonging to groups, such as couples and families, should be sat at the same tables;
- The number of guests per table should be equal;
- If there is any perceived animosity between different guests, these should be sat on different tables; and similarly,
- If guests are known to like one another, they should be sat at the same table.

*Corresponding author. Submitted to GEM'13 - The 2013 International Conference on Genetic and Evolutionary Methods

The WSP can be formally stated as type of graph partitioning problem. Specifically, we are given a graph $G = (V, E)$ comprising a vertex set V and an edge set E. Each vertex $v \in V$ is used to represent a group of guests who are required to sit together (couples, families, etc.), with the size of each guest group denoted s_v. The total number of guests n is thus $\sum_{v \in V} s_v$. Each edge $\{u, v\} \in E$ then defines the relationship between vertices u and v according to a weighting $w_{u,v}$ (where $w_{u,v} = w_{v,u}$). If $w_{u,v} > 0$ we interpret this to mean that we would prefer the guests associated with vertices u and v to be sat on different tables. Larger values for $w_{u,v}$ reflect a strengthening of this requirement. Similarly, negative values for $w_{u,v}$ mean that we would rather u and v were assigned to the same table.

A solution to the WSP is defined as a partition of the vertices into k subsets $\mathcal{U} = \{U_1, \ldots, U_k\}$, such that $\bigcup_{i=1}^{k} U_i = V$ and $U_i \cap U_j = \emptyset$, $i, j \in \{1, \ldots, k\}$, $i \neq j$. The requested number of tables k is defined by the user, with each subset U_i defining the guests assigned to a particular table i.

The quality of a candidate solution for the WSP can be evaluated according to two objective functions, both which we seek to minimise. The first of these, calculated:

$$f_1 = \sum_{i=1}^{k} \sum_{\forall u,v \in U_i : \{u,v\} \in E} w_{u,v} \tag{1}$$

reflects the extent to which the rules governing who sits with who are obeyed. The second objective function then measures the degree to which the number of guests per table deviates from the required number of either $\lfloor n/k \rfloor$ or $\lceil n/k \rceil$:

$$f_2 = \sum_{i=1}^{k} \left(\min \left(\left| \left(\sum_{\forall v \in U_i} s_v \right) - \left\lfloor \frac{n}{k} \right\rfloor \right|, \left| \left(\sum_{\forall v \in U_i} s_v \right) - \left\lceil \frac{n}{k} \right\rceil \right| \right) \right). \tag{2}$$

It is evident that the WSP is intractable since it generalises two classical NP-hard problems:

- If $E = \emptyset$ (or $\forall \{u, v\} \in E$, $w_{u,v} = 0$) then f_1 (Equation (1)) will always equal zero. This means that the only goal is to ensure that the number of guests per table is as equal as possible. Hence the problem reduces to the k-partition problem.[1]
- If $\forall v \in V$, $s_v = 0$ then f_2 (Equation (2)) will always equal zero, implying that the task of balancing the number of guests per table is no longer relevant. In this case the problem becomes equal to the weighted k-colouring problem, which is itself a generalisation of the NP-hard graph k-colouring problem [3].

In this paper we describe a two stage approximation algorithm for the wedding seating problem. This algorithm is currently used on the commercial website www.weddingseatplanner.com. In particular, this approach exploits the underlying graph structures of the problem allowing effective neighbourhood operators to be defined that are able to quickly identify high-quality solutions. In the next section we

[1]Note that the k-partition problem is also variously known as the load balancing problem, the equal piles problem, or the multiprocessor scheduling problem.

	Guest	Companion 1	Companion 2	Companion 3
1	John	Sarah	Jack	Jill
2	Bill	June		
3	Pat	Susan		
4	Una	Tom		
5	Ruth	Kevin	Gareth	
6	Ken	Frank	Bobby	
7	Rod	Dereck	Freddy	
8	Jane			

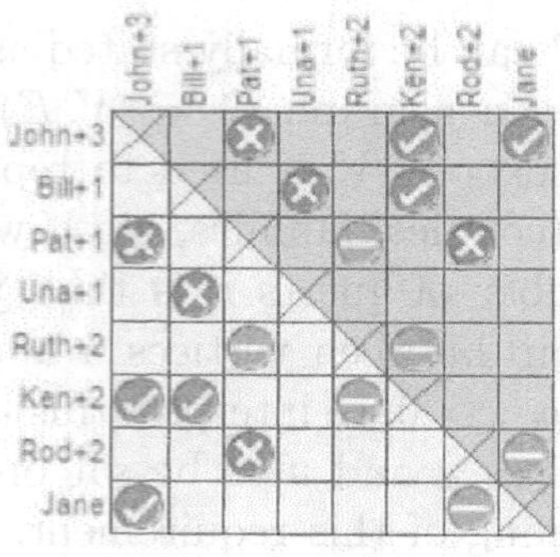

Figure 1: Specification of guest groups (left) and seating preferences (right).

describe the online interactive tool and algorithm in detail, before looking at some its run characteristics in Section 3. Section 4 concludes the paper.

2 Problem Interpretation and Algorithm

On entering the website, the user is asked to input (or import) the names of all guests into an embedded interactive table. Groups of guests that need to be seated together (families etc.) are placed on the same rows of the table, thus defining the various values for s_v. At the next step the user is then asked to define seating preferences between different guest groups.

Figure 1 shows a small example of this process. Here, eight guest groups ranging in size from 1 to 4 have been input, giving 20 guests in total. The right-hand grid then shows how the seating preferences (values for $w_{u,v}$) are defined. If the user wants to define a preference, they do so by clicking on the relevant cells in the grid. Users are limited to three options: (1) "Definitely Apart" (e.g. Pat and John); (2) "Rather Apart" (Pat and Ruth); and (3) "Rather Together" (John and Ken). In our case these are allocated weights of ∞, 1, and -1 respectively. Note that it would have been possible to allow the user to input their own weights here; however it was felt by the website designers that, while perhaps more flexible, this ran the risk of bamboozling the user while not improving the usability of the tool.

The overall strategy of our algorithm is classify the requirements of the problem as either hard (mandatory) constraints or soft (optional) constraints. In our case we consider just one hard constraint, which we attempt to satisfy in Stage 1 – specifically the constraint that all pairs of guest groups required to be "Definitely Apart" are assigned to different tables. In Stage 2 the algorithm then attempts to reduce the number of violations of the remaining constraints via specialised neighbourhood operators that do not allow any of the hard constraints satisfied in Stage 1 to be re-violated. We now describe the two stages of the algorithm in more detail.

2.1 Stage 1

In Stage 1 the algorithm operates on the sub-graph $G' = (V, E')$, where $E' = \{\{u, v\} \in E : w_{u,v} = \infty\}$. That is, G' contains only those edges from E that define the "Definitely Apart" requirement.[2] Using this sub-graph, the problem of assigning all guests to k tables (while not violating the "Definitely Apart" constraint) is equivalent to the graph k-colouring problem.

The graph k-colouring problem is a widely studied combinatorial optimisation problem for which a multitude of different algorithms are available [5]. In our case, we use a variant of the DSATUR heuristic [1] to produce an initial solution. DSATUR is a constructive algorithm that, at each iteration, selects the uncoloured vertex v that currently has the largest number of distinct colours assigned to adjacent vertices. Ties are broken by selecting the vertex with the largest degree. In our case the selected vertex v is then assigned to any colour $i \in \{1, \ldots, k\}$ that currently features no other vertices adjacent to v. If no such colour exists, v is kept to one side and is assigned to a random colour at the end of the construction process, thereby introducing violations of the hard constraint.

If the solution produced by the above process contains hard constraint violations, attempts are next made to eliminate these. This is done using the TABUCOL algorithm of Hertz and de Werra [4, 2] which, while perhaps not as powerful as more contemporary graph colouring algorithms, does have the advantage of being very fast [5]. TABUCOL uses the tabu search metaheuristic to make a series of small changes (moves) to the candidate solution, attempting to find a solution for which the cost function $f_1 = 0$ (using G'). A move in the search space is performed using a neighbourhood operator that takes a vertex v whose assignment to colour i is currently contributing to the cost, and then assigns it to a new colour $j \neq i$. The tabu list is stored in a $|V| \times k$ matrix T and, upon performing this move, the element $T_{v,i}$ is marked as tabu for the next t iterations. In each iteration of TABUCOL all possible moves from the current solution are considered, and the move that is chosen is the one that is seen to invoke the largest decrease (or failing that, the smallest increase) in cost of any non-tabu move. Ties are broken randomly, and tabu moves are also permitted if they are seen to improve on the best solution found so far.

Because speed is an issue with our online tool, TABUCOL is only run for a fixed number of iterations.[3] If at the end of the process a solution with cost $f_1 = 0$ has not been achieved, then it is possible that the user has specified a k-value for which a k-colouring is not achievable (i.e. the number of tables is too small to meet all of the "Definately Apart" constraints). In this case, k is incremented by one and Stage 1 of the algorithm is repeated. This process continues until all hard constraints are satisfied.

[2] For example, using the problem shown in fig. 1, $E' = \{\{1, 3\}, \{2, 4\}, \{3, 7\}\}$.

[3] TABUCOL is executed for $20n$ iterations, using a tabu tenure t that is proportional to the current cost ($t = 0.6f_1 + r$, where r is randomly selected from $\{1, 2, \ldots, 9\}$), as recommended in [2].

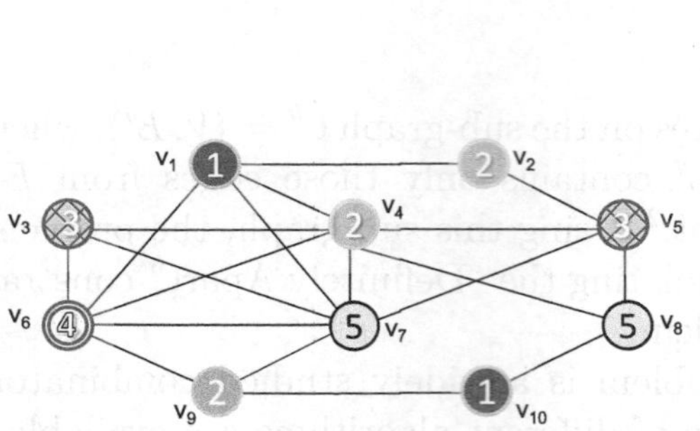

Figure 2: Example of a feasible 5-colouring of graph $G' = (V, E')$.

2.2 Stage 2

At the start of Stage 2 we will have achieved a k colouring of $G' = (V, E')$ for which no pair of adjacent vertices is assigned the same colour. We call such a solution *feasible* as it obeys all of the imposed hard constraints. In this stage we now try to eliminate violations of the soft constraints by exploring the space of feasible solutions. Note that movements in this space might be restricted – indeed the space might not even be contiguous – and so it is necessary to use neighbourhood operators that allow as much freedom-of-movement as possible. In our case this is achieved using tabu search in conjunction with two operators, both that exploit the underlying structure of the graph colouring problem. These are defined as follows:

Kempe-Chain Interchange: Given an arbitrary vertex v currently assigned to colour i, and given a second colour $j \neq i$, a Kempe-chain is defined as a connected subgraph starting from v that only contains vertices coloured with i and j. Such a chain can be denoted $\textsc{Kempe}(v, i, j)$.

A Kempe-chain interchange involves taking a particular Kempe-chain and swapping the colours of all vertices contained within it. For example, in fig. 2, $\textsc{Kempe}(v_7, 5, 2)$ results in a chain involving vertices $\{v_4, v_9\}$ (assigned to colour 2) and $\{v_7, v_8\}$ (assigned to colour 5). When the colours of these vertices are interchanged, we observe that the resultant solution will still be feasible. This is actually the case with all Kempe-chain interchanges [6].

It is also worth noting that Kempe-chains can vary in size, and some combinations for $\textsc{Kempe}(v, i, j)$ will *overlap* in that they result in the same Kempe-chain being identified (e.g. $\textsc{Kempe}(v_7, 5, 2) = \textsc{Kempe}(v_9, 2, 5)$). Indeed, as the number of colours k is reduced, or the density of G' is increased, then so will the size of the chains and the amount of overlap. This feature is relevant with applications of tabu-search such as ours because, with appropriate book-keeping, we can avoid evaluating the effects of a particular interchange more than once when scanning the entire neighbourhood.

Swaps: The swap operator is used for performing further moves not contained within the Kempe-chain neighborhood. Specifically, when scanning the set of Kempe-chain interchanges, we can also identify pairs of non-adjacent vertices u, v that both feature Kempe-chains $\textsc{Kempe}(u, i, j)$ and $\textsc{Kempe}(v, j, i)$ of size 1 (e.g.

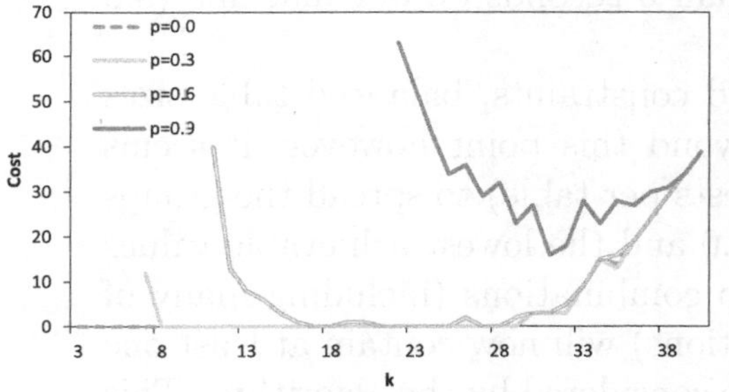

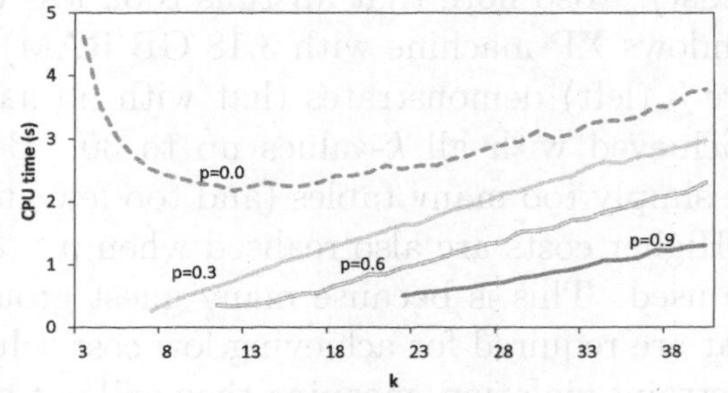

Figure 3: Solution costs (left) and run times (right) for four instances using various k-values. For most of the left figure, the line for $p = 0.0$ is obscured by the line for $p = 0.3$ (i.e. the same results were achieved).

KEMPE$(v_1, 1, 3)$ and KEMPE$(v_5, 3, 1)$ in fig. 2.) In these particular cases u and v can have their colours swapped, but no hard constraint violations will occur as a result.

In each iteration of this stage of the algorithm all possible moves from both neighbourhoods are evaluated and the same acceptance criteria as Stage 1 are applied. Once a move is performed, all relevant parts of the tabu list T are updated to reflect the changes made to the solution.[4] The cost function used is simply $(f_1 + f_2)$ which will always evaluate to a value less than ∞ (since violations of the hard constraints cannot occur).

3 Algorithm Performance

The algorithm and interface described above has been coded in ActionScript 3.0 and can be run via a web browser at www.weddingseatplanner.com. To ensure run times are kept relatively short, and also to allow the interface to be displayed clearly on the screen, problem size is limited to $|V| = 50$ guest groups of up to 8 people, allowing a maximum of $n = 400$ guests.

To gain an understanding of the performance characteristics of this algorithm, a large problem instance of $|V| = 50$ guest groups was constructed, with the size of each group chosen uniform randomly in the range 1 to 8. This instance was then modified such that a each pair of vertices was joined by an ∞-weighted edge with probability p (meaning that a proportion of approximately p guest group pairs would be required to be "Definitely Apart"). Tests were then carried out using values of $p = \{0.0, 0.3, 0.6, 0.9\}$ and number of tables $k = \{3, 4, \ldots, 40\}$.

Figure 3 shows the results of these tests with regard to the costs and run times that were achieved at termination. Note that for $p > 0.0$, values are not reported for the lowest k's as feasible k-colourings were not achieved (quite possibly because they

[4]That is, all nodes and colours effected are marked as tabu in T. For our application a tabu tenure of 10 is used along with an iteration limit of $10n$.

do not exist). Also note that all runs took less than 5 seconds on our machine (3.0 GHz Windows XP machine with 3.18 GB RAM).

Figure 3 (left) demonstrates that with no hard constraints, balanced table sizes can be achieved with all k-values up to 30. Beyond this point however, it seems there are simply too many tables (and too few guests per table) to spread the groups equally. Higher costs are also realised when $p > 0.0$ and the lowest achievable values for k are used. This is because many guest group combinations (including many of those that are required for achieving low cost solutions) will now contain at least one hard constraint violation, meaning they will not be considered by the algorithm. This also explains why low cost solutions are not achieved using $p = 0.9$.

We also note that for more constrained problems (lower k's and/or larger p's), the Kempe-chains in the underlying graph colouring model tend to become larger and less numerous. In practice this means that the size of the neighbourhoods scanned in each iteration of tabu search is reduced, resulting in shorter run times as shown in Figure 3 (right). The exception to this pattern is for low values of k using $p = 0.0$, where the larger numbers of guests per table requires more overheads in the calculation of Kempe chains and the cost function, resulting in an increase in run times.

4 Conclusions

An effective two stage heuristic algorithm has been proposed for the wedding seating problem, making use of concepts taken from the observed underlying graph colouring model. Experiments have been presented to demonstrate factors that influence solution quality and run times.

The described tool has been live at www.weddingseatplanner.com since mid-2011 and receives approximately 1000 hits per month at the time of writing. We have also found that it can be a useful tool for introducing students to many of the issues surrounding combinatorial optimisation.

References

[1] D. Brelaz. New methods to color the vertices of a graph. *Commun. ACM*, 22(4):251–256, 1979.

[2] P. Galinier and J-K. Hao. Hybrid evolutionary algorithms for graph coloring. *Journal of Combinatorial Optimization*, 3:379–397, 1999.

[3] M. R. Garey and D. S. Johnson. *Computers and Intractability - A guide to NP-completeness.* W. H. Freeman and Company, San Francisco, first edition, 1979.

[4] A. Hertz and D. de Werra. Using tabu search techniques for graph coloring. *Computing*, 39(4):345–351, 1987.

[5] R. Lewis, J. Thompson, C. Mumford, and J. Gillard. A wide-ranging computational comparison of high-performance graph colouring algorithms. *Computers and Operations Research*, 39(9):1933–1950, 2012.

[6] J. Thompson and K. Dowsland. A robust simulated annealing based examination timetabling system. *Computers and Operations Research*, 25(7/8):637–648, 1998.

SESSION

SWARM OPTIMIZATION ALGORITHMS AND APPLICATIONS

Chair(s)

TBA

Solving the Traveling Salesman Problem using Reinforced Ant Colony Optimization techniques

N.N.Poddar[1], **D. Kaur**[2]
[1]Electrical Engineering and Computer Science, University of Toledo, Toledo, OH, USA
[2]Electrical Engineering and Computer Science, University of Toledo, Toledo, OH, USA

Abstract - *This paper discusses the results of applying Reinforced Ant Colony Optimization algorithm to solve the Traveling Salesman Problem (TSP), an NP Complete problem. To evaluate the performance of Ant Colony Optimization algorithm, comparative studies were done between research which introduced Hybrid Genetic algorithm [3] to solve the Traveling Salesman Problem and the original Ant Colony Optimization algorithm proposed by Dorigo[1]. After comparing the Hybrid and Genetic algorithms as well as the Nearest Neighbor (NN) algorithm and the original ACO against the reinforced ACO algorithm, it was found that the reinforced ACO algorithm performs the best with the tour length being the shortest. However, the convergence time for the reinforced ACO algorithm increases when the number of cities increases. Thus, although tour length was shorter for the reinforced ACO, for a large number of cities, the reinforced ACO algorithm took a relatively long time to find a tour.*

Keywords: Ant Colony Optimization algorithm, ACO, Combinatorial Optimization problems.

1 Introduction

Ant Colony Optimization uses the behavior of ants as a model for coming up with techniques to solve optimization problems which are difficult to solve in polynomial time using brute force or other advanced algorithms. More specifically, the foraging behaviors of ants were used to develop the Ant Colony Optimization algorithm. This paper discusses the results of applying ACO algorithm to solve the Traveling Salesman Problem.

Some researchers have made attempts to extend the original ACO algorithm [1] to solve the Traveling Salesman Problem. In [2] and [4], Max-Min Ant System is used where only the best ant is allowed to update the pheromone trail, and the pheromone level on the path is kept between a certain lower and upper bound. In [3], hybrid GA was proposed. In [5], a rank-based ACO has been implemented where a few best ants are allowed to update the pheromone trail, and their weight is dependent on their rank, with the best ant being weighted the most. In [6], ants with memory solve a problem in parts, and use the best solutions from that part in later iterations. In [7], entropy is used to measure the information content within the pheromones on a path, and the entropy is used to determine the value for β, one of the parameters for the ACO algorithm. In [8], Ant Colony Optimization is combined with Genetic algorithm in a cooperative manner where information is exchanged between the two algorithms to produce better results. In [9], Ant Colony Optimization is combined with local search which improves the solution found by Ant Colony Optimization algorithm. In [10], a work similar to [8] has been done where genetic techniques were combined with ACO algorithm to yield better results.

This paper is organized as follows. Section 2 discusses TSP and the various methods used to solve TSP. Section 3 discusses the conventional ACO algorithm and the reinforced ACO algorithm. Section 4 discusses the simulation technique. Section 5 discusses the comparative studies between reinforced ACO, conventional ACO and Genetic algorithms. Section 6 discusses the results. Section 7 discusses the conclusion and other future work.

2 Traveling salesman problem

Traveling Salesman Problem is a classic NP Complete problem in the field of Computer Science. It creates a Hamiltonian Tour of all the cities in a graph, where each city is visited once. That is, given a list of cities, the problem is to find the shortest tour that visits all the cities and returns to the first city. Different variations to this problem are there. The problem is NP complete, meaning there aren't any algorithms available to solve the Traveling Salesman Problem in polynomial time. There are many heuristics to solve the TSP which approximate the final answer. Some of the algorithms which approximate the final answer are Nearest Neighbor algorithm, Genetic algorithm, Simulated Annealing, and Ant Colony Optimization to name a few. Genetic algorithm, Nearest Neighbor algorithm, and Ant Colony algorithms are discussed and implemented in this paper. Comparative studies were also done between the above mentioned algorithms, and results of the study have been given in this paper.

3 Ant colony optimization algorithm

Conventional Ant Colony Optimization (ACO) algorithm is a heuristic technique inspired by foraging behavior of ants. It is discussed in section 3.1. The reinforced

ACO algorithm and its simulation are discussed in the following section 3.2 to 3.3.

3.1 Conventional ACO technique

In the ACO algorithm, ants are modeled as agents that search the problem space individually, but communicate with one another the quality of the solution found so far, and thus move towards a better solution. ACO uses a form of communication called "stigmergy". Here, each ant develops a solution to the problem, and communicates with another ant the quality of the solution using pheromone trails. In the Traveling Salesman Problem, each ant starts at a point in the graph, and then the ants build a solution to the Traveling Salesman Problem. As they pass through an edge of the graph, they deposit pheromones on the edge. Another ant trying to create a tour will use the pheromone as a guide. The amount of pheromones deposited depends on the quality of the solution. In the Ant Colony Optimization algorithm, the amount of pheromone deposited is indirectly proportional to the tour length. The smaller the tour length, the more is the pheromone laid on the path. The pheromone also decays along a path with time. This allows for paths less traveled to have a lower pheromone trail as the pheromones evaporates with time.

3.2 Reinforced ACO algorithm

Reinforced ACO was developed by modifying the original ACO. The premise of the original ACO algorithm is that an ant has to find the shortest path from the nest to the food source. However in TSP, this scenario is not true as the objective is to visit all the nodes starting from any node and find the shortest tour distance. The algorithm uses as many ants as the number of cities. The first objective is to go to the nearest node from the starting node. Therefore beta is set high, and a pheromone trail is laid such that the nearest city is the preferred city to visit. Next, beta is decreased so that the pheromone trails can guide the ants. However, this approach has a problem because pheromones evaporate with time. Thus less traveled edges see their pheromones evaporate. To allow less promising edges on the graph to be explored, the reinforced ACO algorithm increases the pheromones on an edge having low pheromone by a factor of 100 once every 10 iterations.

The algorithm implemented is discussed below –

procedure [best] = AS-TSP(max_it)

Randomly initialize τ_{ij} (pheromone on an edge from city i to city j)

Place each ant k on a randomly selected city

Let best be the shortest tour found so far and L_{best} its length.

Initialize L_{best} to a very large value

$t \leftarrow 1$

while t < max_it(maximum number of iterations entered by user) *do*,

For i = 1 to N *do*,

Build $T^k(t)$, the TSP tour created by ant k, by applying (e-1) times, where e is the number of cities, the step below:

At city i, choose the next city j with probability given by equation (1) –

$$P_{ij}^{k}(t) = [\tau_{ij}(t)]^{\alpha}.[\eta_{ij}]^{\beta} / \Sigma_{l \varepsilon J_i^k} [\tau_{il}(t)]^{\alpha}.[\eta_{il}]^{\beta} \quad \text{if } j \varepsilon J_i^k$$

Or 0 otherwise (1)

Equation (1) gives the probability of taking a certain edge(i,j). In the above equation, τ_{ij} is the pheromone trail from node i to node j, and η_{ij} is the visibility of the city which is given by $1/d_{ij}$ where d_{ij} is the distance from city i to city j. J_i^k is the list of cities that are yet to be visited by ant k when it is at city i. α and β are constants defined by the user.

End for

Evaluate the length of the tour performed by each ant k.

If a shorter tour is found,

Then update best and L_{best}

End if

For every city e *do*,

Update pheromone trails by applying the following rule at iteration t:

$$\tau_{ij}(t+1) \leftarrow (1-p)\, \tau_{ij}(t) + \Delta \tau_{ij}(t) + b.\, \Delta \tau^{b}_{ij}(t)$$

where

$$\Delta \tau_{ij}(t) = \sum_1^k \Delta\tau_{ij}^k,\ k = 1, \ldots, N,$$

$$\Delta\tau_{ij}^k(t) = Q/L^k(t) \text{ if } (i, j) \varepsilon T^k(t) \text{ and}$$

0 Otherwise,

$$\Delta\tau_{ij}^b(t) = Q/L_{best}(t) \text{ if } (i, j)\ \varepsilon \text{ best path and 0 otherwise}$$

where p is the forgetting factor, b is a constant, Q is a constant, L^k is the length of the tour performed by ant k, and L_{best} is the best tour length found so far.

End for

For every edge in graph between city i and j

If τ_{ij} < K(constant defined by user)

$\tau_{ij} = \tau_{ij}$ * M every 10 iterations(M is a user defined constant)

End if

End for

$t \leftarrow t + 1$

End while

End procedure

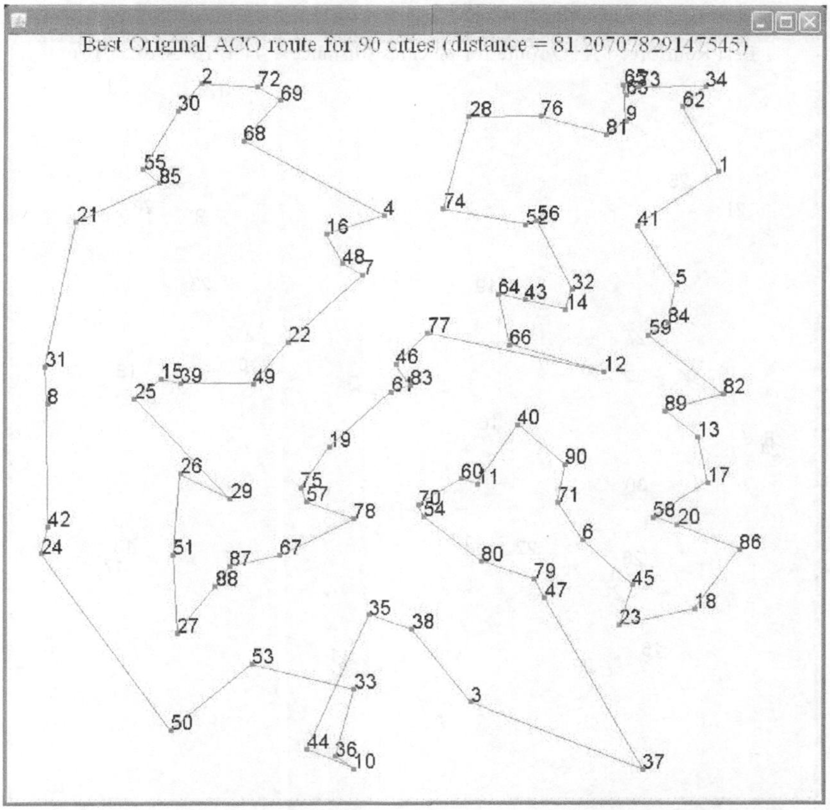

Figure 1: Traveling Salesman tour constructed by the original ACO algorithm for 90-city TSP

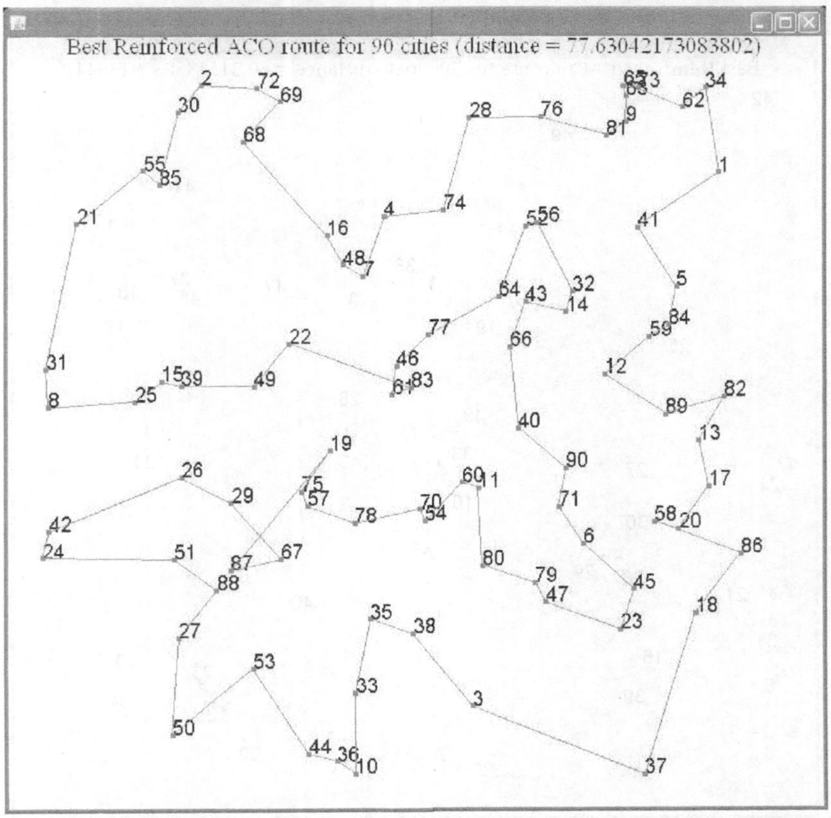

Figure 2: Traveling Salesman tour constructed by the Reinforced ACO algorithm for 90-city TSP

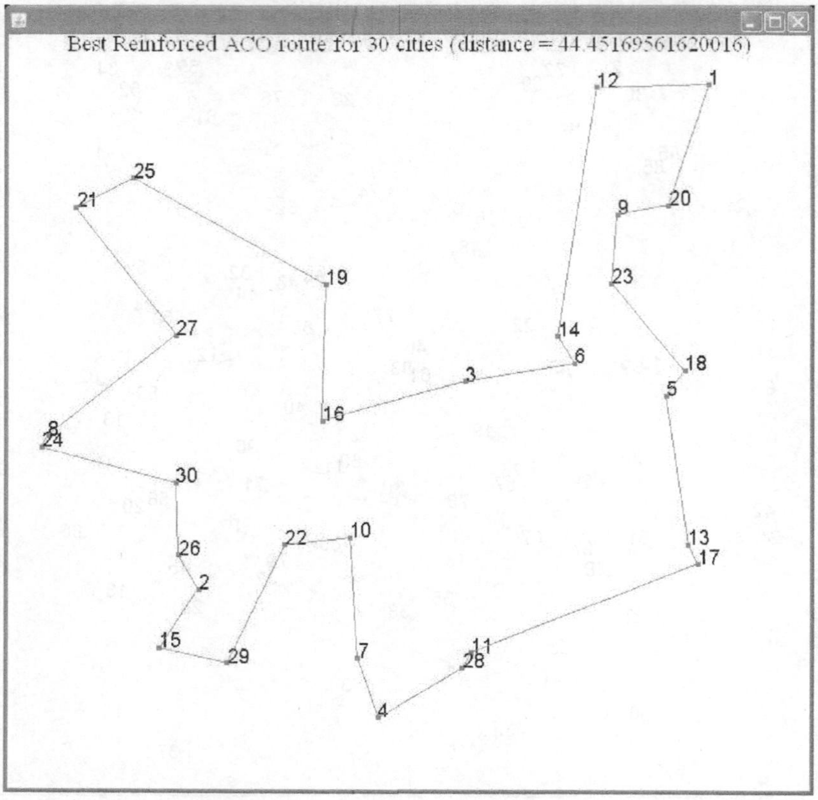

Figure 3: Traveling Salesman Tour constructed by the Reinforced ACO for 30 cities

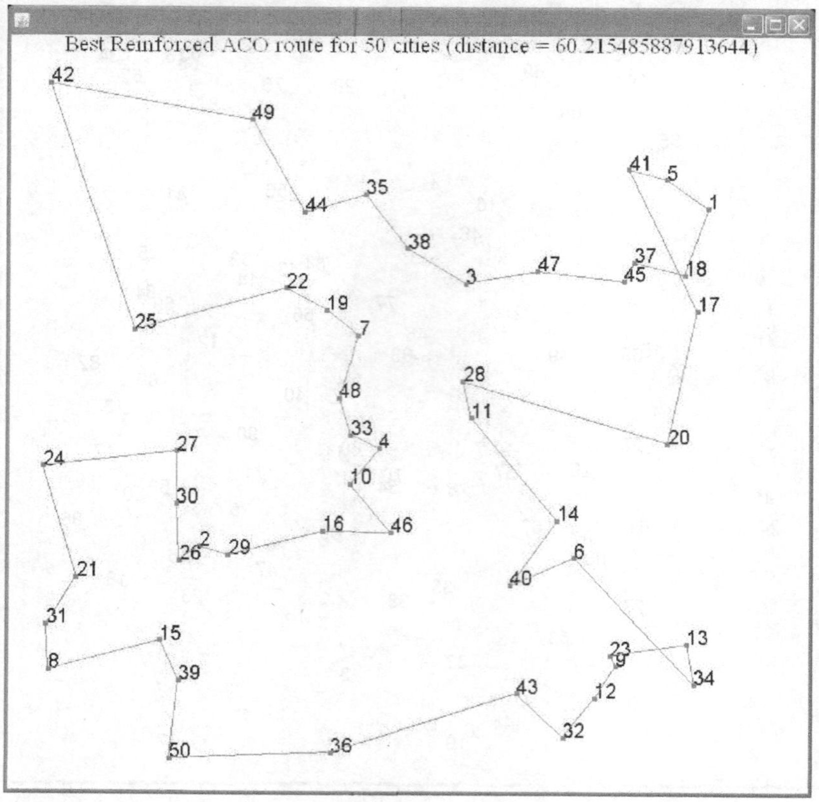

Figure 4: Traveling Salesman Tour constructed by the Reinforced ACO for 50 cities.

3.3 Key features of reinforced ACO algorithm

To get better results than the ACO algorithm which converged to local optimal, changes to the algorithm were made. In the implementation, K was set to 80, and M was set to 100. The value of Q used was 100, while α was set to 1, and β to 100 and then 5. Additionally, to compute the pheromone trail left on the path, a forgetting factor, p, of 0.5 was used. The paths that had a pheromone level less than 80 had their pheromones increased every 10 iterations or time step. It was found that multiplying the pheromone levels by a factor of 100 gave the best results in terms of convergence time. This value is specific to this implementation as the value depends on how the forgetting factor or evaporation rate of the pheromones was set up, as well as other constants. Thus, this modification allowed paths that were less promising to be explored as well, and produce better results.

4 Simulation of reinforced ACO

The reinforced ACO algorithm above was implemented using Java. The tour created visits every city the user wants to visit and ends at the starting city. To compare the results with Hybrid and Genetic algorithms [3], the coordinates of cities from the research in [3] was imported. Also, the original ACO algorithm proposed by Dorigo [1] was implemented. Fig. 1 shows the tour created by implementing the original ACO algorithm with a tour distance of 81.20.

When implementing the original ACO algorithm, it was found that the algorithm got stuck in local optima. That is, only some of the paths were being reinforced. The rest of the paths were slowly dying out, and not being explored at all. The reinforced ACO tries to overcome this pitfall.

Pheromones were initially deposited on each path via a random number generator. The pheromone was updated at the end of each tour by an ant. The number of ants created for the algorithm was equal to the number of cities. The program gives the shortest tour generated by the algorithm along with its tour length. The reinforced ACO algorithm was implemented on a range of cities, and the results of the implementation are shown in Figs. 2, 3, 4 and 5. The tour lengths are shorter than original ACO proposed by Dorigo [1]. Formatting instructions

5 Comparative studies with pure GA, hybrid GA, and nearest neighbor

To evaluate the performance of the reinforced ACO algorithm, comparative studies were done with the original ACO algorithm proposed by Dorigo[1], the Nearest Neighbor algorithm, and Pure and Hybrid GA algorithms proposed by Kaur and Murugappan in [3] The methods and the implementations of the above mentioned algorithms are discussed in the following sections A through C.

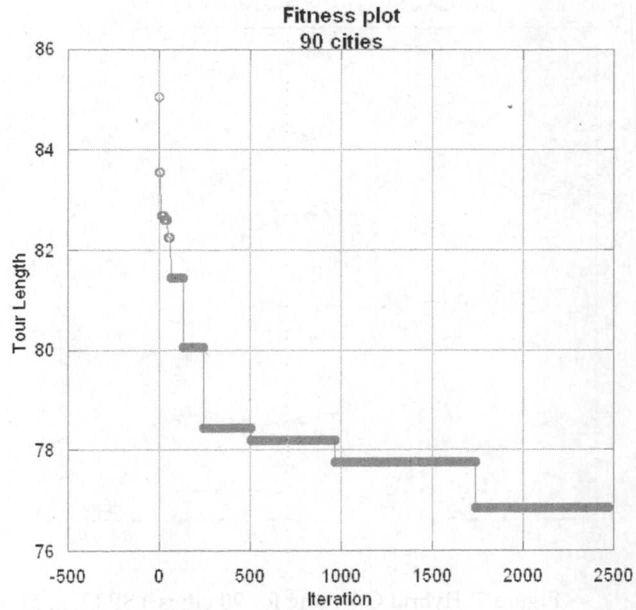

Figure 5: Tour Length vs. Iteration for Reinforced ACO algorithm

5.1 Pure GA

In Pure GA, the initial population was randomly created, and then allowed to reproduce and mutate. The fitness was evaluated based on tour distance with tours having lower distances getting higher fitness values. The result of the experiment is shown in Fig. 6.

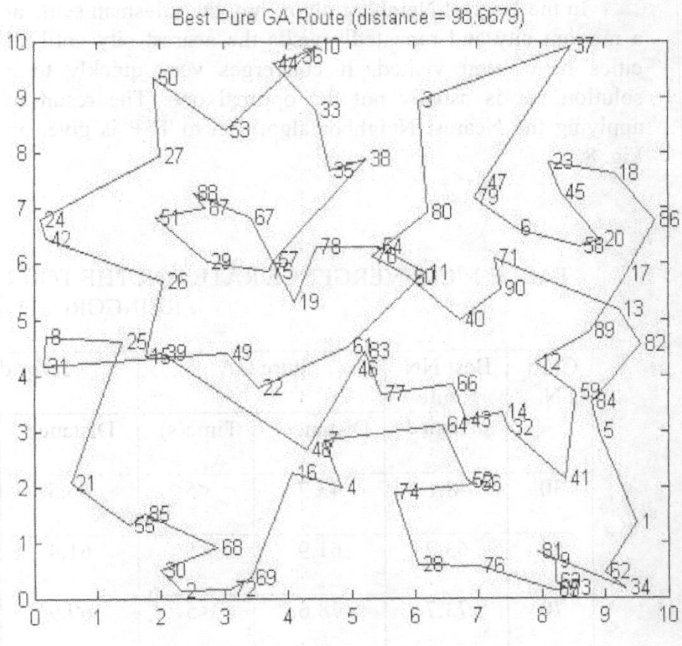

Figure 6 : Pure GA route for 90 cities TSP [2, p. 4]

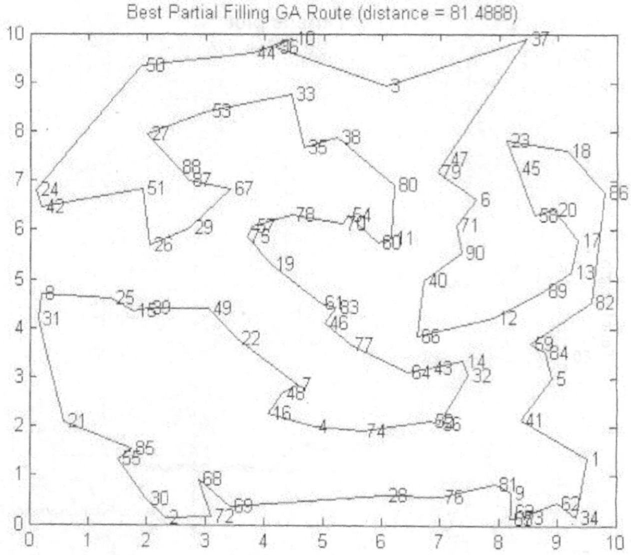

Figure 7: Hybrid GA route for 90 cities TSP [2, p. 5]

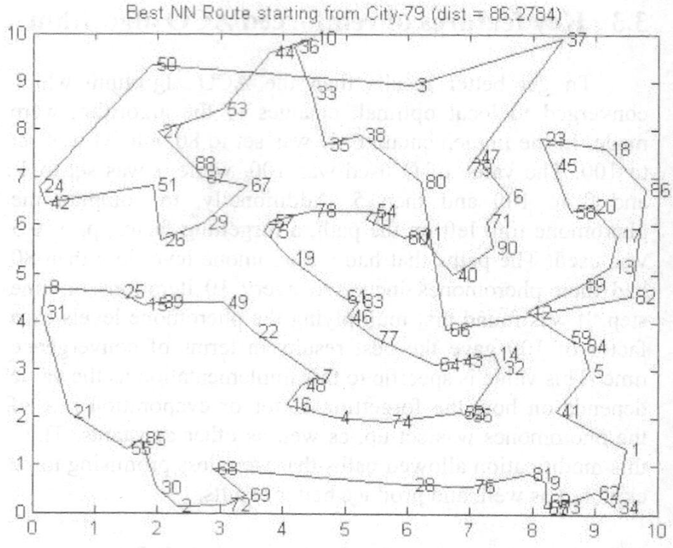

Figure 8: Nearest Neighbor route for 90 cities TSP [2, p.4]

5.2 Hybrid GA

In hybrid GA, the initial population was populated based on the results of Nearest Neighbor algorithm. Thus the initial population was of higher fitness than that of Pure GA. The individuals were crossed over and mutated with one another. The results of the experiment are illustrated in Fig. 7.

5.3 Nearest neighbor algorithm

In the Nearest Neighbor algorithm, the salesman starts at a random city and repeatedly visits the nearest city until all cities have been visited. It converges very quickly to a solution but is usually not the optimal one. The result of applying the Nearest Neighbor algorithm to TSP is given in Fig. 8.

6 Results

The Reinforced ACO algorithm outperformed hybrid GA, pure GA, the conventional ACO and the Nearest Neighbor algorithms by giving the shortest tour distance. This section gives the results of applying the reinforced ACO algorithm on the Traveling Salesman Problem with 30, 50, 70 and 90 cities. Table 1 summarizes the tour distance and the time taken for convergence of the TSP problem for different number of cities using Pure GA, Hybrid GA, the conventional ACO, and the reinforced ACO algorithms. As expected, the time of convergence increased with the number of cities. As can be seen from the Table 1, the reinforced ACO algorithm performs the best in term of tour distance. However, the convergence rate of reinforced ACO is higher than that of hybrid GA or Pure GA as it takes a longer time to find a better tour.

TABLE 1: CONVERGENCE RATE FOR THE TOUR OF N CITIES FOR PURE GA, HYBRID GA, ACO, AND REINCORCED ACO ALGORITHMS

Cities N	Best NN Route distance	Pure GA		Hybrid GA		Original ACO		Reinforced ACO	
		Distance	Time(s)	Distance	Time(s)	Distance	Time(s)	Distance	Time(s)
30	48.1	43.7	<5	45.5	<5	44.71	2.27	44.5	20.18
50	63.2	61.9	<5	61.4	<5	63.05	6.86	60.15	29.25
70	73.7	78.6	<5	69.9	<5	72.68	22.61	68.28	28.6
90	86.3	98.6	<5	81.5	<5	80.31	38.75	78.27	57.3

7 Conclusion and future works

The results show that reinforced ACO algorithm provided the shortest tour length compared with conventional ACO, Hybrid GA, Pure GA and Nearest Neighbor methods. The tour distance of reinforced ACO algorithm becomes significantly smaller as the number of cities increase. As expected, the time of convergence also increases as the number of cities increase. Since the convergence time is high, future work can be done to address that. It would be interesting to embed the solution found from Genetic algorithms to reinforced ACO algorithm where the pheromones obtained from a run of a Genetic algorithm are used by the reinforced ACO algorithm. Also, a different heuristic such as an approximation algorithm can be used in addition to Nearest Neighbor distance. Future works can also include ants with memory.

8 References

[1] Leandro Nunes de Castro."Fundamentals of Natural Computing: Basic Concepts, Algorithms, and Applications: Chapman and Hall, 2006, pp. 210-234.

[2] T. StÄutzle and H.H. Hoos. Improvements on the Ant System: Introducing the MAX-MIN Ant System. In R.F. Albrecht G.D. Smith, N.C. Steele, editor, Artificial Neural Networks and Genetic Algorithms, pages 245-249. Springer Verlag, Wien New York, 1998.

[3] Kaur. D, Murugappan, M.M, "Performance enhancement in solving Traveling Salesman Problem using hybrid genetic algorithm," Fuzzy Information Processing Society, 2008. NAFIPS 2008. Annual Meeting of the North American, May 2008 doi: 10.1109/NAFIPS.2008.4531202.

[4] T. StÄutzle and H.H. Hoos. The MAX-MIN Ant System and Local Search for the Traveling Salesman Problem. In T. Baeck, Z. Michalewicz and X. Yao, editors, Proceedings of the IEEE International Conference on Evolutionary Computation (ICEC'97), pages 309-314.

[5] B. Bullnheimer, R.F. Hartl, and C. Strauss. A New Rank Based Version of the Ant System | A Computational Study. Central European Journal for Operations Research and Economics.

[6] A.Adnan. Ant Colony Optimization and swarm intelligence 4th international workshop, ANTS 2004, Brussels, Belgium, September 5-8, 2004 : proceedings. Berlin New York: Springer, 2004.

[7] Hlaing, Zar, and May Khine. "Solving Traveling Salesman Problem by Using Improved Ant Colony Optimization Algorithm." 2011. Web. 12 Dec. 2012. <http://www.ipcsit.com/vol16/11-ICICM2011M029.pdf>.

[8] Dong, G, Guo, W, & Tickle, K. "Solving the traveling salesman problem using cooperative genetic ant systems". (2012). 39(5), 5006–5011. doi: 10.1016/j.ejor.2012.02.038

[9] Gambardella, L, Montemanni, R, & Weyland, D. (2012). Coupling ant colony systems with strong local searches, 220(3), 831–843. doi: 10.1016/j.ejor.2012.02.038.

[10] Chen, S., & Chien, C. "Parallelized genetic ant colony systems for solving the traveling salesman problem". (2011). 38(4), 3873–3883. doi: 10.1016/j.eswa.2010.09.048

Harmonic Estimation in Radial Distribution Feeders Based on Particle Swarm Optimization

Ricardo A. S. Fernandes
CCET - UFSCar - Brazil
ricardo.asf@ufscar.br

Ricardo A. L. Rabêlo
UESPI - Brazil
ricardor_usp@yahoo.com.br

Ivan Nunes da Silva
EESC - USP - Brazil
insilva@sc.usp.br

Mário Oleskovicz
EESC - USP - Brazil
olesk@sc.usp.br

***Abstract*—This paper presents a method based on the particle swarm optimization algorithm applied to estimate harmonic components in radial distribution feeders. It is important to mention that this method is not applied as harmonic state estimator, neither to estimate the total harmonic distortion at the substation. So, the proposed method can be employed to estimate the harmonic components in specific points of common coupling between the harmonic source and the feeder. In this sense, some case studies were prepared in order to validate the method. The point of common coupling where the harmonic source is located were obtained by means of expert knowledge. Nevertheless, the specialist/engineer should be induced to err the exact position of the harmonic source due to the presence of other harmonic sources with lower levels of distortion. Thus, the precision rate of this method was evaluated in accordance with the uncertainty that can be generated by the expert knowledge. These analysis are crucial to verify the performance of the proposed method, mainly, in the utility's point of view.**

***Keywords*—harmonic components, harmonic estimation, particle swarm optimization, power quality.**

I. INTRODUCTION

Nowadays, the utilities have the concern for the electricity delivered to the consumers. Moreover, we have the energy efficiency, where some linear loads had been replaced by nonlinear loads. Thus, it is possible to observe the increment of current and/or voltage harmonic distortions in the distribution feeders. Given these high level of distortions, it becomes clear the poor power quality which mainly affect the consumers.

In conformity with these premises, some research have been developed with the intuit to reach a precisely harmonic power flow to radial and/or weakly meshed distribution feeders [1-3].

However, in order to employ the above mentioned research, it is necessary a prior knowledge about the harmonic components of each Point of Common Coupling (PCC). Hence, this information is very difficult to obtain due to the absence of power quality monitors installed at these points or smart meters installed at the consumers.

Due to the difficult to determine the harmonic power flow, the research in this area were directed to harmonic state estimation [4-5] and nonlinear load identification [6-7]. It is important to highlight that state estimators need some measurements to determine the harmonic components at each bus.

Among the methods previously cited, we can highlight the research developed by [7], where the authors use the IEEE 34-bus with unbalanced voltages and light loading conditions. So, the proposed method was designated to determine the precise location of harmonic sources based on harmonic power flow calculation. However, this method needs a total of 26 meters located at the feeder. Thus, this kind of method is impractical owing to the high cost for purchase harmonic analyzers.

In [5], a Bayesian method was proposed to estimate the state of the IEEE 13-bus. It is important to say that the authors use pseudo-measurements and the IEEE 13-bus was modified to be a balanced feeder, but this condition is improbable in distribution feeders. Moreover, this method needs 5 harmonic analyzers to realize the state estimation.

Following the context above cited, this paper proposes a method that is capable to determine the harmonic components at a specific PCC. Hence, this technique must be employed to obtain the load with the higher harmonic distortion based on the expert knowledge.

This paper was divided in five sections, where in Section I was given the introduction, Section II presents the characteristics of the distribution feeder modeled and simulated. In the Section III we describe the harmonic estimator aspects. Finally, the Sections IV and V are, respectively, designated to show the results of each case study and the research conclusions.

II. DISTRIBUTION FEEDER MODELED AND SIMULATED

The simulated radial distribution feeder contain 20 buses and consists in a modification of the IEEE 13-bus [8]. Therefore, some characteristics such as transformers, loads, and overhead lines are similar to IEEE 13-bus. Figure 1 shows the 20-bus distribution feeder proposed to evaluate the methodology.

In order to model and simulate the 20-bus distribution feeder, we use the ATP (Alternative Transient Program) software [9]. Despite of this software be employed to transient analysis, in this case it is used to steady-state.

Other features concerning to the 20-bus distribution feeder are described in Table I, where were discriminated: source, transformers, capacitor bank and meters (voltage and current).

The Figure 1 shows the 20-bus line diagram where two power quality meters were allocated (one of them between the buses 10 and P1 and the another one between the buses 50 and P2).

Only the power quality meter at the end of the feeder was randomly allocated. This location was chosen in order to better cover the feeder.

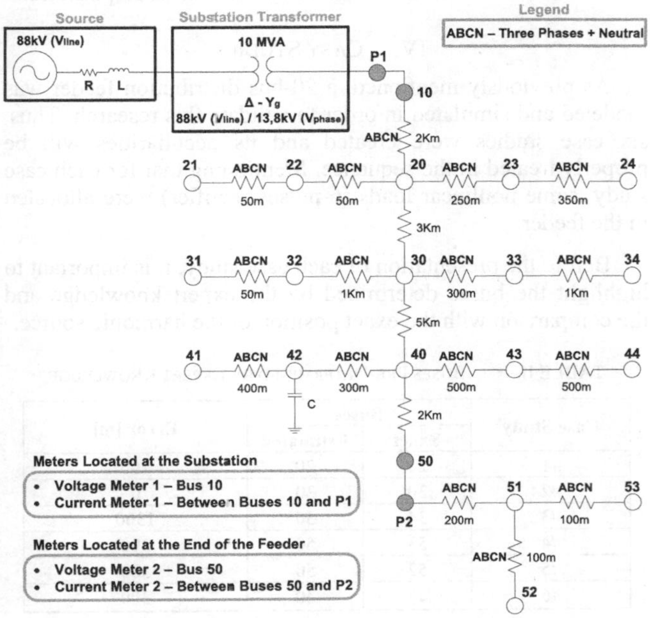

Fig. 1. Line diagram of the 20-bus radial distribution feeder.

Due to this research is focused on the identification of harmonic sources, a 6-pulses rectifier was modeled to supply RC and RL loads. Thus, six case studies were created based on the 20-bus distribution feeder and the 6-pulses rectifier. This case studies will be presented in the Section IV.

III. Harmonic Estimation at the PCC

The harmonic estimator proposed in this paper was addressed to determine a mean harmonic distortion at the PCC. In this sense, the expert knowledge is responsible to define a possible bus where the predominant harmonic source is located. However, it is possible that the expert knowledge is uncertain. So, the harmonic estimator attempts to minimize this uncertainty.

Bearing in mind this pre-determined bus, the estimator follow the procedures shown in Figure 2. These procedures must be done to obtain the mean value of harmonic components at the PCC.

Analyzing the Figure 2, it is possible to note that the harmonic estimator needs the acquisition of actual (measures obtained after entry of the harmonic source) and historical measurements (before the entry of the harmonic source). The historical and actual data are obtained from current and voltage meters allocated at the points highlighted in Figure 1 (P1, 10, P2, 50).

Based on these measurements, the Discrete Fourier Transform (DFT) is applied to obtain the frequency spectrum for each current and voltage acquired. So, the results of the DFT are presented to the power quality engineer in order to support the decision, i.e., the determination of the bus where the harmonic source is probably located.

TABLE I. 20-Bus Radial Distribution Feeder: Meters, Transformers and Source Characteristics.

Source	
Nominal Line-to-Line Voltage (kV)	88.0
Resistance - Zero Sequence (Ω)	20.805
Resistance - Positive Sequence (Ω)	4.062
Inductance - Zero Sequence (mH)	203.721
Inductance - Positive Sequence (mH)	52.540
Nominal Frequency (Hz)	60
Substation Transformer	
Connection	Δ-Yg
Primary Winding - Line-to-Line Voltage (kV)	88.0
Secondary - Winding Line-to-Neutral Voltage (kV)	13.8
Primary Winding - Resistance (Ω)	0.055
Secondary Winding - Resistance (Ω)	0.794
Primary Winding - Inductance (mH)	1.628
Secoundary Winding - Inductance (mH)	23.626
Apparent Power (MVA)	10.0
Capacitor Bank	
Connection	Δ-Yg
Capacitance (μF)	5.965
Voltage and Current Meters	
Sample per Cycle	256
Sampling Rate (Hz)	15360

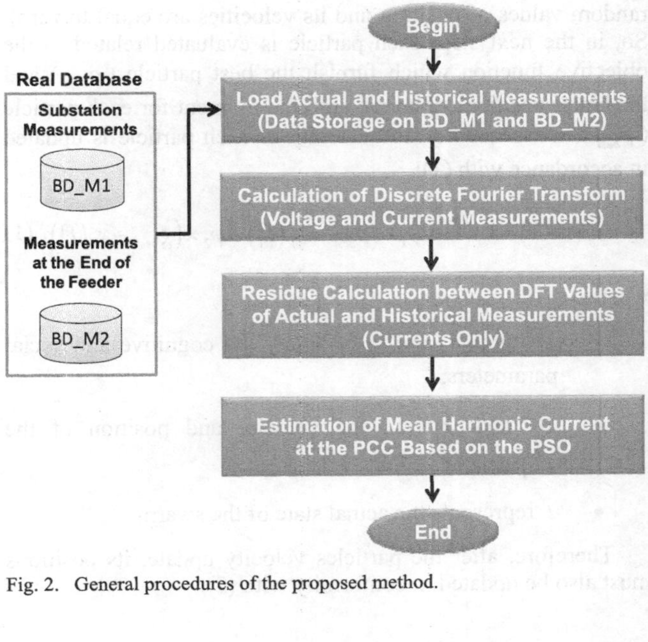

Fig. 2. General procedures of the proposed method.

In the next step, the algorithm performs the residue calculation between the values obtained after the DFT (actual and historical data).

After the procedures above mentioned, the harmonic estimator runs based on the procedures shown in Figure 3.

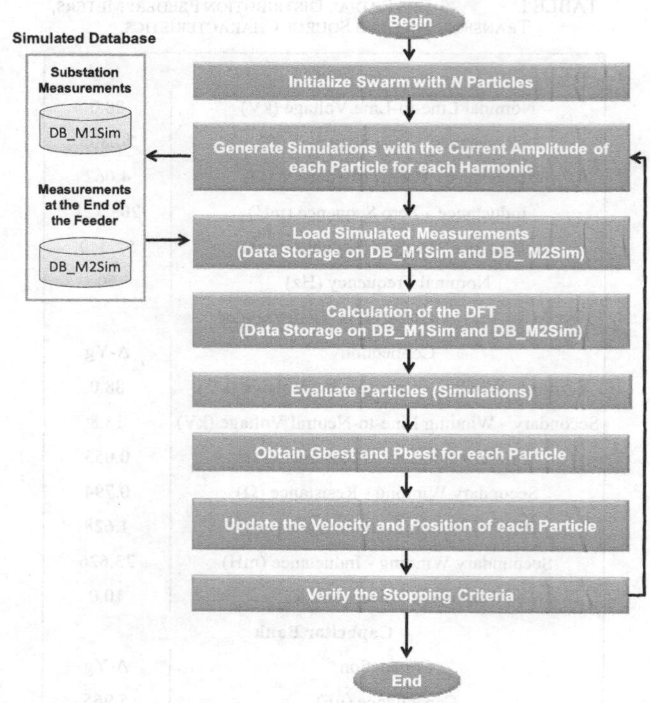

Fig. 3. Flowchart of the harmonic estimator based on particle swarm optimization.

In this paper, as previously mentioned, the estimator is based on Particle Swarm Optimization (PSO). Thereby, the PSO is initialized with N particles (these particles have random values of position and its velocities are equal to zero). So, in the next step, each particle is evaluated related to the objective function which furnish the best particle (g_{best}) and the better positions obtained until the moment for each particle (p_{best}). Consequently, the velocity of each particle is updated in accordance with (1):

$$v_i(t+1) = v_i(t) + \varphi_1 \times (p_{best} - x_i(t)) + \varphi_2 \times (g_{best} - x_i(t)) \quad (1)$$

where:

- φ_1 and φ_2 are respectively the cognitive and social parameters;
- v_i and x_i are the velocity and position of the ith particle;
- t represents the actual state of the swarm.

Therefore, after the particles velocity update, its positions must also be updated in conformity with (2):

$$x_i(t+1) = x_i(t) + v_i(t+1). \quad (2)$$

All the procedures presented must be repeated until the algorithm reach the stopping criteria. This PSO algorithm was implemented based on the foundations proposed by [10-11]. It should be mentioned that was used a swarm with 15 particles.

IV. CASY STUDIES

As previously mentioned, a 20-bus distribution feeder was modeled and simulated in order to validate this research. Thus, six case studies were created and its peculiarities will be properly treated in the sequence. Mentioning that for each case study, some nonlinear loads (6-pulses rectifier) were allocated in the feeder.

Before the presentation of each case study, it is important to highlight the buses determined by the expert knowledge and the comparison with the exact position of the harmonic source.

TABLE II. BUSES PRE-DETERMINED BY EXPERT KNOWLEDGE

Case Study	Buses		Error [m]
	Exact	Estimated	
#1	21	20	100
#2	30	30	0
#3	34	30	1300
#4	53	50	300
#5	52	50	300
#6	42	40	300

A. Case Study #1

In order to obtain the actual measures, a 6-pulse rectifier feeding a inductive load (600 Ω e 200 mH) was allocated on bus 21. Its harmonic current signature can be viewed in the Table III. This is an ideal case study, because the historical measures do not present harmonic distortions (uncommon condition).

TABLE III. RL LOAD (600 Ω E 200 MH) ALLOCATED ON BUS 21

Harmonic Order	Peak Current [A]		
	Phase A	Phase B	Phase C
1	59.935	60.165	59.922
3	0.148	0.268	0.121
5	13.332	13.183	13.316
7	6.896	7.117	6.799
9	0.155	0.244	0.122
11	5.314	5.225	5.275
13	4.055	4.260	3.918

Analyzing the actual signals of voltage and current, it is noted a Total Harmonic Distortion (THD) of voltage about: 1.71% (phase A), 1.91% (phase B) and 1.74% (phase C).

The mean value of exact and estimated harmonic currents obtained for this case can be visualized in the Table IV.

It is important to note that higher harmonic orders (11th and 13th) and those harmonic components with low amplitude presents considerable errors.

TABLE IV. RESULTS OBTAINED TO THE CASE STUDY #1

Harmonic Order	Mean Currents [A]	
	Exact	Estimated
1	60.007	64.464
3	0.179	0.014
5	13.277	13.387
7	6.937	7.172
9	0.174	0.056
11	5.271	0.863
13	4.078	0.932

B. *Case Study #2*

The second case study was generated to present the same historical data of case study #1. The actual state of this feeder has a 6-pulses rectifier allocated in bus 30. This rectifier feed a RL load (900 Ω and 900 mH). Thus, its harmonic currents were measured and can be visualized in the Table V.

TABLE V. RL LOAD (900 Ω E 900 MH) ALLOCATED ON BUS 30

Harmonic Order	Peak Current [A]		
	Phase A	Phase B	Phase C
1	40.183	40.495	40.276
3	0.262	0.340	0.078
5	8.426	8.158	8.356
7	5.220	5.530	5.266
9	0.260	0.337	0.088
11	3.717	3.478	3.643
13	2.892	3.221	2.953

Furthermore, the actual measurements has a voltage unbalance (-5% for the phase B and +10% in the phase C) when compared to historical measurements.

It is important to mention that the percentage of voltage unbalance were randomly generated.

In this case study, it was found THD of voltage at the substation about: 1.36% (phase A), 1.54% (phase B) and 1.39% (phase C). Thus, after perfom the harmonic estimator , it was possible to obtain the exact and estimated mean harmonic currents (Table VI).

TABLE VI. RESULTS OBTAINED TO THE CASE STUDY #2

Harmonic Order	Mean Currents [A]	
	Exact	Estimated
1	40.318	43.750
3	0.227	1.001
5	8.313	8.284
7	5.339	6.018
9	0.228	1.008
11	3.613	1.795
13	3.022	0.123

Analyzing these results, we can see that the harmonic estimator presents the same pattern response shown in the case study #1.

C. *Case Study #3*

This third case study, as well as case studies #1 and #2, was generated to has historical data without harmonic distortion. However, the capacitor bank previously allocated in bus 42 was out of operation.

The simulation that represents the actual state has a 6-pulses rectifier allocated in bus 34. This rectifier has been allocated in the feeder in order to feed a RL load (1300 Ω and 200 mH). Thus, the harmonic signature observed at this PCC can be viewed through the Table VII.

TABLE VII. RL LOAD (1300 Ω E 200 MH) ALLOCATED ON BUS 34

Harmonic Order	Peak Current [A]		
	Phase A	Phase B	Phase C
1	27.922	28.085	27.960
3	0.084	0.175	0.094
5	6.273	6.166	6.290
7	3.005	3.177	3.054
9	0.094	0.182	0.091
11	2.511	2.416	2.564
13	1.686	1.869	1.753

Furthermore, in the actual state of the feeder some RL loads had their impedances changed in order to generate variations in feeder loading. It is worth mentioning that only the resistive part of these RL loads was changed in a randomly way.

The voltage THD for this third case study were calculated at the substation: 0.92% (phase A), 1.11% (phase B) e 0.99% (phase C).

The results obtained by the harmonic estimator based on PSO were those shown in Table VIII.

TABLE VIII. RESULTS OBTAINED TO THE CASE STUDY #3

Harmonic Order	Mean Currents [A]	
	Exact	Estimated
1	27.989	27.354
3	0.118	0.026
5	6.243	6.225
7	3.079	3.103
9	0.122	0.025
11	2.497	2.431
13	1.770	1.658

In this case study, only the estimation pattern related to the harmonic components of low amplitude was maintained.

D. *Case Study #4*

This case study was created to use the same profile of historical measurements presented at this moment (without distortions).

Briefly, it can be said that the actual state of the feeder includes voltage unbalance about: -7% (phase A), 7% (phase B) and -4% (phase C). In addition, variations on the RL loads distributed over the feeder were done and also a 6-pulse rectifier feeding a RC load (800 Ω and 1000 μF) was allocated on bus 53. The harmonic distortions observed at the PCC for this case study can be viewed by means of Table IX.

It was found for this case study voltage THD at the substation about: 1.90% (phase A), 2.46% (phase B) and 1.46% (phase C).

TABLE IX. RC LOAD (800 Ω E 1000 μF) ALLOCATED ON BUS 53

Harmonic Order	Peak Current [A]		
	Phase A	Phase B	Phase C
1	44.446	45.610	44.898
3	0.359	0.444	0.795
5	21.303	21.523	21.765
7	10.675	10.304	10.400
9	0.437	0.149	0.455
11	3.609	3.704	3.840
13	2.481	2.442	2.457

After the estimation of harmonic components (Table X), the proposed method showed a high error to estimate the fundamental component and for those with low amplitude.

TABLE X. RESULTS OBTAINED TO THE CASE STUDY #4

Harmonic Order	Mean Currents [A]	
	Exact	Estimated
1	44.985	79.752
3	0.533	1.437
5	21.530	20.629
7	10.460	9.631
9	0.347	0.140
11	3.718	4.031
13	2.460	2.398

E. Case Study #5

Different from the case studies previously reported, this case had historical data generated with harmonic distortions, i.e., it is assumed that the feeder already has nonlinear loads. Thus, the voltage DHT measured at the substation for the historical simulations were: 0.88% (phase A), 1.04% (phase B) and 0.88% (phase C). Moreover, the capacitor bank was maintained out of operation.

The simulation representing the actual state of the feeder has a 6-pulse rectifier feeding a RL load (1400 Ω e 600 mH) allocated on bus 52. In this way, the fundamental and harmonic components of this load was measured (Table XI).

TABLE XI. RL LOAD (1400 Ω E 600 MH) ALLOCATED ON BUS 52

Harmonic Order	Peak Current [A]		
	Phase A	Phase B	Phase C
1	25.762	25.801	25.852
3	0.085	0.022	0.087
5	5.559	5.562	5.518
7	2.866	2.951	2.990
9	0.077	0.066	0.086
11	2.152	2.176	2.150
13	1.541	1.647	1.685

In the actual state of this case, a voltage unbalance can be verified: +3% (phase A), -6% (phase B) and +9% (phase C); and a loading variation of the feeder.

During the actual state simulation were verified voltage THD at the substation about: 1.38% (phase A), 1.45% (phase B) and 1.28% (phase C). The results obtained for the case study #5 are summarized on the Table XII.

This results are very similar to those obtained for the case study #3.

TABLE XII. RESULTS OBTAINED TO THE CASE #5

Harmonic Order	Mean Currents [A]	
	Exact	Estimated
1	25.805	28.280
3	0.065	0.019
5	5.546	5.304
7	2.936	2.792
9	0.076	0.009
11	2.159	1.979
13	1.624	1.442

F. Case Study #6

Finally, the case study #6 is similar to the case study #5, but the capacitor is in operation and replaced to the bus 20. The historical data was obtained in the same way used to the case study #5. Thus, nonlinear loads were allocated on the feeder and a voltage THD at the substation was measured: 3.58% (phase A), 3.56% (phase B) e 3.49% (phase C).

The actual data was acquired allocating a 6-pulse rectifier on bus 42 to feed a RL load (1200 Ω e 400 mH). Its harmonic components are shown in Table XIII.

TABLE XIII. RL LOAD (1200 Ω E 400 MH) ALLOCATED ON BUS 42

Harmonic Order	Peak Current [A]		
	Phase A	Phase B	Phase C
1	29.650	30.029	29.710
3	0.277	0.437	0.162
5	6.549	6.269	6.489
7	2.974	3.332	2.961
9	0.225	0.355	0.162
11	2.279	2.127	2.263
13	1.438	1.692	1.356

The simulation to the actual scenario of the feeder presents loading variations, voltages unbalance about: +4% (phase A), +2% (phase B) and +2% (phase C), and voltage THD at the substation about: 4.24% (phase A), 4.20% (phase B) and 4.17% (phase C). For this last case study, the harmonic estimator shows high imprecision to determine harmonics with low amplitude and to estimate the fundamental current.

TABLE XIV. RESULTS OBTAINED TO THE CASE #6

Harmonic Order	Mean Currents [A]	
	Exact	Estimated
1	29.796	38.235
3	0.292	2.185
5	6.436	6.169
7	3.089	3.678
9	0.247	0.484
11	2.223	2.205
13	1.495	1.325

V. CONCLUSIONS

Analyzing the six case studies, we can be note that the proposed method is not effective to determine harmonics with low amplitude (less than 1 A). The cases #3 and #5 presents the better estimations, probably due to the absence of capacitor banks. So, the continuation of this research points to the definition of behavioral patterns based on the possible scenarios of load. Moreover, other optimization methods, such as ant colony, genetic algorithm and modified particle swarms must be adequate and tested envisioning results better than these presented on this paper.

ACKNOWLEDGMENT

The authors would like to acknowledge the CNPq (Conselho Nacional de Desenvolvimento Científico e Tecnológico), CAPES (Coordenação de Aperfeiçoamento de Pessoal de nível Superior) and FAPESP (Fundação de Amparo à Pesquisa do Estado de São Paulo) by the financial support.

REFERENCES

[1] K. L. Lian and T. Noda, "A Time-Domain Harmonic Power-Flow Algorithm for Obtaining Nonsinusoidal Steady-State Solutions," *IEEE Transactions on Power Delivery*, Vol. 25, No. 3, pp. 1888-1898, 2010.

[2] M. Valcárcel and J. G. Mayordomo, "Harmonic Power Flow for Unbalanced Systems," *IEEE Transactions on Power Delivery*, Vol. 8, No. 4, pp. 2052-2059, 1993.

[3] L. Sainz and J. Pedra, "Infeasible Harmonic Power Flow Study Solutions," *IEEE Transactions on Power Delivery*, Vol. 10, No. 3, pp. 1621-1627, 1995.

[4] E. F. Arruda, N. Kagan, and P. F. Ribeiro, "Harmonic Distortion State Estimation Using an Evolutionary Strategy," *IEEE Transactions on Power Delivery*, Vol. 25, No. 2, pp. 831-842, 2010.

[5] G. D'Antona, C. Muscas, and S. Sulis, "State Estimation for the Localization of Harmonic Sources in Electric Distribution Systems," *IEEE Transactions on Instrumentation and Measurement*, Vol. 58, No. 5, pp. 1462-1470, 2009.

[6] E. Gursoy and D. Niebur, "Harmonic Load Identification Using Complex Independent Component Analysis," *IEEE Transactions on Power Delivery*, Vol. 24, No. 1, pp. 285-292, 2009.

[7] D. -J. Won, I.-Y. Chung, J. -M. Kim, S. -I. Moon, J. -C. Seo and J. -W. Choe, "A New Algorithm to Locate Power-Quality Event Source with Improved Realization of Distributed Monitoring Scheme," *IEEE Transactions on Power Delivery*, Vol. 21, No. 3, pp. 1641-1647, 2006.

[8] IEEE Distribution Planning Working Group Report, "Radial Distribution Test Feeders," *IEEE Transactions on Power Systems*, Vol. 6, No. 3, pp. 975-985, 1991.

[9] H. K. Hoidalen, ATP Draw version 5 – Users Manual Supplements, Trondheim – Norway, 2007.

[10] J. Kennedy and R. C. Eberhart, "Particle Swarm Optimization," Proceedings of IEEE International Conference on Neural Networks, pp. 1942–1948, 1995.

[11] J. Kennedy, R. C. Eberhart, and Y. Shi, Swarm Intelligence, Morgan Kaufmann/Academic Press, 2001.

Emission Source Localization using the Firefly Algorithm

Darrin M. Hanna[1] **and Michael F. Lohrer**[1]
[1]Department of Electrical and Computer Engineering, Oakland University, Rochester, MI, United States

Abstract – *In this paper two solutions to the emission source localization problem are examined. This problem involves monitoring an environment with a distributed sensor network and processing the data to find the source of an emission. Being able to quickly find the source of a chemical leak or radiological dispersion can save lives, and reducing or eliminating the need for people to be involved in the search process further reduces the danger. Previous work presented the benefits of using the Particle Swarm Optimization for emission source localization. This work presents further benefits by using The Firefly Algorithm. The Firefly Algorithm in general only performs better when dealing with lots of noise from the sensors, but is faster under all circumstances.*

Keywords: Swarm Optimization, Firefly Algorithm, Particle Swarm Optimization, Emission Source Localization

1 Introduction

Tracking and localization of an emission's source is an important safety concern. Whether an accident or terrorist strike causes hazardous material to leak into the surrounding air, finding the source of an emission can be critical. Traditional methods of source localization involve continuously sampling the suspected area and sending in trained personnel to find the source. This is not only time consuming, but very dangerous. One possible solution is to use robots to detect and locate the source, reducing the danger to humans [1]. This can still take a significant amount of time, even if multiple robots are utilized. Another solution is to have many sensors spread throughout the contaminated area, and locate the source by analyzing the data. This method can be very quick, as long as the algorithm performed to analyze the data is efficient.

The US Department of Energy's Oak Ridge National Laboratory (ORNL) is developing a network called SensorNet for the detection and assessment of chemical, biological, radiological, nuclear, and explosive threats [2]. SensorNet consists of many small, distributed sensors for gathering data, and high level nodes for data processing. Various techniques can potentially be applied to the data from these nodes to determine the source of the emission. Previously, we experimented with using Particle Swarm Optimization (PSO) and found that with the proper tuning, PSO performed relatively quickly and located sources accurately [3].

Particle Swarm Optimization is a form of artificial intelligence capable of relatively quickly optimizing a given problem. Recently however, another artificial intelligence algorithm has been shown to outperform PSO [4]. The Firefly Algorithm (FA) is extremely efficient and works well under rugged search conditions. Since sensors involved in the emission source localization will likely have noise in their readings, the search space will not be smooth. It is also of interest to note that with the right parameters, the FA can essentially become PSO, or even Random Search. This means that the FA is a general case of the two, and typically lies somewhere in between, allowing it to potentially outperform both.

The goal of this work is to directly compare the FA to PSO on both benchmark functions and the emission source localization problem. On the benchmark problems, the FA is shown to outperform PSO in every way. For smaller scales of the source localization problem, the Firefly Algorithm only performs better with the more noisy sensors. For larger source localization configurations however, the firefly algorithm produces results similar to PSO in less time.

This paper presents a brief description of the PSO and Firefly algorithms including variations to the initial FA that have been developed by others. Section 3 also presents a new improvement to the FA. Section 4 describes results in benchmarking the algorithm to standard tests and implementation improvements that we have made resulting in faster execution. Section 5 details the source emission problem and results of our firefly implementation compared with the previous PSO work.

2 Particle Swarm Optimization

Particle Swarm Optimization (PSO) models its behavior after the swarming or flocking patterns of animals [1]. PSO has particles that make up its population, called a swarm. Each particle knows its position, velocity, and personal best location found so far, and the global best. The particles use these values to imitate both the social and individual behaviors of a swarm. After a random initialization, the update operation for a particle occurs according to the following function [2]:

$$v_{ij}(t) = v_{ij}(t-1) + \varphi_1 r_1 \left(p_{ij} - x_{ij}(t-1)\right) + \varphi_2 r_2 \left(p_{gj} - x_{ij}(t-1)\right) \quad (1)$$

where i = 1, 2, …, N for N particles, and j = 1, 2, …, D for D dimensions, v_{ij} is the velocity of the particle, t is the generation or time-step, r_1 and r_2 are random numbers in the range (0, 1), p_{ij} is the personal best location found so far, p_{gj} is the global best, x_{ij} is the location of the particle, and φ_1, φ_2 are called learning rates.

3 The Firefly Algorithm

The Firefly Algorithm (FA) is a relatively new swarm intelligence algorithm, developed by Xin-She Yang [3]. The FA is intriguing because its author has shown that it is not only faster than PSO on the functions tested, but also that it is more likely to find the global minimum.

3.1 The Concept behind the Firefly Algorithm

The FA was inspired by the flashing of fireflies in nature. There are over 2000 species of fireflies, most of which produce a bioluminescence from their abdomen [4]. Each species of firefly produces its own pattern of flashes, and although the complete function of these flashes is not known, the main purpose is to attract a mate. The idea of this attractiveness is what leads to the inspiration for the FA.

The FA idealizes several aspects of fireflies in nature. First, real fireflies flash in discrete patterns, whereas the modeled fireflies will be treated as always glowing with a certain brightness. Then, three rules can be made to govern the algorithm, and create a modeled firefly's behavior [5].

1) The fireflies are unisex, and so therefore potentially attracted to any of the other fireflies.
2) Attractiveness is determined by brightness, a less bright firefly will move towards a brighter firefly.
3) The brightness of a firefly is proportional to the value of the function being maximized at its current location.

3.2 The Algorithm

The key to the FA is the encoding of the objective function into the brightness of the fireflies, and in the movement of the fireflies. Initially, all fireflies start in random locations, and are assigned a brightness proportional to the objective function evaluated at their location. After this initialization, the algorithm loops until completion, moving each firefly towards all the other fireflies in the swarm that are brighter than itself. The pseudocode for the FA is given in Figure 3.1. In order to move a firefly towards another, first, the distance between the fireflies, r, has to be calculated. Any form of distance calculation that makes sense for the given problem can be used, but for the general case the Cartesian distance is appropriate. With the distance between two fireflies known, the attractiveness β can be determined. Since the attractiveness is based on the light intensity, two terms go into the calculation of β. These terms account for the light intensity decreasing as distance increases. First, from the inverse square law $\beta_1(r) = I_0/r^2$, where I_0 is the light intensity of the firefly being moved towards. Then due to absorption through the air, $\beta_2(r) = I_0 e^{-\gamma r}$, where γ is the absorption coefficient, and $\gamma \in [0, \infty)$. A γ of 0 yields no absorption, while a large γ relates to the fireflies flying in a heavy fog. Then to produce an approximation of the combined terms, and to avoid the undefined result of $\beta_1(0)$, we obtain $\beta(r) = I_0 e^{-\gamma r^2}$. However, calculating an exponential can be expensive, and $I_0 e^{-\gamma r^2}$ can be approximated by $I_0/(1+\gamma r^2)$ when close to zero, which is not as difficult to calculate. Since the attractiveness is directly related to the light intensity, we can take $\beta_0 = I_0$, where β_0 is the attractiveness at $r = 0$, and typically $\beta_0 \in (0,1]$. Combining the last two remarks results in the expression $\beta(r) = \beta_0/(1+\gamma r^2)$. Changing β_0 changes how attracted fireflies are to others, so lowering β_0 lowers the desire for fireflies to move towards brighter fireflies.

```
Firefly Algorithm
Given:
Objective function f(x), where x = (x1, x2, ..., xd) for d
  dimensions.
Light intensity Ii at xi is determined by f(xi)
Define α, β, γ, δ
Give random locations for N fireflies in D dimensions
Initial evaluation of all N fireflies
while (End condition not met)
    Increment t
    for i = 1 to NumFireflies
        for j = 1 to NumFireflies
            if (Ij > Ii)
                Move firefly i towards j in
                  d-dimension
            end if
        end for j
        Evaluate new objective function solution and
          update light intensity
        Check if the best position found so far
    end for i
    Reduce alpha
    Sort the fireflies
end while
Find the best firefly
```

Figure 3.1. FA Pseudocode

The movement of a firefly towards a brighter firefly is determined by $\beta(r)$ and a random component. The random component is important for all metaheuristic algorithms; it helps the algorithm to escape from local optimums. A simple random movement can be generated with a uniform distribution in the range of $[-0.5, 0.5]$. Another important factor is the scale of the problem. If two parameters of the objective function have different ranges of possible values, a fixed range of random numbers would cause different relative randomness for each dimension. To solve this problem, the generated random numbers can be multiplied with the scale of each dimension, in the form of a vector of scaling values S. With all the terms together, the position update equation for a firefly i being attracted to firefly j becomes:

$$x_i = x_i + \beta_0/(1+\gamma r_{ij}^2)(x_j - x_i) + \alpha S(R - 0.5) \quad (2)$$

where R is a set of uniformly distributed random numbers in the range of $[0,1]$, and α is a parameter controlling the amount of randomness. α is typically in the range [0,1], where 0 corresponds to no randomness and 1 corresponds to being highly random.

3.3 Improvements

On top of the base algorithm, several improvements can be made. The first, suggested by Yang [5], has a major effect. It combines the FA with concepts from simulated annealing (SA). SA models the annealing process of metals, in which there is a given temperature schedule. The temperature starts high, and is decreased as time goes on, and is analogous to the amount of randomness. This idea of reducing the randomness can be applied to the FA as well, and greatly benefits the FA. The best reduction schedule to use varies with the problem at hand, but for the purposes of the experiments undertaken in the next section, the randomness reduction will be determined by the following equation [5]:

$$\alpha(t) = \alpha_0 \delta^t \tag{3}$$

where δ is the randomness reduction parameter, $\delta \in (0,1]$. A δ of 1 corresponds to no reduction, and lowering δ results in a quicker reduction.

A second improvement we developed can help in the case of large differences in the scale of parameters. The random component is already scaled with the scaling vector S, but the distance between fireflies r is not. Thus the attractiveness β is not scaled, since it relies on r. To fix this, the distance calculation can be modified from the standard Cartesian distance equation to

$$r_{ij} = \sqrt{\sum_{d=1}^{D} \left[(x_{id} - x_{jd})/S\right]^2} \tag{4}$$

with the familiar scaling values of S. With this implemented, the entire update equation is scaled to the individual parameters of the objective function.

A last change was simply to notice that the distance r_{ij} is never used in any of the above equations, but rather r_{ij}^2. This implies that the square root does not need to be taken in equation 4, an expensive computation. By removing this, a slight time speedup of the algorithm is achieved.

4 Initial Examination of the Firefly Algorithm

In order to test and verify the FA, there are several benchmark functions that can be used. With benchmark functions both speed and accuracy can be measured and compared. All the functions are usually run with 30 parameters to optimize, except Schaffer's *f6* as it is not generalized for more than two parameters like the rest. All of the functions used have a global minima of $f(x) = 0$, and the ending criteria will be set to a maximum number of 500 generations or when it finds a value at or below the error threshold. The thresholds for each function are given in Figure 4.1. Any execution of the FA that results in finding a value at or below the threshold will be considered to have found the global minimum. All of the function criteria are the same as commonly used in literature, in order to make comparisons easier and more meaningful [6].

Function	Dimension	Range	Error Threshold
Sphere	30	[-100,100]	0.01
Rosenbrock	30	[-30,30]	100
Rastrigin	30	[-5.12,5.12]	100
Griewank	30	[-600,600]	0.1
Schaffer's f6	30	[-100,100]	0.00001

Figure 4.1. Benchmark function parameters

4.1 Benchmark Comparisons to PSO

The Firefly Algorithm was compared with the PSO algorithm results contained in literature [2]. The FA was run with generic parameters of $\alpha = 0.2$, $\beta = 0.2$, $\gamma = 0.8$, and $\delta = 0.97$ for the first testing, and compared against an optimized constriction factor PSO with $V_{max} = X_{max}$ and generic parameters of $\chi = 0.729$ and $\varphi_1 = \varphi_2 = 2.05$. The number of both fireflies and particles used was 30. Further details and full results of the PSO are available in [6]. The parameters listed in Figure 4.1 were again used for these tests. Figure 4.2 shows the comparison between PSO and FA, using the number of generations as a metric. In every case, the FA outperformed the PSO, when each was used with generic parameters. The standard deviations are shown as error bars for all but the generic parameter PSO results, since the standard deviation for the PSO was extremely high in most cases. The fact that the standard deviation is significantly lower for the FA shows its reliability in finding the global optimum.

The generic parameters have been shown to work well, but tuning the parameters based on the objective function can lead to better results. Figure 4.3 Figure 4.2. PSO vs. FA: Number of generations also shows the results of manually tuning the parameters, for both the PSO and the FA. The optimal parameters that were used for the FA, and which were found through trial and error, are shown in Figure 4.4. FA Parameters The results show that in every case, the FA again outperforms the PSO on the benchmark functions. Improvements range from 31-98% fewer generations required to reach the desired result with the tuned algorithms compared to the un-tuned FA. The biggest improvement was seen in Schaffer's *f6* function, which was also the only function with two parameters. So for all tested functions, and particularly the low-dimensional one, the FA is much more efficient than PSO.

Not only is the efficiency of the algorithm important, but so is the accuracy. Figure 4.4 shows the percent failure of the two algorithms, with both the generic parameter and tuned parameter results. The only function that the FA did not find the global minimum 100% of the time was the Rosenbrock function. However, once the parameters were tuned, the FA achieved 100% accuracy on all functions, whereas the PSO failed 10-20% on three of the five functions. This shows that with some careful tuning, the FA can be not only extremely efficient, but also very accurate compared to the PSO.

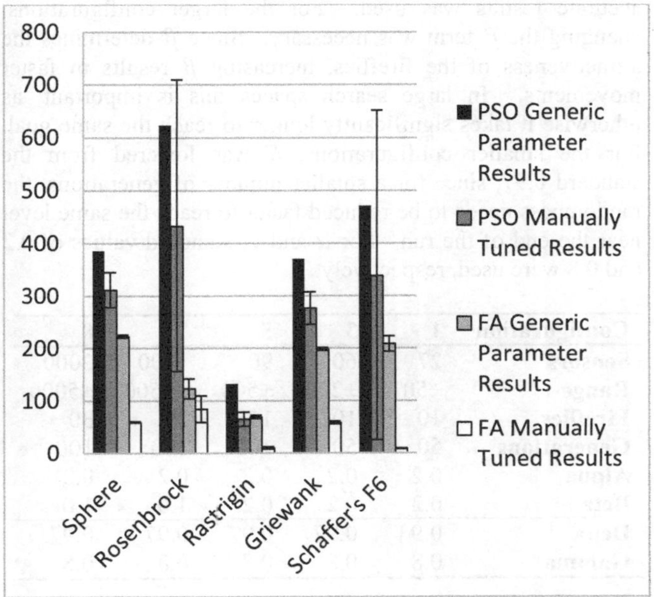

Figure 4.2. PSO vs. FA: Number of generations

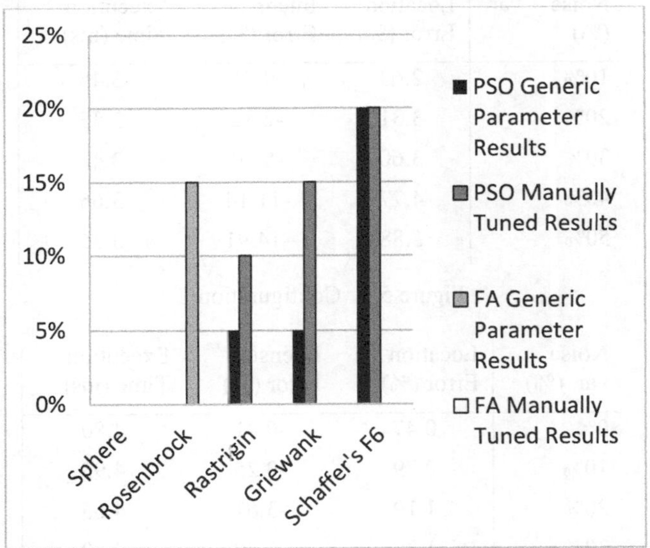

Figure 4.3. Executions that do not find the global minimum

Function	α	β	γ	δ
Sphere	0.2	0.3	0.8	0.89
Rosenbrock	0.02	0.2	0.9	0.9
Rastrigin	0.1	0.5	0.8	0.8
Griewank	0.2	0.2	0.8	0.89
Schaffer's f6	0.6	0.5	0.8	0.3

Figure 4.4. FA Parameters

5 Firefly Algorithm Scalability with Emission Source Localization

The emission source localization problem requires a model of propagation of the emission. From this model and data received from sensors, the source can be located. To model an aerosolized chemical, the intensity at any point away from the source can be assumed to follow the inverse square law [7]. This model ignores possible environmental factors such as air currents, but is a good starting point. It will be assumed that there is only one source, and that the sensors will be scattered randomly around an area known to contain the source. These sensors will also know their own locations, either from GPS or some other sensor localization method. The data from these sensors will be sent to a data processing node, which can then determine the location of the source. For the purposes of this examination, the sensors will be simulated, and varying amounts of additive Gaussian noise will be added to the sensors' readings. With the added noise, and since the propagation is assumed to follow the inverse square law, a sensor's reading can be calculated by:

$$q_j = \frac{Q_0}{d_j^2}(1 + \sigma G) \tag{5}$$

where d_j is the distance to sensor j from the source, Q_0 is the source intensity, σ is the desired standard deviation of the noise, and G is a random number picked from a Gaussian distribution of mean 0 and standard deviation 1. The source is located at (x_0, y_0), which will be determined randomly before the sensors are placed. The sensors will be placed randomly within a fixed square search space. Figure 5.1 shows an example of the placement of sensors with the source located at (-70,80).

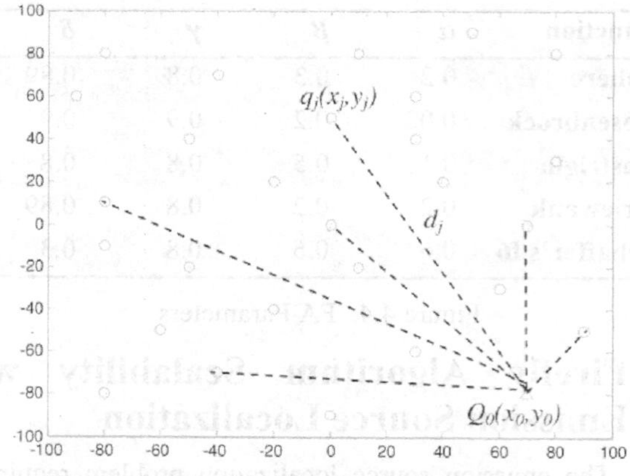

Figure 5.1. Randomly distributed sensors [6]

Then in order to formulate an objective function, the goal becomes to determine the optimal Q_0 and (x_0, y_0) that will provide the closest match between the propagation model and the actual sensor readings. The error between the two can be taken as

$$dQ_j = Q_0 - (q_j d_j^2 + w_j Q_0) \tag{6}$$

where q_j is the intensity reported by sensor j, d_j is the distance between sensor j and the source location (x_0, y_0), and w_j is a weighting factor used to correct for the error in the sensor readings.

Now that the error in an estimate from a single sensor's point of view can be calculated, the least squares method can be used to find the total error of an estimate [7]. The sum of all the squared errors from each sensor will be the objective function, given as [6]:

$$f(Q_0, x_0, y_0, W) = \sum_{j=1}^{N_s} dQ_j^2 = \sum_{j=1}^{N_s} [Q_0 - (q_j d_j^2 + w_j Q_0)]^2 \tag{7}$$

where N_s is the number of sensors, and W is the vector of each w_j for every sensor. So a firefly's position consists of an estimated Q_0, x_0, y_0, and a w_j for every sensor; thus every sensor adds a dimension to the problem.

5.1 Results

The aim of the tests with the FA will be to compare to the PSO results in [3]. Thus, eight different configurations each with a varying number of sensors and range over which the sensors are spread were used to test various scales of the problem, the results of which are given in Figures 5.3-5.7. For each configuration, five tests were performed, with the standard deviation of added noise varied from 0% to 50%. The tests were run 20 times each, and the results shown are the averages. Each test also has its own set of FA parameters. The goal of the parameter choice was to find a set that produced the best results in the least amount of time. The biggest parameter affecting time is the number of fireflies, and so is a good place to start when trying to reduce time taken. Reducing the number of fireflies reduces the number of search agents though, so it is often difficult to still produce accurate results. Once the minimal number of fireflies is determined, the next biggest factor is the number of generations to run. The number of generations also greatly affects the runtime; therefore once again, the minimum amount that still produced accurate results was used. For the larger configurations, changing the β term was necessary. Since β determines the attractiveness of the fireflies, increasing β results in faster movements. In large search spaces this is important, as otherwise it takes significantly longer to reach the same goal. For the smaller configurations, δ was lowered from the standard 0.97, since for a smaller number of generations, the randomness needs to be reduced faster to reach the same level near the end of the run. For α and γ, standard values of 0.2 and 0.8 were used, respectively.

Configuration	**1**	**3**	**5**	**7**	**8**
Sensors	27	60	90	1000	2000
Range	±50	±200	±500	±2500	±5000
Fireflies	10	10	15	25	30
Generations	50	50	100	100	100
Alpha	0.2	0.2	0.2	0.2	0.2
Beta	0.2	0.2	0.2	1.0	1.0
Delta	0.93	0.97	0.97	0.97	0.97
Gamma	0.8	0.8	0.8	0.8	0.8

Figure 5.2. FA parameters used in each configuration

Noise var. (%)	Location Error (%)	Intensity Error (%)	Execution Time (ms)
10%	2.63	-0.71	3.45
20%	3.31	-2.82	3.35
30%	3.60	-5.70	3.40
40%	4.77	-11.14	3.65
50%	5.88	-14.91	3.35

Figure 5.3. Configuration 1

Noise var. (%)	Location Error (%)	Intensity Error (%)	Execution Time (ms)
0%	0.47	-0.71	4.80
10%	0.79	-0.25	4.95
20%	1.19	-3.61	4.65
30%	1.30	-2.70	4.80
40%	1.70	-5.55	4.75
50%	1.80	-4.88	4.55

Figure 5.4. Configuration 3

Noise var. (%)	Location Error (%)	Intensity Error (%)	Execution Time (ms)
0%	0.09	-0.02	28.70
10%	0.29	-0.78	27.50
20%	0.73	-3.12	28.15
30%	1.18	-2.36	27.50
40%	1.52	-5.23	27.25
50%	2.04	-3.69	25.30

Figure 5.5. Configuration 5

Noise var. (%)	Location Error (%)	Intensity Error (%)	Execution Time (ms)
0%	0.05	-0.08	777.9
10%	0.10	-0.54	773.0
20%	0.36	-1.52	768.6
30%	0.43	-1.46	778.0
40%	0.54	-1.51	776.8
50%	0.74	-2.43	689.4

Figure 5.6. Configuration 7

Noise var. (%)	Location Error (%)	Intensity Error (%)	Execution Time (ms)
0%	0.04	0.05	2325
10%	0.06	-0.03	2261
20%	0.15	-0.86	2307
30%	0.48	-1.97	2337
40%	0.53	-1.65	2268
50%	0.73	-2.30	2088

Figure 5.7. Configuration 8

For the first few configurations, the results were fairly similar. In configuration 1, the localization error obtained by the FA is worse for 0-20% noise, but better for 30-50% noise. The intensity error is better under all noise conditions, and the time required is about 13 times lower. Note that much of the time speedup is due to being run on a faster processor, but it is still useful to compare relative speedups between configurations.

In configuration 3, the average localization error is higher for 0-30% noise, but lower for 40 and 50%. The average intensity error is about the same for all noise levels, and the execution time is about 180 times faster. With configuration 5, the FA obtains about the same localization and intensity error for 0-20% noise, but for 30-50% noise the FA obtains better results for both. The speed for this configuration was about 50 times faster than the PSO. Thus, in the smaller configurations 1 through 5, for low noise levels, the PSO seems to find better results, but not always as efficiently. For higher noise levels, the FA wins out in terms of accuracy of the results, and except for the smallest configuration is likely much faster.

Configurations 6-8 provide a better comparison, as tabular data is available. The PSO and FA results are compared in Figures 5.8-5.11. Configuration 6 and 7 show uniformly worse performance for the FA, but in configuration 8 the intensity error is lower for the FA on all but 30% noise. The time speedups, however, are about 34, 23, and 18 times faster, respectively. These times may or may not actually be faster, given that the FA was run on a faster processor, but the difference between speedups of different configurations shows that the FA runs faster on small to medium scale problems compared to the PSO. For the smaller scale problems, the FA performs much better under highly noisy conditions, and in fact gets nearly uniform results across all noise levels, compared to the PSO. These results point to using the FA either when using noisy sensors, or when speed is critical.

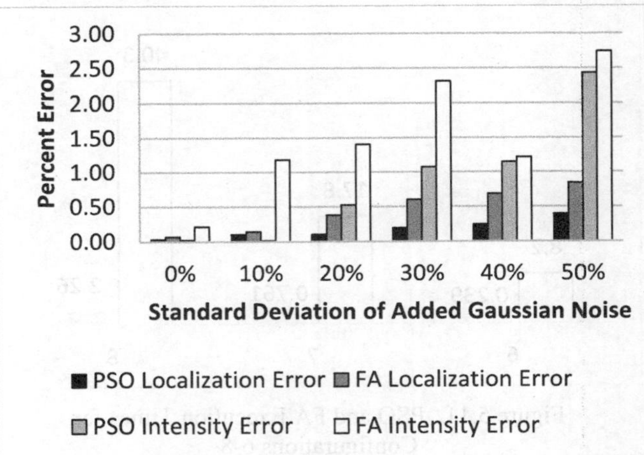

Figure 5.8. PSO and FA on Configuration 6

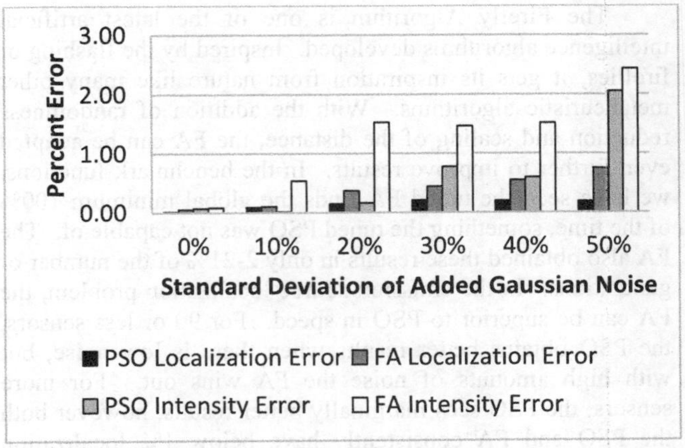

Figure 5.9. PSO and FA on Configuration 7

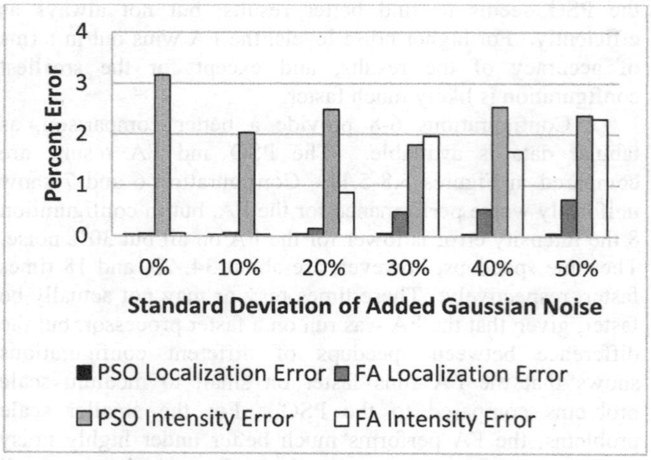

Figure 5.10. PSO and FA on Configuration 8

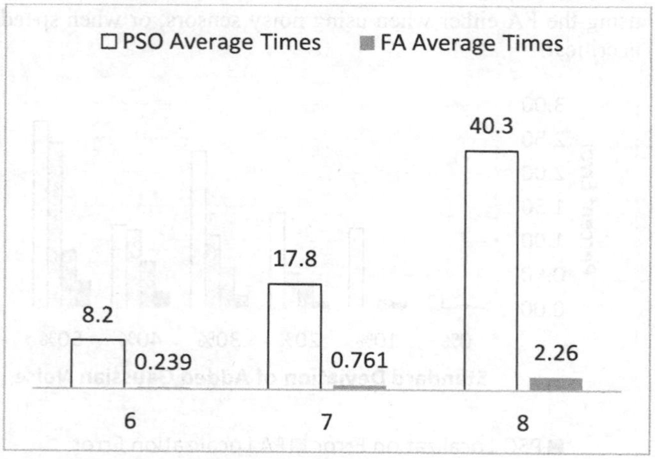

Figure 5.11. PSO and FA Execution Times for Configurations 6-8

6 Conclusions and Future Work

The Firefly Algorithm is one of the latest artificial intelligence algorithms developed. Inspired by the flashing of fireflies, it gets its inspiration from nature like many other metaheuristic algorithms. With the addition of randomness reduction and scaling of the distance, the FA can be adapted even further to improve results. In the benchmark functions, we have seen the tuned FA finds the global minimum 100% of the time, something the tuned PSO was not capable of. The FA also obtained these results in only 2-21% of the number of generations. In the emission source localization problem, the FA can be superior to PSO in speed. For 90 or less sensors, the PSO obtains better results when there is low noise, but with high amounts of noise the FA wins out. For more sensors, the PSO sees marginally better results, however both the PSO and FA consistently have below 1% localization error. It also gives better results when there is a large amount of noise in the sensor data.

In order to speed up the FA even more, we are in the process of implementing it in hardware similar to the architecture that Tewolde and Hanna created for the hardware PSO engine in [8]. A parallel hardware implementation could even further improve speed. To find even better parameters, auto-tuning could be implemented with another FA. As for the algorithm itself, it would be worth investigating possible improvements, such as hybridization with other algorithms. The addition of the randomness reduction concept from simulated annealing helped improve results, and this could be investigated further, such as increasing the randomness at various stages in order to escape local optima. Other such algorithms likely have concepts worth exploring and adapting to the FA.

7 References

[1] J. Kennedy and R. Eberhart, "Particle Swarm Optimization," in *Proceedings of IEEE International Conference on Neural Networks*, Piscataway, NJ, 1995.

[2] G. S. Tewolde, D. Hanna and R. E. Haskell, "Particle Swarm Optimization for Emission Source Localization in Sensor Networks," in *Proceedings of the Conference on Artificial Neural Networks and Intelligence in Engineering (ANNIE) 2009*, St. Louis, Missouri, 2009.

[3] X. S. Yang, Nature-Inspired Metaheuristic Algorithms, Luniver Press, 2008.

[4] S. M. Lewis and C. K. Cratsley, "Flash Signal Evolution, Mate Choice, and Predation in Fireflies," *Annu. Rev. Entomol.*, vol. 53, pp. 293-321, 2008.

[5] X. S. Yang, Engineering optimization: An introduction with metaheuristic applications, Hoboken, NJ: John Wiley & Sons., 2010.

[6] G. S. Tewolde, D. M. Hanna and R. E. Haskell, "Enhancing Performance of PSO with Automatic Parameter Tuning Technique," in *Proceedings of the 2009 IEEE Swarm Intelligence Symposium*, Nashville, TN, 2009.

[7] M. P. Michaelides and C. G. Panayiotou, "Plume Source Position Estimation Using Sensor Networks," in *Proceedings of the 2005 IEEE International Symposium on Intelligent Control, Mediterranean Conference on Control and Automation*, Limassol, Cyprus, 2005.

[8] G. S. Tewolde, "Multi-Swarm Parallel PSO: Hardware Implementation," in *Proceedings of the 2009 IEEE Swarm Intelligence Symposium*, Nashville, TN, 2009.

A Fast Parameter Setting Strategy for Particle Swarm Optimization and Its Application in Urban Water Distribution Network Optimal Design

Xuewei Qi[1], Khaled Rasheed[2], Ke Li[1], Walter Potter[3]
1. College of Engineering, University of Georgia, Athens, 30602, USA
2. Department of Computer Science, University of Georgia, Athens, 30602, USA
3. Institute of Artificial Intelligence, University of Georgia, Athens, 30602, USA

Abstract-*Parameter setting is very essential for the application of particle swarm optimization (PSO), especially the acceleration coefficients. In this paper, we propose a fast estimation strategy of optimal parameter setting for PSO, in which an estimation distribution algorithm (EDA) is used to co-evolve the acceleration coefficients (c_1 and c_2). The proposed algorithm is validated on two numerical optimization problems and then applied to the urban water distribution network optimization problem. The experimental results show that both of these two parameters converge to a fixed value respectively and the achieved values for c_1 and c_2 are consistent as the results of parameter tuning.PSO with the estimated optimal parameters could achieve the best solution on benchmark example and also outperform other methods in terms of reliability and efficiency.*

Keywords: Particle Swarm Optimization, Parameter control, Estimation Distribution Algorithm, Water Distribution Network.

1 Introduction

Particle Swarm Optimization is a population based optimization method inspired by the collective behavior of a bird flock, which was developed by Eberhart and Kennedy[3] in 1995. It is an effective swarm intelligence technique for solving optimization problems. It has shown great potential and perspective for solving various optimization problems [4,5,6,7,8].

A crucial aspect of improving the performance of PSO is parameter setting [9]. PSO can only perform effectively under good parameter settings. There are two primary approaches of setting parameters [10]: parameter tuning and parameter control. Parameter tuning identifies the optimal parameter settings by repeatedly running using different combinations of parameter values. However, this cumbersome method usually takes much time and effort, and relies on luck as exhaustive search of the parameter space is prohibitively expensive. Another more popular approach is parameter control. In this approach, the parameters are not fixed, but changed during the course of the evolutionary process. There are two main approaches of parameter control [10]: adaptive parameter control and self-adaptive parameter control. In adaptive parameter control, the parameter values are adaptively adjusted by heuristic rules based on feedback from previous parameter changes [11]. In this approach, defining the meaning of feedback is a key issue. In general, we often use the current stage of the search, the performance of operators and/or the diversity of the population as the guiding information. Adaptive parameter control is common for PSO and has shown effectiveness in solving various problems in the past [3,12,13]. In self-adaptive parameter control, the parameters and the solutions to the optimization problem evolve together. Self-adaptive parameter control has been used in genetic algorithms in which the parameters are encoded within the chromosomes and evolve with the problem (object) variables [14,15,16,17]. Adopting self-adaptive parameter control in PSO has recently raised much interest [18], which embeds the parameters within the evolution variables. In this way, the parameters are self-adaptively controlled.

Optimal design of water distribution networks (WDN) aims to select a set of pipes (with different diameters) to form a network which satisfies all the hydraulic requirements and also has the minimal total cost, which is also called Pipe Sizing. In the past three decades, a variety of optimization methods have been proposed for the pipe sizing problem. In the past few years, PSO was introduced to optimize WDN. [19] applied a conventional discrete PSO to this problem for the first time in 2008. Shortly afterwards, a diversity enriched PSO variant was proposed [20] to address the premature convergence problem and the performance was improved compared to the conventional PSO. Montalvo et al. [18] improved the performance of PSO further on this WDN optimization problem by introducing a parameter self-adaptive strategy.

2 Methodologies

2.1 Estimation of distribution algorithm

Estimation of distribution algorithms (EDAs) is population based evolutionary algorithm. During the iteration process, EDAs try to estimate the probability distribution by using good individuals to construct a probabilistic model, which is then used to predict the promising positions and generate new individuals of the next generation around that region. The details of implementation of EDA are given in algorithm 1:

Algorithm 1 The EDA algorithm

```
1: P<= Initialize the population
2: Evaluate the initial population
3: While iter_number ≤ Max_iterations do
4:     Ps<= Select the top s individuals from p
5:     M<= estimate a new Model from Ps
6:     Pn <= Sample n individuals from M
7:     Evaluate Pn
8:     P<= Select n individuals from P U Pn
9:     iter_number =iter_number +1
10: end While
```

A very simple model assumes that each of the coefficients follows a simple Gaussian distribution when the parameters are approaching the global optimal settings. Hence, in each iteration of EDA, the top individuals in the population are used to estimate the mean and standard deviation of the distribution of the best parameter settings. On the next iteration, a new population is generated by sampling according to the estimated distribution.

2.2 Particle swarm optimization

In the population of PSO, each particle holds the following information: particle's current positionx_i, particle's current velocity: v_i , the best position that the particle has ever found so far Pbest$_i$ and the best position that the entire swarm has ever found: gbest$_i$

In PSO, each particle updates its position according to the following equations:

$$v_{ij}^{t+1}=wv_{ij}^{t}+c_1r_{1j}(pbest_{ij}^{t}-x_{ij}^{t})+c_2r_{2j}(gbest_{ij}^{t}-x_{ij}^{t}) \quad (1)$$

$$x_{ij}^{t+1} = x_{ij}^{t} + v_{ij}^{t+1} \quad (2)$$

Where j denotes the index of the dimension, i denotes the number of particles, w is the inertia weight and t is the iteration number, r_1 and r_2 are two random numbers uniformly distributed in the range [0,1] and finally c_1 and c_2 are the acceleration factors. After all the particles are updated, the Pbest$_i$ and gbest$_i$ are also updated if better positions are found.

Acceleration coefficients (c_1 and c_2)are most influential to the performance of the algorithm. Much previous research has shown that for different problems, the optimal settings of c_1 and c_2 are different. Therefore, designing an efficient parameter setting strategy for acceleration coefficients has been an active research area in PSO domain.

2.3Parameter co-evolving strategy

In our proposed parameter estimation strategy, there are two iterative loops which run simultaneously. The first loop is PSO which tries to find the optimal solution for the specific problem; the second loop (coevolving loop) is the EDA which tries to optimize the parameter settings (c_1 and c_2) online for each individual in PSO loop. In PSO population, each individual is a candidate solution for the specific optimization problem. In EDA population, each individual is a pair of values for c_1 and c_2. The population size for both PSO and EDA loop are the same and one individual in PSO corresponds to one individual in EDA population respectively. Each individual in PSO is updated based on (1) only using the corresponding pair of c_1 and c_2 in EDA poplation. Each individual in EDA population is updated every generation (see Algorithm 2). But this update is only implemented every M (1-10) generations in PSO loop, which means the parameter values for each individual in PSO keeps unchanged during every M consecutive PSO loop interactions. The fitness used in EDA loop is the progress of the particle under the corresponding parameter settings in PSO loop during M consecutive generations. Therefore, the values of c_1 and c_2 in EDA loop will hopefully converge to the best combination under which the corresponding particle in PSO could achieve the biggest progress in M consecutive generations. There is a assumption behind is that a good setting of parameters for the most recent iterations (e.g. past M iterations) will also be good (at least not worse) for the immediate future iterations. The complete pseudo code is given in following Algorithm 3.

Algorithm 2 Updating process in EDA Loop

1: t is the generation index of PSO loop;
2: x_i^t is the ith individual in P_{eda}at generation t;
3: y_i^t is the ith individual in P_{eda} at generation t;
4: N is populations size;
5: While i ≤ N do
6: $f(y_i^t)= f(x_i^t)-f(x_i^{t-M})$;
7: i=i+1;
8: End While;
9: Rank P_{eda} according to fitness (decsending);
10: Select the top individuals from P_{eda};
11: Estimate the mean and standard deviation for each dimension;
12: Sample N individuals by the estimated distribution;
13: Update all the individuals in P_{eda} with the sample.

Algorithm 3 Parameter co-evolving algorithm

```
t  is the generation index of PSO loop;
N is populations size of both P_pso and P_eda;
Initialize the population for PSO: P_pso;
Initialize the population for EDA: P_eda;
Evaluate the each individual in population P_pso;
While iter_number ≤ Max_iterations do
        Update all the individuals in P_pso according to
          (1)and (2);
          If (iter_number)mod(M)=0
                Update all the individuals in P_eda
                 according to Algorihtm 2;
          End if ;
End While .
```

3 Validation

The proposed method is validated on two different numerical optimization problems. The estimated optimal parameter settings (c1 andc_2) obtained by the proposed algorithm on these problems are compared with the values found by a fine parameter tuning. Ackly's function and Restringing's function are selected in this experiment due to their very rough landscapes with large numbers of local minima which makes any search algorithm vulnerable to being trapped in a local minimum. They are also usually used as benchmark problems for evaluating proposed new optimization algorithms. We use the functions with 30 dimensions and set c1 and c2 in the range of [0, 5] which is normally the range of acceleration coefficients in the literature.

3.1 Parameter fine tuning

A fine tuning experiment was conducted to identify the optimal combination of the parameters c_1 and c_2. The best combinations for c_1 and c_2 were found to be [0.8, 1.8] for Ackley's function and [1.2, 1.6] for Ratrigin's function. Actually, from the 3D scatter plot in Figure 1, we can see that good c_1 and c_2 combination is not just one point, but rather a region in the basin. In other words, there is a family of c_1 and c_2 combinations which could help the PSO algorithm perform best.

3.2 Parameter estimation

For each of the function, the proposed parameter coevolving strategy is used to estimate the best parameter setting. The average values for c_1 and c_2 of 30 runs are taken as the estimated result. From Figures 2 and 3 below, we can see that, for one particle, the c_1 and c_2 converged to almost fixed values at the end of the search process. Also from Figure 4, it is clear that for all the particles tracked, c_1 and c_2 converged to the same or nearly the same values respectively. Table 1 shows both fine-tuned and estimated best combination of c_1 and c_2 for each problem. The differences of between them are all less than 8%. Furthermore, in the 3D plot of the results of parameter tuning, there is an obvious basin which means three are more than one pair of good parameter settings and all the settings located in the basin can be regarded as optimal or near optimal settings. The estimated results are found to be located in the basin area. Therefore, we can say all the estimated results are generally consistent with the results of fine tuning.

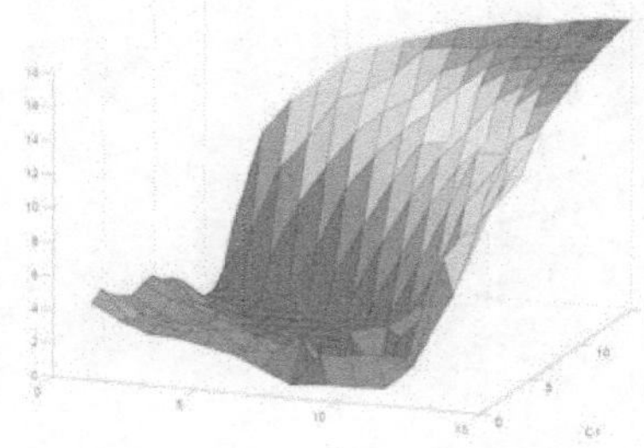

a. Ackley's function

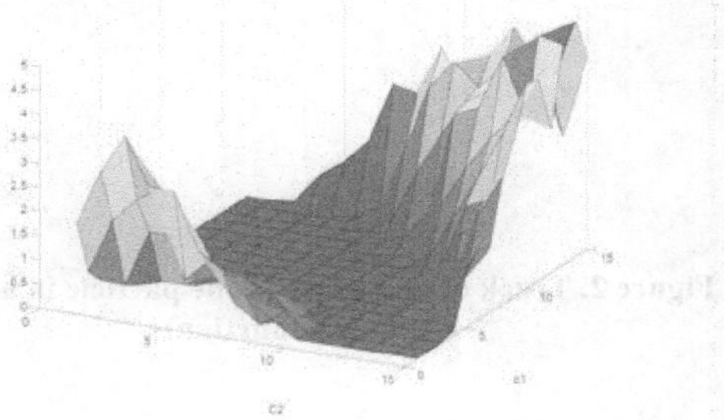

b. Rastrigin's function

Figure 1. Parameter tuning results for two numerical optimization problems

Table 1. Fine tuned and estimated parameters

parameters	Tuned results	
	Ackley's function	Rastrigin's function
C_1	0.8	1.2
C_2	1.8	1.8
	Estimated results and difference	
	Ackley's function	Rastrigin's function
C_1	0.861752 (+7.72%)	1.121347 (-6.6%)
C_2	1.722622 (-4.3%)	1.665069 (-7.4%)

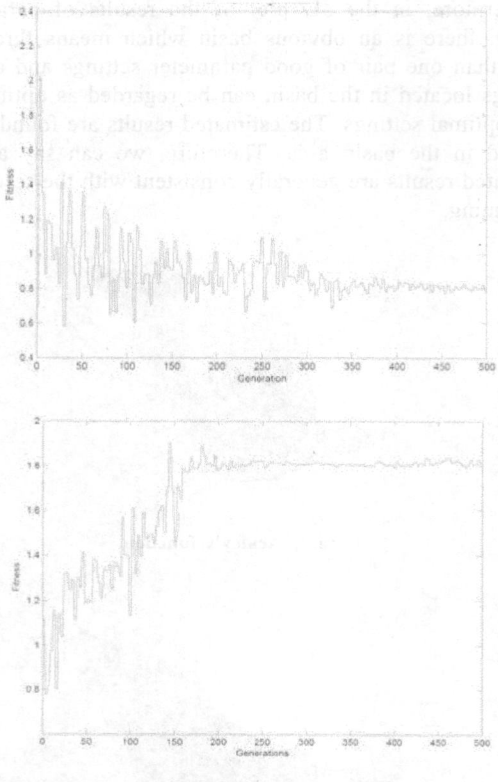

Figure 2. Track of c1 and c2 of one particle in one run (Ackley's function)

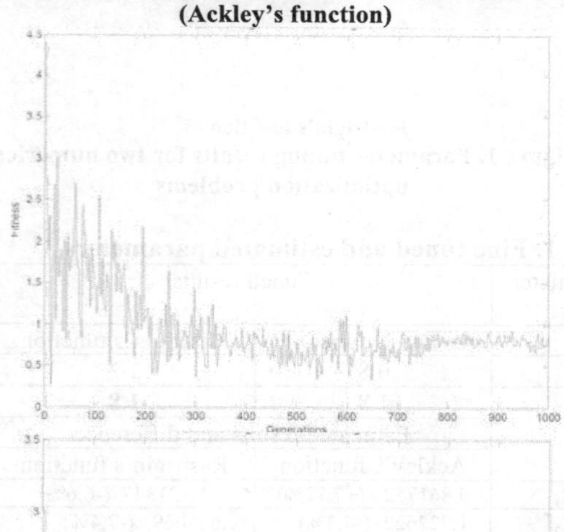

Figure 3. Track of c1 and c2 of one particle in one run (Rastrigin's function)

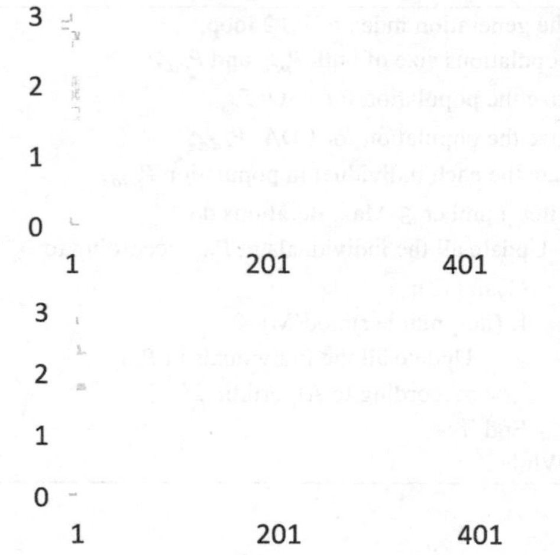

Figure 4. Track of c1 and c2 of 10 particles in one run (Ackley's function)

3.3 Benefits of fast estimation strategy

For most practical optimization problems, especially for engineering design optimization problems, exhaustive parameter tuning is very costly and probably intractable due to the resource limits (time and experimental cost). However, by using this fast parameter estimation strategy, an optimal parameter setting (or near optimal) can be identified in a very short time. Table 2 shows the time consumed by the two methods on different problems.

Table 2. Time consumption by two different methods on different problems

Problem	Tuning	Estimation	Time reduced
Ackley's function	2250 runs (37.5 hours)	10 runs (10 minutes)	99.5%
Rastrigin's	2250 runs (30 hours)	10 runs (8 minutes)	99.5%

4 Optimization of WDN

A water distribution system (WDN) is a network of components (e.g. pipes, pumps, valves, tanks, etc.) that transport water from a source (e.g. reservoir, treatment plant, tank, etc.) to the consumers (e.g. domestic, commercial, and industrial users). The WDN optimization problem here attempts to optimize its pipeline by selecting the lowest cost combination of appropriate pipe sizes such that the criteria of demands and other hydraulic constraints are satisfied.

A free hydraulic solver EPANET2.0 (http://www.epa.gov/nrmrl/wswrd/dw/epanet.html) is used to conduct the hydraulic calculations. In the proposed optimization algorithm, one candidate solution (one particle) is a set of diameters for all the pipes in the water distribution network. The input for the hydraulic simulator

(EPANET2.0) is one candidate solution (diameter set) and its output is the actual head pressure of each node in the network. With these head pressures, the fitness of the solution is calculated. Thus the major task for the hydraulic solver is to compute the fitness of each potential design. A flowchart is given in Figure 5.

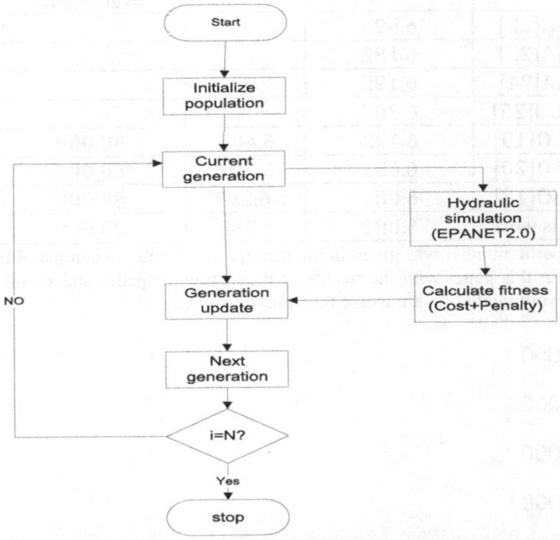

Figure 5. General flowchart of optimization for WDN

4.1 Benchmark network

In this paper, the proposed algorithm is applied to solve a benchmark network from the literature known as the Hanoi network. The Hanoi network (Figure 6), presented by Fujiwara and Khang [21], requires the optimal design of 34 pipes, allowing a minimum hydraulic head of 30 meters for all its 32 nodes, by means of 6 available diameters. The size of the solution space is therefore 6^{34}. It serves as a prototype of a medium sized network for the evaluation of optimization algorithms.

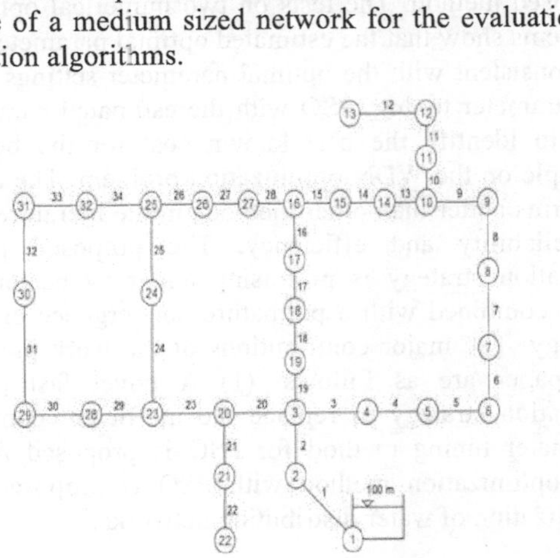

Figure 6. Hanoi Network [21]

4.2 Experimental settings

In addition to the two acceleration coefficients to be estimated by the proposed approach, there are two other important parameters need to be set. For the sake of comparing with previous work, we set all other parameters the same with that in the peer methods: inertia weight is set to be 0.8. The boundary for the updated velocity (see Equation (1)) which is used to constrain the velocity of each particle to the range of [$-V_{max}$, V_{max}], is set to be 50%, because the appropriate range for V_{max} is between 40% and 100% of the variable range, based on the findings by [18].

4.3 Results & discussion

PSO with this parameter setting, PSO is implemented for 30 times on Hanoi network to estimate the optimal parameter settings for this engineering design problem. As we can see from Figure 7, in each single run, there is a clear convergence of both c1 and c2 values during the co-evolution process. The average values of parameters in every implementation are recoded and the results of all 30 runs are displayed in Figure 8. We can see that all the average values are close, which means the estimated results are consistent throughout the experiments. The final average parameter values of the 30 runs are shown in Table 3, which is used as the estimated optimal parameter setting in the subsequent experiments.

Table 3. Estimated results for Hanoi network

Parameters	Mean value	Standard Deviation
c_1	1.186576193	0.228964
c_2	2.057563122	0.423434

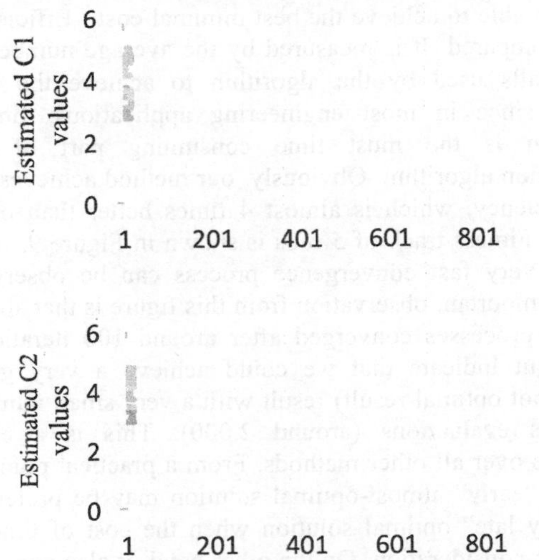

Figure 7. Track of Estimated C1 and C2 values for 10 particles

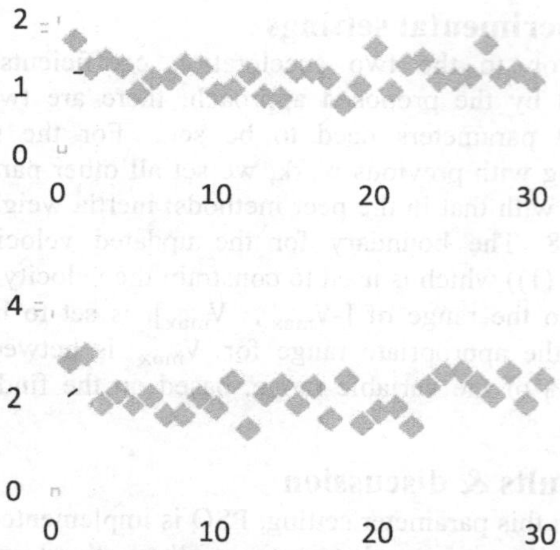

Figure 8. Estimated C1 and C2 values for Hanoi network

With the estimated optimal parameter settings: c1= 1.1866, c2=2.0576, we run the PSO for 30 times on the Hanoi network and the results are summarized in Table 4 below. An extensive comparison previous work from the literature is made. PSO with the estimated optimal parameter settings could achieve the best known minimal cost which is 6.0811(unit cost).

Although the best minimal cost known in the literature is only achieved once out of 30 runs, the reliability and efficiency are better than other methods (Table 4). The reliability of an optimization method could be measured by the average performance achieved by the proposed algorithm in a certain number of runs. Herein, we use the average minimal cost as the indicator of reliability. We know from Table 4 that the proposed algorithm achieves the smallest average cost compared to the other methods which were also able to achieve the best minimal cost. Efficiency is also compared. It is measured by the average number of fitness calls used by the algorithm to achieve the best solution since in most engineering applications, fitness evaluation is the most time consuming part of the optimization algorithm. Obviously, our method achieves the best efficiency, which is almost 4 times better than other methods. Fitness track of 5 runs is shown in Figure 9, from which a very fast convergence process can be observed. Another important observation from this figure is that all the 5 search processes converged after around 100 iterations. This might indicate that we could achieve a very good (usually not optimal result) result with a very small number of fitness evaluations (around 2,000). This is a clear advantage over all other methods. From a practical point of view, an "early" almost-optimal solution may be preferred to a "very late" optimal solution when the cost of time is taken into consideration. On the other hand, it also suggests that premature convergence problem is present, which is a common problem with the application of PSOs. Several researchers have proposed methods to address this problem with no conclusive solution. The major task for our proposed estimation method is to help the PSO obtain a very good parameter setting in a very short time, but it is not able to tackle the premature convergence problem, so more work is required to further improve the performance of PSO.

Table 4. Minimal cost for the Hanoi networks

Methods	Minimal cost ($x10^6$\$)	Average ($x10^6$\$)	Average NO. of Fitness evaluations
GA[22]	6.093		
GA[23]	6.182		
GA[24]	6.195		
ACO[25]	6.367		
PSO[19]	6.133	6.487	80,000
PSO[20]	6.081	6.297	80,000
PSO[18]	6.081	>6.297*	80,000
This work	6.081	6.252	20,000

*no specific number was given in the paper, but the authors compared their results in this paper with the results of their previous paper and found the average minimal costs are worse than previous work.

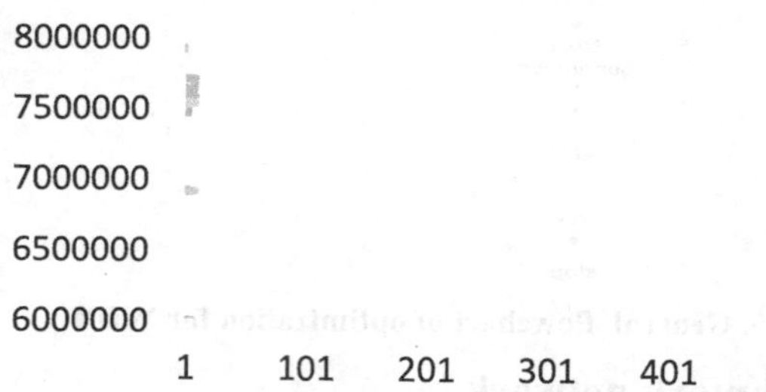

Figure 9. Fitness track of 5 runs optimal parameters

5 Conclusions and future work

In this work, a fast parameter estimation strategy for PSO is proposed to estimate the optimal acceleration parameter settings. Self-adaptive control and co-evolution strategies are used together for the parameter estimation of PSO in the proposed method. The tests on two numerical optimization problems show that the estimated optimal parameter settings are consistent with the optimal parameter settings achieved by parameter tuning. PSO with the estimated parameters is able to identify the best known cost for the benchmark example on the WDN optimization problem. The algorithm performs better than other methods in the literature in terms of reliability and efficiency. The proposed parameter estimation strategy is promising and may perform better when combined with a premature convergence elimination strategy. The major contributions of the work presented in this paper are as follows: (1) A novel fast parameter estimation strategy to replace the inefficient conventional parameter tuning method for PSO is proposed And(2), a new optimization method with PSO is proposed for the optimization of water distribution networks.

Our future work will focus on the following topics: (1) to extend the proposed fast parameter estimation strategy for PSO to other Evolutionary Algorithms where there is a need for parameter tuning. And (2) to apply the proposed algorithm to the design optimization of larger water distribution networks design or other practical engineering design and/or optimization problems.

6 References

[1] Bonabeau E, Dorigo M, Theraulaz G."Swarm Intelligence: from natural to artificial systems."Oxford University Press, New York. 1999.

[2] Kennedy J., Eberhart R.C., Shi Y. "Swarm Intelligence. Morgan Kaufmann, San Francisco" 2001.

[3] Eberhart R.C., Kennedy J." A new optimizer using particle swarm theory." In: 6th International Symposium on Micromachine and Human Science,Nagoya, Japan, pp. 39–43. 1995.

[4] Dong Y., Tang J., Xu B., Wang D. "An application of swarm optimization to nonlinear programming." Computers & Mathematics with Applications 49(11–12). 1655–1668. 2005.

[5] Chau K.W. "Particle swarm optimization training algorithm for ANNs in stage prediction of Shing Mun River." Journal of Hydrology. 329(3–4), 363–367. 2006.

[6] Liao C.J., Tseng C.T., Luarn P. "A discrete version of particle swarm optimization for flowshop scheduling problems. Computers and Operations Research." 34 (10), 3099–3111. 2007.

[7] Izquierdo J., Montalvo I., Pe´rez R., Fuertes V. "Design optimization of wastewater collection networks by PSO." Computers & Mathematics with Applications56 (3), 777–784. 2008.

[8] Izquierdo J., Montalvo I., Pe´rez-Garcı´a R., Fuertes V.S.. "Forecasting pedestrian evacuation times by using swarm intelligence." Physica A: Statistical Mechanics and its Applications 388 (7), 1213–1220. 2009.

[9] Ueno G., Yasuda K., Iwasaki N. "Robust adaptive particle swarm optimization." IEEE International Conference on Systems, Man and Cybernetics, 4, 3915–3920. 2005.

[10] Eiben A.E., Hinterding R., Michalewicz Z. "Parameter control in evolutionary algorithms." IEEE Transactions on Evolutionary Computation 3. 124–141. 1999.

[11] Yen G.G., Lu H. "Dynamic multi-objective evolutionary algorithm: Adaptive cell-based rank and density estimation." IEEE Transactions on Evolutionary Computation 7(3), 253–274. 2003.

[12] Arumugam M.S., Rao M.V.C.. "On the improved performances of the particle swarm optimization algorithms with adaptive parameters, cross-over operators and root mean square (RMS) variants for computing optimal control of a class of hybrid systems." Applied Soft Computing. 8 (1), 324–336. 2008.

[13] Ratnaweera A., Halgamuge S.K., Watson H.C.. "Self-organizing hierarchical particle swarm optimizer with time-varying acceleration coefficients." IEEE Transactions on Evolutionary Computation 8 (3), 240–255. 2004.

[14] Brest J., Greiner S., Boskovic B., Mernik M., Zumer V. 2006. Self-adapting control parameters in differential evolution: A comparative study on numerical benchmark problems. IEEE Transactions on Evolutionary Computation. 10(6), 689–699.

[15] Angeline P.J. "Two self-adaptive crossover operators for genetic programming." Advances in Genetic Programming 2. MIT Press, 89–109. 1996.

[16] Krasnogor N., and Gustafson S. "A study on the use of ''self-generation'' in memetic algorithms." Natural Computing: An International Journal 3 (1),53–76. 2004.

[17] Haupt R.L., Werner D.H.. "Genetic Algorithms in Electromagnetics." John Wiley & Sons, New Jersey. 2007.

[18] Montalvo I., Izquierdo J., Pe´rez-Garcı´a R., Herrera M.. "Improved performance of PSO with self-adaptive parameters for computing the optimal design of Water Supply Systems" Engineering applications of artificial intelligence. 23(5), 727-735. 2010.

[19] Idel Montalvo, Joaquin Izquierdo, Rafael Perez-Garcia, Michael M. Tung, "Particle Swarm Optimization applied to the design of water supply systems." Computers and Mathematics with Applications 56, 769-776, 2008a.

[20] Idel Montalvo, Joaquin Izquierdo, "A diversity – enriched variant of discrete PSO applied to the design of Water Distribution Networks." Engineering Applications 40(7), 655-668,2008b.

[21] Fujiwara, O., and Khang, D. B., "Correction to a two-phase decomposition method for optimal design of looped water distribution networks." Water Resour.Res., 27(5), 985–986. 1991.

[22]Matı´as,A.S.," Disen˜oderedesdedistribucio´ndeag acontemplandola fiabilidad Polite´cnica deValencia.Tesis doctoral." 2006.

[23] Wu, Z.Y., Simpson, A.R., "Competent genetic-evolutionary optimization of water distribution systems." Journal of Computing in Civil Engineering 15 (2), 89–101. 2001.

[24] Savic, D.A., Walters, G.A., "Genetic algorithms for least-cost design of water distribution networks." Journal of Water Resources Planning and Management 123 (2), 67–77. 1997.

[25] Zecchin, A.C., Simpson, A.R., Maier, H.R., Nixon,J.B., "Parametric study for an ant algorithm applied to water distribution system optimization." IEEE Transactions on Evolutionary Computation 9(2),175-191,2005

SESSION

EVOLUTIONAY ALGORITHMS AND STRATEGIES

Chair(s)

TBA

Evolutionary Routing Strategies for Automotive Networks

Martin Dohr, Bernd Eichberger
Institute of Electronics, Graz University of Technology, Austria

Abstract— *The design of efficient communication networks is a challenging task for modern vehicle development. Due to novel technologies and new degrees of freedom in network design, the decision on a bus topology has a severe impact on the overall system cost and performance. In this work, we propose a topology and routing optimization using Evolutionary Algorithms and problem-specific encoding. Our contribution includes a guided topology mutation operator which outperforms standard random mutation. Further, we propose two routing operators for usage during the optimization process and compare their effectiveness on a network application taken from a series vehicle.*

Keywords: Evolutionary computation; communication networks; design optimization; routing;

1. Introduction

Upcoming developments in the automotive industry will have a severe impact on in-vehicle communications. Such developments include advanced driver assistance systems like lane departure warning, night vision or traffic sign recognition. Those systems have in common, that complex sensors such as cameras, RADAR or LIDAR have to be deployed in remote locations within car. In order to convert the raw sensor data into usable information for the driver, sophisticated evaluation algorithms have to be applied. System designers have always been mapping such computational intensive tasks onto central Electronic Control Units (ECUs) for cost reasons. Another argument for centralized processing is, that upcoming functionalities will have a interconnected architecture and rely on multiple distributed sensors as input data sources. However, in contrast to present features, those new developments and sensors will also have much higher communication requirements which cannot be satisfied by well established automotive bus systems like CAN [1]. For example, the raw data transfer of RADAR and LIDAR sensors are comparable to monochrome or colored video stream. In comparison to that, current automotive features such as cruise control or automated headlamp leveling only require a fractional amount of that bandwidth.

There are several solutions to meet the new communication demands in the car. First implementations of rear view cameras were connected by a separate shielded twisted pair or coaxial wire using analog data transmission. While this is cost efficient for a single data source, the cabling effort for several distributed sensors makes this solution impractical for modern automotive architectures. Improved bus systems like MOST [2], FlexRay [3] or Ethernet [4] are better suited for such high bandwidth demands and also satisfy the stringent reliability and real time requirements of automotive applications.

Another aspect are new architecture paradigms to manage the increased complexity of interconnected features. Architectures like AUTOSAR [5] define an interface to separate functional software from the underlying operating system and hardware, thus allowing modular design of software components (SWCs). The advantages of this separation are that software components are now more independent from their location of execution and can be mapped onto different ECUs within the vehicle. At the same time, testability and re-useability of components increases because of the standardized interface and even online relocation of software execution within the car is possible.

However, the architecture and design process of a network is becoming more complex because of such recently introduced degrees of freedom in software mapping. In [6], the authors propose a holistic network architecture process using Evolutionary Algorithms (EAs) and problem-specific encoding. In this paper we will focus on methods to improve the topology and routing optimization of the mentioned approach.

The rest of this paper is structured as follows: Section 2 presents related publications concerning topology optimization using evolutionary methods with a further focus on automotive applications. Our system model and the phases of optimization are explained in Section 3. A more detailed description of our topology mutation and routing operators is then given in Section 4 before presenting our test scenario and results in Section 5. Finally, we give a conclusion of the current work and next plans in Section 6.

2. Related Work

Network topology optimization has been an ongoing research topic for decades as summarized in [7]. Most works focus on multiobjective heuristics to solve such problems [8] with objectives like network cost or message delay. The performance is then verified on realistic traffic models as in [9]. Recent works [10] utilize objective-guided genetic operators in combination with MOEA/D to incorporate problem-specific knowledge into the optimization process.

Several authors have also studied special attributes of automotive networks and how to optimize this specific application. In [11], a repeated-matching method combined with simulated annealing is proposed to optimize task allocation and network assignment. A similar problem was solved in [12] using a sophisticated system model and multiobjective EAs. A hierarchical partitioning is used in [13] in combination with local heuristics for the gateway placement task, a sub-problem which is not addressed in most publications. The authors of [14] propose a combination of Integer Linear Program (ILP) and EAs for topology and routing optimization but also require a given architecture in form of nodes, buses and gateways.

3. Optimization Work Flow and System Model

Our optimization framework distinguishes between two phases, application mapping and signal routing. Both phases run adapted implementations of the SPEA2 algorithm [15] which are extended by application specific network encoding and custom operators. Each phase optimizes the network with respect to different goals by utilizing specific fitness functions and operators suited for the task at hand. The overall work flow is depicted in Figure 1. Our work builds on the 'Metaheuristic Algorithms in Java' framework presented in [16], which was chosen due to the very modular and extendable design.

The aim of the first phase is to map all software components onto ECUs while keeping communication between the nodes at a minimum. On the other hand, the deployment has to respect the processing capabilities of each ECU and safe costs by optimal utilization for each node. Since those goals are contradicting, the result of this phase is a Pareto set of possible software mapping solutions. In our encoding, we call such a mapping candidate an ApplicationMatrix. Therefore, each solution in phase one consists of a common functional description and set of nodes, combined with a unique ApplicationMatrix, which defines the mapping of each SWC onto a node. Further details on the used operators will be published in [17] and are not the focus of this paper. The rest of this section is mainly concerned with input objects and variable encoding for the second optimization phase.

3.1 Input Objects

In order to explain the goals of phase two it is sufficient to know, that the input from phase one is a set of one or many Pareto optimal mapping solutions for a given set of nodes and functional description. The goal of this phase is to create a feasible network topology where all nodes are connected via bus systems or gateways and each communication signal can be routed over this topology. The input parameters shall be defined as follows:

- *NodeDB:* A list of active nodes N where each node $n \in N$ corresponds to an ECU with given coordinates within the vehicle. Note that a model of monetary costs for each node is only required in the first phase of optimization. In phase two, it is sufficient to estimate the additional costs of connecting a node to a bus system which is modeled as bus coupler costs.
- The *FunctionalDescription* is a logical network of all software components C and their corresponding communication signals S. Each signal $s_i \in S$ consists of a set of one or more receiving SWCs C_{s_i} and the corresponding bandwidth requirement in kbit/sec. Since our framework is designed to be used in a very early stage of product development, we provide a rough bandwidth estimation instead of detailed transmission deadline constraints which are generally not known at this time.
- *BusDB:* A database of all available bus systems B with estimated cost factors for bus couplers and wiring effort. Furthermore, each bus system $b \in B$ is defined by a maximum transfer capacity in kbit/sec. This capacity is usually set between 30% and 70% of the theoretical maximum at this stage of development to be prepared

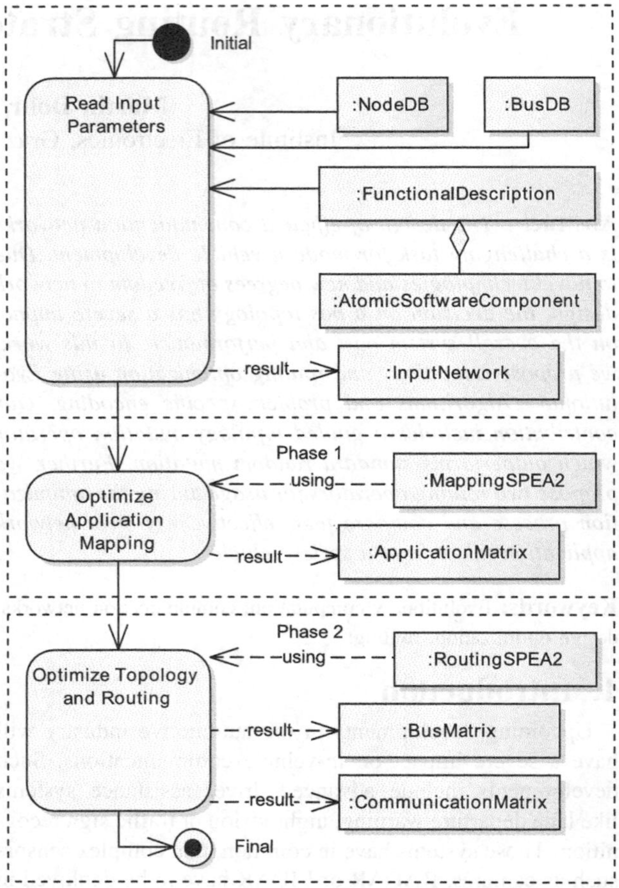

Fig. 1: Workflow of the proposed framework showing input objects and the two phases of optimization

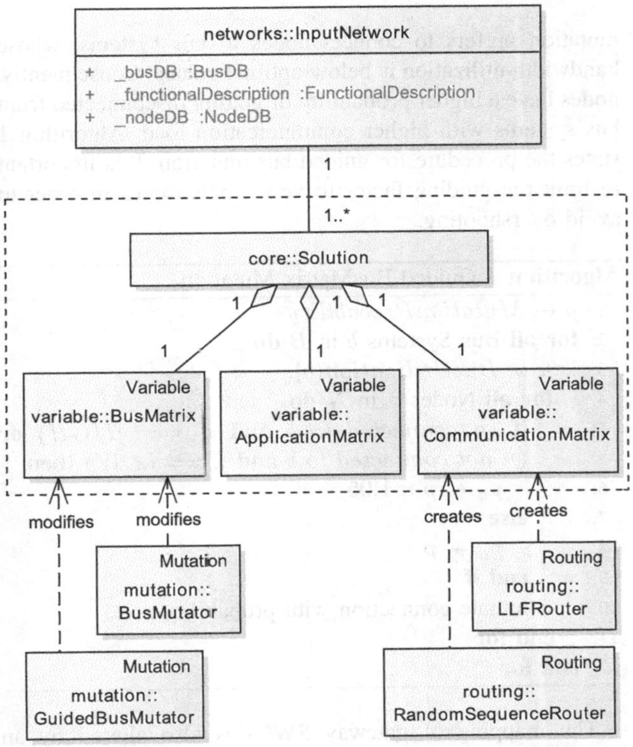

Fig. 2: Diagram of all related input objects, variables and operators

for changes in communication requirements. A detailed schedulability analysis, as presented in [18], is not feasible at this stage of development.

- One or several *ApplicationMatrix* representations of possible solutions from phase one.

3.2 Variable Encoding

A complete solution candidate in phase two consists of common input parameters, a mapping solution from the previous phase and two new variables representing topology and signal routing. First, we define a variable called BusMatrix to model the connections between nodes and buses. The dimension is $|B| \times |N|$ with each entry stating whether the node is connected to this bus system or not. The network topology is therefore defined by this variable with the exception of gateway functionalities. The representation can be altered by mutation operators which is the usual practice in evolutionary algorithms. Since the algorithm can work with several distinct mapping solutions in parallel, a crossover operation would not be suitable in this phase.

It should be noted, that a BusMatrix does not provide a feasible network until a signal path has been found for each communication signal. This is done by a routing operator and results in a CommunicationMatrix, which represents all signal paths and gateways within the network. The routing operator uses a BusMatrix as input but can also add connections to repair infeasible communication paths. Further, the routing procedure can add gateway functionalities onto nodes if needed. We consider gateways as objects derived from software components and only allow a mapping on certain nodes in the system. Those mappings can be created by the router or by a distinct gateway mutation operator. During the routing process, the CommunicationMatrix is filled with signal paths and bandwidth information for all used bus systems accompanied by a set of mapped gateways G and their respective routing tables. In order to preserve feasibility during this process, we define two constraints for the routing algorithm.

1) Signals must not be routed over a bus system if the resulting bandwidth would exceed the maximum bus capacity.
2) To limit complexity and transmission time, a signal route over two or more gateways is not allowed. This is also standard practice for current vehicle networks which utilize one central gateway for all bus systems.

A overview of all mentioned objects is depicted in Figure 2.

3.3 Fitness Functions

The goal of the routing phase is to find feasible networks utilizing availiable bus systems in a cost efficient way. This implies the following statements.

1) Each bus system shall have optimal bandwidth utilization.
2) A balance between faster (more expensive) and cheaper bus technologies has to be found.
3) Wire lengths have to be minimized as the cabling harness is a significant cost factor in modern vehicles.
4) The usage of gateway components doubles the bandwidth requirement for a signal since it has to be transmitted over two bus systems to reach all receiving software components.

Based on those statements we define three objectives to measure the fitness of a solution.

System cost defines the hardware costs for a given topology. The bus coupler cost $BCC(b)$ models the expense of adding a node n to a bus system b. The set $N(b)$ is the set of all nodes that are connected to the bus system b.

$$SystemCost = \sum_{b \in B} BCC(b) \times |N(b)|$$

Wiring cost represents the length of the cable harness. We approximate this length for every bus system as the sum of Manhattan distances between all nodes connected the bus. The Manhattan distance is defined as the path between two nodes, when only moves in direction of the Cartesian axes are allowed.

$$dist(n_1, n_2) = |x_1 - x_2| + |y_1 - y_2| + |z_1 - z_2|$$

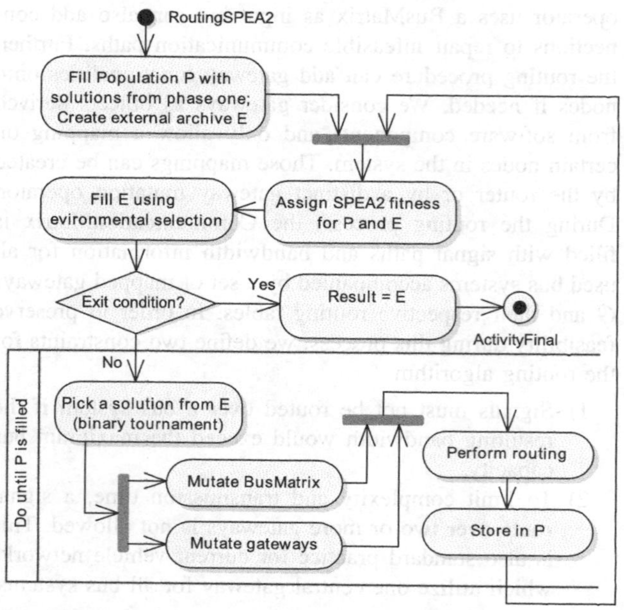

Fig. 3: The routing algorithm with SPEA2 selection methods and custom mutation and routing operators

For certain bus systems like MOST, the wire length can by multiplied by an additional cost factor to reflect the more expensive installation effort for optical cables.

Bus utilization is modeled by a fuzzy set where a consumed bandwidth between 30% and 70% of the maximum speed is considered as optimal load. Those values may vary depending on the bus system in use and can be adapted from 'best practices' in automotive engineering. If a bus utilization is out of this range, we model a penalty value based on the bandwidth mismatch and priority of the bus system. Due to the priority, we can force the optimization process to utilize more expensive bus systems better than cheap ones. The overall fitness function is then the sum over the resulting penalty values for all used bus systems.

4. Mutation and Routing Strategies

As stated before, the algorithm uses mutation operators on a BusMatrix and then creates a CommunicationMatrix by applying a routing operator. The procedure is based on the SPEA2 [15] and employs unaltered fitness assignment and selection implementations from [16]. The principal work flow is depicted in Figure 3.

4.1 BusMatrix and Gateway Mutation

We have developed two mutation operators for the BusMatrix, a random mutation and an advanced guided operator. The random implementation can be compared to a simple bit flip mutation, connecting or disconnecting a node from a bus with a certain probability. In contrast to that, the guided mutation prefers to connect nodes to bus systems, whose bandwidth utilization is below optimal values. Consequently, nodes have a higher probability of getting disconnected from bus systems with higher communication load. Algorithm 1 states the procedure for guided bus mutation. It is important to limit the guiding factor to very small values in order to avoid overshooting.

Algorithm 1 Guided BusMatrix Mutation

$p \leftarrow MutationProbability$
for all Bus Systems b in B **do**
  $u \leftarrow BusUtilization(b)$
  for all Nodes n in N **do**
    if (n *connected to* b **and** $u == HIGH$) **or** (n *not connected to* b **and** $u == LOW$) **then**
      $p_n \leftarrow p \times 1.05$
    else
      $p_n \leftarrow p$
    end if
    mutate connection with probability p_n
  end for
end for

The mapping of gateway SWCs is also altered by an distinct mutation. It is again a random bit flip mutator method but with much lower probability of execution. Like all other genetic operators, the presented mutation functions share the same interface and could be interchanged during runtime of the optimization.

4.2 Routing Strategies

We compared 2 routing operators with different characteristics. The 'Largest Load First Router' (LLFRouter) is specified by a strict deterministic behavior. This means, given the same BusMatrix and ApplicationMatrix as input, the router will always create the same CommunicationMatrix as output. The routing always starts with the signal representing the highest bandwidth requirement and ends with the signal having the lowest. As a consequence, all evolutionary logic is done during the mutation of the BusMatrix. In contrast to that, we also propose a 'Random Sequence Router' (RSRouter), where the order of routed signals does not follow a certain rule. The results are influenced by the given bus topology but can vary depending on the router logic.

Independent of the chosen operator, the router follows 4 steps to find a feasible path on the current topology for each signal:

1) Find a direct connection between source and destination.
2) Find an available gateway connection.
3) Create a gateway connection without adding new bus couplings.
4) Create a new direct connection.

Depending on the current BusMatrix, a step could find more than one feasible path to route a signal. For this case, we define selection schemes which are set globally for the optimization process:

- *BEST_FIT:* The router chooses the bus system in such a way, that the added signal improves the overall bus utilization. A simple local search heuristic was designed to find this system in a time-efficient way.
- *CHEAPEST:* The cheapest available bus system is always chosen.
- *RANDOM:* The router randomly chooses a path. Note that this will force the router into non deterministic behavior.

5. Experimental Results

We evaluated both routing operators using each mutation strategy and path selection schemes defined above. For each operator setup, we calculated the hypervolume indicator or S-metric [19] and generational distance [20] to compare the resulting Pareto fronts after 20.000 evaluations. Since the true Pareto front for the test problem at hand is not known, we estimated it as the global Pareto front of all evaluation runs.

5.1 Input Network

Our test network consists of 15 ECUs executing 284 atomic software components. The overall communication load created by 390 signals equals 281 kbit/sec. Roughly 30% of those signals have more than one receiving software component, for example network management and diagnostic functions. The structure of this network was generated from a middle class series vehicle but bandwidth requirements were greatly increased as to utilize more bus systems and therefore enable a broader spectrum of possible solutions.

5.2 Results

The resulting performance indicators are listed in Table 1 with the best 3 values for each indicator highlighted in gray. The random sequence router runs slightly faster because the bandwidth sorting algorithm in LLF has to be performed for each routing execution. The comparison shows that guided BusMatrix mutation clearly outperforms its random counterpart without a significant impact on execution time. In fact, the fastest runs were also achieved using guided mutation. An exemplary Pareto plot of 3 different operator setups and the global Pareto front is depicted in Figure 4. It shows the trade off between low system costs versus cheap wiring effort and well utilization of bus systems. The LLF router with guided mutation and random path selection has the best overall performance as it covers both parts of the front equally. Only the combination 'RSR / guided mutation / best fit path selection' is closer to the solutions with low system costs but neglects a lot of solutions in the Pareto front.

Table 1: Results for different operator setups after 20.000 evaluations

Router	Mutation	Path	HV	GD	Exec. time [ms]
RSR	Random	Random	0.09356	0.452851	25336
RSR	Random	Cheapest	0.12951	0.095245	26755
RSR	Random	Best Fit	0.35134	0.062998	25414
RSR	Guided	Random	0.46237	0.021208	24048
RSR	Guided	Cheapest	0.19250	0.016120	24946
RSR	Guided	Best Fit	0.19881	0.005960	25304
LLF	Random	Random	0.01778	0.323714	27539
LLF	Random	Cheapest	0.12510	0.050040	26927
LLF	Random	Best Fit	0.37797	0.035734	29095
LLF	Guided	Random	0.51932	0.008477	27354
LLF	Guided	Cheapest	0.18687	0.010839	29407
LLF	Guided	Best Fit	0.19769	0.006498	30078

6. Conclusion

This paper proposes advanced routing methods for evolutionary network optimization. Our work is based on the framework presented in [6] with focus on the application-specific encoding. The framework is designed to optimize the application mapping and topology in the context of in-vehicle communication. Since this is done in a 2-phase approach, our proposals can focus on the topology and routing with a given set of solutions from the mapping process. First, we developed a guided topology mutation operator to even out bandwidth utilization between different bus systems. Secondly, we propose two routing operators where one shows deterministic behavior while the other is non-deterministic by design. As last input, we chose between three different strategies to find feasible communication paths within the network. After evaluating all operator setups, we find that deterministic routing performs better in most cases when combined with guided topology mutation. Further, this guidance does not significantly prolong the execution time of the overall optimization. However, due to the test scenario taken from a series vehicle, it is not clear if the results can be extended to networks of different sizes. In order to ensure stable behavior for other applications, our next goal is to develop generic test cases for a variety of target applications.

References

[1] Robert Bosch GmbH. (2012) CAN - Controller Area Network. [Online]. Available: http://www.semiconductors.bosch.de/en/ipmodules/can/can.asp

[2] MOST Cooperation. (2012) MOST - Media Oriented Systems Transport. [Online]. Available: http://www.mostcooperation.com

[3] FlexRay Consortium. (2012) FlexRay Communications System. [Online]. Available: http://www.flexray.com

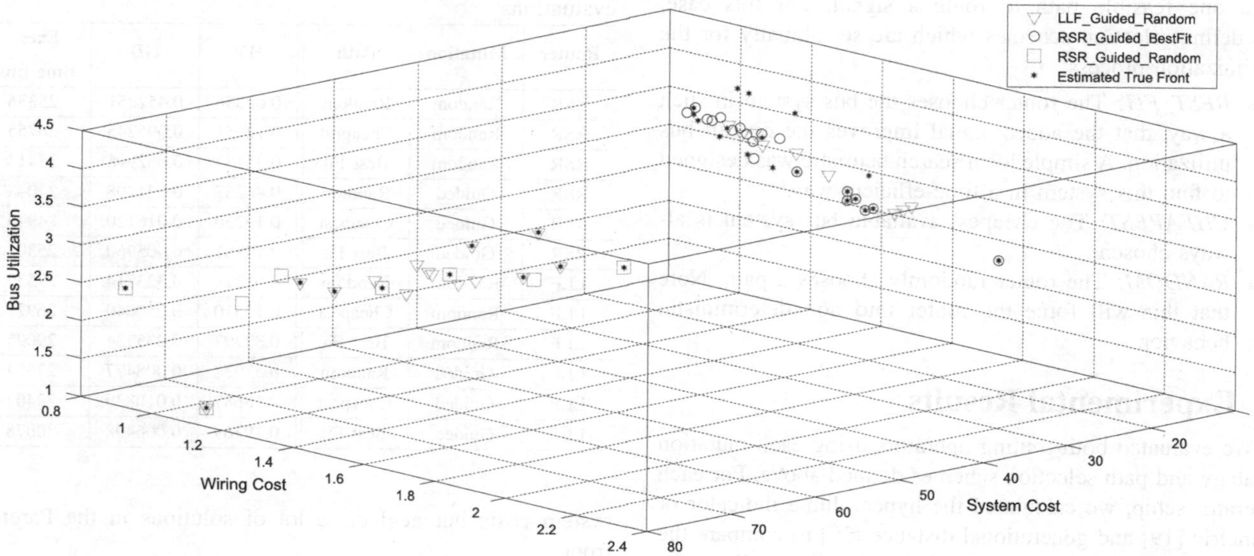

Fig. 4: Pareto plot of 3 operator setups and the estimated global front

[4] H.-T. Lim, L. Volker, and D. Herrscher, "Challenges in a future ip/ethernet-based in-car network for real-time applications," in *Design Automation Conference (DAC), 2011 48th ACM/EDAC/IEEE*, june 2011, pp. 7 -12.

[5] AUTOSAR Consortium. (2012) Automotive Open System Architecture. [Online]. Available: http://www.autosar.org

[6] M. Dohr and B. Eichberger, "An application-specific approach in automotive network optimization," in *Proceedings of the 2012 international conference on genetic and evolutionary methods*, jul 2012, pp. 62–67.

[7] M. Abd-El-Barr, "Topological network design: A survey," *Journal of Network and Computer Applications*, vol. 32, no. 3, pp. 501 – 509, 2009. [Online]. Available: http://www.sciencedirect.com/science/article/pii/S108480450800101X

[8] R. Kumar and N. Banerjee, "Multiobjective network topology design," *Appl. Soft Comput.*, vol. 11, no. 8, pp. 5120–5128, 2011. [Online]. Available: http://dx.doi.org/10.1016/j.asoc.2011.05.047

[9] N. Banerjee and R. Kumar, "Multiobjective network design for realistic traffic models," in *Proceedings of the 9th annual conference on Genetic and evolutionary computation*. ACM, 2007, pp. 1904–1911.

[10] W. Peng and Q. Zhang, "Network topology planning using moea/d with objective-guided operators," in *Parallel Problem Solving from Nature - PPSN XII*, ser. Lecture Notes in Computer Science, C. Coello, V. Cutello, K. Deb, S. Forrest, G. Nicosia, and M. Pavone, Eds. Springer Berlin Heidelberg, 2012, vol. 7492, pp. 62–71. [Online]. Available: http://dx.doi.org/10.1007/978-3-642-32964-7_7

[11] S. Kim, E. Lee, M. Choi, H. Jeong, and S. Seo, "Design optimization of vehicle control networks," *Vehicular Technology, IEEE Transactions on*, vol. 60, no. 7, pp. 3002 -3016, sept. 2011.

[12] T. Streichert, C. Haubelt, and J. Teich, "Multi-objective topology optimization for networked embedded systems," in *Embedded Computer Systems: Architectures, Modeling and Simulation, 2006. IC-SAMOS 2006. International Conference on*, 2006, pp. 93–98.

[13] R. Moritz, T. Ulrich, and L. Thiele, "Evolutionary exploration of e/e-architectures in automotive design," in *Proceedings of the International Conference on Operations Research*, Zurich, Switzerland, 2011, pp. 361–366.

[14] M. Lukasiewycz, M. Glass, C. Haubelt, J. Teich, R. Regler, and B. Lang, "Concurrent topology and routing optimization in automotive network integration," in *Design Automation Conference, 2008. DAC 2008. 45th ACM/IEEE*, june 2008, pp. 626 -629.

[15] E. Zitzler, M. Laumanns, and L. Thiele, "Spea2: Improving the strength pareto evolutionary algorithm for multiobjective optimization," in *Evolutionary Methods for Design, Optimisation, and Control*. CIMNE, Barcelona, Spain, 2002, pp. 95–100.

[16] J. J. Durillo and A. J. Nebro, "jmetal: A java framework for multi-objective optimization," *Advances in Engineering Software*, vol. 42, pp. 760–771, 2011. [Online]. Available: http://www.sciencedirect.com/science/article/pii/S0965997811001219

[17] M. Dohr and B. Eichberger, "Guided mutation strategies for multiobjective automotive network architecture," March 2013, currently under review.

[18] R. I. Davis and A. Burns, "Controller area network (can) schedulability analysis: Refuted, revisited and revised," *Refuted, Revisited and RevisedŤ. Real-Time Systems*, vol. 35, pp. 239–272, 2007.

[19] E. Zitzler and L. Thiele, "Multiobjective optimization using evolutionary algorithms - a comparative case study." Springer, 1998, pp. 292–301.

[20] D. Van Veldhuizen and G. Lamont, "On measuring multiobjective evolutionary algorithm performance," in *Evolutionary Computation, 2000. Proceedings of the 2000 Congress on*, vol. 1, 2000, pp. 204–211 vol.1.

Evac: An Evolutionary Accompanist

Shu Zhang, C. Thomas Bailey, and Khaled Rasheed
Institute for Artificial Intelligence, University of Georgia, Athens, GA, US

Abstract - *Evac (the evolutionary accompanist) is a system that engages in musical improvisation with the user. Evac uses a genetic algorithm (GA) to invent musical phrases that are neither too similar to the user's input, nor too different. It is notable for two reasons. First, it uses a novel, implicitly interactive, genetic algorithm, which allows the user's actions to influence Evac's musical performance without the need for explicit rating of individuals. Second, in contrast to many pieces of software in the world of evolutionary music and art, Evac runs in real time, allowing the user to experience the same kind of exploration that happens in real life improvisation scenarios with other musicians. Evac must also solve the design problems of dynamic environments, since our GA's fitness function relies on the user's input. Sample music resulting from the system is available.*

Keywords
Evolutionary computing, music accompanist, interactive Genetic Algorithm, real time

1. Introduction

Our problem is music composition. In particular, our system allows the user to play music while simultaneously generating impromptu accompaniment to go along with the user's input. The musical "brain" of the system is a genetic algorithm implemented in C#.

Evolutionary computing is a research area which draws inspiration from the process of natural evolution. It reflects the phenomenon of survival of the fittest in nature.

The two cornerstones of evolutionary progress are competition-based selection, and the phenotypic variations among members of the population (Eiben & Smith, 2003). The most important components for any evolutionary algorithm includes: representation (definition of individuals), an evaluation function, population, parent selection mechanism, variation operators, recombination and mutation, and a survivor selection mechanism. Evolutionary algorithms (EA's) have three basic features that distinguish them from other algorithms: EA's are population based; they use recombination, mutation, or other genetic operators; and they are stochastic.

In the literature there have been four main approaches: genetic algorithms, evolution strategies, evolutionary programming (EP), and genetic programming. All these dialects of evolutionary computing follow these general outlines, with differences only in technical detail. For example, the representation of individuals is historically strings over a finite alphabet in GAs, real valued vectors in an evolution strategy, finite state machines in the classical EP, and tree structures in genetic programming (Eiben & Smith, 2003). All of them have been successfully applied to a wide range of problems, with a focus on optimization problems.

When an EA is applied to musical composition, there are three main considerations (Burton & Vladimirova, 1999), namely the search domain, the genetic representation, and the fitness evaluation. For musical composition, the search process is analogous to a combinatorial optimization problem, and because of the infinite combination of melodies, harmonies and rhythms, its search space is unlimited (Tokui & Iba, 2000). Therefore, the composition should be guided by some constraints. By artfully choosing our constraints, we aimed to maximize the musicality of Evac's output, as well as its real-time responsiveness. To this end, we limited our search to melodies of length 16 (i.e., strings of 16 single notes). Each note in the melody can be 1 of 13 pitches. All together this yields roughly 3×10^{17} possible combinations: still quite large, but no longer infinite.

Our goal when designing the representation was to be as simple as possible while maximizing the effectiveness of evolutionary search. Hence we adopted a discrete representation where an integer encodes several properties of a note, and an array of 16 integers represents an individual (musical phrase).

The last topic is fitness evaluation. Since we are generating impromptu accompaniment for the user's music, we incorporate the user's input into the fitness function. Specifically, the music represented by an individual in the GA is compared with the user's input and rated for similarity using music theoretic notions. To determine the individual's fitness, we used a function that assigned low fitness values to those individuals who were either too similar or too different. High fitness individuals were similar but not identical to the user's input. This ensured that the GA favored individuals that were related to the user's input without copying it.

The rest of the paper is structured as follows. The second section gives a brief review of the literature related to evolutionary computation and its application in music and art; the third section describes how the user interacts with Evac; the fourth section offers a detailed description of the Genetic Algorithm used in Evac including: individual representation of music notes, fitness function and genetic operators; the fifth section discusses the results of running and playing with Evac, along with analyses regarding the system; the sixth section presents conclusions about the performance of Evac, and the seventh section discusses future work.

2. Background

Genetic algorithms have been frequently used as an approach to music composition. In a previous study (Matic 2010), position based representation of rhythm and relative representation of pitches (based on distance from a starting pitch), were used to allow flexible encoding of music compositions. Use of a mathematical (i.e., non-interactive) fitness function as well as an initial population with pre-defined rhythm made the GA simpler to implement, and also improved the quality of the final result.

However, strictly non-interactive fitness functions preclude human influence on individuals' fitness. While in some cases this might be desirable, one of the primary goals of art is to give voice to human experience; as such, removing humans entirely from the loop of the fitness calculation represents a serious trade-off. Interactive evolutionary algorithms (IEAs) address that exact issue. Interactive evolutionary algorithms explicitly include the user in the evaluation of individuals, typically by allowing them to select the best individual(s) from a group or assign fitness values based on subjective appeal. In another paper on evolutionary music composition, Tokui and Iba (2000) combined genetic algorithms and genetic programming in an IEA. The GA individuals represented short pieces of rhythmic patterns, while the GP individuals expressed how these patterns were arranged in terms of their functions. Both populations were evolved interactively through user evaluation. The integration of interactive GA and GP has the benefit of allowing search for music structures in large search space.

Interactive evolutionary algorithms have also been used in generating artwork. For example, Graca & Machado used an IEA to generate assemblages (similar to collages) of 3D objects (2008). In their evolutionary art approach, users make the initial choice of source image and object library, then guide the evolutionary process in accordance to their artistic preference, until a desirable distribution of 3D objects is evolved. Several interesting points addressed by this system include: developing masks to allow exploration of details and ignore other regions; conveying different artistic notions such as motion; mimicking texture; and developing overall expressiveness. The limitations of this system include human fatigue, as well as the computational effort required to preview and render the individuals.

User interface design has also been the subject of interactive evolutionary algorithms (Masson, Demeure, & Calvary, 2010). In an evolutionary system called Magellan, the traditional model-based (task-based) approaches and the interactive genetic algorithms were combined to foster the exploration of the design space and inspire the designer. The input of the system was the given user task model, and the output was sketches of UI's, which could be later tuned by human designers. However, as with the previous example, the authors ran up against the human fatigue problem.

To address the issue of human fatigue, one approach that has been used is to hardcode mathematical heuristics of aesthetics. For example, in a proposed jewelry design system, several heuristics functions evaluating aesthetics and morphology were included, which reduced the amount of feedback needed from the user by two orders of magnitude (Wannarumon, Bohez, & Annanon, 2008). It was basically a hybrid approach in which evaluations rely partially on an encoded fitness function (the algorithmic aesthetics), and partially on subjective human feedback. However, this approach is still limited in its need for a hard-coded aesthetical evaluation function, which is something that may not be possible or practical for every situation.

In order to overcome both the human fatigue problem and the hard coded fitness function, Hornby and Bongard (2012) developed The Approximate User (TAU) system, in which a model of the user's preference was built and refined continuously during the search process. This preference model could then be used to drive the search algorithm, decreasing the demand placed on the user. Two variations of a user-modeling approach were compared to determine if this approach can accelerate IEA search. The first approach involved learning classification rules to determine which of two designs is better. The second involved learning a model to predict fitness scores. These two variants were compared against the basic IEA and it was shown that TAU was 2.7 times faster and 15 times more reliable at producing near optimal results.

3. Evac and the user

Evac is simple to operate – after opening the program, a very minimal user interface is displayed and the user begins to hear the tick of a metronome. From this moment, Evac is ready to accept user input. The user treats the Tab, Q, W, E, R, T, Y, U, I, O, P, open-bracket ('['), and close-bracket (']') keys on their computer keyboard like keys on a piano, pressing them to trigger the sound of a flute and releasing them to stop the sound. One note can be played at a time. Each key corresponds to a specific pitch, shown in Table 1.

Table 1: Keyboard keys and pitches.

Keyboard Key	Pitch
Tab	A2
Q	B2
W	C3
E	D3

R	E3
T	F3
Y	G3
U	A3
I	B3
O	C4
P	D4
[	E4
]	F4

After a certain amount of "prep" time, whether the user has played anything or not, Evac will begin playing the output of the genetic algorithm. (In fact, Evac will happily play along with silence forever - the fitness function, described below, has no problem with comparing against silence.)

Evac addresses the human fatigue problem in a novel way. The system does not require the user to evaluate music pieces directly, saving them the mental fatigue of making choice after choice (though the trade-off is that the user has no way to directly control the software's performance). Evac, however, *does* constantly compare its output against the user's input. As a result, the user is kept in the evaluative loop. In this way, Evac dodges the issue of user fatigue - the only human activity involved is playing music, which is quite enjoyable. As a matter of fact, our system can be used as a tool to assist musicians in developing creative accompaniment without much effort; all one needs to do is keep playing.

4. The Genetic Algorithm approach

4.1 Overview

A technical overview of Evac's GA configuration is given in table 2. The major concern when designing Evac's GA was the need to balance the competing demands of high performance with the limited resources available in a real-time environment. A clear microcosm of this issue presents itself in deciding an appropriate population size. Our population size of 100 was chosen to be small enough to prevent undue resource consumption: excessively large populations require more computation per generation, leading to more inertia and less responsiveness. Since Evac operates in real time, this would decrease the value of the system. On the other hand, small population size limits the diversity of the population. This means fewer musical ideas present in the population and a greater risk of stagnation.

Table 2: Technical overview of Evac's GA parameters.

Representation	Discrete. Integers represent pitch. Relative position of integers represents rhythm. (See below.)
Parent selection strategy	Tournament selection with 4 competitors.
Survival strategy	Generational + elitism. (Best individual retained between generations.)
Crossover	Uniform crossover; probability: 90%
Mutation	Uniform mutation; mutation probability per gene: 20%
Population size	100

We were reluctant to use "on-line" forms of parameter control (e.g., self-adaptation, dynamic parameter control) for two reasons. First, some forms of control pose additional challenge to the evolutionary process. Second, others depend on a priori reasoning that was not relevant to Evac's task. For example, a common technique is to use dynamic parameter control to decrease mutation rate as the algorithm progresses. Since Evac operates for as long as the user is entertained, this technique is not appropriate. With that in mind, parameter tuning (i.e., trial and error) was used to determine a reasonable balance between the two demands.

4.2 Representation

Figure 1 shows the representation for a single music note, and for an individual of the GA. As mentioned earlier, the representation for a single note was an 11-bit integer encoding of several values. Specifically, the lowest 6 bits were used to present the pitch of the note, which gave us a range of 64 different pitches (more than sufficient for the thirteen pitches we used). The next 4 bits were used to represent the velocity of the note (i.e., volume, or the strength of the note), which gave us a range of 16 different levels of velocity. If the velocity for a note was 0, that meant it was silent (i.e., a break or rest). The next bit marked whether this note was a new note or a continuation of the previous one. This bit was only meaningful if there were two consecutive notes with the same pitch. In that case, a new note means two notes will be played. If the second one is not a new note, it will not be played; instead, the first note will be played for the duration of two notes.

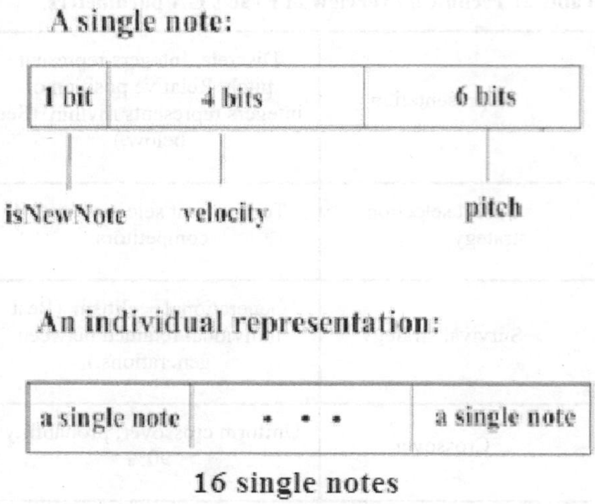

Figure 1: Representation for a single music note and an individual

However, in Evac's GA, an individual is not merely a note, but an entire musical phrase, i.e. a series of notes. We took each individual to be 16 notes long; as in music, these sixteen notes could be played over an arbitrary length of time, depending on Evac's settings. This allowed the user to determine for themselves whether they wanted to play a fast song or a slow song. An example of a musical phrase and the corresponding GA individual representation is shown in Figure 2.

Position	1-5	2	3	4	5	7-16
Velocity	0	1	1	1	1	1
Pitch	12	7	5	3	0	0
isNewNote	n/a	true	true	true	true	False

Figure 2: Musical phrase (above) and corresponding Evac individual representation (below).

4.3 Similarity Rating and Fitness Function

An individual's fitness was achieved by transforming a similarity function. The similarity function was computed by comparing each individual against the user's input for the previous 16 beats, and depended only on the harmonic "distance" (musical term: *interval*) between the pitches at each index. (In our representation, such harmonic distance can be computed by simple subtraction of the integer pitches.) Our similarity weighting function was informed by a musical technique called counterpoint, in which two separate melodies (strings of notes) interweave to form a larger texture. These two separate melodies are harmonically interdependent, but independent in pitch contour and rhythm. In particular, we used a simplistic approach where consonant, "at rest" intervals had a higher similarity rating, while dissonant, "unstable" intervals had a lower similarity rating. Generally for most people, a consonance sounds pleasant whereas dissonance sounds unpleasant or harsh. As Roger Kamien said in his book (2008), "An unstable tone combination is a dissonance; its tension demands an onward motion to a stable chord. Thus dissonant chords are 'active'; traditionally they have been considered harsh and have expressed pain, grief, and conflict." We want our music to be more pleasant to listen to, hence we gave consonant intervals higher similarity ratings, which will lead to higher fitness values in the evolutionary process.

Table 3 presents the 12 different musical intervals and their corresponding similarity values. We adopted these values based on music theory knowledge and our own musical intuition. If two notes have an interval that is higher than 12, their similarity value was calculated in this way: first, a similarity value was calculated based on Table 3 using the remainder of that interval value divided by 12, then the resulting similarity value was decreased by 0.2 to get the final similarity value. Rests have a similarity value of 1 to other rests, and a similarity value of 0 to non-rests.

The similarity value of an individual was the sum of the similarity values calculated for each of the 16 notes within that individual. Once a similarity value had been obtained for an individual, that similarity value was passed through a weighting function (i.e., the fitness function, shown in Figure 4) to calculate the individual's fitness value. The decision of weighting functions was based on the principle that individuals with excessively low or high similarity should receive low fitness values. Individuals with mid-to-high range similarity values should receive higher fitness values. Several fitness functions were tested and the one with the best performance among them, a quadratic function, was chosen.

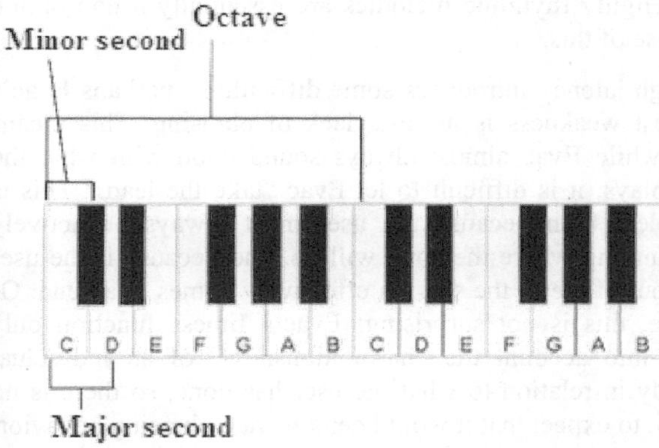

Figure 3: Music intervals shown on piano keyboard

Table 3: Musical intervals and their corresponding similarity values.

Interval : Musical Name	Similarity value
0 : Unison	1
1 : Minor second	0
2 : Major second	0.3
3 : Minor third	0.4
4 : Major third	0.6
5 : Perfect fourth	0.1
6 : Tritone	0
7 : Perfect fifth	0.8
8 : Minor sixth	0.6
9 : Major sixth	0.4
10 : Minor seventh	0.3
11 : Major seventh	0.1
12 : Octave	0.9

To provide a brief idea of how Table 3 works out in practice, assume we are interested in the individual: [0, 3, 5, …]. Furthermore, assume the first three notes of the user's input for the last 16 beats was [0, 10, 22, …]. To determine the similarity rating, simply calculate the absolute value of the differences between each note: [0 - 0, 10 - 3, 22 - 5, …] = [0, 7, 17, …], then compare to table 3. We can see distances of 0 (a unison - i.e., the same note) have a similarity value of 1, distances of 7 have a similarity value of 0.8. For the distances of 17, we first get the remainder of 17 divided by 12, which is 5, and from Table 3 we get distances of 5 have a similarity value of 0.4. We then decrease 0.4 by 0.2 (which is a static value got from experimentation) and get 0.2. Thus, for each interval we have similarities [1, 0.8, 0.2, …]. To obtain the similarity score for an individual, simply sum the similarities of each interval. Thus, assuming the individual in question consisted of only those three intervals listed explicitly above, our example would have a similarity value of 2. To obtain the individual's final fitness score, apply the fitness function shown in Figure 4: $f(2) = -(2 - 10)^2$, yielding -64.

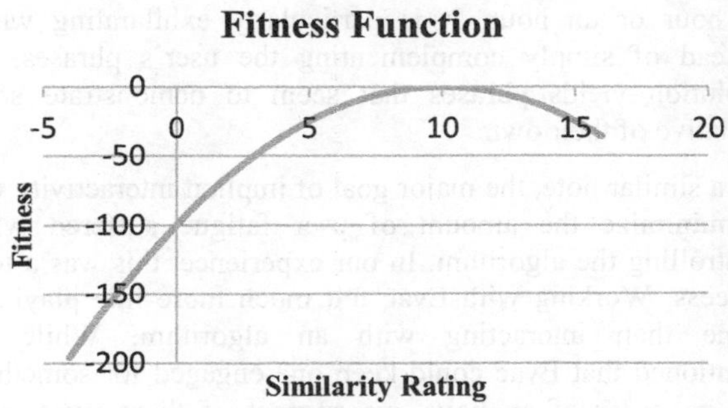

Figure 4: Fitness function: $f(x) = -(x-10)^2$. Input is a similarity rating.

4.4 Genetic Operators

For mutation we used uniform mutation. For each individual (i.e., series of notes), the algorithm goes through each one and decides whether that note will be mutated. Once a certain note is chosen to be mutated, a new random integer will be generated to replace that note. Since all three components (pitch, velocity, isNewNote) are encoded within this integer, we don't need to consider the components separately. A high mutation rate (20%) was chosen to prevent the algorithm from converging on a simple parallel imitation of the user (i.e., shifted up some number of pitches, but otherwise identical).

For crossover, we used uniform crossover. Specifically, we did not do crossover between notes; instead, we performed crossover between different individuals. There are two reasons to adopt this strategy. First, it is simple. Second, and more importantly, we suspect that, in keeping with ideas like the Building Block Hypothesis, recombining effective individuals will allow us to more rapidly reach higher levels of quality.

5. Results and analyses

Four excerpts of Evac sessions are available on the website https://www.dropbox.com/sh/h5cbz756tcyxy6n/vUXrcnmjKg, labeled "Evac Demo 1", "Evac Demo 2", "Evac Demo 3", and "Evac Demo 4." Again, the flute sound is played by a human user and the piano sound is played by the computer. What follows are subjective evaluations of Evac's performance; further research would involve more rigorous measures of quality (e.g., systematically conducted surveys regarding Evac's effectiveness, rating by experts on its degree of musicality and quality of accompaniment, etc.)

The first thing to be said about Evac is that it is surprisingly fun to use. We opted to use a flute as the voice for the user's input, and a piano as the voice for the program. The result was both musical and entertaining. While Evac does not provide hours of entertainment, there are just enough moments of unexpected beauty to keep one engaged for half an hour or an hour. It is particularly exhilarating when, instead of simply complementing the user's phrases, the evolution yields phrases that seem to demonstrate some initiative of their own.

On a similar note, the major goal of implicit interactivity was to minimize the amount of user fatigue suffered while controlling the algorithm. In our experience, this was a total success. Working with Evac felt much more like playing a game than interacting with an algorithm. While we mentioned that Evac could keep one engaged for something on the order of an hour, we suspect, if there were good reason, people would be able to continue significantly longer than that.

We did notice that it takes Evac some time to "catch up" when the user changes musical directions. This is to be expected - the population had optimized for a certain fitness function, and when the user changes their behavior, the algorithm needs time to adapt to the new fitness landscape. Nor, all told, is the time it takes to adapt excessive. Typically within one or two cycles of 16 beats, it has found its way into something that is at least not offensive, if not truly complementary.

Evac also seems to yield a better experience with slower songs. To some degree, this can be attributed to the processing demands - for slower songs, fewer computations need to be performed per second, and as a result the program responds more smoothly and immediately to user input. At the same time, this is also a function of the latency present in the system. Even at modest speeds, there is still appreciable (if not crippling) delay between when the user presses a key and when the corresponding flute sound plays. Slower tempos mean the latency introduces relatively less error, thereby making the delay less intrusive. This latency also limits the user's play style, to some extent. Because of the latency, it is difficult to perform quick, intricate movements while keeping time with the rest of the system. As such, it is simpler and easier for users to play mostly long, sustained notes with some flourishes, either at the beginning or the end. Highly rhythmic melodies are essentially a non-option because of this.

Though latency introduces some difficulties, perhaps Evac's greatest weakness is its utter lack of phrasing. This means that, while Evac almost always sound good with what the user plays, it is difficult to let Evac "take the lead." This is not ideal both because the user must always be actively determining where the song will go, and because if the user runs out of ideas, the session effectively comes to an end. Of course, this is not surprising; Evac's fitness function only takes into account the "harmoniousness" of an individual melody in relation to what the user has done, so there is no reason to expect that it would demonstrate phrasing behavior.

6. Conclusion

Evac is excellent for what it is - a first approximation that demonstrates the power of implicit interactivity. Evac demonstrates satisfying performance on musical improvisation with the user. Evac's ability to run in real time allows the user to experience the same kind of exploration that happens in real life improvisation scenarios with other musicians.

On one hand Evac is able to follow the music that the user plays; on the other hand, Evac is more than a simple reharmonizer. It never copies the user, nor does it repeat its own previous melody. When the user stops playing (while keeping the program running), Evac will also slow down gradually, but it will never completely stop playing – it will play few notes every now and then, as if it is asking and waiting for the user to respond. Once the user starts playing again, Evac will re-start the cooperation with the user, with very short amount of time needed at the beginning to adapt to the user's music style.

7. Future work

The most immediate need is for reduced latency. If Evac responded immediately and effortlessly to user input, we anticipate using it would become even more fun. This in turn would improve the extent to which it fulfilled its original purpose: eliminating user fatigue. There are also some small audio rendering issues (particularly at the end of notes) that could use fixing. These small improvements, together with a strong graphical user interface, would make Evac worthy of public distribution.

If its other operations could be suitably optimized, the next greatest need is for more sophisticated parameter control. Parameter tuning has many downsides, and there is a reasonable chance that well-designed parameter control could reduce or eliminate the issue with Evac not taking the lead (e.g., by increasing mutation rate and number of notes played when user isn't playing much, etc.). Furthermore, sophisticated parameter control could throttle back the GA's resource usage in the event that other, non-Evac processes begin demanding CPU time.

There is also an entire branch of research that we have yet to exploit, despite its great potential relevance: evolutionary computation in dynamic environments. Techniques like storing good solutions to be used in case their environment returns, or using random immigrants to help adapt to a new fitness landscape could be easily applied to our problem domain, since our fitness function changes whenever the user moves in a new musical direction. Using these kinds of strategies would yield serious improvements in Evac's ability to simulate a real human improvisation partner, since a key part of musical improvisation with other people is recognizing song sections which can be returned to or modified.

Finally, the fitness function has several weaknesses that could be addressed in future research. Most obvious is that both the fitness function and the similarity function are hard-coded, and thus rely on human expertise. Minimizing the human involvement in these features would improve Evac's ability to participate in improvisation across different musical traditions and with different individuals. Such an innovation might also be engineered to address the issue with phrasing, or to other musical problems like how to coordinate the actions of more than one automated instrument.

Once Evac or its peers are advanced enough, one might even connect them to one another, and see what kind of music machines would make just for themselves.

8. Acknowledgements

The presented work benefited from http://www.freesound.org/, which provided all the sounds files that are used in Evac.

9. Reference

[1] Burton, A. R., & Vladimirova, T. 1999. Application of Genetic Techniques to Musical Composition. Computer Music Journal , 23.

[2] Eiben, A. E., & Smith, J. E. 2003. Introduction to Evolutionary Computing.

[3] Graca, F. d., & Machado, P. 2008. Evolving Assemblages of 3D Objects. In Applications of Evolutionary Computing (pp. 453-462).

[4] Hornby, G. S., & Bongard, J. C. 2012. Accelerating Human-Computer Collaborative Search through Learning Comparative and Predictive User Models. GECCO .

[5] Masson, D., Demeure, A., & Calvary, G. 2010. Magellan, an Evolutionary System to Foster User Interface Design Creativity. EICS .

[6] Matic, D. 2010. A Genetic Algorithm for Composing Music . Yugoslav Journal of Operations Research , 157-177.

[7] Tokui, N., & Iba, H. 2000. Music Composition with Interactive Evolutionary Computation. Proceedings of the 3rd international conference on generative art , 215-226.

[8] Wannarumon, S., Bohez, E. L., & Annanon, K. 2008. Aesthetic Evolutionary Algorithm for Fractal-Based User-Centered Jewelry Design. Artificial Intelligence for Engineering Design, Analysis and Manufacturing , 19-39.

[9] Kamien, Roger 2008. Music: An Appreciation, 6th Brief Edition, p.41. ISBN 978-0-07-340134-8

Comparison of Uncorrelated and Correlated Evolutionary Strategies with Proposed Additional Geometric Translations

A. Sandra DeBruyne[1], B. Devinder Kaur[2]

[1,2]Electrical Engineering and Computer Science Department, University of Toledo, Toledo, OH, USA

Abstract — *In this paper Evolutionary Strategy for uncorrelated mutations such as self-adaptive one step and self-adaptive k step are compared with correlated mutation. The two offspring selection techniques of direct replacement (μ,λ) and best fit (μ+λ) are used for comparison. These techniques were applied to a standard multi peak function to evaluate their performance. It was found that none of these approaches always found the global maximum. The results were very much dependent on the selection of the initial random parents. Therefore a new approach of correlated mutation using additional geometric translation has been proposed. It is illustrated that this technique was successful in finding the global maximum.*

Keywords: Evolutionary Strategy, Correlated Mutation, Adaptive Algorithm, Artificial Intelligence

1 INTRODUCTION

EVOLUTIONARY strategies are the earliest techniques of evolutionary algorithms first proposed by Rechenberg [6] and Schwefel [10] (1965), initially used for parameter optimization by Beyer (2001) [3], applications in fluid dynamics and function optimization. The idea behind evolutionary strategy is to randomly mutate all of the input parameters in an effort to find the best solution. The amount of mutation is varied in each iteration of the algorithm. Then by applying (μ+λ) or (μ,λ) next generation selection, the resulting parameters are improved further. No recombination techniques were used in the algorithms for this paper. The main objective is to find the set of parameters which will deliver the optimized solution for a problem.

Evolutionary strategies can be developed as uncorrelated and correlated mutations. In uncorrelated mutation the parameters are mutated by a small step size either in the positive or negative direction depending on the fitness value associated with direction. In the uncorrelated one step algorithm one mutation value is calculated during each iteration step and applied uniformly to all parameters being considered. In uncorrelated k step algorithm a vector of mutation values are calculated during each iteration step and added to the vector of parameters. Both of these methods traverse linearly across the x-axis. In correlated mutation angles of rotation are also calculated and applied at each iteration step and used to mutate the parameters with varying orientation from a related correlation matrix. This method makes the parameters sensitive to direction. These methods were all tested using a mutli-peak function (1) commonly used for comparative analysis of algorithms as shown in Fig. 1, this function has a known global maximum 1.0 at x = 0.1. For x □ [0.1]:

$$F(x) = (2^{-2((x-0.1)/0.9)^2})(sin(5\pi x))^6. \quad (1)$$

It was found that both of the uncorrelated algorithms and the correlated did not always reach this global maximum. The correlated mutation had better results but was shown to be a computational intense algorithm requiring more time to run than the uncorrelated algorithms.

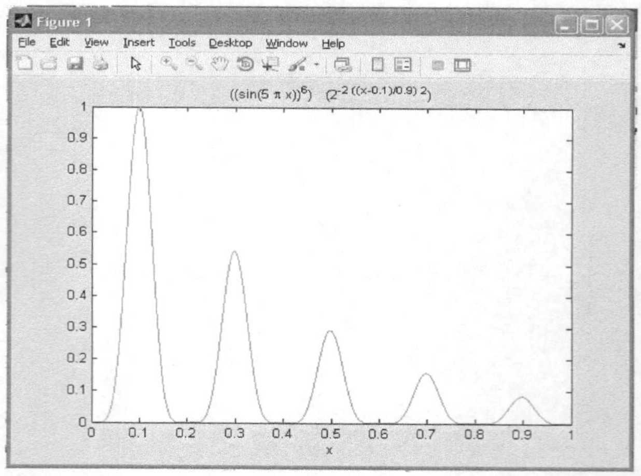

Figure 1. Graph of equation (1) used for evaluation of algorithms.

Both (μ+λ) and (μ,λ) next generation selection techniques were used to compare the performance of the uncorrelated and correlated mutation algorithms. In (μ,λ) the μ parents were directly replaced with their λ children for the next iteration. In (μ+λ) the μ parents and λ children were sorted according to fitness and the candidates with the best fitness were selected for the next iteration. [1] It was found that (μ+λ) had better results.

Therefore in order to search for a better algorithm a proposed new technique of correlated mutation with added geometric translations is introduced. In this technique the ellipses around the parents are translated to a new location in the direction of better fitness. It was found that the results of moving the entire ellipse in this way resulted in finding the global maximum. This was verified by running the same initial sample parent population on both the standard correlated mutation algorithm and the new proposed correlated mutation with added geometric translations.

This paper is organized into seven sections. Section II contains the explanation of the evolutionary strategy algorithms used. Section III discusses uncorrelated mutation with one step size and the shows the results of testing this algorithm. Section IV discusses uncorrelated mutation with individual step sizes and shows the results of testing this algorithm. Section V discusses correlated mutation and shows the results of testing this algorithm. Section VI discusses correlated mutation with proposed translations and shows the results of this algorithm, followed by section VII conclusions.

2 Evolutionary Strategy

In this section the algorithms for evolutionary strategy are presented. Evolutionary strategy algorithms are based on Darwin's theory of evolution. [5] Parents create offspring and the offspring that potentially have stronger features than the parent are chosen to better survive in the environment. Mutations are applied in the creation of these offspring to introduce new features that were not present in the original parents to improve the odds of achieving the desired goal. [1]

2.1 Pseudocode for Evolutionary Algorithms

Using these ideas a computer algorithm can be developed to analyze a problem and its data to achieve an optimal solution to that problem, as shown in Fig. 2. First, an initial population P(t) is generated randomly and evaluated. Second a mutation technique is applied to adjust the children to a new set P'(t). The fitness of those children is evaluated and then children are chosen from the set of parents P(t) and children P'(t) to form the new parent set P(t+1). The loop terminates if either the maximum number of iterations are reached or the desired solution is found. As outlined here by Castro: [1]

```
Initialize P(t)
Evaluate P(t)
While not Terminate do
    P'(t) = mutate P(t)
    Evaluate P'(t)
    P(t+1) = P'(t) or best of {P'(t) U P(t)}
    t = t + 1
Loop
```

Figure 2. Sample pseudo code for evolutionary strategy algorithm [1].

2.2 Next Generation Selection Strategies

Two different selection processes were used to pick the next generation of data to be sent through the algorithm. In standard evolutionary strategy literature "given μ parents generating λ offspring (λ >= μ)" [1] The simplest way is to use the (μ,λ)-ES technique where the new set of children is used as the parents for the next iteration, the algorithm in Fig. 2 would use P(t+1) = P'(t). A second technique is to use (μ+λ)-ES technique [1], by looking at the fitness of the parents and the fitness of the new children and sorting their resulting finesses from best to worst. A next generation set is created from the top μ best parents and children, the algorithm in Fig. 2 would use P(t+1) =best of {P'(t) U P(t)}.

2.3 Geometric Translation

By definition a translation "is a function that moves every point a constant distance in a specified direction"[7]. One of the disadvantages of the evolutionary strategies is that the final results have a good chance of concentrating at a local minimum and never reaching the goal. The advantage of using a translation is to jump the parents that are trapped at a local maximum to a different area of the graph.

3 UNCORRELATED WITH ONE STEP SIZE

As this algorithm loops through each iteration, all parents are being mutated by the same single step size. Using the same standard deviation σ to create all children will have the result that "lines of equal probability density of the normal distribution are hyper-spheres in an l-dimensional space." [1]

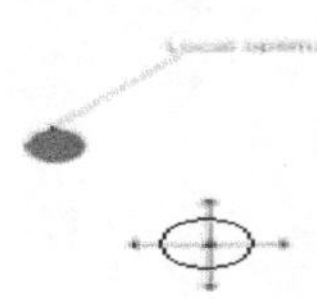

Figure 3. Uncorrelated Mutation with One Step Sizes [11]

3.1 Formulas

Given n parents and the learning rate T suggested by Castro[1] the following formulas are used to compute P'(t):

$$T = 1/\sqrt{n}$$

$$\sigma' = \sigma * e^{(T * N(0,1))}$$

$$P'(t) = P(t) \underline{+} \sigma' * N(0,1) \qquad (2)$$

By multiplying σ by the lgnormal distribution $e^{(\tau * N(0,1))}$ graphed in Fig. 4, and using the normal distribution N(0,1) to modify σ', the standard deviations stays greater than zero and the adjustment being made to σ and σ' are small values. [11]

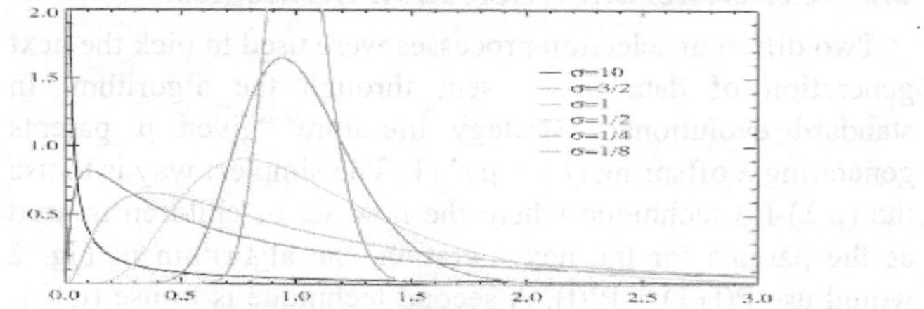

Figure 4. Lognormal Distribution [13]

3.2 Results

Uncorrelated mutation with one step size is shown to be a fast and simple algorithm by the results in Table I. From the tests run it is shown in Fig. 5 and 6 that the algorithm fails to always find a global maximum. As the contours of the graph become more complex the algorithm can tend towards a local maximum and once arriving there concentrates the results at that point. One important determining factor as to whether or not this technique was successful was the selection of the next generation. As shown in Fig. 5, the effect of applying (μ,λ) to the determine the next generation, gives varied results. As shown in Fig. 7, the effect of applying (μ+λ) results in local maximum values. Table I shows the resulting x value of 0.3134 closer to the expected 0.1 value.

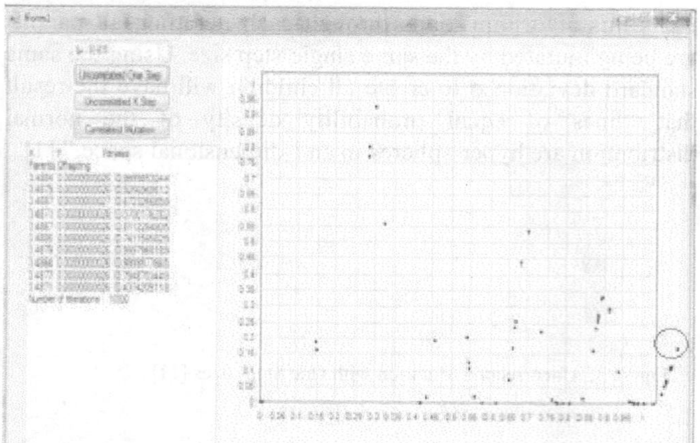

Figure 5. Uncorrelated One Step with No Offspring Sorting after 1000 iterations demonstrating the offspring being continually shifted in the positive direction along the x-axis. Table shows the resulting x value of 3.4884 far from the expected 0.1 value.

4 Uncorrelated Individual Step Size

As this algorithm loops through each iteration, each parent is being mutated by an individual unique step size. Using the different standard deviation σ_i to create each child will have the result that "lines of equal probability density of the normal distribution are hyper-ellipsoids." [1]

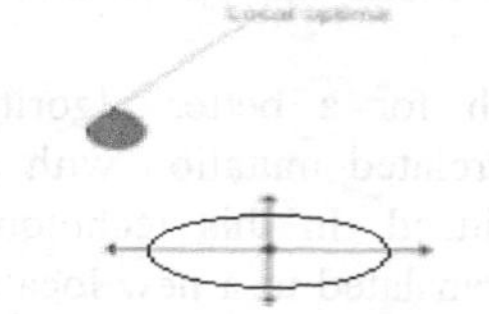

Figure 6. Uncorrelated Mutation with Individual Step Sizes [11]

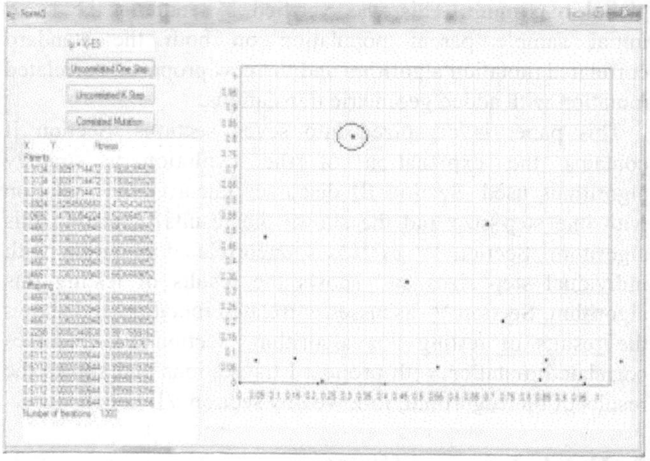

Figure 7. Uncorrelated One Step with Offspring Sorting after 1000 iterations demonstrating the best offspring being selected and used for the next generation. The shift in the positive direction along the x-axis is reduced.

TABLE I. Uncorrelated One Step Results

Method	Next Generation Selector	Change Direction	No Iterations	No Parents	Time (ms)	Result X	Result Y
UnCorrelated One Step							
	(μ,λ)	N	100	10	3.8294	0.960119	0.0114469
			1000	10	28.594	0.945333	0.0553875
			10000	10	190.7619	0.910901	0.2970658
	(μ+λ)	N	100	10	4.119	0.094013	0.9737142
			1000	10	39.0927	0.113978	0.8640433
			10000	10	195.8703	0.89136	0.9157631
	(μ,λ)	Y	100	10	6.4753	0.112	0.8981011
			1000	10	35.22	0.943659	0.0635498
			10000	10	184.0641	0.051005	0.1366517
	(μ+λ)	Y	100	10	4.4389	0.4752	0.4925319
			1000	10	39.0469	0.299784	0.9339375
			10000	10	216.5566	0.296049	0.9255736

4.1 Formulas

Given n parents and the learning rates τ and τ' suggested by Castro[1] the following formulas are used to compute P'(t):

$$T = 1/\sqrt{2\sqrt{n}}$$

$$T' = 1/\sqrt{2n}$$

$$\sigma'(t) = \sigma(t) * e^{(T * N(0,1) + T' * N_t(0,1))}$$

$$P'(t) = P(t) \pm \sigma'(t) * N(0,1) \qquad (3)$$

To ensure that each parent is mutated by a unique step size the algorithm is slightly modified to now use this lognormal distribution $e^{(T * N(0,1) + T' * N_t(0,1))}$ to modify σ. In calculating P'(t) each $\sigma'(t)$is modified by normal distribution N(0,1) to ensure a small adjustment in the mutation.[11]

4.2 Results

Uncorrelated mutation with k step sizes is shown in Table II to be a slightly slower algorithm than the uncorrelated one step algorithm. From the tests run it is shown in Fig. 8 and 9 that this algorithm also fails to always find a global maximum. This algorithm again tends to find a local maximum as the contours of the graph become more complex and once arriving there concentrates the results at that point. The same important determining factor as to whether or not this technique was successful was the selection of the next generation. As shown in Fig. 8, the effect of applying (μ,λ) to the determine the next generation, gives varied results. In comparison by applying (μ+λ) Fig. 9 shows the results concentrating around local maximum values. This technique of calculating the next iteration by modifying the parents with a k sized vector of random values does demonstrate a maximum being discovered in fewer iterations than the previous one step technique, as shown in Tables I & II.

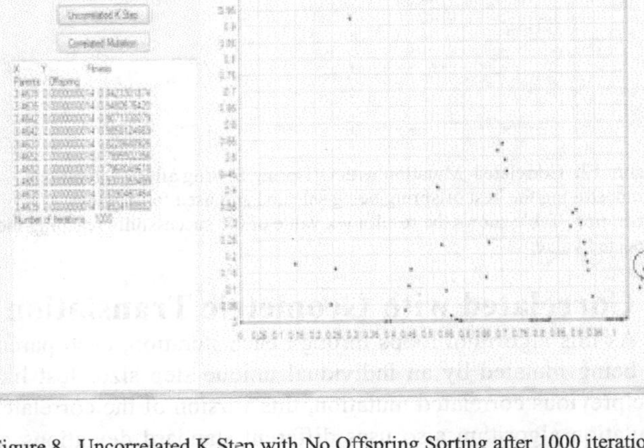

Figure 8. Uncorrelated K Step with No Offspring Sorting after 1000 iterations demonstrating the offspring being continually shifted in the positive direction along the x-axis. Table shows the resulting x value of 3.4639 far from the expected 0.1 value.

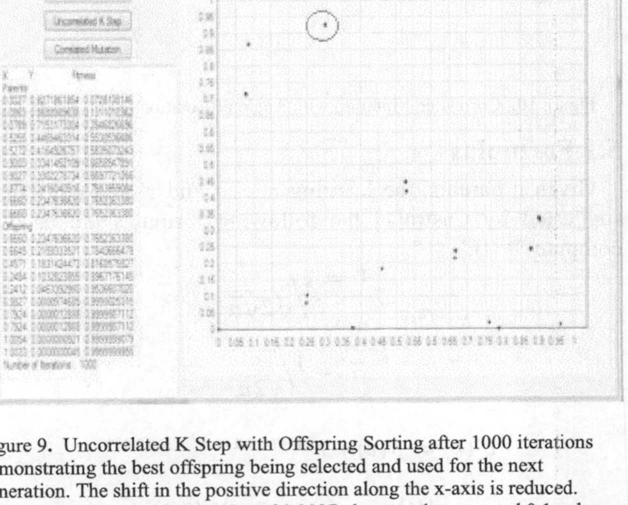

Figure 9. Uncorrelated K Step with Offspring Sorting after 1000 iterations demonstrating the best offspring being selected and used for the next generation. The shift in the positive direction along the x-axis is reduced. Table shows the resulting x value of 0.3027 closer to the expected 0.1 value.

TABLE II. UNCORRELATED K STEP RESULTS

Method	Next Generation Selector	Change Direction	No Iterations	No Parents	Time (ms)	Result X	Result Y
UnCorrelated K Step							
	(μ,λ)	N	100	10	1.6245	0.949158	0.3934992
			1000	10	28.9059	0.927498	0.1737801
			10000	10	150.4814	0.958348	0.0143966
	(μ+λ)	N	100	10	3.7323	0.99746	0.9999520
			1000	10	34.6443	0.286146	0.8166838
			10000	10	161.6135	0.98698	0.9987438
	(μ,λ)	Y	100	10	3.222	0.908266	0.3107350
			1000	10	30.476	0.014095	0.0001107
			10000	10	165.2744	0.118038	0.7829405
	(μ+λ)	Y	100	10	2.9218	0.704934	0.5250089
			1000	10	29.375	0.289595	0.8676037
			10000	10	164.8476	0.116392	0.8174364

5 CORRELATED MUTATION

As this algorithm loops through each iteration, each parent is being mutated by an individual unique step size. Just like the previous uncorrelated mutation with individual step sizes, the formulas use a different standard deviation σ_i to create each child. The correlated mutation formulas add an additional step of introducing rotation angles to "describe the coordinate rotations necessary to transform the uncorrelated mutation vector to a correlated mutation vector. Now the previous hyper-ellipsoids can be rotated randomly at angle α(t) to give the data more freedom of movement through the plane. ".[1]

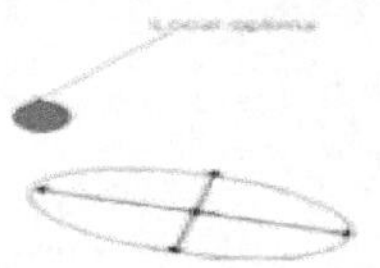

Figure 10. Correlated Mutation with Angle of Rotation [11]

5.1 Formulas

Given n parents, the learning rates τ and τ' and constant β suggested by Castro[1] the following formulas are used to compute P'(t):

$$T = 1/\sqrt{2\sqrt{n}}$$

$$T' = 1/\sqrt{2n}$$

$$\sigma'(t) = \sigma(t) * e^{(T * N(0,1) + T' * N_t(0,1))}$$

$$\alpha'(t) = \alpha(t) + \beta * N_t(0,1)$$

$$\beta = 0.0873$$

$$P'(t) = P(t) \pm \sigma' * N(0, C(\sigma', \alpha'))$$

(4)

Where matrix C(σ', α') is calculated by [1]

$$C = (ST^T ST)$$

S is diagonal matrix of the standard deviations with

$$s_{ij} = \sigma(t)$$

$$T = \prod_{i}^{n-1} \prod_{j=i+1}^{n} R_{ij}(\Theta)$$

$R_{ij}(\Theta)$ is an elementary rotation matrix with

$$r_{ii} = r_{jj} = \cos\alpha(t)$$

$$r_{ij} = r_{ji} = -\sin\alpha(t)$$

(5)

5.2 Results

The time it takes to run the correlated mutation algorithm is significantly higher than the uncorrelated algorithms inn previous sections, as shown in Table III. In contrast the number of iterations required to reach a maximum value is significantly lower. In Fig. 11 and Fig. 12 it is shown that the algorithm had reached a maximum value in fewer than 25 iterations. Fig. 11 and Fig 12 also show that a global maximum is not always reached. Fig. 12 is concentrating the best offspring around x=0.1, the desired value, but Fig. 10 is showing the best offspring concentrating around x=0.5497, a local maximum. Fig. 13 shows the correlated mutation algorithm results with the rotation ellipses displayed. It can be seen in Fig. 13 that the algorithm begins to concentrate its offspring around the maximum peaks of the graph and remains trapped there.

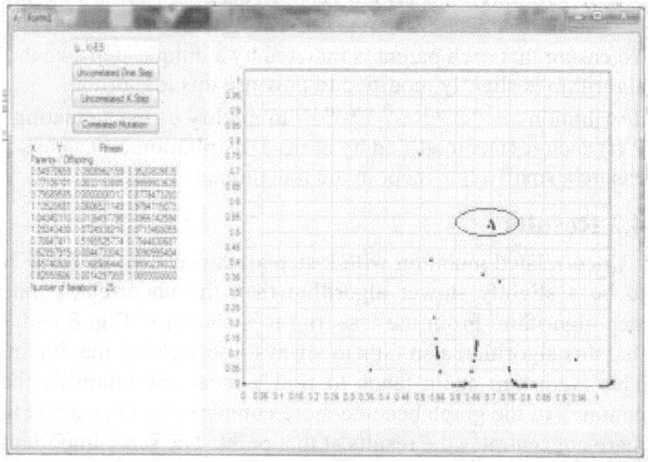

Figure 11. Correlated Mutation with No Offspring Sorting after 25 iterations demonstrating the offspring being continually shifted in the positive direction along the x-axis. Table shows the resulting x value of 0.5497 far from the expected 0.1 value.

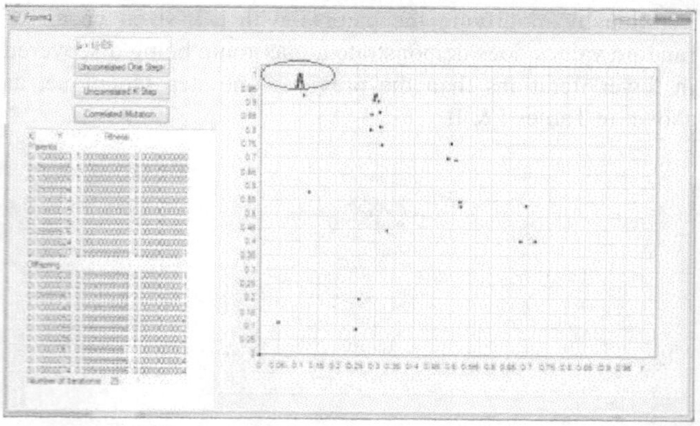

Figure 12. Correlated Mutation with Offspring Sorting after 25 iterations demonstrating the best offspring being selected and used for the next generation. Table shows the resulting x value of 0.1 successfully reaching the expected value.

6 Correlated with Geometric Translation

As this algorithm loops through each iteration, each parent is being mutated by an individual unique step size. Just like the previous correlated mutation, this version of the correlated mutation algorithm also uses different standard deviations σ_i to create each child and calculates the rotation angles for the hyper ellipsoids. The algorithm is further modified by the proposed addition of translating these ellipsoids in the direction of better fitness and reevaluating the translated parameters.

TABLE III. CORRELATED RESULTS

Method	Next Generation Selector	Change Direction	No Iterations	No Parents	Time (ms)	Result X	Result Y
Correlated Mutation							
	(μ,λ)	N	100	10	14.1864	0.0578364	0.2397426
			1000	10	97.73	0.5	0.7603713
			10000	10	2198.9979	0.9431838	0.0659958
	(μ+λ)	N	100	10	16.648	0.299355	0.9339560
			1000	10	91.4732	0.2889162	0.8585757
			10000	10	2240.1232	0.3	0.9335827
	(μ,λ)	Y	100	10	13.0658	0.549034	0.0968278
			1000	10	80.9797	0.696457	0.5389286
			10000	10	1988.959	0.33141	0.4257688
	(μ+λ)	Y	100	10	15.0406	0.1000344	0.9999122
			1000	10	74.5497	0.1	1.0000000
			10000	10	2314.0937	0.9709892	0.9937730

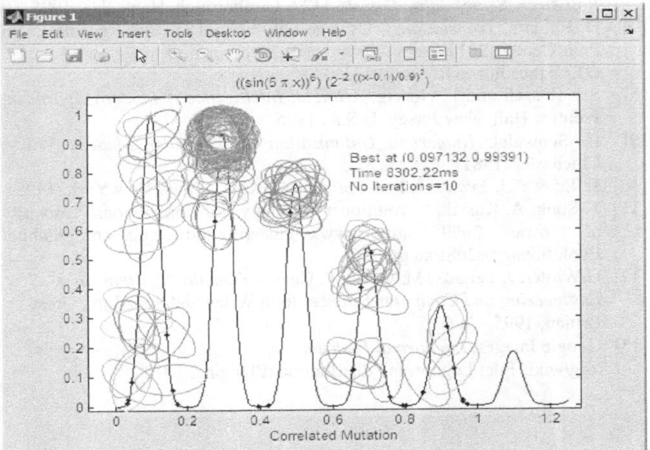

Figure 13. Correlated Mutation with Offspring Sorting after 10 iterations using 25 parents. This graph demonstrates the way correlated mutation uses ellipses. Graph shows the algorithm concentrating at a local maximum of y=0.95.

As shown in standard correlated mutation sample run in Fig. 13, the high concentration of ellipses around x=0.3, the correlated mutation algorithm is shown to get trapped at a local maximum of the graph. Results of this type suggest an additional modification to the correlated mutation algorithm is needed to dissipate these concentrations to other areas of the graph. Since correlated mutation is a computationally intense algorithm, as shown by the time studies in Table III, if the algorithm can be modified to reduce the concentrations of results, time would be saved by computing only sets of unique values.

It is proposed that by adding translations of the ellipse surrounding each of the parents in the directions of each of the four ellipse vertices, parameters will effectively jump out of the areas of local maximums to begin searching for the global maximum in another region of the graph. The vertices are evaluated against for fitness and a decision is made to move the parameters in the direction of best fitness to the next iteration of the algorithm

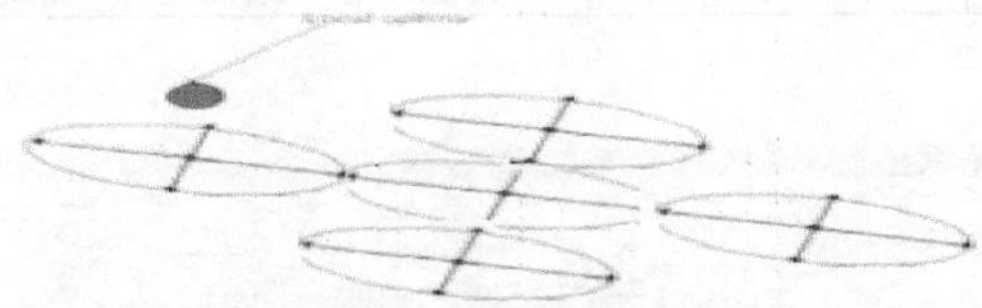

Figure 14. Correlated Mutation with Translation

6.1 Pseudocode

Given the original algorithm in Fig. 2, a test is introduced prior to the selection of the next generation as shown in bold italics in Fig. 15. This test compares the current parents to the newly generated children. If the parents and children are nearly identical a concentration of offspring is developing in the data. Once this situation is identified, new parents are created by translating this set of offspring in the direction best fitness in a series of step sizes. This process removes duplicate parents and replaces them with new unique values to continue on with the search for the goal. The new set of offspring are reevaluated and reselected by the (μ+λ) or (μ,λ) next generation selection techniques and the next iteration of the algorithm begins.

```
Initialize P(t)
Evaluate P(t)
While not Terminate do
    P'(t) = mutate P(t)
    Evaluate P'(t)
    Translate P(t) by step sizes and Reevaluate P'(t)
    P(t+1) = P'(t) or best of {P'(t) U P(t)}
    t = t + 1
Loop
```

Fig. 15. Modification to pseudo code for evolutionary strategy algorithm.

6.2 Results

Figure 16 shows a sample that was run using the standard correlation algorithm starting at x=2.6 for the initial parent parameter. Figure 17 shows a sample that was run using the new proposed correlated mutation with translation starting and the same x=0.26 initial parent value. The result is a shifting of the data and subsequently reaching the global maximum in 4 iterations. Time studies as shown in Table 4 show an increase in the computation time as compared to standard correlated mutation, due to the added step of evaluating and computing the translation values.

TABLE IV. CORRELATED WITH TRANSLATION RESULTS

Method	Next Generation Selector	Chang Direction	No Iterations	No Parents	Time (ms)	Result X	Result Y
Correlated Mutation with Translation							
	(μ+λ)	Y	4	10	575.81	0.1	1.0
			11	10	4235.64	0.10095	0.99933

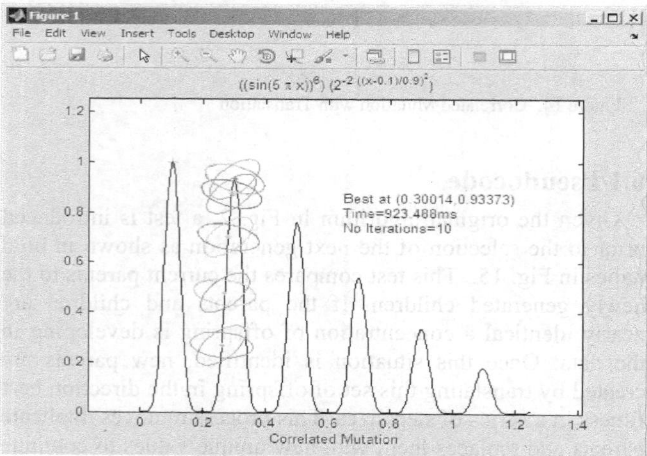

Figure 16. Correlated Mutation with Offspring Sorting and Translation using 1 parent at x=0.26.After 10 iterations maximum found at x= 0.49

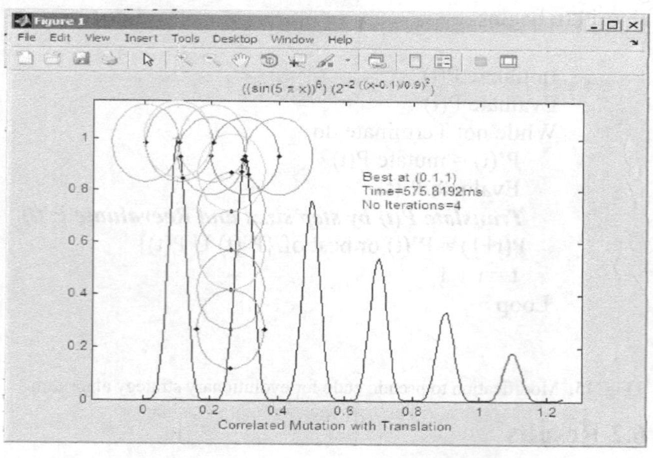

Figure 17. Correlated Mutation with Offspring Sorting and Translation using 1 parent at x=0.26.After 4 iterations maximum found at x= 0.1

7 Conclusion

The Evolutionary strategies were explored to find the global maximum in a mutli-peak mathematical function. An evolutionary strategy with uncorrelated mutation algorithm was shown to reach the global maximum in less than 50% of the test runs, and was shown to be very sensitive to the initial random parent population and next generation selection techniques. Correlated mutation had better results than uncorrelated reaching the global maximum in 90% of the test runs. The correlated algorithm converged on the result in fewer iterations, but each iteration took longer in time to run than the in uncorrelated algorithm. Both uncorrelated and standard correlated algorithms were shown to get stuck in areas of at local maximum values and not reach the global maximum value. The proposed correlated mutation with geometric translation was shown to always reach the global maximum on this multi peak function. The added translations were shown to have an impact on increasing the time to complete each iteration in the search.

References

[1] L. N. Castro, *Fundamentals of Natural Computing, Chapter 3,* Taylor and Francis Group, LLC. New York, 2006.

[2] P.J. Bentley, *Evolutionary Design by Computers,* Morgan, Kaufman, 1999

[3] H. Beyer, *The Theory of Evolutionary Strategies,* Springer-Verlag Berlin Heidelberg, Germany 2001.

[4] D.C. Dennett, *Darwin's Dangerous Idea: Evolution and the Meaning of Life,* Penguin Books. 1995

[5] D. Dumitrescu, B. Lazzerini, L.C. Jain, A. Dumitrescu, *Evolutionary Computing,* CRC Press LLC, 2000, Ch.12.

[6] I. Rechenberg. "Cybernetic Solution Path of an Experimental Problem" *Roy.Aircr. Establ. Libr. Transl.,* 1122, Farnborough, Hants, UK.1995

[7] D. Roberts, *Translations,* Oswego City School District Regents Exam Prep Center, 2012. http://www.regentsprep.org/Regents/math/geometry/GT2/Trans.htm. 11 Mar. 2013.

[8] S.J. Russell and P. Norvig, *Artificial Intelligence A Modern Approach,* Prentice Hall, New Jersey, U.S.A. 1995

[9] H. Schwefel, *Numerical Optimization of Computer Models,* Wiley, Chichester. 1981

[10] H. Schwefel, *Evolution and Optimum Seeking,* Wiley, New York. 1995

[11] Z. Song, A. Kusiak, "Evolutionary Strategy and Applications" Univerity of Iowa. 2009 http://www.engineering.uiowa.edu/~comp/Public/Evolutionary%20Strategy.pdf

[12] G.Winter, J. Periaux, M. Galan, P. Cuesta, *Genetic Algorithms in Engineering and Computer Science,* John Wiley and Sons Ltd., Great Britian, 1995, Ch.6.

[13] Google Images, *Lognormal Distribution,* http://commons.wikimedia.org/wiki/ File: Lognormal_distribution_PDF.png, 2012

Evolutionary Path Algorithm: A Simple and Extensible Metaheuristic for Global Optimization

P. C. Geiger, W. D. Potter, and W. D. Richardson
Institute for Artificial Intelligence, University of Georgia, Athens, Georgia, United States

Abstract - *This paper presents a general-purpose algorithm for finding high-quality solutions to hard optimization problems. The method, called the Evolutionary Path Algorithm, finds high-quality solutions by searching the space that separates solutions within the search space. The Evolutionary Path Algorithm performs random search at the far end of its search path, and then as the path from a random sample back to a Candidate solution is built, the search becomes more local. This path traversal allows the algorithm to explore the search space at the far end and improve a known good solution as it returns to the Candidate solution. Unlike many stochastic search algorithms, the Evolutionary Path Algorithm can be implemented with very limited tuning parameters, making it simpler to use for many practitioners. The Evolutionary Path Algorithm has proven reliable with respect to finding good answers, in the cases presented the best answers, to hard problems. We demonstrate EPA here on an NP hard minimal set cover example with known optima and on an integer valued configuration problem.*

Keywords: Discrete Optimization, Genetic Algorithms, Stochastic Search

1 Introduction

Many real world problems require combinatorial optimization. Examples include scheduling, bin packing, planning, network design, and engineering optimization. What all of these problems share is a search space that is generally too large for exhaustive search methods to find the optimal answer in a reasonable amount of time. Therefore, metaheuristic methods have proven to be useful because they can find good answers in a limited amount of time.

Metaheuristics employing diverse strategies have been developed over the past half century. The most notable being the Genetic Algorithm, Particle Swarm Optimization, Simulated Annealing, and various other swarm techniques such as Ant Colony Optimization [2,3,4,5,6]. These algorithms have produced diverse search strategies, operators for combining answers to form new ones, and new sets of rules for exploring the search space in an efficient manner. Although each of these metaheuristics searches in a different way, they all explore and exploit the search space to find good answers.

The Evolutionary Path Algorithm explores and exploits the search space using a very simple greedy strategy and an exploitation, or intensification, operator called Path Relinking [1]. It does not however, inherit the algorithm as a whole, and instead combines random search with Path Relinking and a moderately greedy strategy. No gradients are computed and directionality is not required. The aim of the development of the algorithm was to make a metaheuristic that was simple to implement for any problem without an abundance of tuning parameters.

In the following we will present the Evolutionary Path Algorithm. It is an algorithm that traces the evolutionary links (differences) between potential solutions to find better solutions to hard problems. In section 2 we describe the Evolutionary Path Algorithm as applied to a minimal set cover problem. Section 3 describes the Evolutionary Path Algorithm as applied to a combinatorial optimization problem using integer values.

Imagine a fishing boat floating on a pond. The pond is the search-space and any potential solution is a fish to catch. The fisherman in the boat can cast anywhere across the open waters in search of the best fish. On each cast the fisherman gets several bites as he reels back to the boat and if he feels a really big fish try the bait, he moves the boat to that location thinking "Where there's one big fish there must be more!" In this way the fisherman moves through the search-space locating his casting point above the best fish he has encountered. After many adjustments of the boat it becomes very likely he has found the best place in the pond. The Evolutionary Path Algorithm adopts this same strategy as it cuts paths through an unknown search-space.

2 Evolutionary Path Algorithm

The Evolutionary Path Algorithm is most simply expressed by the following steps:

1. Initialize a Random Point within the Search Space. This is now the Candidate Solution and the Best Solution.

2. Initialize another Random Point within the Search Space. This is the Random Solution, if it is better than the Candidate Solution, it becomes the Best Solution.

3. An Evolutionary Path is built between the Candidate Solution and the Random Solution. Any solution found that is better than Best Solution replaces Best Solution.

4. Candidate Solution is replaced by Best Solution when the traversal of the Evolutionary Path is complete.

5. The process above is repeated until some stopping condition is met.

The Evolutionary Path Algorithm (EPA) is initialized by choosing a random point within the search space to become the candidate solution. Then, this solution is improved by choosing another random point within the search space and sampling the fitnesses of a randomly generated evolutionary path between the two points. If the best point along the path is better than the candidate solution, the old candidate solution is discarded in favor of the best point seen so far.

This process of traversing an evolutionary path to the best candidate solution is repeated until some stopping criteria, such as a number of fitness evaluations, or a number of paths traversed has been met. At the far end of the path the difference between our candidate solution and the sampled point may be high; this is where exploration of the search space occurs and there is a possibility of leaving local optima in favor of the global optima. As the difference between our candidate solution and points along the evolutionary path decreases, EPA is implicitly performing a local search with a chance of incrementally optimizing our candidate solution.

Creating an evolutionary path is very simple when locations within the search space are represented as binary strings. An XOR of the two strings identifies the bits for which the locations differ. The number of differences is known as the Hamming distance between the two bit strings. Then, one of these bits that differ is chosen at random. The value of the randomly chosen differing bit is then set to match that of the candidate solution. The fitness of this intermediate point along the evolutionary path is evaluated. If the fitness of this intermediate point is better than the fitness of our candidate solution, we remember its location as the "Best Solution".

The evolutionary path is complete when there are no more intermediate points to sample. If, at the end of this process, a best location exists that is not the candidate solution, the candidate solution is replaced by the best solution seen thus far. This process of path building continues until some stopping criteria has been met.

Below is an example path that could be built between two bit strings with a Hamming distance of 3. Although there are multiple possible paths that *could* be built between most solutions, only a single path is traversed in the Evolutionary Path Algorithm.

Step 1 – A Candidate Solution and Random Solution Pairing with Three Differing Bits.

Candidate Solution	1	0	0	0
Random Solution	0	1	0	1

Step 2 – The second bit of the Random Solution was chosen at random to build the second point in the path, reducing the Hamming distance to 2. If the new Random Solution is better than the Candidate Solution it is remembered as the Best Solution but the rest of the path is still built.

Candidate Solution	1	**0**	0	0
Random Solution	0	**0**	0	1

Step 3 – The first bit of the Random Solution was chosen at random and made to match the first bit of the Candidate Solution to build the third point in the path, reducing the differences between the solutions to 1.

Candidate Solution	1	0	0	0
Random Solution	1	0	0	1

Step 4 – The Path is Complete. If no solution along the path was better than the Candidate solution, the algorithm begins again with the Candidate Solution as the Best Solution.

Candidate Solution	1	0	0	**0**
Random Solution	1	0	0	**0**

3 EPA for Multiple Fault Diagnosis

The Evolutionary Path Algorithm has been applied to the Multiple Fault Diagnosis problem (MFD) [8] for characterization. MFD is an NP hard minimum set cover problem in which diagnoses for a set of symptoms are represented by a binary string where an "on" bit represents that the disease is indicated by the symptoms and an "off" bit represents that the disease is not indicated by the set of symptoms. In the problem as presented, there are 10 possible symptoms or 2^10 - 1 (1,023) possible symptom sets. We did not consider the empty set of symptoms because it does not make sense to diagnose people who are well. For this set of symptoms there are 25 possible diseases with 2^25 minus 1 or (33,554,431) possible diagnoses. A set of observed symptoms (*M+*) is evaluated against a diagnosis (set of possible diseases) (*DI*) by the following fitness function:

L(DI; M+) = L1 x L2 x L3

The likelihood of any diagnosis *(DI; M+)* is *L1xL2xL3* where:

L1 is the likelihood that diseases in *DI* cause the symptoms in *M+*.

L2 is the likelihood that diseases in *DI* do not cause symptoms outside of *M+*.

L3 is the likelihood that a highly probable (very common) disease *d* contributes significantly in the overall likelihood of a diagnosis *DI* containing *d*.

The values for calculating *L1, L2*, and *L3* are contained in tables mapping the likelihood of any disease causing a given symptom and the probability of any disease *d* actually occurring in the real world. For example, the table used in *L3* biases the problem towards the common diseases (perhaps the common cold) and away from obscure diseases like the bubonic plague. The effect of the fitness function is to favor diagnoses (*DI*) that explain all of the symptoms present (*L1*) without explaining extra symptoms (*L2*) and contain common diseases instead of rare (*L3*).

Since the search space is made up of possible diagnoses and these are already bit-strings, the set-up for the EPA is minimal. The fitness function, a function that builds evolutionary paths, and a reasonable stopping point are the only functions necessary to build the algorithm.

3.1 Reliability of EPA for MFD

To test the algorithm's reliability it was run against all of the possible symptom set combinations, which is 2^10 - 1 (1023), ten times. The reliability for each run was then computed by dividing the number of times the algorithm found the optimal solution by 1023. For example, if the algorithm found the optimal solution 788 times out of 1023, it would have 77% reliability for that run. Because EPA is a stochastic algorithm, it was run 10 times and the reliability for each of those 10 runs was averaged to determine its reliability.

For this test, the stopping condition was set to a maximum of 18,000 fitness evaluations per symptom set (M+). This number was chosen because it represents the maximum number of fitness evaluations Potter et al [8] allowed for the Genetic Algorithm to test reliability. The Genetic Algorithm represents the algorithm that is most similar to EPA out of those that Potter et al ran (Genetic Algorithm, Discrete PSO, Rain Drop Optimization, and Extremal Optimization). Because the optimal fitness values are known for this problem, the algorithm was stopped for each symptom set *(M+)* if the known best fitness was found before 18,000 fitness evaluations had been performed.The reliability statistics for other algorithms were provided by Potter et. al [8].

Table 1. Comparison of Reliabilities for MFD

EPA	GA	DPSO	EO
97%	85%	98%	100%

EPA's reliability is comparable to the DPSO's reliability for this problem and is far better than the GA's with a similar number of fitness comparisons. Extremal Optimization has a reported 100% reliability on this problem with a similar number of evaluations as allowed. It is likely that EPA's reliability is higher than the GA's with a similar number of fitness evaluations due to the fact that the GA has many redundant fitness evaluations as it nears convergence whereas the EPA continually builds evolutionary paths to random possible solutions so the likelihood of redundancy is extremely small.

3.2 EPA Efficiency for MFD

To test the efficiency of EPA on the MFD problem, the algorithm was run 10 times over all 1023 symptom sets. The stopping condition for these runs was the optimal solution *DI,* so the algorithm was forced to find the global optima for each symptom set. This experiment was done to replicate an earlier reliability experiment for several algorithms [8].

On average the EPA took 5971 fitness evaluations to find the optimal solution. Potter et. al. did not provide average fitness evaluations to find optimal solutions for the MFD for any of the algorithms compared for the MFD. However, 5971 fitness evaluations is considerably less than the maximum allowed by Potter et. al., because a GA with 300 individuals run for 60 generations allows for a maximum of 18,000 fitness evaluations per solution.

Figure 1. Optimization Curve of EPA for MFD

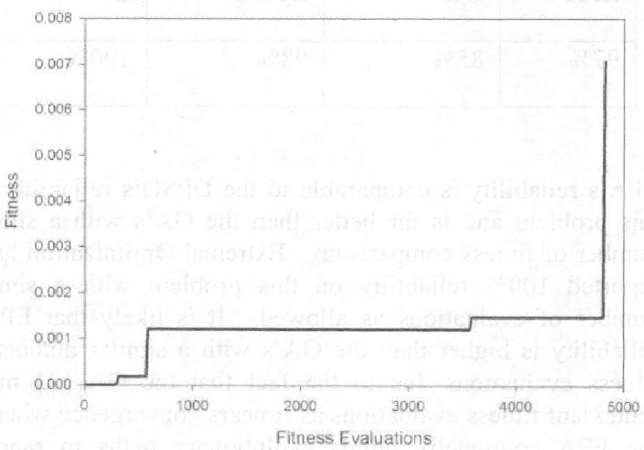

4 EPA With Integer Representation

4.1 Mobile Subscriber Equipment Problem

The mobile subscriber equipment problem (MSE) is a configuration problem in which the best mobile communications network must be assembled within the constraints of component connectivity, mission requirements, and U.S. Army doctrine. Although the networks being configured are now outdated, the MSE represents a classic configuration problem in which an expert's knowledge can be translated to a fitness function for optimization.

Army networks configured using MSE were in use in the early 1990s. A single network could support troops over a 15,000 square mile radius. At the heart of any MSE system was the Node Center. Each network could contain up to 42 Node Centers. There are six other modules that attach to this backbone to form the rest of the network. Both large and small extension nodes expanded the number of wire subscribers by big and small amounts respectively, with two types of small extension nodes offering different combinations of connectivity. Radio subscribers were supported by Remote Access Units, Control Centers were necessary for connectivity, NATO interface units allowed the system to be patched into NATO communications systems.

Using the fitness function laid out by Chang and Potter it is possible to optimize a network given the number of wire and radio subscribers [9]. However, the search space is very large due to the combinatorial explosion that is created. The minimum number of units allowed for most of the equipment is zero, with the exception of the Node Center and System Control Center. At least one of these is required for each network. The maximum number of allowed units ranges from the low end at four NATO Interfaces to 168 small extension nodes.

4.2 EPA Set-Up for MSE

Building an evolutionary path between two lists of integer values is almost as simple as building a path between two bit strings. Originally, a naïve scheme of iteratively setting the values of the random sample to those of the candidate solution, in the same way that the bits were switched in the binary example, was tried. This did not yield positive results. The second scheme worked in the following way:

While stopping criteria not met:

1. Select a Random Solution
2. While Path not Complete (Random and Candidate Equal):
    a. Find differences between the Random Solution and the Candidate Solution
    b. Select a differing component at random.
    c. Choose a random value between the Candidate solution's assignment for the differing component and the Random solution's assignment for differing component.
    d. Evaluate the new Random Solution: if this point has the highest fitness seen so far, save it as the Best solution.
3. Restart randomly if stagnation is detected.

An upper bound of 300,000 evaluations was used because early runs suggested that this represented the near upper bound for the number of evaluations the algorithm would take. However, the average number of evaluations needed to find the optimal answer was much lower than this. The fitness function needs a number of wired subscribers and a number of wireless subscribers to evaluate a candidate solution. The number of wired subscribers was set to 1,495 and the number of wireless subscribers was set to 672. This combination has an optimum fitness of 327.35689.

Random restarts were also introduced due to the observed possibility of stagnation. For these experiments, stagnation was assumed if the algorithm had not found the optimal answer by 125,000 fitness evaluations.

Obviously building paths between solutions with very different component values can get quite long. Below is a sample path built between two solutions with just a single component that differs in value.

Path Point 1 – a Candidate Solution and Random Solution Pairing with a Single Component that Differs.

Candidate Solution	100	14	**98**	0
Random Solution	100	14	**12**	0

Path Point 2 – Since the Third Component Differs, a random value between the Candidate's (98) and the Random's (12) value assignment is selected to replace the Random Solution's current value for the third component.

Candidate Solution	100	14	**98**	0
Random Solution	100	14	**72**	0

Path Point 3 – Random Solution's Third Component is Still not Equal to Candidate Solution's Third Component, so the process is repeated again.

Candidate Solution	100	14	**98**	0
Random Solution	100	14	**97**	0

Path Point 4 – The Two Solutions are Now Identical. If Any Point Along the Path Had a Higher Fitness Than The Candidate Solution, it Would Now Become the New Candidate Solution.

Candidate Solution	100	14	**98**	0
Random Solution	100	14	**98**	0

4.3 Reliability of EPA for MSE

To test the reliability of EPA, the algorithm was run 1,000 times. The stopping condition for these 1,000 runs was 300,000 evaluations or the optimal solution. This experiment replicated a previously published reliability experiment for several other popular optimization algorithms run on the same problem [8]. For this experiment reliability was calculated as the number of times the algorithm found the optimal solution, divided by the number of runs.

Table 2. Comparison of Algorithm Reliabilities for MSE

EPA	GA	DPSO	EO
99.3%	99.6%	99.85%	100%

The EPA found the optimal solution 993 times out of 1000, missing the optimal solution just 7 times. In each of these 7 times a random restart was initiated, and the second or third best solution was found. All of the algorithms had less than a 1% margin of difference in reliability for this problem. The real difference between the algorithms' performances was in efficiency.

4.4 EPA Efficiency for MSE

To test the efficiency of the EPA for MSE the algorithm was run 1,000 times with the optimal solution as the only stopping condition. This setup was used to force the algorithm to find an optimum even in a badly performing run.

The EPA took an average of 49,906.5 evaluations to find the optimum solution for this problem, with a minimum of 1,675. This is larger, but similar to the number of evaluations that the DPSO and GA took in reported results [8]. These are presented in the table below. There were no results for the number of fitness evaluations for EO.

Table 3. Average Fitness Evaluations to Find Optimum

EPA	GA	DPSO
49,906.5	12,000	31,500

The observed difference in efficiency for this problem is due to the observed possibility of spending a great deal of time on a good, but not globally optimum point. In later experiments, not presented here, random restarts were introduced when this situation was detected, which improved efficiency greatly for this problem. However, the basic algorithm remains less efficient than both GA and DPSO for this problem.

Figure 2. A Selected Optimization Curve for MSE

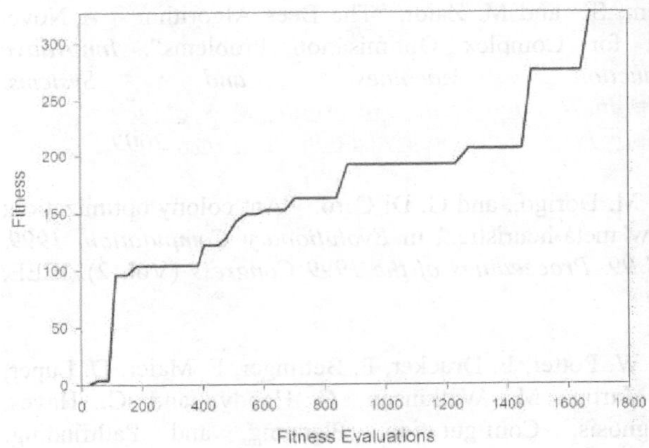

5 Conclusions

This paper has presented a new optimization algorithm designed particularly for discrete optimization. The Evolutionary Path Algorithm requires no tuning parameters, but still performs well in comparison to other well-known stochastic optimization algorithms. It is reliable and reasonably efficient. Although the algorithm may not be as efficient on real-valued optimization problems as competing algorithms, it is likely that small modifications could greatly improve this performance.

The algorithm finds good solutions without calculating any gradient information, using tuning parameters, or keeping a large population in memory. Because it continually samples the whole search space it is able to continue to search for and find good solutions long after other methods have converged. Future work should extend the path-building operators to include other representations and look for extensions of the algorithm that tailor it to specific optimization problems.

6 References

[1] F. Glover. "Tabu Search—part I." *ORSA Journal On Computing* , Issue 3, 190-206, 1997.

[2] S. Boettcher & A. G. Percus. " Extremal Optimization: Methods derived from co-evolution." *Modeling and Simulation Design.* AK Peters Ltd. 1999.

[3] S. Kirkpatrick, and M.C. Vecchi. "Optimization by simulated annealing." *Science,* 220 (4598), 671-680, 1983.

[4] J.H. Holland, *Adaptation in natural and artificial systems.* University of Michigan Press, Ann Arbor. 1975.

[5] Kennedy, J. and Eberhart, R.C. 1995. "Particle swarm optimization. " *Proc. IEEE International Conference on Neural Networks,* Picataway NJ: IEEE Service Center, 1942-1948. 1995.

[6] D. T. Pham, E. Ghanbarzadeh, A. Koc, E. Otri, S. Rahim, S. and M. Zaidi. "The Bees Algorithm – A Novel Tool for Complex Optimisation Problems". *Innovative Production Machines and Systems. DOI=http://conference.iproms.org/the_bees_algorithm_a_novel_tool_for_complex_optimisation_problems. 2009.*

[7] M. Dorigo,, and G. Di Caro. "Ant colony optimization: a new meta-heuristic." In *Evolutionary Computation, 1999. CEC 99. Proceedings of the 1999 Congress* (Vol. 2). IEEE. 1999.

[8] W. Potter, E. Drucker, P. Bettinger, F. Maier, D. Luper, M. Martin, M. Watkinson, G Handy, and C. Hayes. "Diagnosis, Configuration, Planning, and Pathfinding: Experiments in Nature-Inspired Optimization." *Natural Intelligence for Scheduling, Planning and Packing Problems,* R. Chiong, ed., Springer-Verlag. 1999.

[9] F.L. Chang and W. Potter. "A genetic algorithm approach to solving the battlefield communication network configuration problem." In *Yfantis, EA (ed) Intell Sys. Third Golden West Intern Conf* (Theory and Decision Library D, Vol 15). Kluwer,Dordrecht. 1995.

SESSION

GENETIC ALGORITHMS AND APPLICATIONS + GENETIC PROGRAMMING

Chair(s)

TBA

Genetic Programming using the Karva Gene Expression Language on Graphical Processing Units

A.V. Husselmann and K.A. Hawick
Computer Science, Massey University, North Shore 102-904, Auckland, New Zealand
email: {a.v.husselmann, k.a.hawick }@massey.ac.nz
Tel: +64 9 414 0800 Fax: +64 9 441 8181

Abstract— *Genetic Programming (GP) has been employed in many problem domains, and as a result, it has been the subject of much scientific inquiry. The extensive literature body of GP has reported applications in algorithm discovery, image enhancement and cooperative multi-agent systems, as well as many other areas and disciplines, such as agent-based modelling in Geography and Social Science. As models become more complex, further research toward higher efficiency have been warranted. We discuss solutions to large-scale systems which require automatic programming, and present results of a modified data-parallel implementation of GP based on Gene-expression Programming for Graphical Processing Units (GPUs), as well as a modified Santa Fe Ant Trail problem to measure the efficacy of this algorithm. We present results on algorithm convergence as well as timing performance on both GPU and CPU implementations.*

Keywords: karva language; CUDA; genetic programming; gpu; parallel; optimisation.

1. Introduction

Genetic Programming (GP) was the combinatorial optimiser specially adapted for evolving programs by way of natural selection and evolutionary processes [35]. It was the result of John Koza's paradigm altering work of 1995 [20], the same year that saw parametric optimisation take a great leap forward with the advent of the particle swarm optimiser, due to Kennedy and Eberhart [18]. Combinatorial optimisation had been a problem under careful research for many years, with classic problems such as the Traveling Salesman Problem [38], Prisoner's Dilemma [1] and the Knapsack problem[10]. Many of these problems are representative of real-world applications, and advancements in solutions to these are beneficial to finding effective solutions for other problems. GP has been applied to intrusion detection [5], soccer playing "softbots" [25], [24], models of land change in Mexico [27], team learning [26], algorithm discovery [2] and even image enhancement [36]. Cooperative multi-agent systems also benefit from the use of genetic programming [34], as well as classification for data mining [40].

Since the introduction of Genetic Programming in 1995, the canonical algorithm has been the subject of many enhancements and alterations, as is the case with related parametric optimisers [17], [15]. Some of these modifications include Linear GP [3] and Cartesian GP [30]. Some modifications are very extensive, such as more restrictive versions of GP [4] and also complete overhauls of the original representation of programs, such as that in Ferreira's Gene Expression Programming (GEP) [7]. Many of these modifications were intended to combat common problems in GP, which have precluded more extensive use. O'Neill et al describe these problems in detail [33]. The most prominent of which is code size; in which there exists a drift in the population towards larger and more redundant programs [37].

GP is a population-based optimiser, in which a set of programs are improved upon successively, by replacing it with a set of new programs, with genetic operators applied in a bid to drift away from bad solutions. A set of programs in this context is usually referred to as a generation. Each program represents a specific candidate solution to the problem at hand. Typically the most computationally expensive aspect of genetic algorithms in general, is the fitness evaluation of each of these candidate solutions. A fitness metric is necessary to guide the genetic operators in a way that is analogous to the concepts of natural selection and "survival of the fittest" in biology. The most common genetic operators considered are known as selection, mutation and crossover, where mutation perturbs a candidate solution in the search space, and crossover combines two candidate solutions to hopefully obtain a new single candidate with a slight improvement. Selection is simply a mechanism to obtain inputs for the crossover operator.

Gene Expression Programming (GEP) [7], [8] is one algorithm which departs from the traditional representation of programs in GP. It replaces the tree-based representation with a linear one, which still encodes an abstract syntax tree (AST). Perhaps the greatest advantage to GEP is its inherent support for introns: non-coding sections of the genotype. When the linear representation is interpreted to obtain the phenotype, certain introns may not make it into the tree. As well as being more representative of actual biological systems [30], this also brings a great simplification to mutation and crossover.

In this article we present a modified GP using the *k-expression* program representation from GEP, and accel-

Fig. 1: A 3D rendered version of the classic genetic programming test environment known as the Santa Fe Ant Trail. This visualisation[16] is a frame taken after random initialisation of the 256 agents. This representation casts light on the computationally expensive process of evaluating program individuals.

erate this using Graphical Processing Units (GPUs). Our rationale for using GPUs are two-fold: commodity pricing on GPUs is very favourable for the computing power that can be exerted on these platforms, and second, the inherent parallelism in population-based optimisers such as the GP allow not only parallel fitness evaluation, but also parallel selection, crossover and mutation. Most other data-parallel implementations of GP focus on accelerating fitness evaluations [21]. We make a calculated effort to accelerate the genetic operators in our implementation. Other GPU-based GPs include efforts in acceleration on GPU clusters [12] and different representations [22]. Interestingly, there have also been parallelisation research inspired by quantum computing, most notably the evolution of CUDA (Compute Unified Device Architecture) PTX programs by a quantum-inspired linear GP [6].

Our article is structured as follows: In Section 2 we present some background on GEP, its operators, and various specifics on the algorithm. We also introduce the Compute Unified Device Architecture (CUDA) and the idiosyncrasies of efficient data-parallel simulations designed for this. In Section 3 we describe our modifications to GP and also the method by which we measure the efficacy of this algorithm. Following this, we use Section 4 to present our results and then discuss these in Section 5, then finally we conclude and present some possible future work in Section 6.

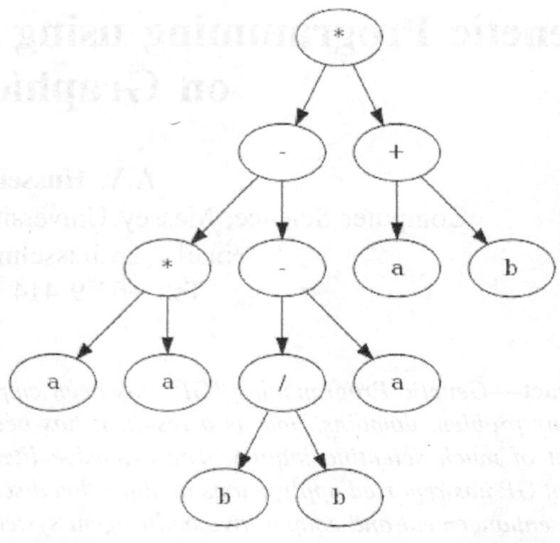

Fig. 2: Phenotypic AST built from genotype represented by the *karva*-expression *-+*-abaa/abbacda.

2. Gene Expression Programming

We provide some background to gene-expression programming (GEP) and mechanisms for implementing it. Perhaps the most advantageous feature of Gene Expression Programming (GEP) is its representation of candidate programs[8]. Ferreira [7] designed a language named *Karva*, and candidate programs are represented in the form of *karva*-expressions, or sometimes shortened to *k*-expressions. These expressions take the following form:

```
01234567890123456
*-+*-abaa/abbacda
```

The first line is simply used as an indexing convenience. The second line is the genotype of the candidate solution to a particular problem. The distinction between *genotype* and *phenotypes* in GP in general is simply the interpretation of a representation into an executable program. This is not always necessary, especially in Linear GP, where candidates are stored in the same form as they are executed (namely, sequences of instructions executed successively).

The symbols used in the *k*-expressions are either terminals or non-terminals; and in this case, the terminals are `a`, `b`, `c` and `d`. In this example, all the non-terminals are self-explanatory and of arity 2, except `Q`, which is the square root function, of arity 1. GEP has support for any set of function terminals of any arity, provided that the expression length is long enough to give each function its required arguments. This will be made clear in how the genotype is interpreted into a phenotype. This *k*-expressionis shown in its phenotypic form in Figure 2.

The tree is built by reading the *k*-expressionfrom left to right and filling the arguments of the non-terminals in the tree level by level. Upon careful inspection, it is noteworthy

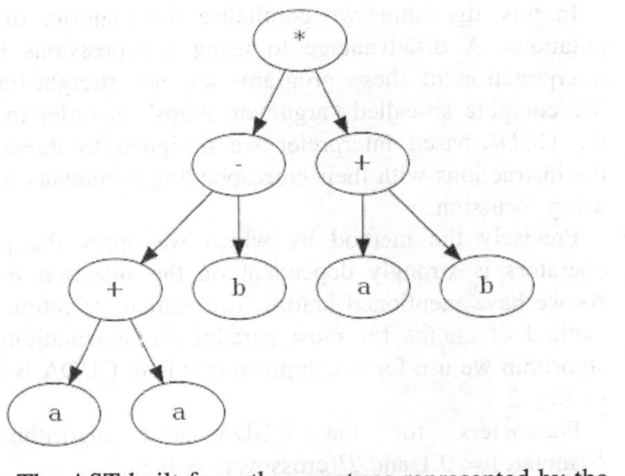

Fig. 3: The AST built from the genotype represented by the *karva*-expression *-++babaa/abbacda.

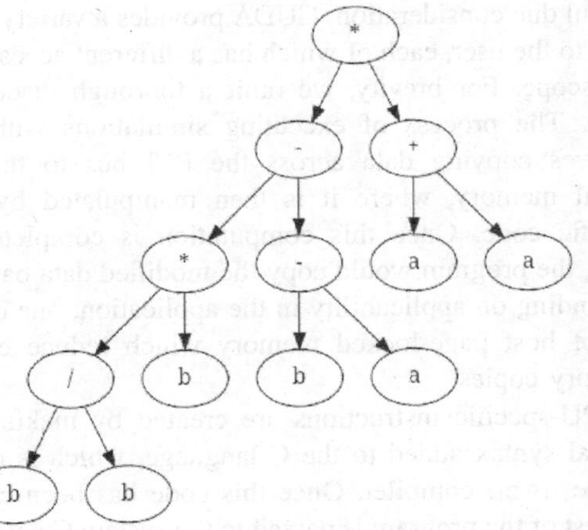

Fig. 4: The phenotypic AST built from the genotype represented by the *karva*-expression *-+*-aa/bbabbacda.

that the terminal `d` is an intron, and hence not in the phenotype. Ferreira proposes several genetic operators and leaves the selection of these to the user and their specific application.

For ease of reference, we provide here a brief overview of the mutation and crossover operators. Our selection operator is tournament selection; as it most closely aligns with our needs in data-parallel computation. Details on this is provided in Section 3.

Crossover of two *k*-expressions is simple. We elect to use a one-point recombination (for its simplicity), which involves selecting a crossover point at random, and then creating two new candidates from the recombination about that point. Consider the *k*-expressionshown in 2. If it were recombined with another expression at index 5, such as:

```
01234567890123456
*-++baa/bbabbacda
```

Then the results would be the following:

```
01234567890123456
*-++babaa/abbacda
*-+*-aa/bbabbacda
```

Which, when interpreted, are shown in Figs. 3 and 4.

Mutation of a *k*-expressionis simple. By using a uniform random number, a random symbol in the expression is chosen, and that symbol switched for another terminal or non-terminal.

The most popular method of selecting pairs of candidates to pass through the crossover operator is Roulette Selection[11]. Candidates are chosen at random throughout the population, but the probability of selecting each candidate is proportional to their fitness. This is usually accomplished by choosing a random number in $(0, 1)$ and mapping this to a hypothetical "roulette" wheel where the range of $(0, 1)$ is divided up in such a way that the probabilities of choosing each candidate are correct relatively.

The Roulette selection method does not parallelise extremely well. Most parallel GP algorithms make use of a selection method named "Tournament Selection"[29]. In this scheme, every candidate is compared against another uniform-randomly selected candidate, and the best candidate (by fitness) is chosen as one of a crossover pair. Once this process is complete, two candidates at a time are recombined and then the mutation operator is called.

Genetic Programming responds very well to parallelisation. We use NVidia's Compute Unified Device Architecture (CUDA) platform [32], [23] to accelerate our algorithm. The CUDA platform arose from a very effective arrangement of MIMD and SIMD processors, which were intended for processing large numbers of pixel data as fast as possible. General-Purpose Graphical Processing Units (GPGPU) has gained much interest since the advent of CUDA, particularly in light of the fact that using pixel and fragment shaders for simulation is an arcane and difficult affair. CUDA makes this process much more accessible and purpose-built[31].

The CUDA-enabled GPU consists of several Streaming Multi-processors (SMs) which have a certain number of "CUDA cores". These SMs process work units known as "blocks", which represent a 1D, 2D or 3D grid of threads. These blocks are sized by the user, and typically coincide with simulation-specific requirements. An SM computes a block until completion, and then, if available, carries on to the next block. During execution, threads are divided into groups of 16, known as "warps". Warps are the smallest unit of execution in CUDA. Warps are executed in a SIMD fashion on the CUDA cores on each SM (sometimes known as SIMT). The combination of all SMs are therefore MIMD.

CUDA-enabled GPUs have some idiosyncratic behaviour including memory access penalties and scoping among others. These can sometimes be problematic when not given careful due consideration. CUDA provides a variety of memories to the user, each of which has a different access penalty and scope. For brevity, we omit a thorough discussion of these. The process of executing simulations with CUDA involves copying data across the PCI bus to the GPU's global memory, where it is then manipulated by device-specific code. Once this computation is complete on the GPU, the program would copy the modified data back again. Depending on applicability in the application, one can make use of host page-locked memory which reduce expensive memory copies.

GPU-specific instructions are created by making use of special syntax added to the C language, which is compiled by the `nvcc` compiler. Once this code has been compiled, the rest of the program is passed to the system C compiler for normal compiling. This allows the CUDA device drivers to copy device specific instructions to the GPU for computing.

3. CUDA Implementation

Apart from our use of The *Karva* language for expressing candidate solutions, we also make special effort in order to accelerate the process by which a new generation is computed. It should be noted that sometimes the fitness function can greatly outweigh this computation.

It appears then that k-expressions are naturally well-suited to being used in CUDA. This is because they can be stored as sequences of (independent) characters or integers. Furthermore, crossover and mutation are almost trivially easy, bearing in mind the head and tail requirements. Our method for combining the traditional GP algorithm and GEP-style k-expressions is shown in Alg. 1.

Algorithm 1 The parallel implementation of GP on GEP k-expressions.

allocate & initialise space for n candidate programs

allocate space for random deviates
while termination criteria not met **do**
  call CURAND to fill the random number array with uniform deviates in the range [0,1)

  copy candidates and candidate bests to device
  CUDA: compute_argument_maps()
  CUDA: interpret/execute programs
  CUDA: update food locations/fitness
  copy back to host

  if end-of-generation then **then**
    CUDA: apply genetic operators to programs
    replace old programs with new ones
  end if
  visualise the result
end while

In this algorithm, we parallelise the majority of computations. A disadvantage to using k-expressions is that interpretation of these programs are not straight-forward. We compute so-called "argument maps" in order to allow the CUDA-based interpreter we designed to directly fill the instructions with their corresponding arguments without using recursion.

Precisely the method by which we apply the genetic operators is strongly dependent on the selection method. As we have mentioned before, Tournament selection is the method of choice for most parallel implementations. The algorithm we use for accomplishing this in CUDA is shown in Alg. 2.

Parameters for the CUDA-based algorithm are $P(\text{mutate}) = 0.1$ and $P(\text{crossover}) = 0.8$.

Algorithm 2 Parallel Tournament Selection

launch a CUDA kernel with $n/2$ threads
assign thread candidate $x/2+1$ and $x/2$
set a to random index
if candidate a beats candidate $x/2+1$ **then**
  replace candidate $x/2+1$ with a
end if

set b to random index
if candidate b beats candidate $x/2$ **then**
  replace candidate $x/2$ with b
end if

recombine candidates $x/2$ and $x/2+1$
mutate the two resultant candidates
save results over the original two candidates

To facilitate comparison, we have implemented a single-threaded CPU-based GP optimiser, with the exact same objective function, but computed in a serial fashion. Parameters are similar to the CUDA-based modified GP, with $P(\text{crossover}) = 0.8$ and $P(\text{mutation}) = 0.01$. The CPU-based GP makes use of the canonical tree-based representation with a depth restriction of 4. The same number of agents were used (1024). Tournament selection is also used, and initialisation/point mutation is done by the Full method. Crossover is implemented as a subtree swap. To avoid program bloat, we prune the trees following the genetic operators to a maximum depth of 4, where leaves are replaced by random terminal symbols.

4. Convergence & Performance Results

We present some convergence data showing how the various algorithmic implementations behave as well as some timing performance data for a GPU/CUDA implementation compared with a conventional serial CPU implementation.

Convergence results for the CUDA-based GP (based on k-expressions) as well as the CPU-based GP with canonical

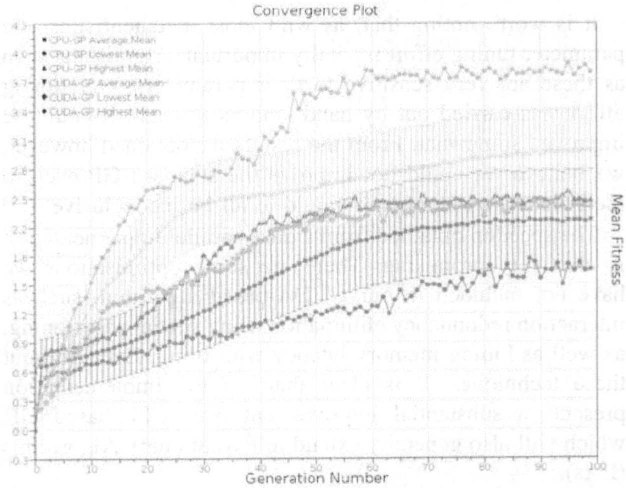

Fig. 5: Convergence results for the CUDA-based GP with k-expressions and the CPU-based GP with the canonical tree-based representation. The graph shows the average mean value of each generation, from 100 independent runs. The error bars represent the average standard deviation of the 100 runs in each generation. Lowest and highest population means are also shown.

	Frame Time (μ sec)	Gen. Time (μ sec)
CUDA-GP (k-exp)	1160 ± 40	423.2 ± 0.5
CPU-GP	48000 ± 8300	2600 ± 300

Table 1: Performance data for the CPU-based canonical GP and the k-expression GPU-based GP algorithm.

representation is shown in Fig. 5. The plot shows the average mean values of each generation for both algorithms. Each of these data points has been averaged across 100 independent runs. The error bars on the average mean line represents the average standard deviation of the population fitness across all 100 separate runs.

It is clear from this graph that the CUDA-based GP with k-expressions clearly outperform the standard GP. At around generation 20, the CUDA-GP seems to have a larger spread in the average mean. We believe that this may be indicative of a local minimum, analogous to the same phenomenon in parametric optimisation. It is interesting to note that, because of the difference in representation between the CUDA-GP and the standard GP, at generation 20, the standard GP shows the same increase in spread of mean, albeit, less pronounced.

The spread of the mean towards the end of the simulation is smaller for the standard GP than for the CUDA-GP. Although a smaller spread is much more desirable, the highest mean of the standard GP only barely surpasses the score of the lowest mean in the CUDA-based GP.

Performance data for each of these algorithms were also collected. These are shown in Tab. 1. We averaged the frame

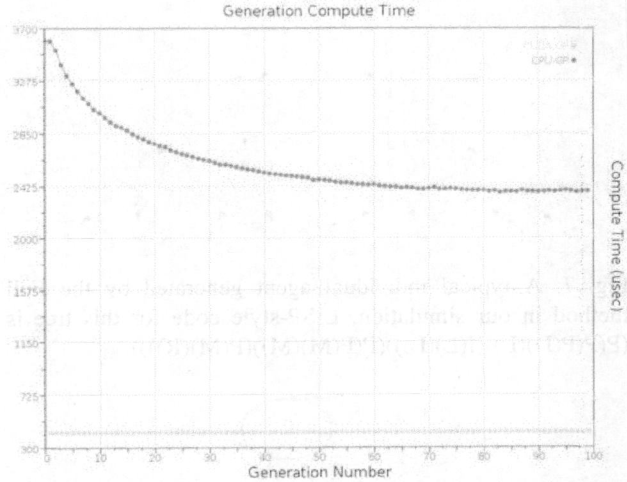

Fig. 6: Wall-clock performance of the CUDA and CPU-based algorithms by generation.

compute time across the 300 frames in each generation, and then across all 100 independent runs. The generation compute time represents the time it took the algorithms to compute a new population only. This was also averaged over the 100 separate runs. The data is of the form mean $\pm$ std. dev.

From this data, the CUDA-based algorithm achieves a speedup of 6 times over the CPU algorithm for computing new populations, and 41 times over the CPU algorithm for computing a single frame of the simulation.

Fig. 6 shows the time taken by each algorithm for computing a new population for fitness evaluation. This process is mostly just the genetic operators; selection, crossover and mutation. It is interesting to note that the compute time for the CPU-based standard GP is nonlinear, while the CUDA-based GP (with GEP-style k-expressions) is practically linear. This is not an artifact of the plot itself. The mean generation compute time for the CUDA algorithm has a standard deviation of just 40μ sec, whereas the CPU algorithm has a much larger 8300μ sec, even taking into account the fact that its frame time is 41 times larger.

We believe that this may be due to the initialisation method (Full) of the GP algorithm. Fig. 7 shows what form a typical initialised agent would take. This is in sharp contrast with Fig. 8 which depicts a much more effective solution. As can be seen from the initial program, they can potentially contain more `IfFoodAhead` functions, which are far more computationally expensive. This explains why initialised programs are often more expensive to evaluate, and hence increase the overall generation compute time for early generations.

From observation, it seems that highly effective programs generally take a certain form. An `IfFoodAhead` function

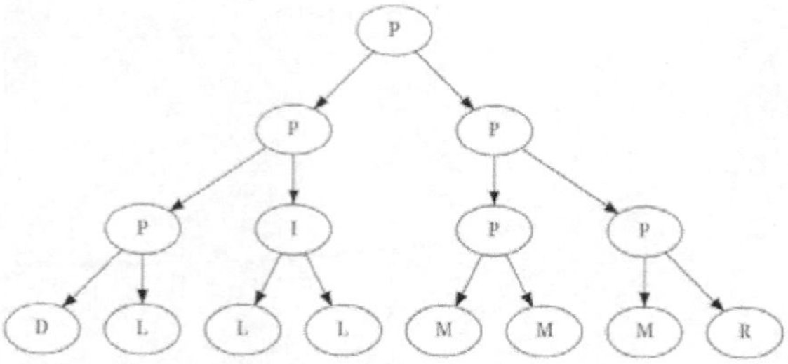

Fig. 7: A typical individual agent generated by the Full method in our simulation. LISP-style code for this tree is (P(P(P(D)(L))(I(L)(L)))(P(P(M)(M))(P(M)(R)))).

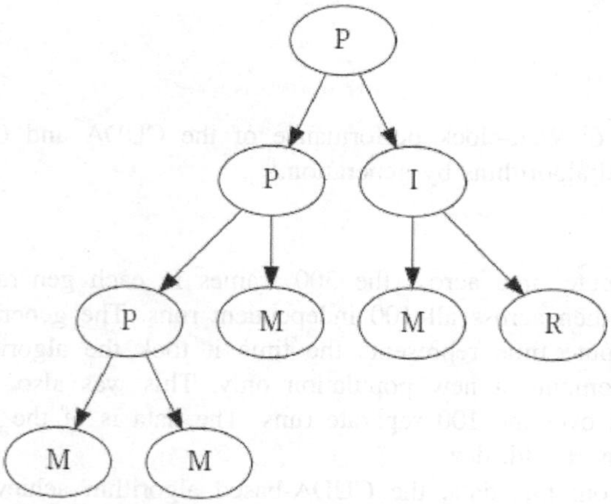

Fig. 8: A highly effective generated agent. The LISP-style code for this is (P(P(P(M)(M))(M))(I(M)(R))).

is used to cause movement in a direction other than straight, and the rest of the program is simply `Move` terminals. The reason why more `Move` terminals are beneficial is because it allows the agent to move faster, and hence potentially reach more food.

5. Discussion

By using the *Karva* language from within Ferreira's Gene Expression Programming algorithm, we believe we may have attained better convergence for a particular reason; crossover with k-expressions is a lossless matter. During mutation in the standard GP, code bloat occurs, which is generally remedied by using a pruning method, which forces trees to be of a certain maximum depth. This is accomplished by simply replacing functions with terminals which are just above the maximum depth. The trees are also pruned after crossover, since subtrees are chosen at random, and destination nodes are also chosen at random. In other words, one tree can be virtually appended to another, causing a program that is twice the size of the original. Every time pruning is applied, potentially valuable information is lost. By using k-expressions, we avoid this problem.

It is worth noting that, as with most metaheuristics, the parameter tuning effort is vitally important. Algorithms such as these are very sensitive to their parameters. Our tuning effort was carried out by hand, and as a result, it could be improved somewhat. From the results we obtained however, we believe we could not improve the standard GP even to the point where the result would at all be inconclusive.

The speedup obtained from a data-parallel implementation is also very promising. There are some optimisations we have not included in our CUDA-based algorithm, such as interaction redundancy elimination using spatial partitioning, as well as hiding memory latency with tiling. Even without these techniques, it is clear that a GPU implementation presents a substantial improvement over CPU-based GP, which will also generally extend to Evolutionary Algorithms (EAs).

The notion of evolving a grammar is a powerful one providing there is sufficient expressivity in the grammar itself to accommodate appropriate features. Programming grammars and formats such as Extended Backus-Naur Form (EBNF) and Backus Naur Form (BNF) and their various derivatives[39], [19] may offer some interesting possibilities if appropriate genetic operators can be applied to language evolution. Although there is work reported in the literature on parsers that learn a language based on examples[28] in (E)BNF the notion of evolving languages themselves based on such a representation does not yet seem to have been explored. Given the recent interest in the literature on domain-specific languages (DSLs) [9], [13], [14] and their use for reducing code complexity in a wide range of applications, there is scope for applying the techniques we have discussed to DSLs expressed in an appropriate grammar that can be subsequently evolved and investigated for fitness metrics such as compactness.

6. Conclusions and Future Work

We have presented a CUDA-based Genetic Programming algorithm using the *Karva* language from Gene Expression Programming for program representation. We have characterised and compared this algorithm against the canonical CPU-based Genetic Programming algorithm both with the same modified Santa Fe Ant Trail objective function. Our results suggest that using *Karva* provides a great benefit towards convergence aspects of the algorithm, as well as towards improving the wall-clock performance.

We have also discussed our method of selection, as well as crossover and mutation in the context of k-expressions. The resultant programs we obtained from both the CPU and CUDA-based were competitive with hand-tuned programs for the given restrictions. In our results, the best wall-clock performance was achieved by the CUDA-based algorithm, and we also discussed some irregularities in the CPU performance data for population computations.

There is scope for further work towards extending or improving Grammatical Evolution in a similar manner, especially taking into account its highly desirable attribute in making use of BNF grammars. We also belive it possible to develop tools that will support visualision of this sort of program space in a more appropriate fashion.

References

[1] Axelrod, R.: The emergence of cooperation among egoists. The American Political Science Review 75, 306–318 (1981)

[2] van Berkel, S.: Automatic Discovery of Distributed Algorithms for Large-Scale Systems. Master's thesis, Delft University of Technology (2012)

[3] Brameier, M.: On Linear Genetic Programming. Ph.D. thesis, University of Dortmund (2004)

[4] Castle, T., Johnson, C.G.: Evolving high-level imperative program trees with strongly formed genetic programming. In: Proceedings of the 15th European Conference on Genetic Programming, EuroGP. vol. 7244, pp. 1–12. Springer (April 2012)

[5] Crosbie, M., Spafford, E.H.: Applying genetic programming to intrusion detection. Tech. rep., Department of Computer Sciences, Purdue University, West Lafayette (1995), aAAI Technical Report FS-95-01

[6] Cupertino, L., Bentes, C.: Evolving cuda ptx programs by quantum inspired linear genetic programming. In: Proceedings of GECCO'11 (2011)

[7] Ferreira, C.: Gene expression programming: A new adaptive algorithm for solving problems. Complex Systems 13(2), 87–129 (2001)

[8] Ferreira, C.: Gene Expression Programming - Mathematical Modeling by an Artificial Intelligence. Springer, 2nd edn. (2006), iSBN 3540327976

[9] Fowler, M.: Domain-Specific Languages. No. ISBN 0-321-71294-3, Addison Wesley (2011)

[10] Garey, M.R., Johnson, D.S.: Computers and Intractability: A Guide to the Theory of NP-Completeness. W.H. Freeman (1979)

[11] Goldberg, D.E.: Genetic Algorithms in Search, Optimization and Machine Learning. Addison-Wesley (1989), iSBN 0201157675

[12] Harding, S.L., Banzhaf, W.: Distributed genetic programming on gpus using cuda, submitted to Genetic Programming and Evolvable Machines, 2009

[13] Hawick, K.A.: Engineering domain-specific languages for computational simulations of complex systems. In: Proc. Int. Conf. on Software Engineering and Applications (SEA2011). pp. 222–229. No. CSTN-123, IASTED, Dallas, USA (14-16 December 2011)

[14] Hawick, K.A.: Fluent interfaces and domain-specific languages for graph generation and network analysis calculations. In: Proc. Int. Conf. on Software Engineering (SE'13). IASTED, Innsbruck, Austria (11-13 February 2013)

[15] Husselmann, A.V., Hawick, K.A.: Levy flights for particle swarm optimisation algorithms on graphical processing units. Tech. rep., Computer Science, Massey University (2012), submitted to J. Parallel and Cloud Computing

[16] Husselmann, A.V., Hawick, K.: 3d vector-field data processing and visualisation on graphical processing units. In: Proc. Int. Conf. Signal and Image Processing (SIP 2012). pp. 92–98. No. CSTN-140, IASTED, Honolulu, USA (20-22 August 2012)

[17] Husselmann, A.V., Hawick, K.A.: Parallel parametric optimisation with firefly algorithms on graphical processing units. In: Proc. Int. Conf. on Genetic and Evolutionary Methods (GEM'12). pp. 77–83. No. CSTN-141, CSREA, Las Vegas, USA (16-19 July 2012)

[18] Kennedy, Eberhart: Particle swarm optimization. Proc. IEEE Int. Conf. on Neural Networks 4, 1942–1948 (1995)

[19] Knuth, D.E.: Backus normal form vs. Backus Naur form. Commun. ACM 7(12), 735–736 (Dec 1964), http://doi.acm.org/10.1145/355588.365140

[20] Koza, J.R.: Genetic programming as a means for programming computers by natural selection. Statistics and Computing 4(2), 87–112 (June 1994)

[21] Langdon, W.B.: A many-threaded cuda interpreter for genetic programming. In: Esparcia-Alcazar, A.I., Ekart, A., Silva, S., Dignum, S., Uyar, A.S. (eds.) Proceedings of the 13th European Conference on Genetic Programming, EuroGP. pp. 146–158. Springer (April 2010)

[22] Langdon, W.B., Banzhaf, W.: A simd interpreter for genetic programming on gpu graphics cards. In: O'Neill, M., Vanneschi, L., Esparcia, A., Gustafson, S. (eds.) Proceedings of the 11th European Conference on Genetic Programming, EuroGP (March 2008)

[23] Leist, A., Playne, D.P., Hawick, K.A.: Exploiting Graphical Processing Units for Data-Parallel Scientific Applications. Concurrency and Computation: Practice and Experience 21(18), 2400–2437 (25 December 2009), CSTN-065

[24] Luke, S.: Genetic programming produced competitive soccer softbot teams for robocup97. In: Koza, J.R., Banzhaf, W., Chellapilla, K., Kumar, D., Deb, K., Dorigo, M., Fogel, D., Garzon, M., Goldberg, D., Iba, H., Riolo, R. (eds.) Genetic Programming 1998: Proceedings of the 3rd annual conference. pp. 214–222. Morgan Kaufmann, San Mateo, California (1998)

[25] Luke, S., Hohn, C., Farris, J., Jackson, G., Hendler, J.: Co-evolving soccer softbot team coordination with genetic programming. Robocup-97: Robot soccer world cup I 1, 398–411 (1998)

[26] Luke, S., Spector, L.: Evolving teamwork and coordination with genetic programming. In: Proceedings of the First Annual Conference on Genetic Programming. pp. 150–156. MIT Press (1996)

[27] Manson, S.M.: Agent-based modeling and genetic programming for modeling land change in the southern yucatán peninsular region of mexico. Agriculture Ecosystems & Environment 111, 47–62 (2005)

[28] Mernik, M., Gerlic, G., Zumer, V., Bryant, B.R.: Can a parser be generated from examples? In: Proceedings of the 2003 ACM symposium on Applied computing. pp. 1063–1067. SAC '03, ACM, New York, NY, USA (2003), http://doi.acm.org/10.1145/952532.952740

[29] Miller, B.L., Miller, B.L., Goldberg, D.E., Goldberg, D.E.: Genetic algorithms, tournament selection, and the effects of noise. Complex Systems 9, 193–212 (1995)

[30] Miller, J.F., Smith, S.L.: Redundancy and computational efficiency in cartesian genetic programming. IEEE Transactions on Evolutionary Computation 10(2), 167–174 (2006)

[31] Nickolls, J., Buck, I., Garland, M., Skadron, K.: Scalable parallel programming with CUDA. ACM Queue 6(2), 40–53 (March/April 2008)

[32] NVIDIA® Corporation: NVIDIA CUDA C Programming Guide Version 4.1 (2011), http://www.nvidia.com/ (last accessed April 2012)

[33] O'Neill, M., Vanneschi, L., Gustafson, S., Banzhaf, W.: Open issues in genetic programming. Genetic Programming and Evolvable Machines 11, 339–363 (2010)

[34] Panait, Luke: Cooperative multi-agent learning: The state of the art. Autonomous Agents and Multi-Agent Systems 11, 387–434 (2005)

[35] Poli, R., Langdon, W., McPhee, N.: A field guide to genetic programming. lulu.com (2008), http://www.gp-field-guide.org.uk

[36] Poli, R., Cagnoni, S.: Genetic programming with user-driven selection: Experiments on the evolution of algorithms for image enhancement. In: Genetic Programming 1997: Proceedings of the 2nd Annual Conference. pp. 269–277. Morgan Kaufmann (1997)

[37] Soule, T., Foster, J.A.: Code size and depth flows in genetic programming. In: Koza, J., Deb, K., , Dorigo, M., Fogel, D., Garzon, M., Iba, H. (eds.) Proceedings of the 2nd Annual Conference on Genetic Programming. pp. 313–320. MIT Press (1997)

[38] Wilson, G.V., Pawley, G.S.: On the stability of the travelling salesman problem algorithm of Hopfield and Tank. Biol. Cybern. 58, 63–70 (1988)

[39] Wirth, N.: What can we do about the unnecessary diversity of notation for syntatic definitions. Communications of the ACM 20(11), 822–823 (November 1977)

[40] Zhou, C., Xiao, W., Tirpak, T.M., Nelson, P.C.: Evolving accurate and compact classification rules with gene expression programming. IEEE Transactions on Evolutionary Computation 7, 519–531 (December 2003)

A Genetic-Based Nurse Rostering Tool: A Riyadh Hospital Case

Manar Hosny[1] , **Najla Al Turiki** [1]
[1]College of Computer and Information Sciences, King Saud University, Riyadh, Saudi Arabia
mifawzi@ksu.edu.sa, najla_m_t@yahoo.com
P.O.Box 57395 Riyadh 11574
GEM'13 Conference

Abstract—*Recently, many healthcare institutions became interested in automating the process of personnel scheduling. Nurse Rostering is a difficult scheduling problem, which is defined as generating rosters by assigning working shifts to a number of nurses over a certain planning period, such that a predefined set of constraints is satisfied. There is a high demand to automate this process, since many healthcare institutions still make nurse rosters manually. In this research we design a scheduling tool that is based on a Genetic Algorithm (GA) approach to solve the nurse rostering problem for the surgical unit in a Riyadh hospital. Our GA-based tool will automatically create a schedule while taking into account a number of difficult constraints. Some constraints are specified by the hospital, and mainly relate to maximizing the coverage of shifts and adhering to workload requirements and certain shift succession patterns. Other constraints relate to preferences of the nurses regarding their annual leave and weekly days off. The main contribution of this research is in proposing new GA solution representation and problem specific operators that are specially designed to handle the difficult problem constraints and satisfy the requirements of the hospital. The automatically generated schedule will save time and reduce the planner workload.*

Keywords: Nurse Rostering, Scheduling, Heuristics, Metaheuristics, Genetic Algorithms, Combinatorial Optimization

1. Introduction

The Nurse Rostering Problem (NRP) is a personnel scheduling problem that became essential for modern hospitals and medical institutions. Currently, many hospitals make nurse rosters manually. The process of building efficient and balanced rosters is time consuming and needs a lot of experience. Therefore, there is a high demand for automated nurse rostering tools. The automation of this task will minimize the time and effort needed to create high quality and flexible schedules. High quality rosters produced automatically will overcome the problems resulting from poor rostering, such as career leakage due to fatigue and stress from overwork.

The NRP is complex and difficult to solve. It belongs to the category of NP-Hard problems [1], where a set of difficult rules and constraints need to be simultaneously satisfied. The NRP is defined as generating rosters by assigning the required shifts to nurses over a certain planning period (typically one month or one week), such that some predefined rules and constraints are satisfied [1]. In the schedule, each day consists of a number of shifts, for example: a day shift, a night shift and a late shift. Each shift must be assigned to sufficient nurses to cover the demand of the ward or the hospital.

There are many constraints that make this problem challenging. Usually, work regulations, hospital rules and preferences of nurses define the constraints of the problem. Secondly, there is a specified number of hours a nurse can work in a week, which should not be exceeded. Also, some nurses are not qualified to work in certain shifts. In general, the constraints are classified into two types: *hard constraints* and *soft constraints*.

Hard constraints are the constraints that must be satisfied at all times in order to create a feasible solution. A solution in which all hard constraints are satisfied is called a *feasible solution*. Hard constraints are usually defined by law and hospital requirements. For example, the minimum and maximum number of hours that should be worked by a nurse, and assigning certain shifts to qualified nurses, to achieve the desired level of care quality [2][3].

Soft constraints are not mandatory but violations of these constraints need to be avoided as much as possible. The quality of a generated roster is determined by the degree of violation of soft constraints. Common soft constraints are those related to nurses' requests for days off on particular days of the week, and balancing the work load efficiently among the available nurses. Some of the common problem constraints are listed below [3]:

1) Coverage: defines the required number of nurses to work on each shift type per day.
2) Max (Min) Hours: defines the maximum (minimum) number of hours a nurse must work over a period of time.
3) Personal Preference: defines the nurses' requests for day and night shifts or off days.
4) Succession: defines the legal and illegal successions of shifts, for example a night shift cannot be followed by a day shift.

Many techniques were introduced in the literature to solve the NRP. For example, operational research optimization methods have been used including: goal programming [4], column generation [5], and Lagrangian heuristic [6]. In addition, many Meta-heuristic based methods that are used for combinatorial optimizations are also applied for nurse scheduling problems such as tabu search, simulated annealing, variable neighborhood search and genetic algorithms.

In this research we propose a GA approach to solve the NRP. Although the general framework of GAs is standard, there is a great potential for innovation when applying GAs to a difficult problem like nurse rostering. In addition, most papers in the literature focused on developing new algorithms for solving the problem, rather than building a system for the practical use of a certain healthcare institution.

This research is based on an MSc graduation project in the College of Computer and Information Sciences at King Saud University, Riyadh, Saudi Arabia. A user-friendly GA-based system was designed in order to automatically generate nurse schedules for the surgical department in a famous hospital called "Riyadh Care" (denoted hereafter by RC) hospital. The main objective of the research is to automatically create an efficient nurses' schedule that takes into account a number of difficult constraints. The generated schedule should fulfill the needs of the hospital by maximizing the coverage of shifts, and adhering with the workload requirements and the personal preferences of nurses. In this paper we provide the early results of theoretical experimentation with the designed tool before actual hospital implementation, and try to highlight both the promising outcomes of the research as well as areas of possible future improvement.

The rest of this paper is organized as follows: Section 2 gives a brief overview of some solution methods from the literature to the NRP. Section 3 defines the NRP handled in this research, as described by the RC hospital in Riyadh. Section 4 describes in detail the proposed GA solution, including the representation, the initial population, the fitness function and the crossover and mutation operators. Section 5 shows the experimental results obtained by testing the proposed approach. Section 6 summarizes the results and proposes some future improvements. Finally Sect. 7 concludes this paper with a brief summary.

2. Related Work

The nurse rostering problem requires a robust and efficient algorithm that can effectively handle the difficult problem constraints. Heuristics are the most common methods that have been applied to the nurse rostering problem. One popular group of heuristics is population based heuristics like genetic algorithms. In this section we will give examples of two of the most commonly used heuristic methods in the literature to tackle the NRP: Variable Neighborhood Search (VNS), and Genetic Algorithms (GAs).

2.1 Variable Neighborhood Search (VNS)

[7] presented a VNS approach for the nurse rostering problem. In this approach, a wide variety of constraints are considered. The presented approach allows accessing the hidden parts of the search space by applying suitable problem specific neighborhoods. Shortsighted neighborhoods and very greedy ones are combined to achieve better exploration of the search space. The design of a cost function of the nurse rostering model is simply assigning a cost parameter set by the user to each constraint. Each violation of constraints is then penalized. The cost of the entire schedule is calculated as the summation of penalties associated to each personnel schedule. The neighborhood structures of their VNS method are of four types, inspired from the manual scheduling process: single-shift day, soft constraints related neighborhoods, swapping large sections of personnel schedules, and shaking the solution. Experimental results have shown that it will be useful to apply local search in the neighbors of the roster until a local optimum is reached, then the search expands to wider area.

[8] presented an approach that hybridizes heuristic ordering with variable neighborhood search. They have shown how combining the repeated use of heuristic ordering and backtracking will extend the search and improve the solution quality. They also presented an analysis and discussion about the allowed computational time and the significant role it plays. They have compared the proposed VNS algorithm with a genetic algorithm on commercial data. The results have shown that the VNS algorithm outperform the genetic algorithm.

2.2 Genetic Algorithms

[9] defined the problem of nurse rostering as assigning shifts to qualified personnel using a given timetable under some hard and soft constraints. They presented a method based on genetic algorithms to solve nurse scheduling in Fatih Sultan Mehemet Hospital. The standard GA is used, and the fitness value is obtained for each individual in the population by calculating the summation of its penalty scores. Each hard and soft constraint is associated with a weight value. The success ratio of finding a good solution increases by the use of a hill climbing operator. They used two techniques for handling the constraints: repair technique, and normalization of fitness values and parameter settings. Experimental results have shown that normalizing penalty scores and the repair of violations and adaptive weights of constraints will increase the quality of generated schedules.

[10] presented a research for designing and developing a system for nurse schedules to be used in public hospitals. They defined the nurse rostering problem as the problem that occurs when one or more nurses cannot work on shifts that were scheduled for them. This means that the current roster must be rebuilt if there are no reserve nurses available to cover these shifts. The paper applied constructive heuristics

with different versions of genetic algorithms to solve the problem of nurse rostering. In the presented GA approach, the individual is represented as a pair of chromosomes, and each chromosome is represented as permutation, one for nurses and one for tasks. The presented versions of GAs differ in the encoding of permutations and the implementation of genetic operators. The approaches were tested using real data form Lisbon Hospital and produced good quality solutions within time limits specified by the hospital.

A genetic algorithm approach for the NRP is introduced by [11] which is based on an indirect encoding of solutions. The objective of their study is not to guarantee finding feasible solutions, but they focus on using the problem constraints in an active way to minimize the need for penalty functions. Their problem definition is based mainly on two constraints. First, the nurses of higher grades can replace nurses of lower grades. Second, most of nurse contracts involve special day-night structure in which the nurse can work either day shifts or night shifts in a week but not both. The crossover operator used is order-based crossover. In addition, there are three decoders presented for their indirect encoding. Experimental results have shown that the indirect GA approach is more flexible than Tabu Search.

3. NRP for the Riyadh Care Hospital

Our system was designed based on real-world data of the surgical unit in the Riyadh Care (RC) hospital, where currently nurse rosters are made manually. The aim is to generate weekly schedules for the surgical department in the hospital for a predetermined number of nurses. The day's schedule consists of two types of shifts: *day* (from 7:00 am to 7:00 pm) and *night* (from 7:00 pm to 7:00 am). There are two main types of nurses: *head nurse* and *staff nurse*. The regular nurse can have three days off in a week while the head nurse can have only one day off.

For a feasible schedule, qualified nurses are assigned to cover the required shifts, such that each nurse is only assigned one shift per day. Some of the nurses are assigned to a predetermined number of on-call shifts according to the hospital demand. In addition to the coverage constraint, there is a number of constraints that make this problem challenging: (1) a night shift cannot be followed by a day shift; (2) the nurse should take a day off after working on two consecutive day shifts; (3) when a nurse is assigned a night shift followed by a day off, the following shift (after the day off) should not be a day shift. This is intended to give the nurse a chance to adjust her sleeping pattern after working a night shift, before assigning a day shift to her; and (4) the nurse can request certain days off according to her preference. A sample roster for two staff nurses for a week starting at Saturday and ending at Friday is shown in Table 1.

Symbols used in formulating the problem are:

Table 1: Sample Roster

	Sat	Sun	Mon	Tue	Wed	Thu	Fri
SN1	D	D	/	N	N	*	/
SN2	N	/	N	N	N	#	/

- SN: Staff Nurse
- D: Day Shift
- N: Night Shift
- /: Day Off
- ∗: Day On-Call
- #: Night On-Call
- PL_j: Preference list of off days requested by nurse j

The constraints of the problem can be summarized as follows, in order of importance as expressed by the schedule planner of the hospital:

1) Number of night and day shifts in a day ($d_i, i = 1, 2, ...7$) of a weekly schedule should differ by at most one:
$C_1 : |\sum_{d_i} D - \sum_{d_i} N| <= 1, \forall_{i=1,2,...7}$
2) A nurse working in a night shift of some day should not work in a day shift the day after:
$C_2 : N \rightarrow N$ or $N \rightarrow O$, where $O \in \{/, *, \#\}$
3) After working two consecutive day shifts, the nurse should take a day off:
$C_3 : D \rightarrow D \rightarrow O$, where $O \in \{/, *, \#\}$
4) An off day preceded by a night shift should be followed by a night shift or another off day:
$C_4 : N \rightarrow O \rightarrow N$ or $N \rightarrow O \rightarrow O$, where $O \in \{/, *, \#\}$
5) Days off should meet the preference of each nurse:
$C_5 : O_j \in PL_j$, where $O_j \in \{/, *, \#\}$

In our approach, we assume that all constraints are soft constraints. However, the constraints are assigned different weights according to the importance of each constraint as indicated by the listing order above.

4. Proposed GA Solution

In our GA approach to solve the NRP, we propose a new problem specific heuristic to initialize the population. We also introduce problem specific crossover and mutation operators which are basically dependent on the rules and constraints of the RC hospital. The solutions generated are evaluated by a fitness function that assigns weighs to the given constraints and penalizes the violations of each constraint.

The solution is represented as a 2-D array which represents a schedule of one week. The scheduling process starts by generating the initial population as described in Sect. 4.2. Then each individual in the population is evaluated and assigned a fitness value by the fitness function which is defined in Sect. 4.3. Individuals with high fitness values are selected to be recombined and mutated to generate new offspring (details of crossover and mutation operators are given in Sections 4.4 and 4.5 respectively). Bad individuals with low fitness values are eliminated from the new population and replaced with the newly generated offspring. The rest of the individuals will survive to the next generation. Then the process is repeated from the fitness evaluation phase for each generation until a high quality schedule is found or a specified number of generations is reached.

4.1 Representation

The individual in the population represents a one week schedule for the department with a given number of nurses. The individual is represented as a 2-D array where one dimension denotes the nurses, and the other dimension denotes the shifts assigned to nurses on every day of the week. A sample individual representation for four nurses is shown in Table 2, where D denotes a day shift, N denotes a night shift and / denotes a day off [1].

Table 2: Solution Representation

Nurses \ Week Days							
	D	N	/	D	/	/	N
	D	/	N	/	D	N	/
	N	D	/	/	D	/	D
	D	/	D	N	/	D	/

4.2 Initial Population

The initial population is created using a heuristic that will try to satisfy some of the problem constraints in the initially generated schedules. First, to calculate the total number of shifts per week, we multiply the total number of nurses in the surgical unit with 7 days (shifts), since each nurse can be assigned a maximum of one shift per day:
$TotalShifts = TotalNurses \times 7$
To compute the required number of day and night shifts in a week according to the coverage constraint of the hospital, we will first assign the Annual Leave (AL) days of nurses, if any, in the week to be scheduled. After assigning the AL days for nurses, the off days are assigned randomly to each nurse in the initial schedule, where the staff nurse will be assigned three days off and the head nurse will have one day off. Then, to calculate the remaining number of shifts we subtract the assigned AL days and off days from the total number of shifts:
$RemainingShifts = TotalShifts - (TotalAL + TotalOff)$
Then we can calculate the number of night shifts ($TotalN$) as 1/3 of the remaning (required) number of shifts:
$TotalN = \lceil (RemainingShifts/3) \rceil$
Finally, the number of day shifts ($TotalD$) is calculated as:
$TotalD = RemainingShifts - TotalN$
Following this, $TotalD$ (number of day shifts) and $TotalN$ (number of night shifts) are assigned randomly to nurses in the initial schedule. Note that in the initial solution, more day shifts are assigned than night shifts in the weekly schedule (night shifts are 1/3 and day shifts are 2/3 of the total number of shifts). This was suggested to try to achieve the desired balance between the number of day and night shifts during the evolutionary process, since the mutation operator, which will be described in Sect. 4.5, mainly converts violating day shifts into night shifts to try to repair constraints violation in the solution. The initial population of schedules is created using the initial schedule algorithm described above.

[1] In our representation we assume that a day off represents on-call days as well, since the planner can easily change selected days off to on-call days according to the need of the department.

4.3 Fitness Function

The fitness function assigns a fitness value to each individual in the population to measures its quality. The quality of the schedule in our approach depends on the number of constraints violations found in the schedule. We penalize the violations by assigning a weight value to each constraint. The weight value represents the significance of the constraint. So, the coverage constraint C_1 is assigned higher weight values than the other constraints.

Constraint C_1 is checked by subtracting the number of day and night shifts in each day (d_i) of the schedule as shown in (1).

$$V_1 = \sum_{i=1}^{7} |\sum_{d_i} D - \sum_{d_i} N| \tag{1}$$

The number of violations of C_2, C_3, C_4 and C_5 are calculated for each nurse. The weight associated with each constraint C_k is then multiplied by the corresponding number of violations V_k. The summation of the results of this operation for all constraints gives the fitness value of the nurse's schedule as shown in (2), where $F(N_j)$ is the fitness of the schedule of nurse j in the evaluated schedule.

$$F(N_j) = \sum_{k=2}^{5} W_k * V_k \tag{2}$$

Summing fitness values of all nurses' schedules, and the fitness of the whole schedule in terms of the difference in the number of day and night shifts gives the fitness of the entire schedule as shown in (3), where $F(S)$ is the fitness function of the schedule and n is the number of nurses.

$$F(S) = W_1 * V_1 + \sum_{j=1}^{n} F(N_j) \tag{3}$$

It is important to mention that when evaluating a schedule we assume that the schedule of the previous week is already present and is used by the fitness function to check constraint violations between the last day of the previous schedule and the first day of the current schedule.

4.4 Crossover Operator

High quality schedules are selected for recombination by crossover. The crossover operator proposed in our GA approach is a problem specific operator that helps to improve solutions with respect to one constraint of our problem. This constraint is C_5, the preferences of each nurse for off days. Two parent solutions are recombined by swapping a specified number of nurses[2] from one solution with the same number of nurses of the other solution. The number of nurses swapped between the two parents is according to a given probability, such that a maximum of half the number of nurses in a given solution can be swapped. The swapping of nurses is performed under one condition which is as follows:

If group1 contains nurses selected randomly from parent1 and group2 contains nurses selected from parent2, then the total numbers of day and night shifts in each day of group2 must be equal to the total numbers of day and night shifts in each day of group1.

This condition will try to maintain the feasibility with respect to the coverage constraint C1 as much as possible. An example of the crossover operator is shown in Figure 1.

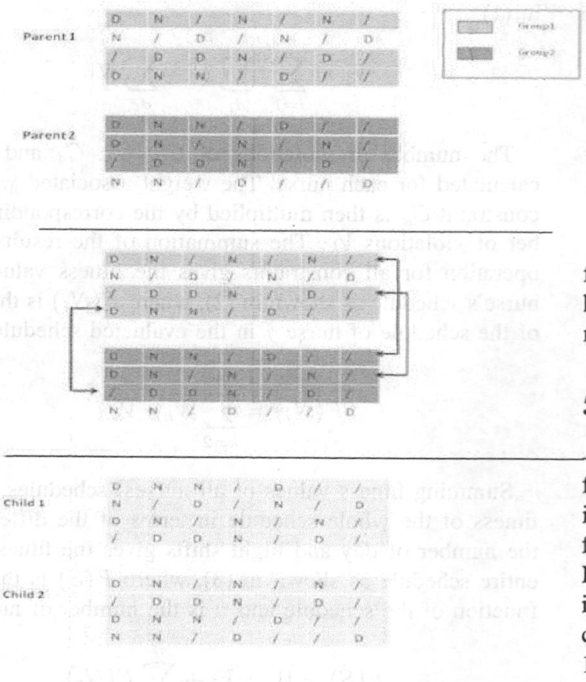

Fig. 1: Crossover Operator

[2]For simplicity hereafter we use the term "nurse" to refer to a "nurse schedule", i.e., the crossover operator swaps the "schedules" of two nurses, one nurse selected from each parent

4.5 Mutation

After applying crossover, the generated offspring can be mutated under a given mutation probability. The mutation operator proposed in our approach is a repair mutation. It repairs the violations of the constraints C_2, C_3 and C_4 found in the schedule. In the mutation operator, some nurses' schedules will be selected for repair according to a certain probability. The mutation operator will repair the selected nurses' schedules by correcting the violations as it moves through the schedule of each nurse from left to right. The mutation operator will proceed in two passes:

- **Pass 1:** moving through the schedule of the nurse from left to right, the mutation will correct the violation of constraint C_3, which happens when two consecutive day shifts are followed by a third day shift or night shift. This violation can be repaired by swapping the third day/night shift with a day off found anywhere in the schedule of that nurse:
  $D \rightarrow D \rightarrow N$ OR $D \rightarrow D \rightarrow D \Longrightarrow D \rightarrow D \rightarrow O$
- **Pass 2:** moving through the schedule of the nurse from left to right for the second time, the mutation will try to correct the following two violations at the same pass:
  - Constraint C_2 (a night shift followed by day shift): This violation can be repaired by changing the day shift to night shift:
    $N \rightarrow D \Longrightarrow N \rightarrow N$
  - Constraint C_4 (a night shift followed by an off day and the latest is followed by a day shift). This violation is repaired by changing the day shift to night shift, as shown below:
    $N \rightarrow O \rightarrow D \Longrightarrow N \rightarrow O \rightarrow N$

It is important to stress that fixing the schedule is done forward from left to right in order not to disturb what has been previously fixed in the schedule. An example of mutating an individual is shown in Figure 2.

5. Experimental Results

To measure the performance of the proposed GA approach for the nurse rostering problem, we performed several experiments with different test cases. All experiments were performed with Intel (R) 2 Duo (2.53GHz) processor, 4.00 GB RAM, 32-bit Windows 7 Operating system. The experiments include 10 test cases with 10 runs for each case. The test cases are different with respect to the number of nurses (from 10 to 100). The preferences of each nurse for the days off are created randomly in each test case. Initially we performed tuning of GA parameters following the method suggested by [12], which presented three main measures to evaluate the performance of Genetic Algorithms. According to [12], these measures are proved to evaluate GAs in terms of solution quality regardless of convergence. The measures include: *likelihood of optimality*, *average fitness value* and *likelihood*

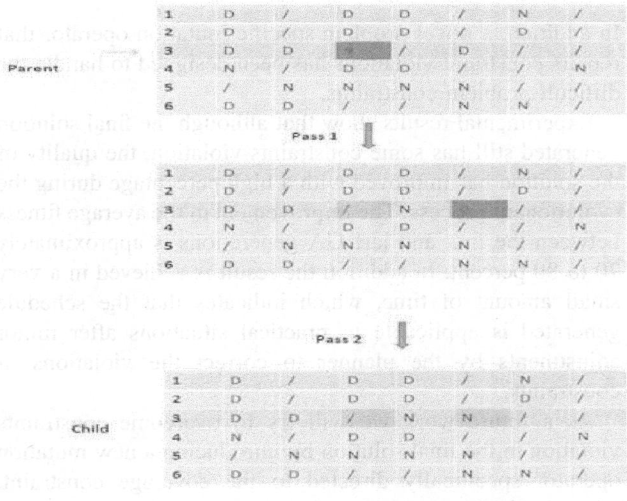

Fig. 2: Mutation Operator

of evolution leap. After tuning, the following values were used for GA parameters:

- Population Size = 50
- Number of Generations = 50
- Crossover Probability = 0.2
- Mutation Probability = 0.8

In addition, the selection method used was *Tournament Selection* and the termination condition was reaching a maximum pre-specified number of generations.

Regarding the weights of the constraints violations in the fitness function. The following values were selected empirically: $W1 = 0.5$, $W2 = W3 = 0.24$, and $W4 = W5 = 0.01$.

Figure 3 shows the experimental results of our GA in terms of the average fitness values of both the first generation and the last generation over the 10 runs. As can be seen in Figure 3, the solution is improved with a high percentage during the evolutionary process. The improvement in the average fitness is approximately between 70 to 80 percent for the 10 test cases.

Table 3 shows the average number of constraints violations (over the 10 runs) in the last generation of each test case. It can be observed from this table that the resulting average number of violations for the most important constraint C1 is always less than 5.0 violations. This is considered a good achievement for the GA given the difficulty of the problem and the conflicting nature of the constraints. For example, the planner who is responsible for putting the schedule of 100 nurses (the last test case) will only need to adjust on average 2-4 violations for the constraints C1, C2, and C3 in the resulting schedule. The less important constraint C4 on the other hand has a reasonable number of violations for the small test cases, but is more difficult to satisfy for the largest two test cases as indicated by the

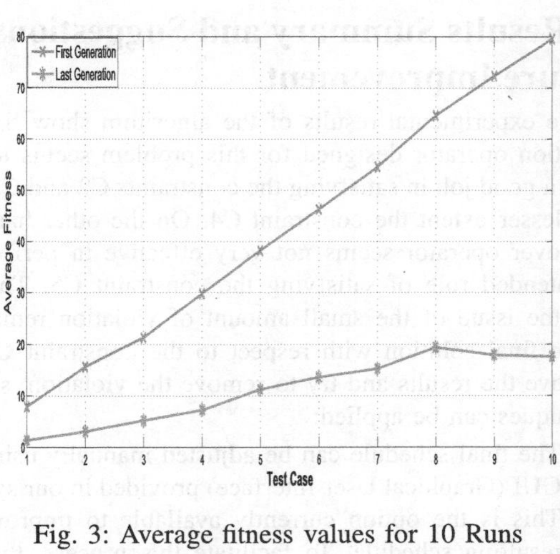

Fig. 3: Average fitness values for 10 Runs

results in the table.

Table 3: Average number of constraints violations

Num Nurses	C1	C2	C3	C4
10	0.5	1.7	0.5	0.9
20	1.5	1.4	2.0	2.5
30	2.3	3.1	1.5	1.9
40	3.0	3.9	2.8	3.4
50	3.5	5.7	4.1	6.0
60	3.8	3.3	3.2	5.0
70	4.6	7.6	5.0	6.9
80	4.4	9.3	5.4	6.2
90	3.8	2.3	1.8	16.2
100	4.1	2.0	1.9	16.6

Regarding the constraint C5, which is the preferences of the nurses for the days off. The algorithm was able to satisfy on average between 2-3 preferences only. This indicates that the algorithm was not very successful in satisfying the preferences of the nurses in terms of the days off. The reason is obviously the small weight assigned to this constraint in the objective function. Another reason is the restricting condition in the crossover operator that requires swapping only nurses that have the same number of day and night shifts in each day of the week . This condition seems seldom satisfied, which renders the crossover operator almost useless.

On the other hand, the average execution time is quite fast. It ranged from 5.7 seconds for the smallest test case to 46.4 seconds for the largest test case. This is indeed a lot of time and effort saving compared to the manual planning process needed to prepare a weekly schedule for 100 nurses.

6. Results Summary and Suggestions for Future Improvement

The experimental results of the algorithm show that the mutation operator designed for this problem seems to perform a good job in satisfying the constraints C2 and C3, and to a lesser extent the constraint C4. On the other hand the crossover operator seems not very effective in performing its intended role of satisfying the constraint C5. There is also the issue of the small amount of violation remaining in the final solution with respect to the constraint C1. To improve the results and try to remove the violation, several techniques can be applied:

- The final schedule can be adjusted manually using the GUI (Graphical User Interface) provided in our system. This is the option currently available to improve the resulting schedule. To facilitate this process, the tool can be modified to highlight locations of violation so that the planner can easily spot them and manually correct infeasibility.
- A new mutation operator can be added which is specifically designed to repair the violation of the constraint C1.
- The final best solution obtained by the GA can undergo another optimization process using a simple technique like hill climbing or simulated annealing. In this process, some small changes may be applied to day and night shifts, depending on which number is higher. The new schedule is then evaluated in each iteration in order to decide whether it can replace the old schedule or not. In our opinion this seems to be the most promising approach to correct the violation in constraint C1.

Regarding the constraint C5 which is related to satisfying the preferences of nurses in the selected days off, it appears that this constraint should be removed from the fitness function, since it is difficult to satisfy simultaneously with the other more important constraints of the problem. A better approach could be to try to improve the last obtained schedule by replacing some days off with days off belonging the nurse's preference list, provided that this change does not violate the other problem constraints. We expect a significant improvement in the results, if some or a combination of these techniques is applied to the algorithm. We plan to try some of these approaches in the near future.

7. Conclusions

In this paper we proposed a GA approach to solve the nurse rostering problem. The aim is to automate the process of nurse scheduling. The main contribution of this research is in the design of complete system that can be used in practical situations to generate fast and effective nurse rosters. The algorithmic component of the system was based on a GA in which a new heuristic approach for constructing the initial schedules was devised to create the GA population. In addition, a novel problem specific mutation operator that repairs constraint violations has been designed to handle the difficult problem constraints.

Experimental results show that although the final solution generated still has some constraints violation, the quality of the solution has improved with a high percentage during the evolutionary process. The improvement in the average fitness between the first and last GA generations is approximately 70 to 80 percent. In addition the result is achieved in a very small amount of time, which indicates that the schedule generated is applicable in practical situations after minor adjustments by the planner to correct the violations of constraints.

As a future work we will try to overcome constraints violation in the final solution by introducing a new mutation operator specifically directed to the coverage constraint. Also, the final best solution obtained by the GA can undergo another optimization process using a simple technique like hill climbing or simulated annealing to improve the result and get rid of constraints violation.

References

[1] E. Burke, P. De Causmaecker, G. Berghe, and H. Van Landeghem, "The state of the art of nurse rostering," *Journal of scheduling*, vol. 7, no. 6, pp. 441–499, 2004.

[2] E. Burke, P. De Causmaecker, and G. Vanden Berghe, "A hybrid tabu search algorithm for the nurse rostering problem," *Simulated evolution and learning*, pp. 187–194, 1999.

[3] S. Petrovic and G. Berghe, "Comparison of algorithms for nurse rostering problems," in *Procedings of the 7th International Conference on the Practice and Theory of Automated Timetabling*, 2008, pp. 1–18.

[4] M. Azaiez and S. Al Sharif, "A 0-1 goal programming model for nurse scheduling," *Computers & Operations Research*, vol. 32, no. 3, pp. 491–507, 2005.

[5] J. Bard and H. Purnomo, "Preference scheduling for nurses using column generation," *European Journal of Operational Research*, vol. 164, no. 2, pp. 510–534, 2005.

[6] ——, "Cyclic preference scheduling of nurses using a lagrangian-based heuristic," *Journal of Scheduling*, vol. 10, no. 1, pp. 5–23, 2007.

[7] E. Burke, P. De Causmaecker, S. Petrovic, and G. Berghe, "Variable neighbourhood search for nurse rostering problems," *MCG Resende & J. Pinho de Sousa (Eds.), Metaheuristics: Computer Decision-making, Chapter 7, Kluwer*, 2002.

[8] E. Burke, T. Curtois, G. Post, R. Qu, and B. Veltman, "A hybrid heuristic ordering and variable neighbourhood search for the nurse rostering problem," *European Journal of Operational Research*, vol. 188, no. 2, pp. 330–341, 2008.

[9] Ö. Kelemci and A. Uyar, "Application of a genetic algorithm to a real world nurse rostering problem instance."

[10] M. Moz and M. Vaz Pato, "A genetic algorithm approach to a nurse rerostering problem," *Computers & Operations Research*, vol. 34, no. 3, pp. 667–691, 2007.

[11] U. Aickelin and K. Dowsland, "An indirect genetic algorithm for a nurse-scheduling problem," *Computers & Operations Research*, vol. 31, no. 5, pp. 761–778, 2004.

[12] K. Sugihara, "Measures for performance evaluation of genetic algorithms," in *3rd Joint Conference on Information Science, JCIS '97*, 1997, pp. 172–175, extended Abstract.

A Genetic Algorithm for Multiprocessor Task Scheduling

Tashniba Kaiser, Olawale Jegede, Ken Ferens, Douglas Buchanan
Dept. of Electrical and Computer Engineering, University of Manitoba, Winnipeg, MB, Canada
Ken.Ferens@ad.umanitoba.ca

Abstract—The goal of task scheduling in a multiprocessor system is to schedule dependent tasks on processors such that the processing time is minimized. This ensures optimal usage of the processing systems. However this problem is NP-hard in nature and heuristic based techniques are used to obtain a good schedule in polynomial time. Genetic Algorithms (GA) have been proposed over other heuristics because it can use its genetic processes to find multiple solutions faster. The GA proposed is based on a non-pre-emptive precedence relation between tasks in the task graph. Tasks assignment is prioritized based on the number of tasks dependencies (NTD) and the earliest start time (EST) of each task. For tasks with multiple possible earliest start times, the minimum earliest start time is chosen for such tasks. Java simulations compared the results obtained using the minimum EST and the maximum EST. Our simulation shows that the proposed algorithm with minimum EST achieves faster processing periods compared with the maximum EST.

Keywords—Genetic Algorithm, Number of Task Dependencies, Total Finishing Time, Multiprocessor Scheduling.

I. Introduction

The need to achieve optimal usage of a multiprocessing system for task allocation cannot be overemphasized. The aim is to ensure that the processing period is minimized by scheduling tasks on time. However this problem of obtaining optimal task scheduling in the multiprocessing system is reported to be NP hard [1]. There are different scheduling algorithms such as First-in-First-Out, Shortest-Job-First, Priority based scheduling, Round-robin scheduling, Multilevel Queue scheduling etc. It is important that any algorithm chosen is able to address the scheduling problem in polynomial time. Due to the computational complexity however, different types of machine learning techniques have been proposed. Some of the heuristics that have been widely used for this problem are simulated annealing, tabu search, ant colony optimization, and genetic algorithms among others. Genetic algorithms are efficient in solving NP hard problems especially in parallel computing such as any multiprocessing system.

The common approach to this problem has been to use the precedence-relations between tasks to prioritize task assignment on the processors. This is also known as the height-based tasks assignment, somewhat similar to the first-in-first-out method as tasks with higher heights are given priority than those down the tasks-graph. However to further improve the optimization process (by further reducing the makespan), a new approach is to assign tasks based on the number of task dependencies (NTD) of each task. Which means a task must be executed before all the other tasks that depends on it can be executed. Thus, irrespective of a task's height in a task graph, priority is given to tasks with higher number of task dependencies. This ensures a decrease in the total finishing time (TFT) of the schedule.

The remaining sections of this paper are organised as follows. Section 2 represents related work on multiprocessor task allocation problem and our contribution to this work. Section 3 discusses the GA approach to the multiprocessor task allocation problem and methodology. In Section 4, we discuss the simulations and results obtained using genetic algorithm. Section 5 concludes the paper and gives future work.

II. Related Work

There have been several approaches to the tasks allocation problem in a multiprocessing systems. Most of the approaches have been based on non-pre-emptive precedence relations between tasks in the task graph. Jin et al [2] carried out a comprehensive survey of nine scheduling algorithms which are frequently used to solve the multiprocessor task scheduling problem and compared the performance of each of the algorithms. The nine algorithms considered were min-min, chaining, A*, genetic algorithms, simulated annealing, tabu search, Highest Level First Known Execution Times (HLFET), Insertion Scheduling Heuristic (ISH), and Duplication Scheduling Heuristics (DSH) with task duplication. The performance of the nine algorithms was benchmarked against two widely used algorithms in linear algebra which are the LU decomposition and the Gauaa-Jordan elimination. With task duplication, the DSH performed best while the ISH performed best without task duplication. It was also reported that the GA and tabu search obtained the best solution out of all the iterative search algorithms considered. However, in this work task duplication was not considered. Other works have been done reporting the performance of the GA. Majority of the works [1] [3] [4] [5] [6] assume non-pre-emptive precedence relations between tasks in the task graph as well as non-duplication of tasks. Wu et al [7] however assumed duplication of tasks. The non-preemptive characteristics of tasks in the task graph ensures that precedence relations are adhered to. This necessitates the priority-based task scheduling. The most common scheduling method is to prioritise task based on their height [1]. The height is used to denote the precedence relations between tasks in a task graph. The higher a task is in the task graph, the higher the priority given to it in allocating it to the multiprocessing systems. However, as a result of tasks dependencies, the height-based task scheduling can be inefficient. Tasks at a higher height with no task dependencies will be scheduled ahead of tasks at a lower height with task dependencies. This increases the makespan of the processor. Abdeyazdan and Rahmani [8] proposed a new algorithm which prioritizes tasks scheduling based on the number of task dependencies of each task and the earliest start time of each task. This ensures that tasks having higher task dependencies are given higher priority irrespective of their height on the precedence graph thereby resulting in a further decrease in the makespan of the processing system.

In this work, we have considered the algorithm proposed by [8]. We observed that in the task graph, there may be tasks with multiple possible earliest start times. Our contribution is that for tasks with multiple possible earliest start times, our algorithm choses the minimum earliest start time for such tasks as against the maximum earliest start time used by [8]. This is akin to choosing the shortest path as against the longest path in a routing problem. Our algorithm ensures a further decrease in the makespan.

III. GA MULTIPROCESSOR TASK SCHEDULING

The main goal of a scheduling problem is to reduce the schedule length (makespan) of the processor. For a multiprocessing systems N processors, the time it takes for the last on a processor to finish executing is termed the *finishing time* FT. The maximum finishing time among the *m* processors in any schedule is termed the Total Finishing Time TFT of that schedule. For *k* number of schedules, the TFT can be represented as in (1) below.

$$TFT_k = \sum_{1}^{k} Max\,\{FT\ of\ Processor_i\} \quad for\ m \geq i \geq 1 \qquad (1)$$

Height-Based Scheduling

Hou and Ansari [1] based their task priority-scheduling in a multiprocessor system on the task height of each task. In this model, tasks that are higher up the task graph are given priority compared to tasks on lower levels. In a task graph where there is a sequence of directed edges from task, say t_i to t_j, then t_i is higher up the graph while t_j is lower down the graph. This precedence relation implies that task t_i has to be executed before tasks t_j and other tasks that precede that task t_i. According to [1], if PRED(t_i) is a set of preceded tasks of t_i, then we can obtain the height of any of the preceding tasks using equation (2).

$$height\ (t_i) \begin{cases} 0 & if\ PRED(t_i) = \emptyset, \\ 1 + \max\{height(t_j)\} & otherwise.. \\ \quad t_j\ \in PRED(t_i) & \end{cases} \qquad (2)$$

The height function given above is a mathematical representation of the precedence relations between the tasks in the task graph. Since the task height increases from 0 to a finite length, the preceding tasks to the task(s) at height 0 will have heights greater than 0. Therefore the lower the task height of any task, the higher up the task graph the task is. In other words, if task t_i is preceded by tasks t_j, then t_i will be executed before t_j and height(t_i) < height(t_j). However if there is no precedence relation between any two tasks, the order of execution can be arbitrary.

Problem with Height-Based Scheduling

To explain the drawback of a height-based scheduling algorithm, we have used the task graph below [8]. Each of the tasks t0 to t15 will have a height and an execution time. Task t0 is at height 0 (highest), t1 and t2 have height 1, etc. as shown in the table 1 below. The execution time of each task is assigned randomly ranging from 0 to 15. The height-based scheduling is such that tasks at higher heights are scheduled before task at lower heights. However for tasks at same heights, any of them is randomly chosen to be scheduled on the processor.

The implication is that: "tasks such as t7 will be scheduled before tasks such as t14."

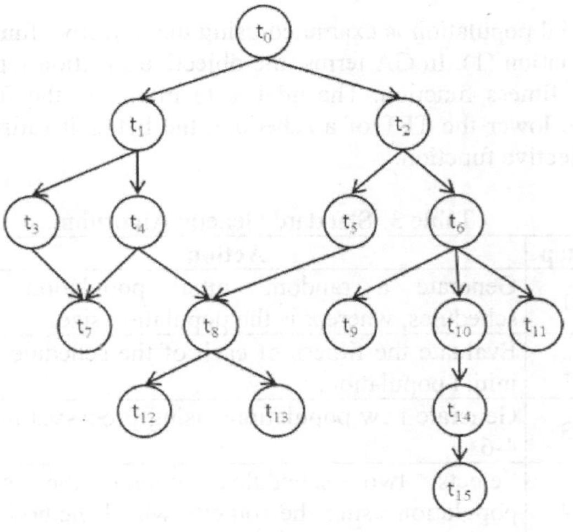

Fig. 1 A task graph, from [8].

Table 1. Height and Execution time of tasks in Fig. 1.

Task	Height	Execution time
t_0	0	3
t_1	1	2
t_2	1	4
t_3	2	1
t_4	2	10
t_5	2	3
t_6	2	6
t_7	3	9
t_8	3	7
t_9	3	11
t_{10}	3	5
t_{11}	3	5
t_{12}	4	8
t_{13}	4	10
t_{14}	4	15
t_{15}	5	2

It is observed that task t_7 has no task dependency, meaning there is no task that needs task t_7 to complete before it can start. However, tasks t_{14} has task dependency; task t_{15} cannot be scheduled unless task t_{14} finishes execution. Therefore, scheduling based on height increases the FT of a processor and consequently the TFT. For a task graph with a high percentage of task dependencies, the height-based scheduling will not be suitable to achieve optimal scheduling. This is why a new algorithm is needed for optimal task scheduling in a multiprocessing systems.

Task Dependency-based Scheduling

The main goal of a scheduling problem is to reduce the TFT (makespan) of the processor. To further reduce the TFT, Abdeyazdan and Rahmani [8] proposed a new algorithm which prioritizes tasks scheduling based on the number of task dependencies and earliest start time (EST) of each task. This ensures that tasks having higher task dependencies are given higher priority irrespective of their height on the precedence graph. For any task t_i with a j number of outgoing edge, i.e. tasks that directly depends on t_i, the Number of Task Dependency (NTD) for such task t_i is mathematially obtained by equation (3).

$$NTD(t_i) = \begin{cases} 0 & ; if\ NTD(t_i) = \emptyset, \\ \sum_{j=1} \{1 + NTD(t_j)\}\ otherwise. \\ t_j\ directly\ depends\ on\ t_i; \end{cases} \tag{3}$$

The NTD function above represents the total number of tasks that depends on a task t_i whether directly or indirectly, this [8] termed as number of children. With this, a task with more number of tasks dependencies will be scheduled earlier than one with lower number of task dependencies. The concept of Earlier Start Time was introduced to ensure that tasks are scheduled with respect to the earliest time for which they are available to be scheduled. The EST of any task is a function of the summation of the execution time of all the tasks that precedes such tasks. However, because there could be one or more path on the task graph along which a task could be executed, this implies that there will be multiple EST for such task. Our algorithm selects the minimum EST. An algorithm to produce the schedule based on the number of task dependencies is as below:

1. Arrange the tasks in descending order based on the number of task dependencies of each task.
2. Put tasks with the same NTD in a single group and perform steps a and b for all the groups in order of higher NPD until every group is empty.
   a. Randomly select a task from the group and then delete it from the group.
   b. Allocate the selected task to one of the processors based on the EST method such that the starting time of the task on that processor is less than other processors.
      i. For tasks with multiple EST, choose the minimum EST in performing *b*.
3. Repeat steps 'a' and 'b' until all the tasks have been selected.

The algorithm is such that every task is assigned only once to a processor as there is no repetition of same task on the task graph. From the task graph in figure 1, we can arrange the tasks according to the NTD of each tasks. The execution time of each task is used to compute the EST of each task. Table 2 shows the EST of each tasks arranged according to the descending order of the NTD of each tasks. From Table 2, we see that each of tasks t_8, t_7, t_{12}, and t_{13} have two ESTs because there are two possible path from which the EST can be obtained. For instance task t_8 have an EST of 10 along the path $t_4 \rightarrow t_1 \rightarrow t_0$ and an EST of 15 along the path $t_5 \rightarrow t_2 \rightarrow t_{10}$. Our algorithm always chooses the minimum EST.

Scheduling using GA

The goal of the combinatorial optimization problem in this work is to find optimal task schedule in a very short time. Since this problem is NP-complete, we have chosen the GA to do the task scheduling. GA is a subset of evolutionary algorithms that models biological processes to optimize highly complex functions.

Table 2. Task Order based on NTD.

Task	NTD	EST
t_0	15	0
t_2	10	3
t_1	6	3
t_6	5	7
t_4	4	5
t_5	3	7
t_8	2	10,15
t_{10}	2	13
t_3	1	5
t_{14}	1	18
t_7	0	6,15
t_9	0	13
t_{11}	0	13
t_{12}	0	17,22
t_{13}	0	17,22
t_{15}	0	33

The GA allows a population composed of many individuals to evolve under specified selection rules to a state that maximizes the "fitness" (i.e. minimize the objective function). It is important that a solution is found in good time because time plays an important role in real time applications for task scheduling in multiprocessing system. The main advantage of using GA over other stochastic techniques is its parallelism which enables faster convergence. GA therefore outsmarts all other meta-heuristic techniques in terms of the time it takes to arrive at a good solution. The GA is able to provide a list of optimum solutions at a single iteration; this is particularly good for our application because we have multiple processors on which the scheduling is done. GA's are also less likely to get stuck in local minima because of its crossover and mutation processes. GA is therefore well suited to our problem. The GA procedure is shown in Table 3.

The initial population consists of solutions in the search space. A solution represents a schedule generated every time the algorithm in section 3.3 is run. In GA term a solution is termed a chromosome. A particular population size is chosen depending on the problem size. Each of the solutions in the initial population is examined using the objective function in Equation (1). In GA terms, the objective function represents the fitness function. The goal is to minimize the function. The lower the TFT of a schedule, the better it satisfies the objective function.

Table 3. Standard Genetic Algorithm.

Step	Action
1	Generate a random initial population of n schedules, where n is the population size.
2	Evaluate the fitness of each of the schedule in the initial population.
3	Generate new populations using processes in steps 4-6
4	Selects two schedules among the current population using the roulette wheel method based on fitness of each schedule.
5	Crossover the two selected schedules considering the crossover probability, to form the schedules for the next generation
6	Mutate the one of the selected schedules at each defined mutation point, considering the mutation probability and place it in the new population.
7	Evaluate the fitness of each of the schedules in the new population
8	Repeat steps 3-7 until the stopping criteria have been met.

GA uses selection, crossover and mutation processes to generate new solutions (schedules) in the search space.

- **Selection** deals with the probabilistic survival of the fittest, in that the fittest schedules are chosen to survive. Fitness is a comparable measurement of how well a schedule satisfies the objective function. Once the schedules with the better fittest are chosen, others will be eliminated. Simply, the probability of a chromosome to be selected is proportional to the quality value/fitness; this is also called the roulette wheel selection method. There are various selection methods but we propose to use the roulette wheel selection algorithm because it gives every chromosome a chance of survival. The lower the TFT of a schedule, the larger the slot it occupies in the roulette wheel and consequently the higher the chances of being selected for every spin.

- **Crossover** is a technique considered to be the most important step in the context of GAs. At a certain crossover rate, GA selects two schedules from the population based on roulette wheel method. After selecting these two schedules, using the roulette wheel, a task is randomly selected from the ordered set of tasks based on their NTD. In one of the schedule (first schedule), the algorithm will choose all the tasks that have equal or lower number of NTD to the selected task. For each processor in the first schedule, the chosen tasks are exchanged with the other tasks on corresponding processor in the second schedule. This produces two new schedules with most likely varying TFT to the initial schedules.

• **Mutation** is a genetic operator used to maintain genetic diversity, at a certain mutation rate, from one generation of a population of schedules to the next. Mutation alters one or more gene (task) values in a chromosome from its initial state. In mutation, the solution may change entirely from the previous solution. Hence GA can come to better or worst solution by using mutation. Consequently, mutation aids GA to avoid getting stuck in local minimal. To do mutation, the two different schedules and task selected for the crossover process are used. In the first schedule, the selected task is exchanged with another task with equal NTD on another processor in the same schedule. This same mutation process is done for the second schedule. Like the crossover, this procedure also produces two new schedules with most likely varying TFT to the initial schedules.

After each cycle of selection, crossover and mutation, the newly generated sets of solutions (schedules) are termed *new generation*. Every *generation* is evaluated based on the fitness function to determine if they represent a good enough solution to satisfy the fitness function. This determines if the GA can stop searching, or if otherwise, for the GA to continue searching until the set stopping criteria is met. The stopping criteria could be *the number of generations, or evolution time, or fitness threshold, or fitness convergence, or population convergence.* In our case, the *number of generations* was set as the stopping criteria. The schedule obtained after the stopping criteria will be the optimal or near optimal schedule.

IV. EXPERIMENTAL RESULTS

The GA Simulation was done in Java to evaluate our algorithm. Task graphs were created with number of tasks in the graph ranging from 16, 21, and 30. The task dependency percentage range between 20 and 60 and the execution time for each task is random between 1 and 15 s. The task graphs are scheduled on a multiprocessor system with 3 processors for the two genetic-based algorithms with maximum earliest start time and our algorithm minimum earliest start time. The genetic algorithm parameters chosen are population size of 40, crossover rate of 0.8 and the mutation rate of 0.1, number of generations of 50.

Table 4 shows the schedules and the TFT for each of the Max-EST and the Min-EST algorithm. The results shows that the Min-EST can schedule tasks either with same TFT or lower TFT compared to the Max-EST. The computation time is however the same for both algorithms.

Table 4. Schedules for the 2 Algorithms.

Algorithms	Total Finish Time (seconds)		
	Number of Processors = 3		
	Number of Tasks		
	16	21	30
Max-EST	40	76	146
Min-EST	40	75	134

Table 5. Schedule with varying NTD of tasks.

Algorithms	Total Finish Time (seconds)		
	Number of Processors = 3		
	Number of Tasks = 30		
	Increase NTD of Tasks with Multiple ESTs		
	20%	40%	60%
Max-EST	146	187	209
Min-EST	134	162	176

Table 5 shows the results obtained when the number of task dependencies (NTD) of tasks with multiple ESTs is considerably large compared with other tasks in the graph with single EST. With a task graph containing 30 tasks, our algorithm (Min-EST) outperforms the Max-ESTs algorithms with increasing NPD of tasks with multiple ESTs. This occurs because since both algorithms are based on NTD, tasks with higher NTDs are given priority than those with lower NTDs. In effect, if a task with multiple ESTs have a higher NTD, it will be scheduled earlier and the minimum EST of such task is likely to be less than the current available start time on any of the processor. In the same vein, if the NTD of a task with multiple ESTs is considerably small compared to other tasks with single EST, then such tasks will be scheduled late at which time the minimum ESTs will be insignificant because the current available start time on any of the processors would have exceeded the minimum EST. Therefore our algorithm outperforms the Max-EST algorithm only when the NTD of tasks with multiple ESTs is considerably high compared to that for tasks with single EST.

V. CONCLUSIONS AND FUTURE WORK

This paper presents a simulation of multiprocessor tasks scheduling based on the number of task dependencies using GA. GA was used because this problem is NP_Hard and a an optimal-or near-optimal schedule is needed in good time. Tasks with higher number of task dependencies were given priority independent of the height of such tasks. This helps to further ensure that all the tasks in the tasks graph are scheduled on time using the earliest start time of each task. It was observed that some tasks can have more than one EST as a result of multiple path of reaching such tasks in the tasks graph. Our idea ensures that the minimum of the multiple ESTs is chosen. Choosing the minimum ESTs is only significant when the tasks with multiple ESTs are given priority in scheduling which occurs only when the number of task dependency is considerably high compared to tasks with single ESTs. Simulation shows that our algorithm will outperform the Max-EST algorithm only when the tasks with multiple ESTs have higher task dependency compared to other task with single EST in the task graph. For future work, an adaptive adjustment of the algorithm parameters (crossover and mutation rate) proposed by Yun-Xiao [9], can be implemented in order to reduce the vector distance between individual schedules. This should reduce the convergence time for our proposed GA.

REFERENCES

[1] E. S. Hou, N. Ansari and H. Ren, "A Genetic Algorithm for Multiprocessor Scheduling," in *IEEE Transactions on Parallel and Distributed Systems*, 1994.

[2] S. Jin, G. Schiavone and D. Turgut, "A Performance study of multiprocessor task scheduling algorithms," *Journal of Supercomputing,* vol. 43, no. 1, pp. 77-97, January 2008.

[3] M. U, C. Ho, S. Funk and K. Rasheed, "GART: A Genetic Algorithm based Real-time System Scheduler," in *IEEE Congress on Evolutionary Computation*, 2011.

[4] D. Montana, G. Bidwell and S. Moore, "Using Genetic Algorithms for Complex Real Time Scheduling Applications," in *IEEE Network Operations and Management Symposium*, 1998.

[5] R. M. Miryani and M. Naghibzadeh, "Hard Real-Time Multiobjective Scheduling in Heterogenous Systems Using Genetic Algorithms," in *International CSI Computer Conference*, 2009.

[6] Y. Monnier, J.-P. Beauvais and A.-M. Deplanche, "A Genetic Algorithm for Scheduling Tasks in a Real-Time Distributed System," in *Euromicro Conference*, 1998.

[7] A. S. Wu, H. Yu, S. Jin, K.-C. Lin and G. Schiavone, "An Incremental Genetic Algorithm Approach to Multiprocessor Scheduling," in *IEEE Transactions on Parallel and Distributed Systems*, 2004.

[8] M. Abdeyazdan and A. M. Rahmani, "Multiprocessor Task Scheduling using a new Prioritizing Genetic Algorithm based on number of Task Children," in *International Conference on Distributed and Parrallel Systems*, 2008.

[9] Z. Yun-Xiao, Z. Jie and Z. Chang-Chang, "Cognitive Radio Resource Allocation based on Coupled Chaotic Genetic Algorithm," in *IOP Science Chinese Physics B*, 2010.

Prediction of Potential Human West Nile Virus (WNV) Disease Distribution in the US Based on Year 2000 New York State Avian WNV Mortality

Jack K. Horner
P.O. Box 266
Los Alamos NM 87544 USA

GEM 2013

Abstract

West Nile Virus (WNV) disease is caused by a flavivirus that is transmitted primarily by the bites of mosquitoes that have bitten infected birds. It was first detected in the US in New York City in 1999. By 2003, it had spread across the state; by September 2012, it had spread to the contiguous 48 states. Given the WNV disease surveillance record, it is now possible to assess how well ecological niche modeling (ENM), given the observed Year 2000 New York State WNV bird-mortality distribution, would have predicted the distribution of the virus across the US. Here I compare a genetic-algorithm- rule-production ENM predictions of the potential geographic distribution of the US avian WNV mortality with the observed distribution of human WNV disease in the US in early October 2012.The analysis shows that despite significant limitations of the WNV surveillance protocols in the US, ENM would have correctly predicted the potential presence or absence, by state, of human WNV disease in the US.

Keywords: West Nile Virus, ecological niche modeling. epidemiology

1.0 Introduction

1.1 Overview of West Nile Virus disease

WNV disease is a viral disease that is typically spread by the bites of mosquitoes that have bitten birds infected by the virus. Humans and other mammals, and ~50 species of common birds in the US, are susceptible to the disease.

About 20% of humans infected with WNV develop mild WNV disease. Mild WNV disease in humans can have any of the following non-specific symptoms:

- Abdominal pain
- Diarrhea
- Fever
- Headache
- Lack of appetite
- Muscle aches
- Nausea
- Rash
- Sore throat
- Swollen lymph nodes
- Vomiting

These symptoms usually last for 3 - 6 days.

Severe WNV disease in humans can have any of the following symptoms:

- Confusion or change in ability to think clearly
- Loss of consciousness or coma
- Muscle weakness
- Stiff neck for no apparent reason
- Weakness of one arm or leg

Only about 1% of humans infected by WNV will develop severe WNV disease.

There is no vaccine to help protect against, or drug to treat, human WNV disease. Treatment of severe forms WNV disease in humans often involves hospitalization, intravenous fluids, respiratory support, and prevention of secondary infections.

WNV was first detected in 1937 in Uganda. It was first detected in the United States in the summer of 1999 (in New York City). As of 18 September 2012, all contiguous 48 states had reported WNV infections in people. A total of 3,142 cases of WNV infection in people, including 134 deaths, had been reported to the Centers for Disease Control (CDC). Of these, 1,630 (52%) were classified as severe ("neuroinvasive") disease (such as meningitis or encephalitis) and 1,512 (48%) were classified as non-neuroinvasive cases ([8]).

Two-thirds of the reported US cases are from seven states (Texas, Mississippi, Michigan, South Dakota, Louisiana, Oklahoma, and California). Almost 40 percent of all reported cases are from Texas, particularly in the Dallas and Houston areas ([8]).

Mosquitoes carry the highest WNV load in late summer/early autumn -- generally August through early September.

1.2 Overview of ENM

The general problem of ENM can be stated as follows. Given the distribution of a set S of species in a geographic region G (e.g., New York state) with associated ecological variables E (e.g., temperature, precipitation, slope, aspect, altitude), predict the potential distribution of S in geographic region G' ≠ G (e.g., the US) . Roughly speaking, this amounts to predicting which parts of G' have an ecological system state "like" that part of G which is populated by S. "Like" in this context is cast in terms of statistical measures.

There are several ENM algorithms ([11]); among the more widely used is genetic algorithm rule-production (GARP, [5]). In general terms, the GARP algorithm applies a genetic algorithm ([12]) to optimize a set of inference rules on a set of training data, then applies that optimized set of rules to infer features of a set of test data. A flowchart of the generic GARP algorithm is shown in Figure 1.

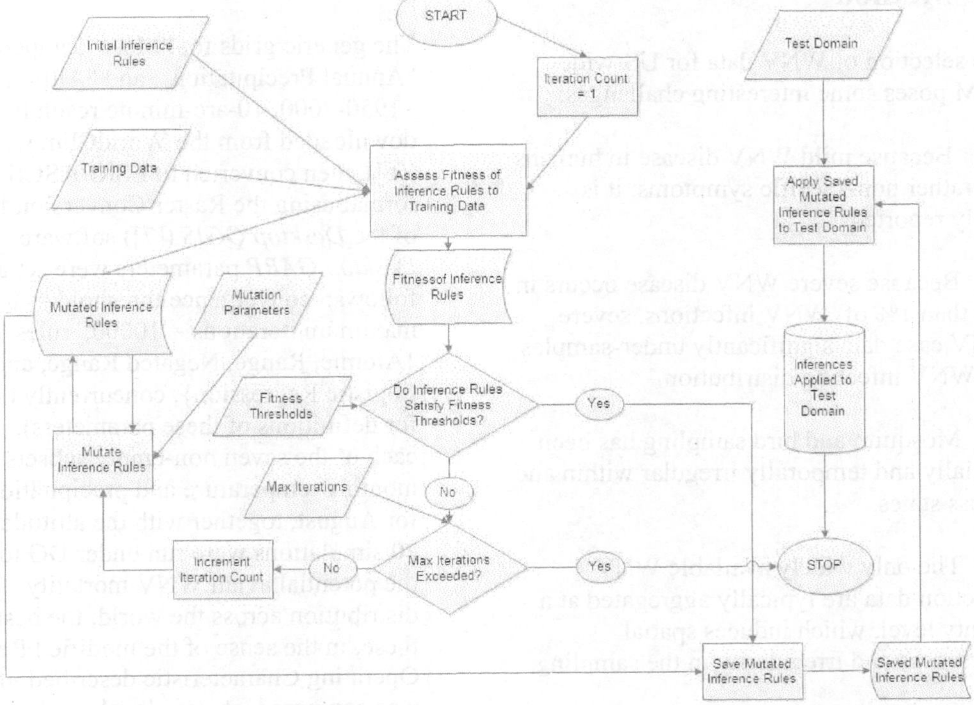

Figure 1. Generic GARP algorithm flowchart. A parallelepiped represents data, a rectangle represents a process or action, a diamond represents a test, a symbol that is convex on the left and concave on right represents an intermediate store, and a cylinder represents a permanent store. An arrow represents dataflow, or transfer of control, depending on context, from the entity at the tail, to the entity at the head, of the arrow.

In GARP ENM, the Training and Test Data consist of assertions about the geographic locations (e.g., latitude and longitude) of a set of species, together with a description of an ecological state at those locations (i.e, the values of a set of ecologically significant variables such as temperature and precipitation at those locations). The Inference Rules allow one to infer the likelihood that a given species will be at a location, given the ecological state of that location. A nominal GARP Inference Rule might have the form "If region R has temperature T and precipitation P, then the probability that species K can survive in R is S" (see [5] for further detail). The ENM GARP algorithm first assesses how well an initial set of Inference Rules predict a part of the Training Data. If the prediction satisfies some prescribed Fitness Threshold, the Inference Rules are then applied to Test Data of interest, and the algorithm terminates. If the Rules do not satisfy the Fitness Threshold criteria, the Inference Rules are automatically modified ("mutated") and again tested against a portion of the Training Data. This process is iterated until the Fitness Criteria are satisfied or the number of iterations of the process exceeds some pre-established maximum (Max Iterations).

2.0 Method

The selection of WNV data for US-wide ENM poses some interesting challenges:

1. Because mild WNV disease in humans has rather non-specific symptoms, it is rarely reported.

2. Because severe WNV disease occurs in less than 1% of WNV infections, severe WNV case data significantly under-samples the WNV infection distribution.

3. Mosquito and bird sampling has been spatially and temporally irregular within and across states.

4. The only widely available WNV infection data are typically aggregated at a county level, which induces spatial coarseness and irregularity in the sampling.

Because of (3) and (4), only WNV presence-absence data (as opposed to observed case-counts) were used in the present study. Because of (3), a resolution of 10 arc-minutes was selected for the ecological variables considered in the study. (This choice corresponds to roughly 0.1 of the distance from the average county centroid to its borders.)

The annual aggregated distribution of avian WNV mortality by county in New York state in 2000 was obtained from [2]. County coordinates (Internal Point Latitude and Longitude, essentially a centroid) were obtained from the US Census Gazetteer for Year 2010 ([3]). Case-occurrences from [2] were reduced to present|absent by county (i.e., multiple cases in a single county were counted as only one occurrence), yielding one mortality-occurrence "case" in each of 58 counties. The resulting present|absent distribution was then exported to an Excel spreadsheet to produce a *Desktop GARP* (DG; [1],[5])-compatible avian-mortality-occurrence training data file.

The generic grids for "Mean Temperature", "Annual Precipitation", and "Altitude", ~1950-2000, 10-arc-minute resolution were downloaded from the WorldClim web site ([6]), then converted to ESRI/ASCII GIS format using the Raster/Conversion function of the *Desktop QGIS* ([7]) software. *Desktop GARP* parameters were set as follows: convergence threshold = 0.01, maximum iterations = 10000, rules = {Atomic, Range, Negated Range, and Logistic Regression}, concurrently (see [5] for definitions of these parameters). For each of the seven non-empty subsets of the monthly temperature and precipitation grids for August, together with the altitude grid, 20 simulations were run under DG to project the potential avian WNV mortality distribution across the world; the best of these, in the sense of the modified Receiver Operating Characteristic described in [9] was compared, at state-level resolution, with the US human WNV distribution reported in [10] for 2012.

All software was executed on a Dell Inspiron 545 with an Intel Core2 Quad CPU Q8200 clocked at 2.33 GHz, with 8.00 GB RAM, under *Windows Vista Home Premium/SP2.*

3.0 Results

The best prediction of the US distribution of WNV avian mortality cases, in the sense of the modified Receiver Operating Characteristic described in [9], used only the August mean temperature as an environmental variable (all other combinations of the variables described in Section 2.0 produced worse results). Figure 2 shows this best prediction.

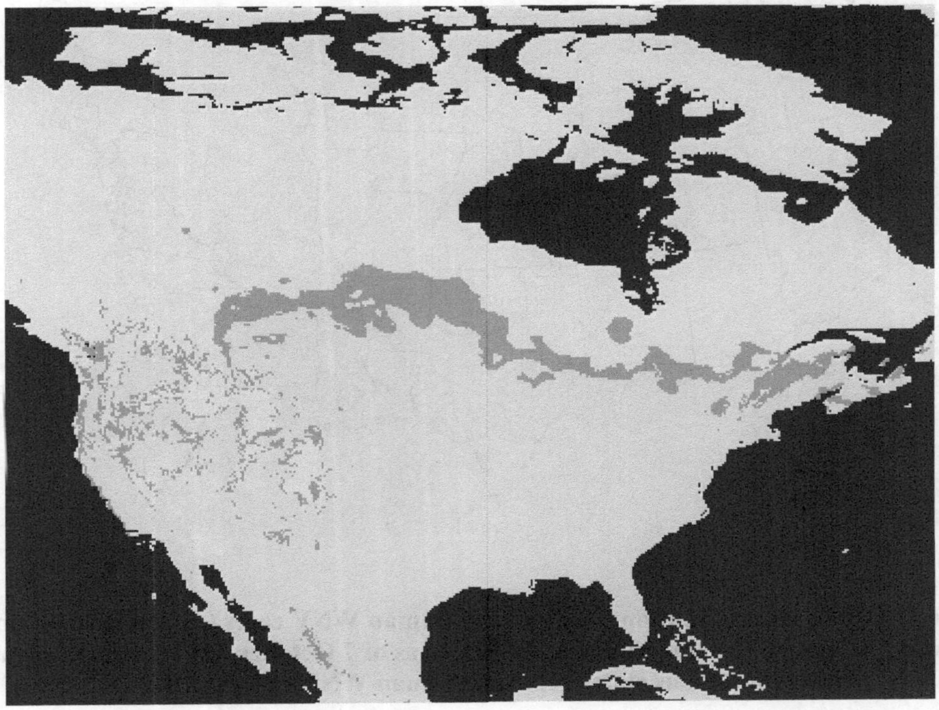

Figure 2. Predicted potential distribution of avian WNV mortality (shown in medium grey in the US) in North America, given the 2000 New York State county-level avian WNV mortality distribution (58 total WNV-mortality-occurrences) and the WorldClim world August mean monthly temperature ("tmean8"), 10-arc-minute resolution. The simulation predicts that all 48 contiguous states have the potential for avian WNV mortality. Note the absence of mortality predicted for the highest elevations of the Rocky Mountains and for the driest/hottest parts of the US deserts. The training accuracy of this scenario is ~0.72; the test accuracy, ~0.70.

Figure 3 shows the observed distribution of US human WNV disease as of early October 2012.

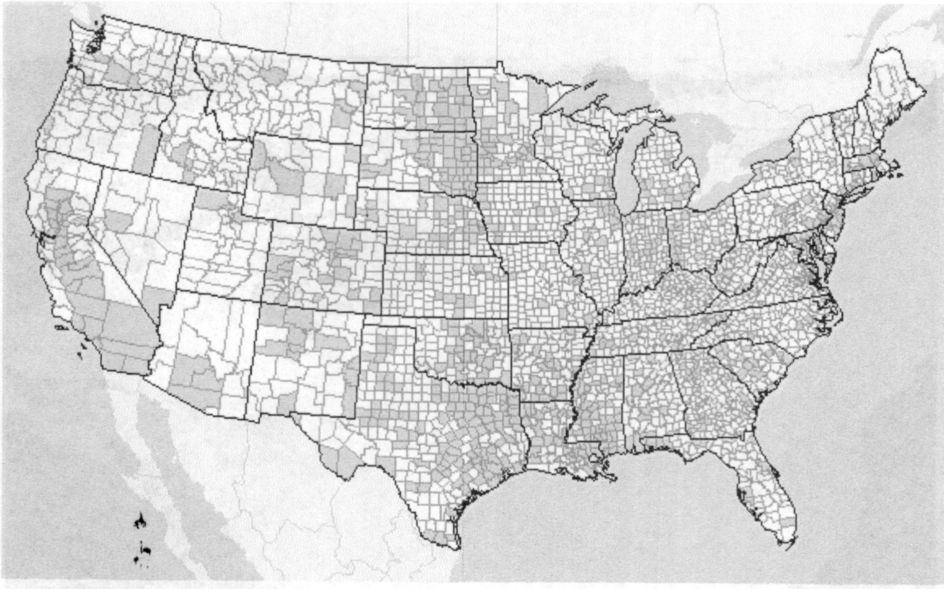

Figure 3. Observed distribution of confirmed human WNV cases (shown in medium grey, by county) in 2012 in the contiguous 48 US states as of 7 October 2012 (adapted from [10]). All 48 contiguous states reported human WNV cases in 2012 ([8]).

The computation utilized ~25% of the CPU and ~2 GB memory on the platform described in Section 2.0, as measured on the system monitor. The time to solution for each of the seven setups described in Section 2.0 on that platform was 5-30 minutes, depending on the list of environmental variables ("layers" in ENM jargon) in a setup. The time to solution decreased as the number of environmental variables increased.

4.0 Conclusions and discussion

If we posit that avian WNV mortality in a state is sufficient to predict that a human WNV case could occur in that state, the analysis above suggests that ENM could have predicted the potential presence or absence, by state, of human WNV disease, given the Year 2000 New York avian WNV mortality presence|absence distribution by county.

The method described in Section 2.0, however, raises at least one serious question. The spatial and temporal sampling irregularities described in that section could in principle give rise to nearly arbitrary noise in the data, and consequently induce arbitrary noise in the predictions.

At least one consideration helps to mitigate this concern. The simulation produces the observed distribution at state-level resolution, and correctly predicts the absence of WNV disease from the highest elevations in the Rocky Mountains and the hottest parts of the US deserts (the temperatures and precipitation of these regions lie well outside those of the training data set).

5.0 Acknowledgements

This work benefited from discussions with Town Peterson and Jorge Soberón of the

University of Kansas Biodiversity Institute and with Desmond Foley of the Smithsonian Institution. For any problems that remain, I am solely responsible.

6.0 References

[1] Pereira RS. *Desktop Genetic Algorithm for Rule-set Production (Desktop GARP)* v1.1.6. http://www.nhm.ku.edu/desktopgarp/. 2004. (Note: this software is no longer supported. An implementation of the GARP algorithm can be found in Reference [4].)

[2] New York State Department of Health. 2000 West Nile Virus Summary. WNV Positive Test Results 01/01/2000 - 12/31/2000. http://www.health.ny.gov/diseases/west_nile_virus/update/2000/today.pdf.

[3] US Census Bureau. http://www.census.gov/tiger/tms/gazetteer/county2k.txt. 2010.

[4] Muñoz MES, De Giovanni R, Sutton T, Pereira RS, Ruland K, Brewer P, Jardim AC, Yamamoto M, Bellini DJS, da Cunha Rodrigues ES, Stanzani SL, Avilla AO, Lin C-T, Oberender J, Elwertowski T, Yesson C, and Bruy A. openModeller. http://openmodeller.sourceforge.net/. Circa 2009.

[5] Stockwell DRB. Genetic algorithms II. In A. H. Fielding, ed. *Machine Learning Methods for Ecological Applications*. Kluwer. 1999. pp. 123-133.

[6] WorldClim. Global Mean Temperatures. ~1950-2000. Generic grid, 10-arc-minute resolution. URL http://www.worldclim.org/current.

[7] The Quantum GIS Project. *Desktop QGIS* v 1.8.0. URL http://www.qgis.org/. 2012.

[8] US Center for Disease Control. Division of Vector-Borne Diseases. West Nile Virus. URL http://www.cdc.gov/ncidod/dvbid/westnile/index.htm. 2012.

[9] US National Library of Medicine. PubMed Health. West Nile Virus. URL http://www.ncbi.nlm.nih.gov/pubmedhealth/PMH0004457/.

[9] Peterson AT, Papeş M, and Soberón J. Rethinking receiver operating characteristic analysis applications in ecological niche modeling. *Ecological Modeling* 213 (2008), 63-72.

[10] US Geological Survey. West Nile Virus 2012 disease map. http://diseasemaps.usgs.gov/wnv_us_human.html.

[11] Peterson AT, Soberón J, Pearson RG, Anderson RP, Martínez-Meyer E, Nakamura M, and Araújo MB. *Ecological Niches and Geographic Distributions.* Princeton. 2011.

[12] Poli R, Langdon WB, and McPhee NF. *A Field Guide to Genetic Programming*. Lulu Enterprises. 2008.

A Chaotic Genetic Algorithm for Radio Spectrum Allocation

Olawale David Jegede, Ken Ferens, Witold Kinsner
Dept. of Electrical and Computer Engineering, University of Manitoba, Winnipeg, MB, Canada
{jegedeo@cc.umanitoba.ca, Ken.Ferens@ad.umanitoba.ca, Witold.Kinsner@ad.umanitoba.ca}

Abstract—A Chaotic Genetic Algorithm (CGA) for Cognitive Radio spectrum allocation procedure is presented. The development of the Cognitive radio system puts emphasis on the efficient utilization of spectrum for both primary and secondary users. Secondary users make use of the spectrum without degrading the quality of service of the primary user(s). We assume that spectrum sensing has been done; thus a secondary user can specify the Quality of Service (QoS) requirements for a particular application at any given time. A Genetic Algorithm is used for the spectrum allocation. We have compared the performance of a Traditional Genetic Algorithm (TGA) with the chaotic counterpart. The simulation shows that the CGA converges faster with better fitness than the TGA. The simulation has been modeled using MATLAB.

Keywords— Cognitive Radio, Quality of Service, Genetic Algorithm, Traditional Genetic Algorithm, Chaotic Genetic Algorithm, Adaptive Genetic Algorithm.

I. INTRODUCTION

In the past two decades, the use of wireless applications has increased rapidly eventually leading to an increased demand of bandwidth. This higher demand of bandwidth has resulted in two main problems: spectrum scarcity and underutilization. Cognitive Radio (CR) concept was introduced to solve this problem. Cognitive radio involves secondary users borrowing free spectrum not being used by the primary users without degrading the quality of service of the primary user's communication. The CR therefore must be able to sense available spectrum, establish and maintain quality of service (QoS) requirements for user's application, meet service level agreement (SLA) and understand its own operational capabilities such as radio parameters [1].

The underlying objective of this work is to use a chaotic genetic algorithm (CGA) to implement a spectrum allocation process in which decisions to assign a spectrum are made according to the radio user's QoS requirements. Genetic algorithm (GA) is a subset of evolutionary algorithms that models biological processes to optimize highly complex functions. A GA allows a population composed of many individuals to evolve under specified selection rules to a state that maximizes the "fitness" (i.e. minimize the objective function). The main advantage of using GA over other stochastic techniques is its parallelism, which speeds up the simulation results leading to faster convergence. It is important that a solution is found in good time because time plays an important role in real time applications especially for a CR. Some other significant advantages of using of the GA include its ability to deal with a large number of variables [1]. While GA can provide a single solution, it can also provide a list of optimum solutions; this is particularly good for multi-objective problems. Continuous or discrete variables can be optimized with the GA and it can also encode variable so that the optimization is done with the encoded variables. Moreover, genetic algorithms are less likely to get stuck in local minima owing to its crossover and mutation processes. Therefore, it is a suitable approach to the spectrum allocation problem. For the purpose of distinguishing between a chaotic genetic algorithm and a typical GA, the typical GA will be referred to as traditional genetic algorithm (TGA).

Traditional Genetic Algorithms use a random process to generate parameter values for the selection, crossover and mutation processes. Random number generators are designed to result in either uniform distributions or Gaussian distributions [2]. We conjecture that selection, crossover and mutation in genetics are driven by a random non-linear dynamics process rather than a random process. Therefore in the spectrum allocation process, a chaotic logistic map is incorporated into the initial population generation as well as in the crossover and mutation processes of TGA. We have compared results obtained through the chaotic process with that obtained using the traditional genetic algorithm process. A coupled chaotic genetic algorithm (CGA) strategy is therefore proposed [3].

Chaotic phenomena, which exists in nonlinear systems is an irregular motion, seemingly unpredictable random behavior under deterministic conditions [4]. Introducing chaos into the whole process of a traditional genetic algorithm may help improve convergence time and accuracy. The CGA takes full advantage of the chaotic characteristics of the logistic map. The logistic chaotic map was used in the following processes of the GA: *population generation, crossover* and *mutation*. The chaotic iterative generates variables with unique probability distributions that are different from typical uniform or Gaussian distributions, and may be better suited for specific problems [4]. The algorithm runs crossover and mutation simultaneously thus reducing the run time and reduce the computational complexity of the TGA. Simulation was implemented in MATLAB to compare the results obtained for CGA and TGA.

The remaining sections of this paper are organised as follows. Section 2 presents related work in the application of TGA and CGA to similar spectrum allocation problem. The contribution of this work is stated hereafter. Section 3 discusses the cognitive radio technology and the spectrum allocation optimization problem to which we have applied the CGA algorithm. Section 4 describes the TGA approach to the spectrum allocation problem. We then describe the proposed CGA approach used for the spectrum allocation problem. In Section 5, we have compared the results obtained using the TGA to the ones obtained with the CGA. Conclusion is given in Section 6.

II. Related Work

Genetic Algorithm has been applied to spectrum optimization in cognitive radio networks. Siddique and Azam [1] applied GA to optimize spectrum allocation where a secondary user specifies the QoS and the GA is then used for the spectrum allocation. Kaur et al [5] also proposed an Adaptive Genetic Algorithm (AGA) to optimize QoS parameters in a cognitive radio. The AGA is such that, unlike the TGA that uses a constant crossover and mutation rates throughout the evolution process (iterations), it allows different crossover and mutation rates so that the algorithms can transverse different directions in the search space. This ensures improved performance as well as represents a response to the cognitive radio's need to adapt to a changing environment. Yun-Xiao et al [3] introduced Chaos into GA processes and applied it to Cognitive radio resource allocation. The coupled CGA succeeded in reducing the total transmission power, bit error rate, and convergence speed in the cognitive system compared to the simple GA (TGA) and dynamic allocation algorithm. Min-Yuan and Kuo-Yu [4] also proposed K-means clustering and Chaos Genetic (KCGA) for Non-linear optimization. The KCGA was shown to enhance the diversity of the GA as well as improve on the limitations of the TGA in terms of convergence time and local optima. The KCGA has an improved accuracy and faster convergence time compared to the TGA. There are several papers [2] [6] [7] [8] that have applied chaos to other stochastic methods for different applications. The work presented in this paper integrates chaos into the processes of genetic algorithm for the purpose of spectrum allocation using the QoS requirements of the secondary user and the sensed spectrum environment. We have used chaotic sequence to generate the initial population and also incorporate chaos into the crossover and mutation processes.

III. Cognitive Radio Spectrum Allocation

Cognitive radio (CR) was developed to meet the increasing demands of QoS in wireless communications [9]. The QoS of a network application can be defined as "the set of quantitative and qualitative characteristics of the communication system required to achieve desired functionality of that application" [10]. A CR has been defined as a radio that understands the context in which it finds itself and as a result can tailor the communication process in line with that understanding [11]. The focal objective of CR is to address the underutilization of the electromagnetic (EM) spectrum to meets today's increased needs in wireless communications. A CR can also recognize the radio environment, can predict the future events, and can learn from previous behaviors. Thus, the main cognition capabilities of the CR are *learning, sensing, awareness and reasoning*. A cognitive radio works in a cycle i.e. *observe* (learning and sensing the environment), *decide* and *act* [11]. The observed results in the environment are given as input to the CR and a decision is made on the basis of a mechanism and finally an action will be taken as to allocation of spectrum. We have chosen GA as the mechanism for the spectrum allocation. The process of making a decision is seen to be the "heart of the cognitive radios". The set of choices for our application represents QoS parameters. The process involved in selecting the best 'choice' from the list of available choices (search space) in order to reach some kind of goal that is very near as possible to the optimal goal is an "*optimization process*".

We assume that the possible number of secondary users is finite and the spectrum resources (QoS) will always be countable, therefore our problem becomes that of combinatorial optimization. A combinatorial optimization problem will always have an objective function and a solution space. The solution space for our problem is a set of parameters of the QoS. The objective function is the difference between the available QoS parameters and that requested by the secondary user. The closer this difference is to zero, the closer the optimization process is to optimality. The goal of the combinatorial optimization problem in this work is to find optimal spectrum allocation for CR secondary users in a very short time without degrading the quality of service of the primary user's communication. It has been proven that the problem of finding the optimal spectrum allocation to CR users is NP-complete [12] [13] [14]. Heuristics approach can be used to solve NP-complete problems because they produce quickly enough a good solution the problem. There are several heuristics available, and we have chosen the genetic algorithm because it is faster than most other heuristics and it is equally less likely to get stuck in local minima compared to other heuristics.

A Secondary user (SU) specifies QoS requirements (values) and transmits it to the CR; the CR has sensed information about the whole radio environment. This sensed information represents a pool of available solutions for spectrum allocation for the secondary user, and from this pool the initial population for the GA can be selected randomly. After selecting the initial population, spectrum allocation decision takes place following certain genetic algorithm processes discussed in section 4. We have considered five radio frequency (RF) QoS parameters; they are: data rate, signal power, bit error rate, operating frequency and modulation technique. The QoS requirements of the application are compared with several available solutions in the pool and then the best possible optimized solution is to be taken. In this work, we have used the objective function developed by Siddique and Azam [1] to analyse the performance of the proposed CGA.

IV. Spectrum Allocation Optimization Solution

In this section we describe how the traditional GA algorithm can be applied to find an optimal solution to the optimization problem. Then the CGA is described and applied to the problem.

The TGA and CGA starts with a randomly generated set of solutions (initial population) each of which represents a possible solution to the allocation problem. The objective function in equation (1) is used to test for the fitness of each of the possible solutions. In GA terms, a possible solution is also called a chromosome. For a multi-objective problem, each of the objectives is known as 'gene' in GA terms. Therefore the GA chromosome for this problem will have five genes, each gene representing each of the five RF parameters. The GA procedure applied to the spectrum allocation problem is shown in Table 1.

Table 1. Genetic Algorithm.

Step	Action
1	Generate a random initial population of n solutions, where n is the population size.
2	Evaluate the fitness of each of the solutions in the initial population.
3	Generate new populations using processes steps 4-6.
4	Selects two solutions among the current population using the roulette wheel method based on fitness of each solution.
5	Crossover the two selected solutions considering the crossover probability, to form new solutions for the next generation.
6	Mutate the new solution at each defined mutation point, considering the mutation probability and place it in the new population.
7	Evaluate the fitness of each of the solutions in the new population.
8	Repeat steps 3-7 until the stopping criteria have been met.

Chromosome Structure

The five radio parameters to be optimized are arranged in the following order (Table 2). We have used the same simulation parameters as in [1] because we will be comparing their TGA with our proposed CGA. Each of the radio parameters are described in the following section.

Table 2. Chromosome Structure.

Data Rate	Signal Power	Bit Error Rate	Operating Frequency	Modulation Technique

Data Rate

The Data Rate, measured in bps, is the first gene of the chromosome; we choose a range from 0-2M bps with a step size of 125 kpbs. This implies that we have 16 decimal values from 0 – 15 where '0' is assigned to the 1st data rate band (0-125 kpbs), '1' to the 2nd data rate band (126-250 kbps) etc., (Table 3).

Table 3. Data Rate Gene.

Index	0	1	2	...	15
Data Rate	0-125kbps	126-250Kbps	251 – 275 Kbps	...	1.876–2.000 Mbps

Signal Power

This is the specific power range that permits users to communicate without any error; it boosts the probability of successful communication. It is the second gene of the chromosome. In like manner, we have chosen *Signal Power* ranging from -31dBm to 31dBm, step size of 1dBm resulting into 63 decimal values from 0 – 62 required for chromosome representation. This is shown in Table 4.

Table 4. Signal Power Gene.

Index	0	1	2	...	62
Power	-31 dBm	-30 dBm	-29 dBm	...	31dBm

Bit Error Rate

This is the third gene of the chromosome. It stands for the bit error rate (BER) which is the number of bit errors divided by the total number of transferred bits during a studied time interval. It ranges from 10^{-1} to 10^{-16}, step size of 10^{-1}

resulting into 16 decimal values required for chromosome representation. This is shown in Table 8.

Table 5. Bit Error Rate Gene.

Index	0	1	2	...	15
Bit Error Rate	10^{-1}	10^{-2}	10^{-3}	...	10^{-16}

Operating Frequency

This is the fourth gene of the chromosome. It is the specific frequency at which information is transmitted and received. It ranges from 0-20MHz with a step size of 40 KHz producing 500 frequencies resulting in decimal values representation from 0 to 499. This is shown in Table 6.

Table 6. Operating Frequency Gene.

Index	0	1	2	...	499
Operating Frequency	0-40 KHz	41-80KHz	81-120KHz	...	19.9 – 20MHz

Modulation Technique

This is the fifth gene in the chromosome. It is the process of varying one or more properties of a high-frequency periodic waveform, called the carrier signal, with a modulating signal which typically contains information to be transmitted. Eight Modulation Techniques have been considered and their equivalent decimal values range from 0 to 7 in the following order in which they are listed in Table 7. The values of the respective parameters above have been coded in decimal for the purpose of initial population generation, selection and crossover.

Table 7. Modulation Technique Gene.

Modulation Technique	Decimal Value
BPSK	0
QPSK	1
GMSK	2
16 QAM	3
DPSK	4
MSK	5
OFDM	6
OOK	7

However, mutation process requires the binary form of any value encoding adopted. Therefore each of the genes to be mutated will need to be represented in their binary form. Table 8 shows the configuration of the chromosome in decimal and the number of bits used for the binary representation of each of the genes.

Table 8. Chromosome Configuration.

Gene No.	Gene	Decimal Values	Number of Bits
1	Date Rate	0 – 15	4
2	Signal Power	0 – 62	6
3	Error Rate	0 – 15	4
4	Frequency Band	0 – 499	9
5	Modulation Technique	0 – 8	3

A pseudorandom initial population of 100 chromosomes was generated with a GA breeding rate of 50 generations. In formulating the fitness function (objective function) used in the algorithm, [1] considered the magnitude of the difference between the values of each parameter (or gene) that is requested by the user (QoS) and the corresponding values of the parameter available in the solution search space.

$$G_f = |G_{gen} - G_{su}| \quad (1)$$

G_{gen} = randomly generated gene

G_{su} = secondary user`s QoS requested gene

The fitness function is derived in such a way that it minimizes the chances of the selection of the most terrible chromosomes for the next generation of population. Notably this work also considers the number of bits used to represent each gene in the chromosome as part of the fitness measure of each of the gene.

The number of bits used to represent each of the genes is termed the *Weight* of the gene denoted by 'GW'. The weight of the gene is represented by GW1, GW2, GW3, GW4 and GW5 for the date rate (2a), the signal power (2b), the error rate (2c), the operating frequency (2d) and the modulation technique (2e), respectively. The detailed weight for each gene represents the percentage ratio of the number of bits used to represent each gene to the total bits (26) of the chromosomes.

$$\text{GW1} = (4/26) * 100\,\% \quad (2a)$$

$$\text{GW2} = (6/26) * 100\,\% \quad (2b)$$

$$\text{GW3} = (4/26) * 100\,\% \quad (2c)$$

$$\text{GW4} = (9/26) * 100\,\% \quad (2d)$$

$$\text{GW5} = (3/26) * 100\,\% \quad (2e)$$

Another important constant used in calculating the fitness measure is a *fitness point* (FP). This FP will have an integer value within the range defined for each gene in their respective decimal representation part. This value is purely the developers own choice. The FP is meant to *limit* the search process of the algorithm on both side of the required gene decimal value range. In Fitness Measure equations for each gene these fitness points are represented by FP1, FP2,

FP3, FP4 and FP5 for the date rate, the signal power, the error rate, the operating frequency and the modulation technique respectively with chosen values being 6, 20, 7, 20 and 1 respectively. If we denote the fitness measure of a gene as fm, then fm can be given as in (3a) and (3b).

$$fm = [(GW * G_f)] \; for \; FP > (1) \tag{3a}$$

$$fm = [GW] \; for \; FP \leq (1) \tag{3b}$$

The total fitness of the chromosome Tfm is then calculated by summing up all the fitness of each of the genes and then subtracting from 100. The Tfm is given in (4) and the aggregated weighted sum of each of the gene fm_{aws} is given by (5).

$$Tfm = 100 - fm_{aws} \tag{4}$$

$$fm_{aws} = fm_{dr} + fm_p + fm_{ber} + fm_{fb} + fm_{ms} \tag{5}$$

fm_{aws} is the aggregated weighted sum of each parameter's fitness. fm_{dr} is the fitness measure of the data rate parameter. fm_p is the fitness measure of the signal power parameter. fm_{ber} is the fitness measure of the bit error rate parameter. fm_{fb} is the fitness measure of the frequency band parameter. fm_{ms} is the fitness measure of the modulation scheme parameter. The lower the value of the fm_{aws}, the higher the fitness measure of the chromosome.

Elitism method of selection was used to copy the best fit set of chromosomes from one generation to another without altering the genes. The roulette wheel method of selection was used to choose the two chromosomes that will be crossed-over. The roulette wheel was chosen because the probability of any chromosome being chosen for crossover is directly proportional to its relative fitness with respect to the total sum of fitness of the complete chromosome population. GA uses crossover and mutation processes to generate new population. Crossover involves the exchange of genes between two chromosomes. This allows for diversity within the solution as well as prevents the GA from getting stuck in local minima. Two point crossover technique and a crossover rate of 0.9 was employed as proposed by Hasancebi and Erbatur [15]. Mutation is a genetic operator used to maintain genetic diversity from one generation of a population of algorithm chromosomes to the next. It alters one or more gene values in a chromosome from its initial state. Mutation is applied on genes of the child after crossover, altering a binary bit of 0 to 1 or vice versa [16]. In mutation, the solution may change entirely from the previous solution. Hence GA can come to better solution by using mutation. Mutation occurs during evolution according to a user-definable mutation probability. This probability should be set as low as possible. If it is set too high, the search will turn into a primitive random search. We have used a mutation rate of 2%. The chromosomes are converted to binary form for the purpose of mutation and converted back after mutation is done. The stopping criteria used is the number of generations which was set at 50.

Chaotic GA (CGA) Method

Chaos refers to apparent randomness (but definitely not true randomness), or irregularity, or unpredictability that arises in deterministic dynamical systems [17]. According to Kinsner [17], the properties of a chaotic system that provide additional benefits over randomly generated solutions are sensitivity to initial conditions, topological density and topological transitivity. These ensure that CGA is able to explore the entire solution space. The initial population of size N was generated using the coupled logistic chaotic sequence. The elitism method of selection is used to ensure that best fit n chromosomes are copied to the next generation. The decisions as to which of the genes to be crossed over and mutated of the remaining N-n chromosomes are also taken using a chaotic sequence. The results obtained from this procedure are explained in Section V. The important steps in the CGA include: establishing the logistic chaotic sequences, using the sequence to initialise population, using the chaotic sequences to run crossover and mutation. The behavior of any chaotic systems is governed by deterministic equations. Chaotic systems have a sense of order or pattern even though they appear to be disorderly. The first chaotic system can be produced by the well-known one-dimensional logistic map which is defined in (6) as:

$$z_{k+1} = \mu z_k(1 - z_k) \quad \text{for } \mu = 4 \tag{6}$$

The z_k represents the value of the variable z at the kth iteration; z_k is in the interval [0,1]; and μ is a so-called bifurcation parameter of the system. We have employed a new chaotic map proposed by Mingjun and Huanwen [7] because it has a better probability distribution. This new chaotic map is defined in (7) as:

$$z_{k+1} = \eta z_k - 2tanh(\gamma z_k)e^{-3z_k{}^2} \tag{7}$$

$$\eta=0.9, \gamma=5.$$

For 100,000 points (solutions), the probability distribution of the solutions generated by the logistic map is shown in Fig. 1 below, while that for the new chaotic map is shown in Fig. 2. A GA combined with chaotic operator has several advantages such as large solution search space, reduced similarity among individual solution and fast convergence speed [3]. As explained by Mingjun and Huanwen [7], the logistic map of Fig. 1 shows a lot of the points on the distribution are near the edges, meaning that it can escape local minima although it is difficult to seek for the global optimum solution. Figure 2 shows that point distribution of the new chaotic map is similar to uniform distribution with two peaks near -0.8 and 0.8. This means that the new chaotic map has the ability to escape local optimum as well as converge to the global optimum at the same time. This is the motivation for using the new chaotic map. We observe that for an initial population size of 5000 there is a significance difference pictorially between the ones generated using the new chaotic map shown by Fig. 3 compared to those generated using the pseudo-random process shown in Fig. 4.

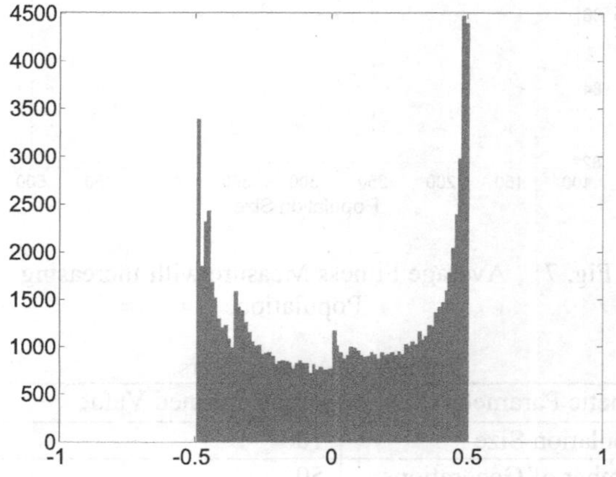

Fig. 1 Probability distribution of Logistic map.

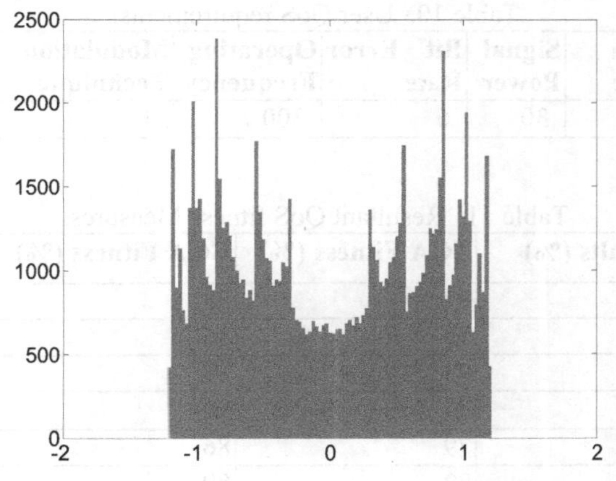

Fig. 2 Probability distribution of new chaotic map.

V. Experimental Results

Simulation was done in MATLAB in order to compare the performance of the CGA against the TGA. We have used the same GA parameters and secondary user`s QoS requirement used by Siddique and Azam [1]. Table 9 shows the GA parameters while Table 10 represents the secondary user`s QoS requirements. The algorithm was run ten times and the results (fitness) obtained are shown in Table 11 and plotted in Fig. 5.

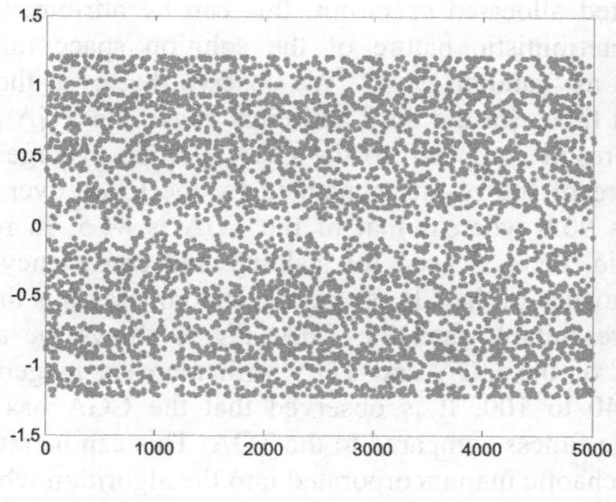

Fig. 3 Initial population with new chaotic map.

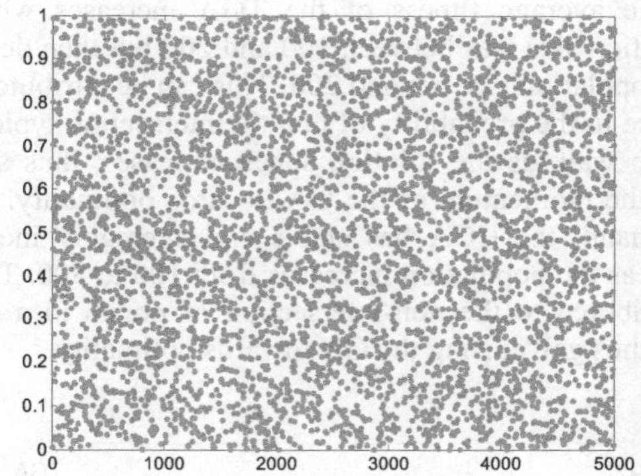

Fig. 4 Initial population with random generator.

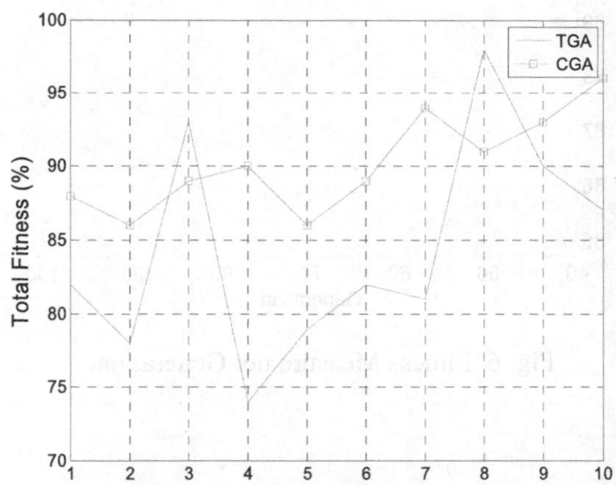

Fig. 5 Total Fitness Measure of Resultant Chromosome.

The result shows that every time the algorithm is run, the results generated by the CGA is more stable compared to the TGA. The TGA has high swings and large variability in the outputted allocated spectrum; this can be attributed to the non-deterministic nature of the solution space otherwise known as "random walk". We observe that even though at certain times (in the third and eight runs), the TGA gives a better result compared to the CGA, yet the average fitness measure of the results generated by the CGA over the 10 runs is 90.6 whereas that of the TGA is 84.5. In real life scenario, there is need for stability and consistency in the performance of the CR as against randomness; thus the CGA is more suitable than the TGA. Fig. 6 shows the average fitness of the CGA and TGA with increase in generation from 40 to 100. It is observed that the CGA has higher average fitness compared to the TGA. This can be attributed to the chaotic map incorporated into the algorithm which has been reported to aid the speed of convergence as reported in section 2 of this work. Fig. 7 shows the performance of the algorithms with increased population size. The result shows that the average fitness of the TGA increases when the population size was between 100 and 200 but then decreases with population size beyond 200. This can be attributed to an increase in the probability of point's intersection typical of a random walk as the solution space increases, thus slowing down the momentum of the GA towards optimality. On the other hand, the CGA has stable and averagely increasing fitness as the population increases from 100 to 500. This can be attributed to the non-intersection of points in a chaotic walk; thus galvanising the GA towards optimality.

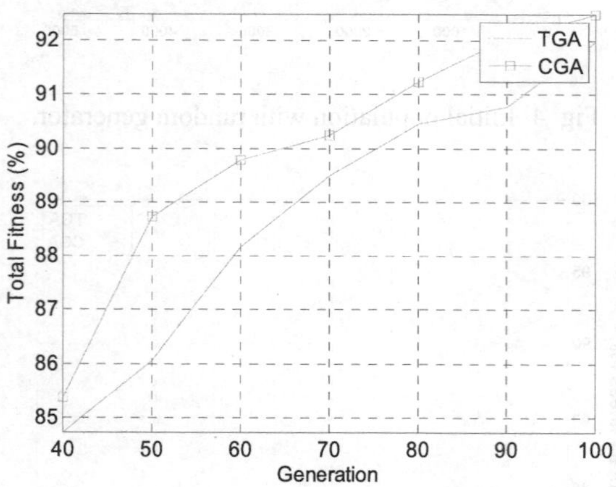

Fig. 6 Fitness Measure per Generation.

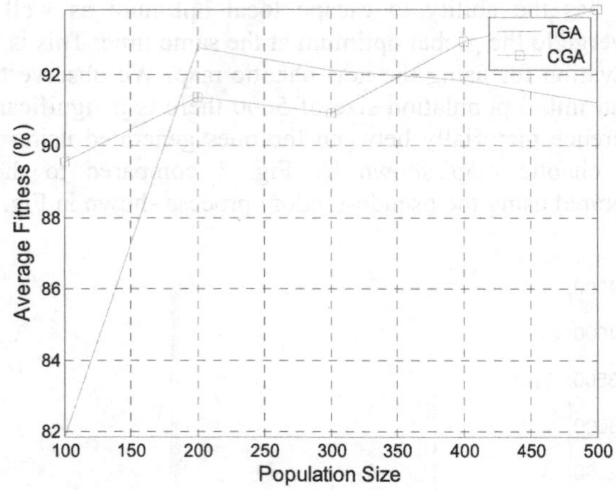

Fig. 7 Average Fitness Measure with Increasing Population.

Table 9. GA parameters.

Genetic Parameters	Predetermined Value
Population Size	100
Number of Generations	50
Crossover Rate	0.9
Mutation Rate	0.02

Table 10. User QoS requirements.

Data Rate	Signal Power	Bit Error Rate	Operating Frequency	Modulation Technique
6	30	6	300	4

Table 11. Resultant QoS fitness Measures.

Results (%)	TGA Fitness (%)	CGA Fitness (%)
R1	82	88
R2	79	86
R3	93	89
R4	74	90
R5	79	86
R6	82	89
R7	81	94
R8	98	91
R9	90	93
R10	88	95

VI. CONCLUSIONS AND FUTURE WORK

A Chaotic genetic algorithm was developed and used to find good solutions to the radio spectrum allocation problem. The CGA is based on the new chaotic map proposed by Mingjun and Huanwen [7] because it has a better distribution compared to the logistic map. The new chaotic map has the ability to escape local optimum and converge to the global optimum simultaneously unlike the logistic map. The chaotic sequences generated by this map were used to generate the initial population of the solution space and to run the crossover and mutation processes of the genetic algorithm. The experimental results showed that the CGA gives a stable and better result compared to the TGA for the spectrum allocation problem. For future work, an adaptive adjustment of the algorithm parameters (crossover and mutation rate) proposed by Yun-Xiao [3], can be implemented in order to reduce the vector distance between individual solutions. This should further reduce the convergence time for our proposed CGA.

REFERENCES

[1] T. Siddique and A. Azam, "Spectrum Optimization in Cognitive Radio Networks Using Genetic Algorithms," Blenkinge Institute of Technology, Sweden, 2010.

[2] D. Cook, K. Ferens and W. Kinsner, "Application of Chaotic Simulated Annealing in the Optimization of Task Allocation in a Multiprocessing System," in *IEEE International Conference on Cognitive Informatics and Cognitive Computing*, 2013.

[3] Z. Yun-Xiao, Z. Jie and Z. Chang-Chang, "Cognitive Radio Resource Allocation based on Coupled Chaotic Genetic Algorithm," in *IOP Science Chinese Physics B*, 2010.

[4] C. Min-Yuan and H. Kuo-Yu, "K-Means Clustering and Chaos Genetic Algorithm for Nonlinear Optimization," in *The International Symposium on Automation and Robotics in Construction (ISARC)*, 2009.

[5] M. Kaur and M. Uddin, "Optimization of QoS Parameters in Cognitive Radio Using Adaptive Genetic Algorithm," *International Journal of Next-Generation Networks (IJNGN)*, vol. 4, no. 2, pp. 1-15, 2012.

[6] D. Shaw and W. Kinsner, "Chaotic simulated annealing in multilayer feedforward networks," in *Canadian Conference on Electrical and Computer Engineering*, 1996.

[7] J. Mingjun and T. Huanwen, "Application of chaos in simulated annealing," vol. 21, no. 4, pp. 931-944, 2004.

[8] H. Meng, P. Zheng, R. Wu, X. Hao and Z. Xie, "A Hybrid Particle Swarm Algorithm with Embedded Chaotic Search," in *IEEE Conference on Cybernetics and Intelligent Systems*, 2004.

[9] F. Bruce, "Introducing Adaptive, Aware, and Cognitive Radios," in *Cognitive Radio, Software Defined Radio, and Adaptive Wireless Systems*, Springer, 2007, pp. 1-16.

[10] A. Vogel, B. Kerherve, G. von Bochmann and J. Gecsei, "Distributed Multimedia and QoS: A Survey," in *IEEE Multimedia 2*, 1995.

[11] D. Linda, Essentials of Cognitive Radio, New York: Cambridge University Press, 2009.

[12] F. Wu and N. Vaidya, "SMALL: A Strategy-Proof Mechanism for Radio Spectrum Allocation," in *IEEE International Conference on Computer Communications*, 2011.

[13] D. Cox and D. Reudink, "Dynamic channel assignment in high capacity mobile communication system," *Bell System Technical Journal,* vol. 50, no. 6, p. 1833–1857, 1971.

[14] W. Yue, "Analytical methods to calculate the performance of a cellular mobile radio communication system with hybrid channel assignment," *IEEE transactions on vehicular technology,* vol. 40, no. 2, p. 453–460, 1991.

[15] O. Hasancebi and F. Erbatur, "Evaluation of crossover techniques in genetic algorithm based optimum structural design," *Computer and Structures (Elsevier) 78*, p. 435 – 448, 2000.

[16] C. Reeves and J. Rowe, Genetic Algorithms: Principles and Perspectives A Guide to GA Theory, AA Dordrecht: Kluwer Academic Publishers, 2003.

[17] W. Kinsner, "Fractal and chaos engineering," Dept. Electrical and Computer Eng., Univ. Manitoba, Winnipeg,, 2010.

A Genetic Algorithm for Node Localization in Wireless Sensor Networks

Olawale David Jegede, Ken Ferens
Dept. of Electrical and Computer Engineering, University of Manitoba, Winnipeg, MB, Canada
Ken.Ferens@ad.umanitoba.ca

Abstract— A wireless sensor network is a collection of nodes organised in into a cooperative network. Knowing the locations of the wireless sensor nodes is central to accurate information gathering. Conventional location detection technique such as global positioning system (GPS) and infrared are expensive to deploy. This paper proposes the use of a genetic algorithm (GA) to learn the environment impairments within a wireless sensor network for the purpose of localization for data management. For each coordinate in the grid network area, random perturbations of received signal strength (RSS) were supplied to the GA. The GA is able to learn the environment and reduce the possible errors inherent in the RSSI measurement taken per coordinate. Our simulation modeled in MATLAB shows that the GA can achieve acceptable node location detection with the aid of three anchors.

Keywords— Wireless Sensor Networks, Genetic Algorithm, Received Signal Strength, Global Positioning System.

I. Introduction

A Wireless Sensor Network (WSN) is simply a collection of devices organized into a cooperative network. It is a network consisting of spatially distributed autonomous devices that use sensors to monitor physical or environmental conditions. Node localization has been a topic of active research in recent years. Accurate network self-localization capability is highly desirable in wireless sensor network [1]. Each device within the WSN consists of processing capability (one or more microcontrollers, CPUs or DSP chips), may contain multiple types of memory (program, data and flash memories), have a RF transceiver (usually with a single omni-directional antenna), have a power source (e.g., batteries), and accommodate various sensors and actuators. The devices can communicate with their neighbours within a limited radio range, and by relaying information to each other, they can transmit signals to anywhere within the network. WSNs are potentially important enablers for many applications in areas such as military, environment or industrial control and monitoring, telecommunications, security monitoring etc. A common location detection technique is the use of the global positioning system (GPS). The GPS is a satellite navigation system based. GPS provides accurate location information and can be installed in wireless sensor network nodes so that each node can locate itself and be able to report its location. However, installing GPS on every node in a WSN system with large number of nodes is expensive. Therefore there is a need to explore cheaper means of locating sensor nodes. One way is to install GPS on a few sensor nodes which are generally regarded as *anchor nodes.* Typically, the anchor nodes in a network should be at least 3 or more. Then each of the remaining sensor nodes in the network can then find their coordinate in the network by triangulating around the anchor nodes. Triangulation can be done using either range-free or range-based algorithm [2]. A range-free algorithm does not measure absolute distance between nodes but it acquires location information by using estimated distance between nodes [3]. Range-free algorithm includes DV-hop [4], APIT [2] and so on. The performance of the range-free algorithm decreases with increasing sensor nodes. A range-based algorithm however uses the actual distance measured between the anchor nodes and the sensor nodes to calculate the position of the unknown nodes [3]. The methods used for the range-based algorithm includes RSS, Angle of Arrival (AOA), Time Difference of Arrival (TDOA), and Time of Arrival (TOA). Range-based algorithm is more accurate than the range-free algorithm. However, to deploy range-based algorithm requires additional hardware which makes it more expensive especially in large sensor networks. In this work our localization algorithm is based on the received signal strength. We have used GA to estimate the accurate location using the received signal strength. The set of received signal strengths received per sensor position is fed into our proposed GA. The GA uses the Euclidean distance objective function to find the accurate position of the sensor nodes.

The remaining sections of this paper are organised as follows. Section 2 represents related work on wireless sensor network localization methods and our contribution to this work. Section 3 discusses the GA approach to the localization problem and methodology. In Section 4, we have discussed the simulation and results obtained using genetic algorithm. Section 5 concludes the paper and gives future work.

II. RELATED WORK

There have been several approaches to the localization of sensor nodes in a WSN including range-free and range-based algorithm. Our optimization algorithm is range-based because range-based algorithm is more accurate than the range-free algorithm. The methods used for the range-based algorithm includes RSS, Angle of Arrival (AOA), Time Difference of Arrival (TDOA), and Time of Arrival (TOA). Compared to the other methods, RSS-based ranging method can be a cheap alternative. Therefore our algorithm is RSS-based. Ash and Moses [5] evaluated the feasibility and quality of self-localization that can be obtained using received signal strength measurements from array of directional antennas on each sensor node. The results were found to be favourable when benchmarked against the Cramer-Rao bound. Goldoni et al [6] used RSS range-based localization methods in low power IEEE 802.15.4 WSN to obtain positioning information. The algorithms used were trilateration, min-max and the maximum-likelihood. The results obtained were not without considerable errors. In general the localization problem NP-hard [7]. It is important that location of sensor nodes is done in quick time especially very sensitive applications such as military operations. Stochastic processes have been aplied to reduce the computational time to locate sensor nodes. Simulated Annealing [8], Artificial Neural Network [9], Particle Swarm Optimization [10], and Ant Colony Optimization [11] are among other approaches that have been used for the localization problem. However, these techniques can easily get stuck in local minima. This is why we have approached the problem using Genetic Algorithm. Zhang et al [1] and Li and Zhou [3] have proposed the GA for this problem. Zhang et al [1] reported a better performance compared to the gradient search localization (SPDL) while Li and Zhou [3] reported a better performance compared to the range-free DV-hop approach. However it is unclear what range-based method was used to obtain the euclidean distance of the unknown nodes position in the network. As stated earlier, we have used the RSS as a measure to obtain sensor node position in the network.

III. GA APPROACH

The approach we have used is the RSS-based method of localization. The RSS obtained from a next-hop sensor node is used to determine the location of the sensor node. In our own case we make use of a one-hop connection where a sensor node is directly connected to each of the anchor nodes. Since the sensor nodes are within transmission range of each of the anchors, the signal strength of the sensor nodes received at each of the anchor is used to find the coordinate of the sensor node in the network. There is a relationship between the transmit power of the sensor nodes and the RSS at the anchor nodes. This is estimated as contained in [12]:

$$RSS(d) = 10n \log \frac{d_0}{d} + A \tag{1}$$

A is the RSS at distance d_0 from the transmitter; d_0 is the reference distance (usually 1m away from the transmitter); and d is the distance of each sensor node to each anchor. We solve (1) for *d*.

We consider that our sensor network has a total of ***r*** sensors, comprising of ***k*** anchor nodes with known locations and ***r-k*** sensor nodes with an unknown locations. Since we have ***r-k*** sensor positions with unknown coordinates, we move a sensor around in each of the ***r-k*** positions and capture several readings of each the signal strength at each of the ***r-k*** positions. Based on the RSS, let the estimated distances of the mobile sensor node from each of the ***r-k*** positions to the anchor nodes be given by (2):

$$d_{i,\ i=1\ to\ r-k} \tag{2}$$

If the absolute positions of the mobile sensor node in the grid are (**x_i, y_i**), i=1 to r-k and the positions of the anchor nodes in the network is given by (**X_j, Y_j**), j=1 to k, then the Euclidean distance between the mobile sensor node and any of the anchor nodes is given by (3):

$$D_{ij} = \sqrt{(X_j - x_i)^2 + (Y_j - y_i)^2} \tag{3}$$

The objective function is primarily to minimize the difference between the actual and estimated distance between the anchor node and the mobile sensor node at each r-k positions. Therefore, we can formulate the objective function as given by (4).

$$\sum_{j=1}^{k} \sum_{i=1}^{r-k} (D_{ij} - d_{ij})^2 \tag{4}$$

Motivation for using Genetic Algorithms (GA)

Since the problem formulation in (1) has been regarded as an NP-Hard [7], we are using the genetic algorithm to optimize the objective function. For this problem it is imperative that we get the desired solution (location) within a very short time. This is the motivation for proposing GA to solve this problem. GAs can explore large solution space in multiple directions, a feature which accounts for its speed. GAs can also strike a perfect balance between the global optimum and many local optima. Genetic Algorithms (GAs) are adaptive heuristic search algorithm based on the evolutionary ideas of natural selection and genetics. They represent an intelligent exploitation of a random search used to solve optimization problems. GAs, although randomized, exploit historical information to direct the search into the region of better performance within the search space. It has been successfully applied in many search, optimization, and machine learning problem as discussed in section 2.

For this problem, every possible location in the network represents a possible solution which in GA term is known as a *chromosome* and the set of chromosomes for each grid point is designated as the *population* for that grid point. Since for each grid point(locations) we have the x and y coordinate, our chromosome therefore is made up of two genes, one for the x axis the other for the y axis. The GA procedure applied to the localization problem is as shown in Table 1.

Table 1. Genetic Algorithm.

Step	Action
1	Generate a random initial population of n chromosomes, where n is the population size.
2	Evaluate the fitness of each of the chromosomes in the initial population
3	Generate new populations using processes in steps 4-6
4	Selects two chromosomes among the current population using the roulette wheel method based on fitness of each solution.
5	Crossover the two selected chromosomes considering the crossover probability, to form the off springs for the next generation
6	Mutate the new offspring at each defined mutation point, considering the mutation probability and place it in the new population.
7	Evaluate the fitness of each of the chromosomes in the new population
8	Repeat steps 3-7 until the stopping criteria have been met.

Standard GA applies genetic operators such as *Selection*, *Crossover* and *Mutation* on an initially random population in order to compute a whole generation of new strings. The first phase of the GA is to generate a population of individuals (chromosomes), after which evaluations will be made to know if such chromosome has reached the desired solution sufficient enough to be considered a good solution. Otherwise, such chromosome will need to go through the Selection, Mutation and Crossover Process in as many times as possible to be able to select the best result – in this case the best RSS in order to compute the particular location.

• **Selection** deals with the probabilistic survival of the fittest, in that the fittest chromosomes are chosen to survive. Fitness is a comparable measurement of how well a chromosome solves the problem at hand. Once the chromosomes with the better fittest are chosen, others will be eliminated. Simply, the probability of a chromosome to be selected is proportional to the quality value/fitness; this is also called the roulette wheel selection method. There are various selection methods but we propose to use the roulette wheel selection algorithm because it gives every chromosome a chance of survival.

• **Crossover** is a technique considered to be the most important step in the context of GAs. At a certain crossover rate, GA takes individual chromosomes from relevant data and combines them to form new ones in the hope that the new chromosomes will have better fitness compared to the previous ones.

• **Mutation** is a genetic operator used to maintain genetic diversity, at a certain mutation rate, from one generation of a population of algorithm chromosomes to the next. It is analogous to biological mutation. Mutation alters one or more gene values in a chromosome from its initial state. In mutation, the solution may change entirely from the previous solution. Hence GA can come to better solution by using mutation. Mutation simply aids GA to avoid getting stuck in local minimal.

After each cycle of selection, crossover and mutation, the newly generated sets of solutions are termed *new generation.* Every *generation* is evaluated based on the fitness function to determine if they represent a solution good enough for the problem so the GA can stop searching, or if otherwise, for the GA to continue searching until the set stopping criteria is met. The stopping criteria could be *the number of generations, or evolution time, or fitness threshold, or fitness convergence, or population convergence.* In our case, the *number of generations* was set as the stopping criteria.

IV. Experimental Results

Simulation was done in MATLAB to determine the location of the wireless device using the genetic algorithm.

Generation of Data

Experiment was carried out in a chamber free from wireless interference. A 5m by 5m grid was created with coordinates ranging from [0, 1], [0, 2] to [5, 5]. The RSS captured at each of the coordinates in the grid points were fed into the GA as input. A Spectrum Analyzer was used to measure the RSS at each of the three anchor nodes. Because RSS is susceptible to attenuation and reflection, we captured 10 readings per coordinate per testing period over 10 test periods. We averaged the RSS values per coordinate per one test period and used it to determine the behaviour of the RSS with distance; this is in order to ascertain the amount of signal interference in the chambers. Figure 1 shows the graph of the captured RSS against distance averaged over one test period. Figure 1 shows a decrease in RSS with increasing distance with the exception of three out of the twenty five points in the grid. The readings obtained at each of these three points were consistent over several test periods. We conjecture that there is a deflection or reflection at these points as a result of the obstructing steel elements present at the specific points.

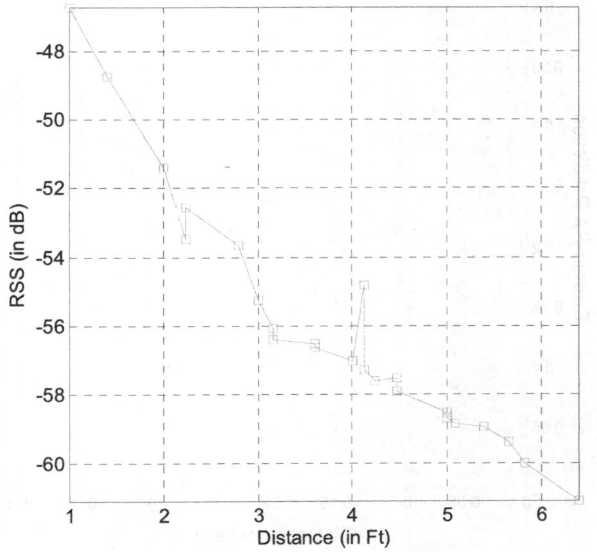

Fig. 1 Average RSS vs. Distance.

Since Fig. 1 shows a relatively acceptable RSS behavior with distance, we were able to ascertain that the room is largely free from other signals apart from that from our mobile sensor. The GA parameters are as follows: Population Size is 100, Number of generations is 100, Crossover rate is 0.6 and Mutation rate is 0.01.

The results obtained are as shown in Tables 2 to 5. Each Table shows the error in the predicted location of the GA for each target positions as well as the relative percentage error to the grid. Table 3 shows the results in the GA predictions for each target when each of the target's initial positions is increased by 10cm. Table 4 shows the results in the GA predictions for each targets when each of the target's initial positions is increased by 20cm. Table 5 shows the results in the GA predictions for each targets when each of the target's initial positions is increased by 30cm. Figure 2 shows the error in GA predictions for target 1 with increased distance. Figure 3 shows the error in GA predictions for target 2 with increased distance. Figure 4 shows the error in GA predictions for target 3 with increased distance. Figure 5 shows the error in GA predictions for target 4 with increased distance. Figure 6 shows the error in GA predictions for target 5 with increased distance.

Table 2.

GA PREDICTED	ACTUAL Targets Initial Positions	ERROR in GA Prediction	Percentage Error (Relative to total Grid)
(2.47, 1.35)	(2.5, 1.4)	0.05	1.25
(1.16,2.37)	(1.2, 2.4)	0.05	1.25
(0.4,2.96)	(0.4,3.0)	0.04	1
(2.51,3.23)	(2.5,3.2)	0.05	1.25
(3.54,3.56)	(3.6,3.5)	0.08	2

Table 3.

ACTUAL Targets' Initial Positions + 10cm	ERROR in GA Prediction	Percentage Error (Relative to total Grid)
Target 1	0.212	5.3
Target 2	0.191	4.78
Target 3	0.108	2.7
Target 4	0.095	2.38
Target 5	0.165	4.125

Table 4.

ACTUAL Targets' Initial Positions + 20cm	ERROR in GA Prediction	Percentage Error (Relative to total Grid)
Target 1	0.340	8.5
Target 2	0.332	8.3
Target 3	0.312	7.8
Target 4	0.275	6.88
Target 5	0.295	7.38

Table 5.

ACTUAL Targets' Initial Positions + 30cm	ERROR in GA Prediction	Percentage Error (Relative to total Grid)
Target 1	0.481	12.03
Target 2	0.474	11.85
Target 3	0.453	11.33
Target 4	0.396	9.9
Target 5	0.433	10.825

Each of the graphs shows an approximately linear relationship between the errors in prediction with increasing distance. This stems from the RSS relationship with increasing distance in Fig. 1.

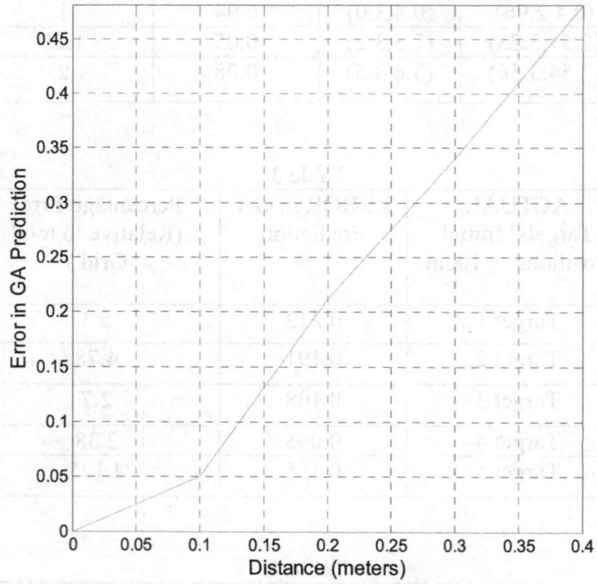

Fig. 2 Target 1.

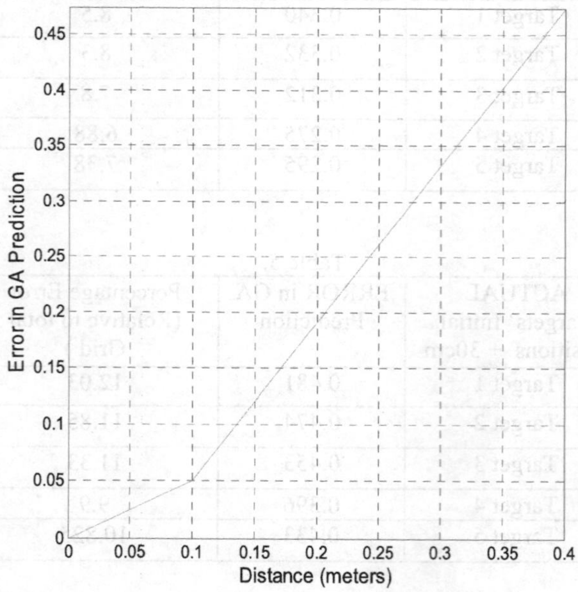

Fig. 3 Target 2.

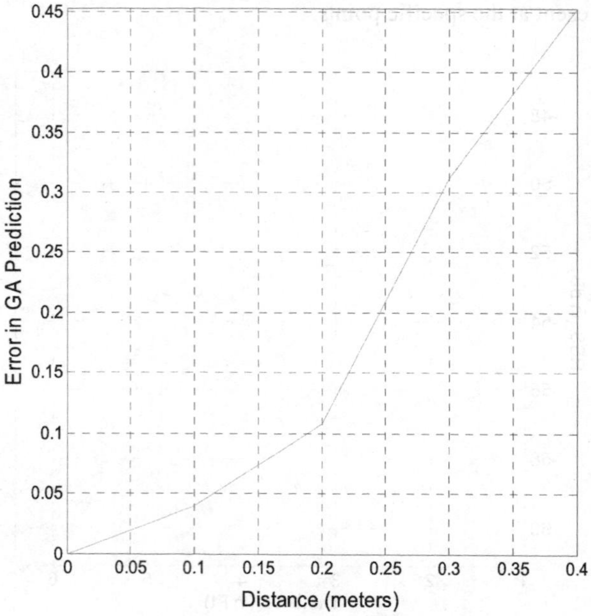

Fig. 4 Target 3.

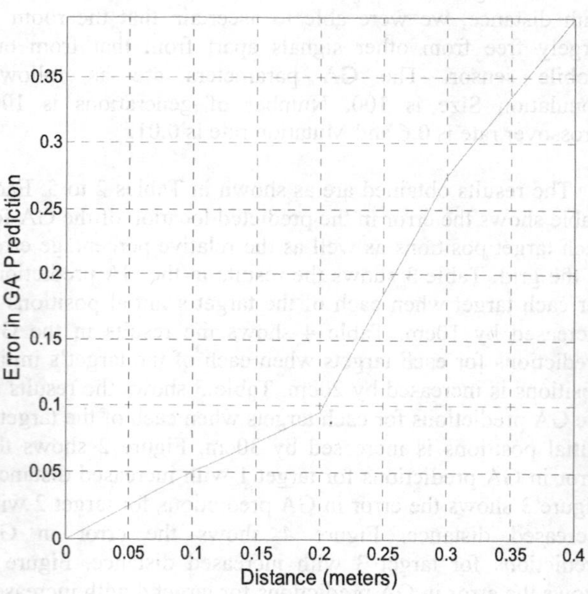

Fig. 5 Target 4.

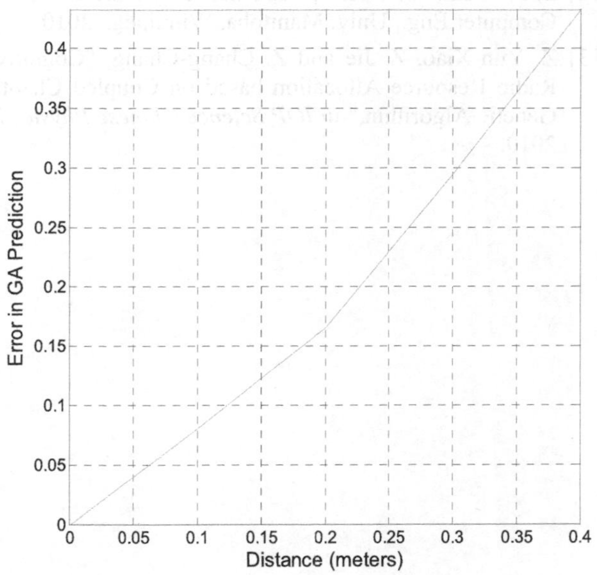

Fig. 6 Target 5.

The Average Error which shows the difference between the GA predicted results and the expected ones is shown in Fig 7 below. We can see that the error decreases with increase in the number of generations. At around the 33rd generations, the GA had found a good solution of less than 0.01. This is a practically acceptable result.

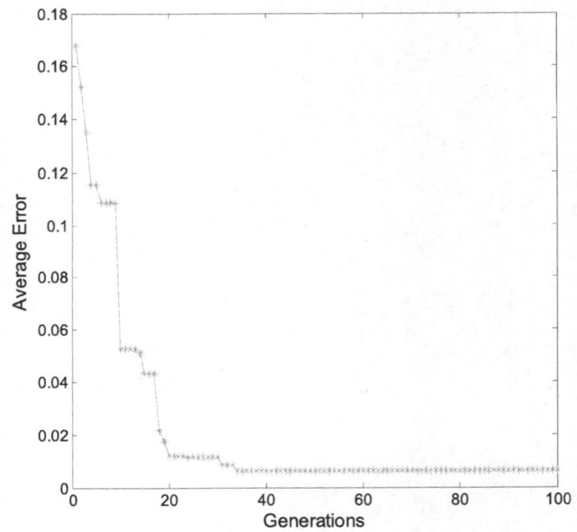

Fig. 7 Average Error for Target nodes per Generation.

V. Conclusions and Future Work

This paper presents a simulation of wireless sensor network node localization using the GA. We used the received signal strength captured at each of the anchor nodes from a mobile sensor node for the purpose of estimating the coordinate of the mobile sensor node at any point within the grid. The test was carried out in a chamber free from any other wireless signals apart from the signals from the mobile sensor node. The GA algorithm was allowed to run for 100 generations giving acceptable results of less than one percent average error in a very short time. This is good for practical purpose in a wireless sensor network. For future work, an adaptive adjustment of the algorithm parameters (crossover and mutation rate) proposed by Yun-Xiao [13], can be implemented in order to reduce the vector distance between individual solutions. This should further reduce the convergence time for our proposed GA.

References

[1] Q. Zhang, J. Wang, C. Jin , C. Ma and W. Zhang, "Genetic Algorithm based Wireless Sensor Network Localization," in *IEEE Fourth International Conference on Natural Computation*, 2008.

[2] T. He, C. Huang, B. Blum, J. Stankovic and T. Abdelzaher, "Range-free Localization Schemes for Large Scale Sensor Networks," in *9th Annual International Conference on Mobile Computing and Networks (Mobicom)*, 2003.

[3] W. Li and W. Zhou, "Genetic Algorithm-Base Localization for Wireless Sensor Networks," in *7th International Confercence on Natural Computation*, 2011.

[4] D. Niculescu and B. Nath, "DV Based Positioning in Ad hoc Networks," in *Journal of Telecommunication Systems*, 2003.

[5] J. N. Ash and L. C. Potter, "Sensor Network Localization via Received Signal Strengths Measurements with Directional Antennas," [Online]. Available: www2.ece.ohio-state.edu/~ashj/pubs/allerton04.pdf. [Accessed 13 March 2013].

[6] E. Goldoni, A. Savioli, M. Risi and P. Gamba, "Experimental Analysis of RSSI-based Indoor Localization with IEEE 802.15.4," in *European Wireless Conference*, 2010.

[7] J. Saxe, "Embeddability of weighted graphs in k-space is strongly np-hard," in *17th Allerton Conference in Communications, Control and Computing*, 1979.

[8] A. A. Kannan, G. Mao and B. Vucetic, "Simulated Annealing based localization in wireless sensor network," in *The 30th IEEE Conference on Local Computer Networks*, 2005.

[9] T. Kaiser, P. Card and K. Ferens, "Environment Feature Map for Wireless Device Localization," in *The*

2012 International Conference on Security and Management, 2012.

[10] X. Lei, Z. Huimin and S. Weiren, "Mobile Anchor Assisted Node Localization in Sensor Networks Based on Particle Swarm Optimization," in *6th International Conference on Wireless Communications Networking and Mobile Computing (WiCOM)*, 2010.

[11] S. Niranchana and Dinesh E, "Object Monitoring by Prediction and Localization of Nodes by Using Ant Colony Optimization in Sensor Network," in *IEEE Fourth International Conference on Advanced Computing (ICoAC)*, 2012.

[12] E. Hossain, "Wireless Networks," Dept. Electrical and Computer Eng., Univ. Manitoba, Winnipeg,, 2010.

[13] Z. Yun-Xiao, Z. Jie and Z. Chang-Chang, "Cognitive Radio Resource Allocation based on Coupled Chaotic Genetic Algorithm," in *IOP Science Chinese Physics B*, 2010.

SESSION

EVOLUTIONARY OPTIMIZATION AND GENETIC ALGORITHMS

Chair(s)

Prof. Hamid Arabnia
University of Georgia

Multi-objective Evolutionary Optimization of Cloud Service Provider Selection Problems

Cheng-Yuan Lin
Dept of Computer Science and Information Engineering
Chung-Hua University
Hsin-Chu, Taiwan
m09902021@chu.edu.tw

Jian-Hung Chen*
Dept of Computer Science and Information Engineering
Chung-Hua University
Hsin-Chu, Taiwan
jh.chen@ieee.org*

***Abstract*—This paper describes a multi-objective evolutionary approach for solving cloud computing service provider selection problems with dynamic demands. In this investigated problem, not only the service purchase costs and transmission costs of service providers are different, but the demands of service requests also change over the given periods. The objective of this problem is to select a number of cloud service provider while optimizing the total service distance, the total number of serviced demand points, the total service purchase costs, and total transmission costs simultaneously in the given continuous time periods. A multi-objective genetic approach with an inheritance mechanism is proposed to solve the investigated problems. Four trail benchmark problems are designed and solved using the proposed multi-objective evolutionary algorithm. The results indicate that the proposed approach is capable of obtaining a number of non-dominated solutions for decision makers.**

I. INTRODUCTION

With the rapid development of computing hardware, high-speed network, web programming, distributed and parallel computing, and other storage technologies, cloud computing has recently emerged as an effective reuse paradigm, where hardware computing power, software functionality, and other computing resources are delivered as integrated services through Internet [1]. There are many global and local commercial cloud service providers, offering various kinds of delivered services such as Infrastructure-as-a-Service (IaaS), Platform-as-a-Service (PaaS) and Software-as-a-Service (SaaS). Recently, the advantages and features of cloud services has arisen the interests of digital entertainment/media/content suppliers to integrate cloud computing services into their content delivery networks [2].

Consider a national-wide area with a number of service request points, the requests at each point usually changes in time; and within this area, a number of cloud service providers with different locations and pricing options of services are available for chosen. From the point view of digital entertainment/media content suppliers, it is an important issue to select suitable cloud computing service providers, which can deliver their contents to massive customers rapidly and smoothly. Therefore, maximizing some expected Quality-of-Service (QoS) indictors and minimizing services related costs are crucial considerations for decision makers. As a result, considering the requirements of content supplier and the conditions of cloud service providers, we formulated such problems to multi-objective dynamic *p*-median problems in this paper.

The classical *p*-median problem consists of selecting *p* facilities in a given space which minimizes the total costs of serving *m* demand points at a time. *P*-median problem is prominent combinatorial optimization NP-hard problem in location science and cluster analysis [3-9]. Many exact and heuristic approaches have been proposed for solving *p*-median problems. In traditional approaches, the planning of service facility centers usually considers the demand of consumers as constant values. However, it is not true in the real world applications, because the demands of consumers may change by environments and time. The dynamic *p*-median problem is applicable to all situations modeled by the standard *p*-median problem whenever demand changes over time in a predictable way.

In this paper, a multi-objective *p*-median model with dynamic demands which optimizes the total QoS distance, the total number of serviced demand points, the total service purchase costs, and the total network transmission costs is investigated. Considering four different geographical features, we propose an efficient approach based on genetic algorithms for content providers to determine the selection of service providers in different periods and satisfying the dynamic demands of customers. The proposed approach can also provide decision-makers a set of non-dominated solutions for the selection processes.

This paper is organized as follows: Section 2 describes the investigated dynamic *p*-median problem and multi-objective optimization. Section 3 describes the mathematical model of the investigated problem. Section 4 presents the proposed multi-objective genetic algorithm MOGA for solving investigated problems. Section 5 gives the experimental results and analysis of the proposed algorithm. Section 6 concludes our paper.

II. RELATED WORK

A. P-median Problems

The classical p-median problem consists of locating p facilities (medians) in a given space (e.g. Euclidean space) which minimizes the total costs of serving m demand points, where the pair-wise cost of servicing each point from all facilities is given. Each demand point is only served by a single facility and services to demand points are not combinable [3-10].

Exact methods for solving p-median problems include linear programming approaches, dual-based algorithms. However, these exact methods suffer from the curse of dimensionality since the computation costs of calculating all demand points' expectations over all possible future combinations increases exponentially in the number of demand points. Many heuristic approaches have been proposed to solve p-median problems, including greedy heuristic, variable neighbor decomposition search, cooperative parallel variable neighborhood search, and Lagrangian-surrogate heuristic. Modern meta-heuristics have been applied to solve p-median problems as well [8], such as tabu search approaches, simulated annealing approaches and genetic algorithms approaches.

Recently, considering the real-world conditions, various models of p-median problems are proposed in the literature, including stochastic p-median problems, progressive p-median problems [3], dynamic p-median problems, and bi-objective p-median problems [9].

B. Multi-objective Evolutionary Optimization

Assume the multi-objective functions are to be minimized. Mathematically, MOOPs can be represented as the following vector mathematical programming problems

$$\textit{Minimize}\quad F(Y) = \{F_1(Y), F_2(Y), ..., F_i(Y)\}, \qquad (1)$$

where Y denotes a solution and $f_i(Y)$ is generally a nonlinear objective function. Pareto dominance relationship and some related terminologies are introduced below. When the following inequalities hold between two solutions Y_1 and Y_2, Y_2 is a non-dominated solution and is said to dominate Y_1 ($Y_2 \succ Y_1$):

$$\forall i : F_i(Y_1) > F_i(Y_2) \wedge \exists j : F_j(Y_1) > F_j(Y_2). \qquad (2)$$

When the following inequality hold between two solutions Y_1 and Y_2, Y_2 is said to weakly dominate Y_1 ($Y_2 \succeq Y_1$):

$$\forall i : F_i(Y_1) \geq F_i(Y_2). \qquad (3)$$

A feasible solution Y^* is said to be a Pareto-optimal solution if and only if there does not exist a feasible solution Y where Y dominates Y^*, and the corresponding vector of Pareto-optimal solutions is called Pareto-optimal front.

By making use of Pareto dominance relationship, multi-objective evolutionary algorithms (MOEAs) are capable of performing the fitness assignment of multiple objectives without using relative preferences of multiple objectives. Thus, all the objective functions can be optimized simultaneously. As a result, MOEA seems to be an alternative approach to solving the investigated service provider selection problems on the assumption that no prior preference and domain knowledge is available [10-11].

III. PROBLEM STATEMENT

In this paper, the investigated dynamic service provider selection problem (DSPSP) is to select p service providers from n service providers in each quarter, in order to satisfy the dynamic demands of m service requests from end-users. The following conditions are assumed in this problem:

1) Each service provider has different pricing options for purchasing services and network transmission.
2) Although contents can be deliver to anywhere though internet, end-users still expects no delays during network transmission. Therefore, each service provider has a pre-assumed maximum Quality-of-Service (QoS) distance.
3) The number of demand points that a service provider can service is unlimited.
4) The Euclidean distance is used to calculate the distances between demand points and points of service provider.
5) Each demand point can only serviced by a nearest point of service provider within the maximum QoS distance.
6) In order to satisfying the dynamic demands, content supplier may select p different service providers in the next following quarter.

The investigated problem can be formulated to multi-objective p-median problems with dynamic demands. The objectives of DSPSP are while optimizing four competing objective functions: the total QoS distance, the total number of serviced demand points, the total service purchase costs, and the total network transmission costs.

A. Problem Notations

i, j : $i \in \{1,2,3,...m\}$, $j \in \{1,2,3,...,n\}$.

m : The total number of demand points.

n : The total number of service provider points for selection.

L_i : The index of demand points, $L_i = i$.

S_j : The index of the service provider points. Service providers points usually co-locate with some demand points, therefore $S_j \in \{L_1, L_2, ...L_m\}$.

D_j : The maximum Quality-of-Service (QoS) distance of the service provider point j.

T : The total service periods.

t_j : The time period that the service provider S_j served, $0=t_1<t_2<...<t_p<t_{p+1}<T$.

d_{ij} : The distance between L_i and S_j.

md_{ij} : The nearest distance of the demand point L_i between the nearest service provider point, $md_{ij}=min\{d_{ij}\}$.

$w_i(t)$: The demanding function of the demand points L_i at time t, $0 \leq t < T$.

w_{ij} : The total demanding amount of the demand point L_i from time t_j to time t_{j+1}, $w_{ij} = \int_{t_j}^{t_{j+1}} w_i(t)\,dt$.

A_j : The network transmission cost of the service provider point S_j per demand unit.

C_j : The monthly service purchase cost of the service provider point S_j.

X_i : The serviced index of the demand point L_i. If the demand point service L_i is serviced within the maximum QoS distance of a provider point, then $X_i = 1$, otherwise $X_i = 0$.

Z_j : The selection index of the service provider point S_j. If the service provider point S_j is chosen and serves demand points in the specific time period, then $Z_j = 1$, otherwise $Z_j = 0$.

B. Problem objectives

1) Minimization of QoS distance

In the classical *p*-median problem, the demands in each demands points are usually considered to a constant. However, considering the real-world applications, demands are known to be changed dynamically. Given the demanding function of each demand points, the Quality-of-Service distance of each demand to its nearest service provider points can be expressed as follows:

$$Minimize\ F_1 = \sum_{j=1}^{n}\sum_{i=1}^{m} w_{ij} \times md_{ij} \times X_i \times Z_j . \quad (4)$$

2) Minimization of network transmission cost

Considering the cloud computing environments, the costs of network transmissions between service provider points and demand points are not fixed. Given the network transmission cost of each service point per time unit, the transmission costs of each facility can be expressed as follows:

$$Minimize\ F_2 = \sum_{j=1}^{n}\sum_{i=1}^{m} w_{ij} \times A_j \times X_i \times Z_j . \quad (5)$$

3) Minimization of service purchase cost

In additional to the network transmission cost, the service purchase cost on a specific service provider point is also an important factor for content suppliers, because the service cost in different service provider point are different. Given the service purchase cost for each service provider points, the total service purchase costs of selected service provider points can be expressed as follows:

$$Minimize\ F_3 = \sum_{j=1}^{n} C_j \times Z_j . \quad (6)$$

4) Maximum of total number of serviced demand points

Because different service providers has different QoS distance, therefore the number of demand points that a service provider points may serviced could be different. Given the maximum QoS distance of each service provider, the number of serviced demand points can be calculated as follows:

$$Maximize\ F_4 = \sum_{i=1}^{m} X_i . \quad (6)$$

C. An Illustrative Example

An example is given here to explain our mathematical formation. Assumed that a content supplier plans to select three service provider points (p=3) from six providers (n=6) within twelve months (T=12), in order to service ten demanding points (m=10). The maximum Quality-of-Service (QoS) D_j is 3 for all the service provider points. The coordination, demanding function of demand points, the service purchase costs and transmission costs of service provider points are listed in Table I. Assumed a selection plan for four quarters is determined as shown in Table II, three service provider S_2, S_3, S_6 are select in the first quarter, and finally three service provider S_1, S_3, S_5 are select in the fourth quarter.

Take the selection plan of Quarter 4 for example, the total amount of each demand points during Quarter 4 can be calculated, as shown in Table III. The distance of each demand point to different service provider points can be calculated, as shown in Table IV. The demand points with D_j are marked as bold. Hereafter, according to all the tables, the objective functions in Quarter 4 can be calculated, F_1 = 10.12242, F_2= 1507.5, F_3= 1650, F_4= 8.

TABLE I. THE INFORMATION OF DEMAND AND SERVICE POINTS L_i, S_j

L_i	S_j	coord.	$w_i(t)$	A_j	C_j
L_1	S_1	(1,8)	10+6t	1	500
L_2	S_2	(2,5)	3+4t	1	700
L_3		(0,9)	16+2t	1	
L_4		(10,2)	25+3t	1	
L_5	S_3	(4,5)	50-2t	1	700
L_6	S_4	(3,7)	99-3t	1	450
L_7	S_5	(12,3)	6+7t	1	450
L_8		(6,16)	24+4t	1	
L_9		(2,10)	10+10t	1	
L_{10}	S_6	(8,4)	5+5t	1	500

TABLE II. REPRESENTATION OF FOUR SELECTION PLAN FOR FOUR QUARTERS

QUARTER 1	QUARTER 2	QUARTER 3	QUARTER 4
2, 6, 3	3, 6, 4	5, 4, 3	3, 1, 5

TABLE III. THE TOTAL AMOUNT OF DEMANDS IN QUARTER 4, ACCORDING TO THE SELECTION PLAN

	t = 0~3	t = 3~6	t = 6~9	t = 9~12
L_1	57	111	165	219
L_2	27	63	99	135
L_3	57	75	93	111
L_4	88.5	115.5	142.5	169.5
L_5	141	123	105	87
L_6	283.5	256.5	229.5	202.5
L_7	49.5	112.5	175.5	238.5
L_8	90	126	162	198
L_9	75	165	255	345
L_{10}	37.5	82.5	127.5	172.5

TABLE IV. THE DISTANCE OF EACH DEMAND POINT TO SELECTED SERVICE PROVIDER POINTS IN QUARTER 4

	$S_3(=L_5)$	$S_1(=L_1)$	$S_5(=L_7)$
L_1	4.24264	**0**	12.083
L_2	**2**	3.16228	10.198
L_3	5.65685	**1.41421**	13.4164
L_4	6.7082	10.8167	**2.23607**
L_5	**0**	4.24264	8.24621
L_6	**2.23607**	**2.23607**	9.84886
L_7	8.24621	12.083	**0**
L_8	11.1803	9.43398	14.3178
L_9	5.38516	**2.23607**	12.2066
L_{10}	4.12311	8.06226	4.12311

IV. THE PROPOSED MULTI-OBJECTIVE GENETIC ALGORITHM

In this section, the proposed multi-objective genetic algorithm to find a selection plan within four quarters for DSPSP is described.

A. Chromosome Representation

A chromosome has gene information for solving the problem in DSPSP. In the proposed approach, each chromosome of has p genes. When a quarter is finished, the non-dominated solutions will be stored and inherited to the next population of the next quarter. The chromosome can be regarded as a selection plan for a quarter.

B. Fitness Assignment

We use a generalized Pareto-based scale-independent fitness function (GPSIFF) considering the quantitative fitness values in Pareto space for both dominated and non-dominated individuals [10]. GPSIFF makes the best use of Pareto dominance relationship to evaluate individuals using a single measure of performance. The used GPSIFF is briefly described below. Let the fitness value of an individual Y be a tournament-like score obtained from all participant individuals by the following function:

$$F(X) = Np - Nq + c. \tag{7}$$

, where Np is the number of individuals which can be dominated by the individual Y, and Nq is the number of individuals which can dominate the individual Y in the objective space. Generally, a constant c can be optionally added in the fitness function to make fitness values positive. c is usually set to the number of all participant individuals.

C. Genetic Operators

The genetic operators used in the proposed approach are widely used in literature. The selection operator uses a binary tournament selection without replacement, which works as follows. Choose two individuals randomly from the population and copy the better individual into the intermediate population. The crossover operator is uniform crossover and the mutation operator is single point mutation without duplicated genes.

D. Procedure of MOGA

The procedure of MOGA is written as follows:

Input: population size N_{pop}, recombination probability p_c, mutation probability p_m, the number of maximum generations G_{max}. Current Quarter Index q=1.

Output: The optimum solutions ever found in P.

Step 1: Initialization Randomly generate chromosomes to fill in the population P until N_{pop} individuals are reached. Each chromosome is consists of p genes for a quarter.

Step 2: Evaluation For each individual in the population, compute all objective function values F_1, F_2, F_3.and F_4.

Step 3: Fitness Assignment Assign each individual a fitness value by using the equation (7) GPSIFF.

Step 4: Selection Select N_{pop} individuals from the population to form a new population using the binary tournament selection.

Step 5: Recombination Perform the uniform crossover operation with a recombination probability p_c.

Step 6: One Point Mutation Apply the one point mutation operators to each gene with a mutation probability p_m. If the mutated gene is duplicated with other genes in the same chromosome, mutate the gene again.

Step 7: Termination test If the maximum generations have reached, store all the non-dominated solutions in quarter q, and then go to Step 8. Otherwise, go to Step 2.

Step 8: Inheritance $q=q+1$. If $q>4$, stop the algorithm. Otherwise, inherit and copy non-dominated solutions to the population of the next quarter, if the number of non-dominated solutions exceed the population size N_{pop}, randomly delete solutions and reduce the size to N_{pop}. Then, go to Step 1.

V. RESULT AND DISCUSSIONS

A. Simulation Environment and Parameter Settings

In this paper, four benchmarks are designed for experiments, as shown in Figure 1. Each problem has different distribution of demand points on different grid sizes, described as follows:

1) *Circle.* 100 demand points and 36 service providers on a 18*18 grid. The number of providers to be chosen p=10, and the maximum QoS distance D_f=2.2.

2) *Rectangele.* Square with empty space. 100 demand points and 36 service providers on a 16*16 grid. The number of providers to be chosen p=10, and the maximum QoS distance D_f=3.

3) Square. 100 demand points and 36 service providers on a 110*110 grid. The number of providers to be chosen p=10, and the maximum QoS distance D_j=10.

4) Triangle. 100 demand points and 36 service providers on a 14*14 grid. The number of providers to be chosen p=10, and the maximum QoS distance D_j=2.

Ten service providers will be select for each quarter. The total number of quarter is 4. The parameter settings of MOGA are listed as follows: population size N_{pop}=100, recombination probability p_c=0.9, mutation probability p_m=0.1, the number of maximum generations G_{max}=100. Fifteen independent runs are conducted for each problem.

B. Disscussions

Figure 2-5 depicts the average values of objective function F_1, F_2, F_3, and F_4 of non-dominated solutions obtained MOGA in solving the circle benchmark from 15 runs. Figure 6-9 depicts the average values of objective function F_1, F_2, F_3, and F_4 of non-dominated solutions obtained MOGA in solving the square benchmark from 15 runs. Figure 10-13 depicts the average values of objective function F_1, F_2, F_3, and F_4 of non-dominated solutions obtained MOGA in solving the square benchmark from 15 runs. The results indicate that the proposed MOGA is capable of solving DSPSP and optimize four objectives simultaneously, considering different geographic distribution of demand points.

VI. CONCLUSIONS

In this paper, a multi-objective evolutionary approach is proposed to solve dynamic service provider selection problems. Experimental results demonstrated the proposed approach is capable of optimizing the quality-of-service distance, the total network transmission cost, the total service purchase cost, and the total number of demands points simultaneously. Moreover, the proposed approach can provide mission planers a set of non-dominated solutions for construction plan of service facilities. Our future work is to apply our approach in solving some real cases.

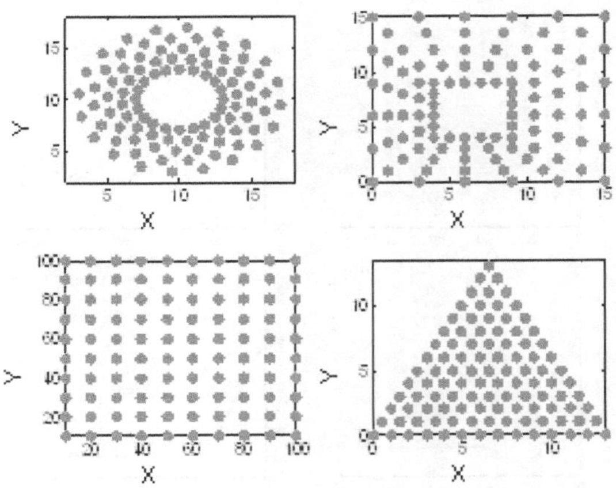

Figure 1. Distributions of demand points in four benchmark problems.

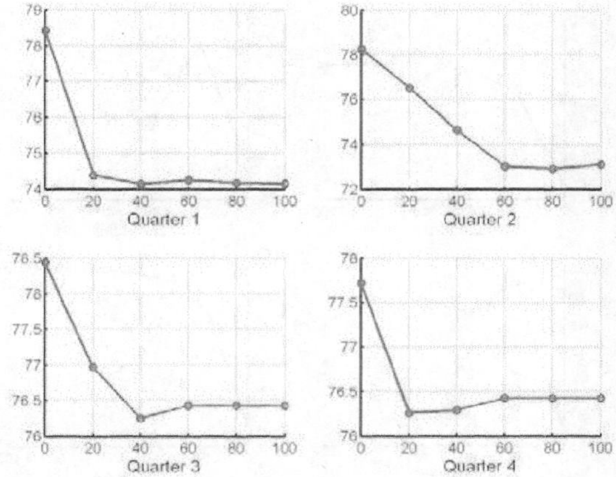

Figure 2. The average service distance of non-dominated solutions in different generations for the circle benchmark.

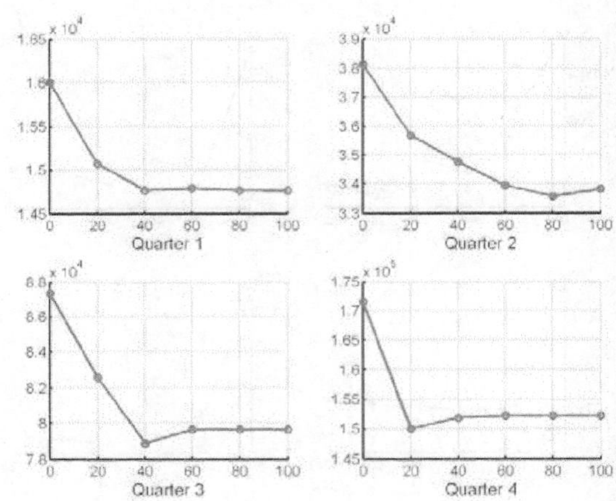

Figure 3. The average network transmission cost of non-dominated solutions in different generations for the circle benchmark.

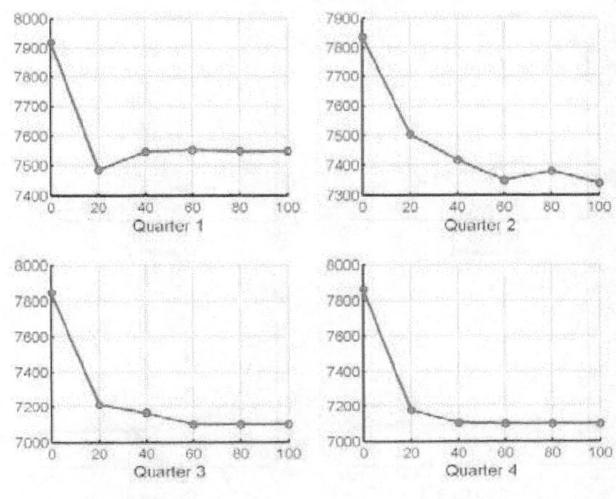

Figure 4. The average service purchase cost of non-dominated solutions in different generations for the circle benchmark.

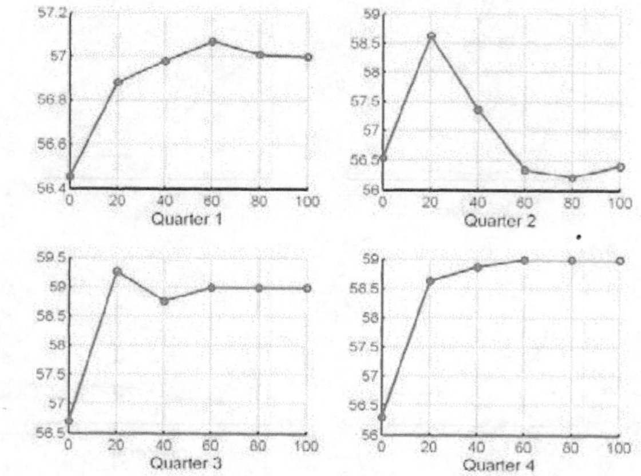

Figure 5. The average total number of serviced demand points of non-dominated solutions in different generations for the circle benchmark.

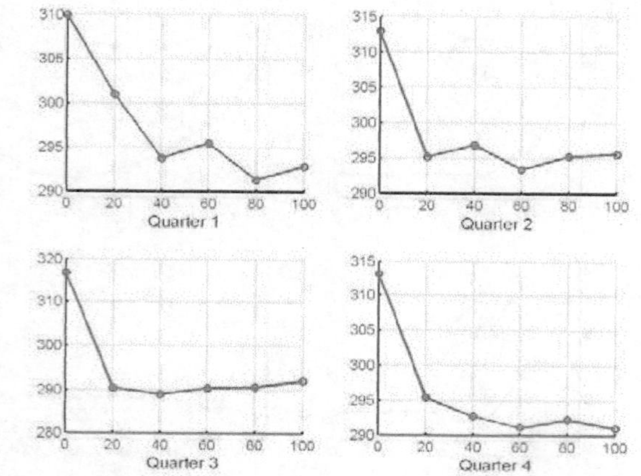

Figure 6. The average service distance of non-dominated solutions in different generations for the square benchmark.

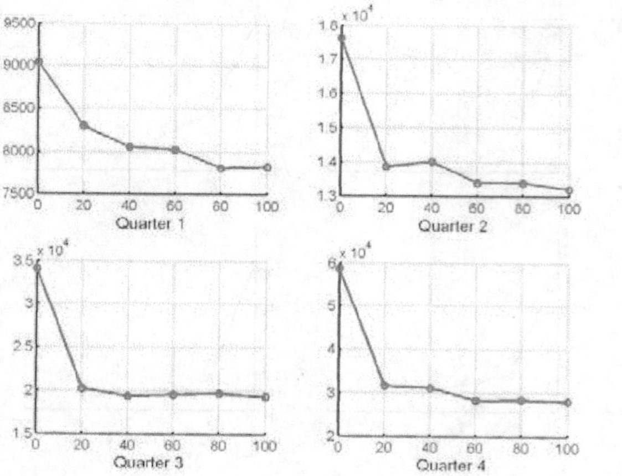

Figure 7. The average network transmission cost of non-dominated solutions in different generations for the square benchmark.

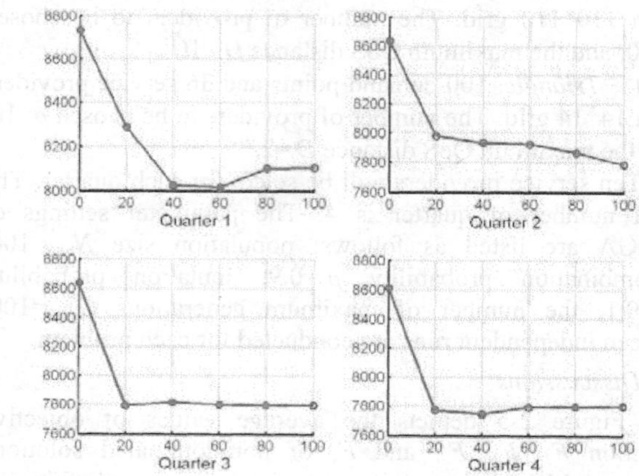

Figure 8. The average service purchase cost of non-dominated solutions in different generations for the square benchmark.

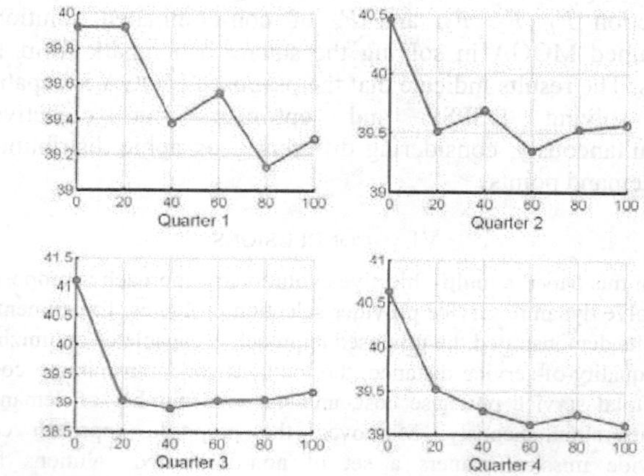

Figure 9. The average total number of serviced demand points of non-dominated solutions in different generations for the square benchmark.

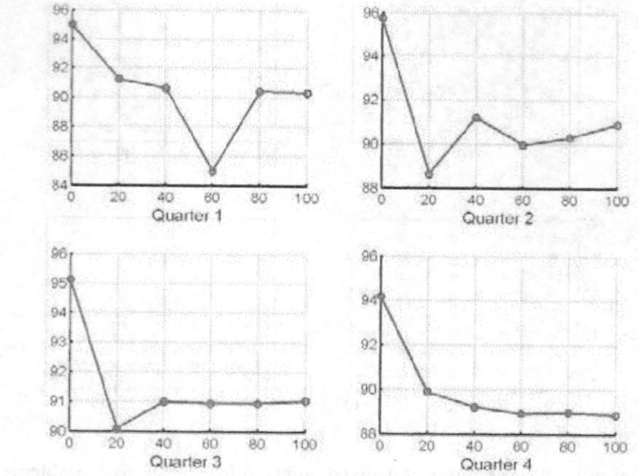

Figure 10. The average service distance of non-dominated solutions in different generations for the triangle benchmark.

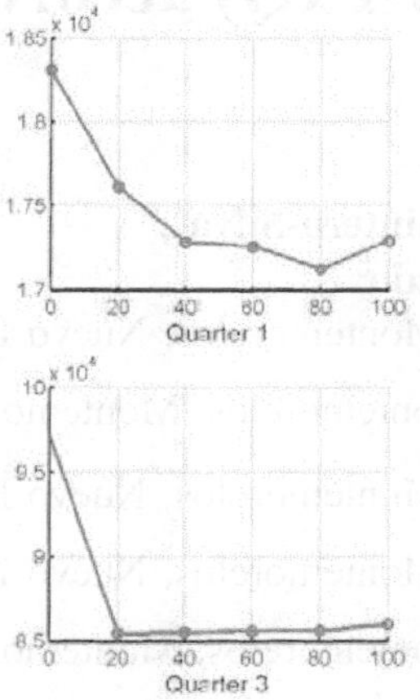

Figure 11. The average network transmission cost of non-dominated solutions in different generations for the triangle benchmark.

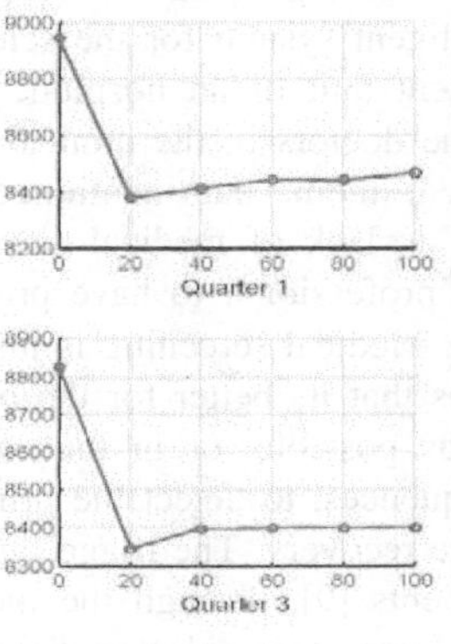

Figure 12. The average service purchase cost of non-dominated solutions in different generations for the triangle benchmark.

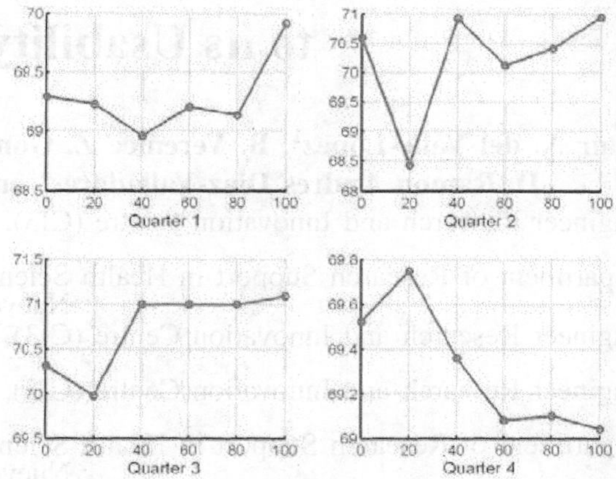

Figure 13. The average total number of serviced demand points of non-dominated solutions in different generations for the triangle benchmark.

REFERENCES

[1] I. Foster, Y. Zhao, I. Raicu, and S. Lu, "Cloud Computing and Grid Computing 360-Degree Compared," *Proceeding of Grid Computing Environments Workshop*, 2008. GCE '08, Nov. 2008, pp. 1-10, 12-16.

[2] Y. Li, Y. Shen, and Y. Liu, "Utilizing Content Delivery Network in Cloud Computing,", *Proceeding of 2012 International Conference on Computational Problem-Solving (ICCP)*, Oct, 2012, pp. 137-143.

[3] Z. Drezner, "Dynamic Facility Location: The Progressive *p*-median Problem," *Location Science*, Vol.3, No.1, 1995, pp.1-7.

[4] S. H. Own, and M. S. Daskin, "Strategic Facility Location: A Review," *European Journal of Operational Research* Vol. 111, 1998, pp.423-447.

[5] G. O. Wesolowsky, "Dynamic Facility Location," *Management Science*, Vol. 19, No.11, 1973, pp.1241-1248.

[6] G. O. Wesolowsky, and W. G. Truscott, "The Multiperiod Location-Allocation Problem with Relocation of Facilities," *Management Science*, Vol.22, No.1, 1975, pp.57-65.

[7] S. D. G. Francisco and E. C. Maria, "A Heuristic Approach for the Discrete Dynamic Location Problem," *Location Science*, Vol. 6, 1998, pp.211-223.

[8] W. Pullan, "A population based hybrid metaheuristic for the p-median problem," in *Proceedings of IEEE Congress on Evolutionary Computation*, June 2008, pp.75-82.

[9] J. E. C. Arroyo, M. dos Santos Soares, P. M. dos Santos, "A GRASP heuristic with Path-Relinking for a bi-objective p-median problem," in *Proceedings of 10th International Conference on Hybrid Intelligent Systems (HIS)*, Aug. 2010, pp.97-102.

[10] S.-Y. Ho, L.-S. Shu and J.-H. Chen, "Intelligent Evolutionary Algorithms for Large Parameter Optimization Problems," *IEEE Transaction on Evolutionary Computation*, Vol.8, No.6, Dec.2004, pp.522-541.

[11] E. Zitzler and L. Thiele, "Multiobjective evolutionary algorithms: a comparative case study and the strengthen Pareto approach," *IEEE Transaction on Evolutionary Computation*, Vol. 3, No. 4, 1999, pp. 257-271.

Validation of an Attributes Selection System Through Genetic Algorithms for ICU on Severely Burnt Patients (AG-PxQ) according to its Usability on the Clinic

A. Jair A. del Valle-Lopez[1], B. Verenice Z. Gonzalez Mejia[2], C. Brenda R. Quintero-Silva[3], D. Ramon Andres Diaz-Valladares[4] and E. Hector A. Olivas Namorado[5]

[1]Engineer Research and Innovation Centre (CI3), Universidad de Montemorelos, Montemorelos, Nuevo Leon, Mexico
[2]Department of Research Support in Health Sciences (DAICS), Universidad de Montemorelos, Montemorelos, Nuevo Leon, Mexico
[3]Engineer Research and Innovation Centre (CI3), Universidad de Montemorelos, Montemorelos, Nuevo Leon, Mexico
[4]Engineer Research and Innovation Centre (CI3), Universidad de Montemorelos, Montemorelos, Nuevo Leon, Mexico
[5]Department of Research Support in Health Sciences (DAICS), Universidad de Montemorelos, Montemorelos, Nuevo Leon, Mexico

Abstract— *On the practice of clinical medicine, decisions that involve high uncertainty must be taken [12], according to this, the medical diagnose may be described as the attempt of taking right decisions despite the use of inadequate information [11]. Reduction of processes is one of the most frequent applications of Artificial Intelligence (AI), there are several methods to achieve this, one of which is the Genetic Algorithm Optimizing Method (GAOM), that searches for the best solution to a problem in a set of multiple possible options. In the specific case of the medical duty, developing intelligent systems should be considered in terms of credibility, to reach this, the objective is to value an algorithm previously developed, measuring its functionality in the clinical medicine by its utility for diagnosing, it is done through contingency charts in order to know: (a) sensibility, (b) specificity, (c) predictive positive value y (d) predictive negative value.*

Keywords: Genetic Algorithms, Medical Screening, Artificial Intelligence

1. Introduction

"Artificial Intelligence, does not imply mere information" [4]

Artificial Intelligence AI is a science that designs systems capable to show human behavior features as: (a) language, (b) ratio or intelligence and (c) apprenticeship, among other things [1]. Due to this, AI is applied on different science and technology activities, not excluding Bio-science, it has been applied in the medical area to: (a) search for ideal solutions and for (b) agility and prevention in medical processes. An intelligent system is not conscious about its processes. Although the increasing incursion of this systems in the medical area [6], [7], [8]. , only few of them specify the requirements to make this intelligent system a functional system and with a certain level of credibility. For example, the implementation of the genetic algorithm AG-PxQ, that shows the results of an intelligent system for the selection of features in the burnt patient unit of an hospital; when this results were shown to the doctors in the clinical field, they approved and amazed at them, but mentioned that it cannot be applied due to its lack of medical screening bases, disabling the medical professional to have practical use of this intelligent system. Medical screening is justified on the statement that declares that its better for the patient to detect a disease as fast as possible, or in the case of patients with accident consequences, to detect the principal problems that may complicate recovery. The triage, method to categorize emergency patients [9], through the medical screening employes methodologies that validate diagnostic tests for its use on diseased or healthy patients; one of these methodologies is the contingency chart.

2. Methodology for validation of diagnostic test

On the validation of a diagnostic test, statistical perspective plays a very important role. On statistics, contingency charts are used to analyze relations between nominal or ordinal variables. A contingency chart is defined by the number of variables to analyze. Therefore a 2x2 contingency chart will analyze relations between two variables, being compound by rows for information of one of the variables and columns for information of the other variable; lines and columns form cells, where frequencies of each combination of the analyzed variables will be set, as shown on Figure 1.

The statistics with medical utility that can be obtained from a contingency chart, are: (a) sensibility, (b) specificity, (c) predictive positive value y (d) predictive negative value, among others.

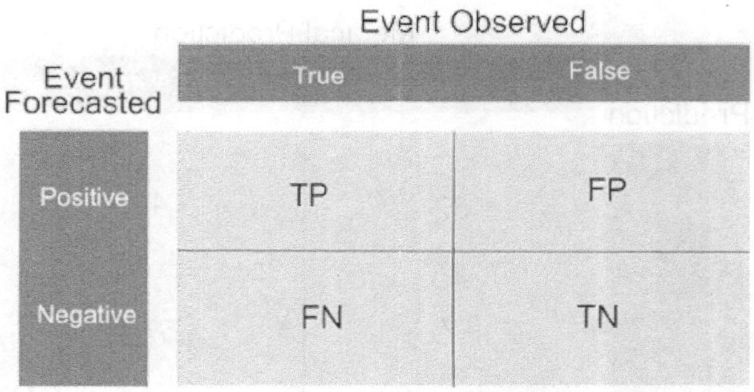

Fig. 1: Contingency Table

One of the aspects that require validation on medical ambit is the capability to diagnose diseased patients as diseased, in other words, certainty that the patient has a disease or is dying. This measurement is called sensibility, and is defined as the probability of having a diagnose with positive results when the disease is present or there's the possibility that the patient will die; this group can be defined on a contingency chart as true-positive. Then, it can be declared that sensibility is the total percentage of diseased patients that have a positive diagnostic result. [12] If the diagnostic of the diseased patients can be validated, then the diagnostic of the healthy patients can be validated also. This measurement is called specificity, and is defined as the probability of having a negative result if the patient is not been infected or diseased; this group is called true-false on a contingency chart. Then, it can be declared that specificity is the total percentage of non-diseased (healthy) patients that have a negative diagnostic result. [12]. Another aspect that requires validation in the medical field is the certainty that the obtained result of a diagnostic test is correct. Probability of having the when the result of a diagnostic test is positive is known as Positive Predictive Value (+PV). On the other hand, probability of not aving the disease when the result of a diagnostic test is negative is known as Negative Predictive Value (-PV). [12]

3. Short explanation of the results of the AG-PxQ intelligent system

The genetic algorithm, one of the best known models of evolutionary computation suggested by Holland in 1975 [3], works with a set (population) of possible solutions (individuals) with the best capacity (adaptation/fitness). Population changes according to an iterative process (generations) where individuals with best proficiency have the chance to survive, go through the next generation, and take part with genetic operators [5]. Table 1 shows the AG-PxQ attributes that medical specialists consider as parameters that collect relevant clinical evidence to establish burnt-patients survival.

After creating the Initial population for the AG-PxQ based on a data base of 100 patients, Successor populations were generated using different seeds, which is a specific space to start searching for an ideal solution; seed1 was selected as the most promising location, generating multiple combinations (individuals) that might be the ideal solution, in other words, the attributes combination that may present the higher probability patient survival.

Table 1: Considered parameters for serious burnt patients.

Name	Description
Genre	Genre of the patient
Age	Age of the patient
Tot	Burnt surface in porcent
Prof	Burnt surface in depht
Weight	Weight of the patient
SAPS	General severity indicator
Inh	Inhibitor utilisation
BACTEREMIA	Bacterian presence in blood
PNEUMONIA	Pulmonary infection
WOUND INFECTION	Surgical infection
Comorbilidad Cardiaca	Previous cardiopathy
Comorbilidad Respiratoria	Respiratory problems
Comorbilidad Hepatica	Previous hepatic problems
HTA Arterial	hypertension
Diabetes	Diabetic patient
Sida drogas	Drug consumption with HIV
Comorbilidad Renal	Kidney problems
muere	Decease foresight

The result after different tests, as shown in Table 2, suggested that the 5 variables (0, 1, 3, 5, 14) that match with: (a) total burnt surface, (b) burnt surface depth, (c) patient's weight, (d) pulmonary infection and (e) Arterial hypertension are the best options to apply on a patient with severe burns, since it gets the better adaptation percentage according to the experiment.

Table 2: Considered parameters for serious burnt patients.

Experiment Adaptation	Variables	Matching tests
0.9545	1	5
0.9545	2	5 10
0.9545	3	5 14 16
0.9545	4	5 10 12 13
1.0000	5	0 1 3 5 14
0.9545	6	5 10 12 13 14 15
0.9545	7	5 10 12 13 14 15 16
0.9545	8	1 5 10 12 13 14 15 16
0.9545	9	1 5 8 10 12 13 14 15 16
0.9545	10	0 1 3 5 10 12 13 14 15 16
0.9545	11	0 1 2 3 4 5 10 12 13 14 15
1.0000	12	0 1 2 3 4 5 7 8 9 10 11 15
0.9545	13	0 1 3 4 6 7 8 9 11 12 13 15 16
1.0000	14	0 1 2 3 4 5 7 8 9 10 11 12 13 15
0.9090	15	0 1 2 3 6 7 8 9 10 11 12 13 14 15 16
0.9090	16	0 2 3 4 5 6 7 8 9 10 11 12 13 14 15 16
0.9090	17	0 1 2 3 4 5 6 7 8 9 10 11 12 13 14 15 16

4. Application of the validation method

AG-PxQ uses an original data base of about 100 severe burnt patients, on which is indicated the medical appreciation about the patient's triage, with a nominal dichotomic attribute of the decease foresight. This attribute is used as

System Prediction \ Medical Prediction	True	False
Positive	TP	FP
Negative	FN	TN

Fig. 2: Contingency Table Design with AG-PxQ

System Prediction \ Medical Prediction	True	False
Positive	32	4
Negative	7	57

Fig. 3: Contingency Table Values with AG-PxQ

one of the variables that occupy the columns at the 2x2 contingency chart. AG-PxQ uses the data collector tool WEKA, specifically the NSGA II method, as the method which features will calculate and classify the adaptation/fitness level of each individual; wherefore original data base is passed through WEKA to see how it develops patient's triage, this will produce information that will be used to fill up the lines on the contingency chart corresponding to the diagnostic test that is going to be compared to the medical triage, as shown on Figure 2.

The formulas to get validity and security (reliability) in the area of public health are (1) Sensibility (S), (2) Specificity (SP), (3) Positive Predictive Value (+PV),
(4) Negative Predictive Value (-PV).

$$S = (TP/(TP + FN)) * 100. \quad (1)$$

$$SP = (TN/(FP + TN)) * 100. \quad (2)$$

$$+PV = (TP/(TP + FP)) * 100. \quad (3)$$

$$-PV = (TN/(FN + TN)) * 100. \quad (4)$$

5. Validation results

As seen on Figure 3, the design of the contingency chart facilitates calculation of statistic values for AG-PxQ validity and reliability.

Using the previously described formulas the following values are obtained:

$$S = (32/(32 + 7)) * 100 = 82.05 \quad (5)$$

$$SP = (57/(4 + 57)) * 100 = 93.44 \quad (6)$$

$$+PV = (32/(32 + 4)) * 100 = 88.89 \quad (7)$$

$$-PV = (57/(7 + 57)) * 100 = 89.06 \quad (8)$$

6. Conclusions and future projects

Once the results of the tests for validity and reliability of the AG-PxQ have been described and analyzed, the conclusion is:

a) The total percentage of diseased patients that have a positive diagnostic (sensibility) is 82.05%, which is a very acceptable value of validity.

b) The total percentage of non-diseased (healthy) patients with a negative diagnostic (specificity) is 93.44%, which is a very acceptable value of validity.

c) Probability of presenting certain disease when the result is positive in the diagnostic test (test) (Positive Predictive Value or +PV) is 88.89% Which is a very acceptable value of reliability on diagnostic testing.

d) Probability of not presenting certain disease when the result is positive in the diagnostic test (test) (Negative Predictive Value or -PV) 89.06%, which is a very acceptable value of reliability on diagnostic testing.

As future projects, the following topics are proposed:

- Utilization of the proposed algorithm using an enlarged data base.
- Application on real cases and valuation of results on a ICU supplied clinic.
- Application of the methodology of this system in other medical areas.

References

[1] Petot GJ, Marling C, Sterling L. (1998). *An artificial intelligence system for computer-assisted menu planning. J Am Diet Assoc* 98:1009- 14 8.

[2] Bell AJ. (1999). Levels and loops: the future of artificial intelligence and neuroscience. 354:2013- 20.

[3] Holland, J.H. (1975). *Adaptation in Natural and Artificial Systems.* Ann Harbor, MI: Univ. Of Michigan Press.

[4] Javier Caballero Villarraso, Antonio Romero Tabares, Francisco J. Gavilán León, Manuel Baena García, Francisco Javier Díez Vegas, Sevilla. (2011). *Aplicación de algoritmos genéticos y sistemas expertos en medicina asistencial.* Agencia de Evaluación de Tecnologías Sanitarias de Andalucía

[5] J.A. Del Valle-López, R.A. Díaz-Valladares, B.R. Quintero-Silva, J.A. Serrano-Martínez. (2013). *Aplicación de los algoritmos genéticos a la UCI para la clasificación de pacientes.* 978-607-95255-4-5

[6] Holman JG, Cookson MJ. (1987). *Expert systems for medical applications.* J Med Eng Technol. 11:151-9.

[7] Edwards M, Morse DR, Fielding AH. (1987). *Expert systems: frames, rules or logic for species identification?* Computational Applied Bioscience. 3:1-7.

[8] Flouris AD, Duffy J. (2006). *Applications of artificial intelligence systems in the analysis of epidemiological data* (Eur J Epidemiol). 21:167-70

[9] María M. Abad-Grau, Jorge S. Ierache, Claudio Cervino. (2007). *Modelado de Sistema Experto para Triaje en Servicios de Urgencias Médicas* Universidad de Granada, Facultad de Informática Ciencias de la Comunicación y Técnicas Especiales, Universidad de Morón. p. 1734-1744

[10] L. Salleras. (1994). *La medicina clínica preventiva: el futuro de la prevención.* Med Clin (Barc). 102 Supl 1: 5-12.

[11] Riegelman RK, Hirsch RP. (1989). *Studying a Study and Testing a test: How to read the medical literature.* Boston: Little Brown.

[12] Á. Ruiz Morales, L.E. Morillo Zárate. (2004). *Investigación clínica: epidemiología clínica aplicada.* Edición Médica Panamericana p.576.